CO-AYJ-592

Dangerous Territories

Dangerous Territories

Struggles for Difference and Equality in Education

~

Edited by

Leslie G. Roman and Linda Eyre

Routledge
New York and London

Published in 1997 by

Routledge
29 West 35th Street
New York, NY 10001

Published in Great Britain by

Routledge
11 New Fetter Lane
London EC4P 4EE

Library of Congress Cataloging-in-Publication Data

Dangerous territories: struggles for difference and equality in
  education / edited by Leslie G. Roman and Linda Eyre.
     p. cm.
   Includes bibliographical references and index.
   ISBN 0-415-91595-3 (alk. paper). -- ISBN 0-415-91596-1 (pbk.:
alk. paper)
   1. Critical pedagogy. 2. Educational equalization. I. Roman,
Leslie G.   II. Eyre, Linda.
   LC196.D35   1997
   370.11'5--dc21   97-16909
                                                            CIP

Dedication

We dedicate this book to our mothers, Miriam Edelman (1932–) and Alice Seckington (1914–1995), who in their own ways have taught us a great deal about equality and social justice. May their legacy continue in our work and in future struggles for equality and difference.

March 1997

Leslie G. Roman and Linda Eyre

Contents

PART II
Inside-Out: Transgressive Pedagogies and Unsettling Classrooms

PART III
Shifting Courses, Directions, and Policies:
Out from the Ghetto of Pedagogy

Preface

Dangerous Territories, Territorial Power, and Education

Chandra Talpade Mohanty
Hamilton College (United States)

territory, -ies 1: a geographical area belonging to or under the jurisdiction of a governmental authority 2: a part of the U.S. not included within any state but organized with a separate legislature 3: REGION, DISTRICT; also: a region in which one feels at home 4: a field of knowledge or interest 5: an assigned area 6: an area occupied and defended by one or a group of animals— territorial (adj)
—Websters New American Dictionary, *1995*

Dictionaries are very useful indices of truth/falsehood making. Educational institutions also operate in the realm of ideology and truth-making, consolidating regimes of power and domination in the name of civility and democracy. In *Dangerous Territories* we have a complex, richly textured collection of essays that analyze and challenge the various lies nation-states, educational institutions, and educators knowingly, and unknowingly enact through the formalized use of a rhetoric of difference and equality. In this brief essay I add my unruly voice to the conversation so carefully crafted by the authors in this volume.

In fact, almost all the meanings, and inflections I want to highlight are embedded in the epigraph: territory in terms of relations of rule and authority, as the geography of a nation or the possession of one, as the psychic economy of home, as an epistemological map, as occupation. In what follows, I weave some of the insights from this collection into a reflection on the "dangerous territories" encountered by radical educators in Eurocentric educational institutions at the end of the twentieth century. Specifically, I am interested in the question of cultures and politics of dissent in increasingly conservative national and transnational educational locations. What is at stake in the way intellectual, institutional, pedagogical, and relational territories are drawn, legitimated, regulated, and consolidated in educational institutions and systems? What dangers inhere in these cartographies? To whom? What knowledges and identities are legitimated/delegitimized as a result of the struggles over territorial boundaries and borders?

In the introduction to this volume, Leslie Roman and Linda Eyre tell us that *Dangerous Territories* began with a conversation about the effects of a Right-wing "backlash" on "anti-oppression pedagogies, equity policies, and non-traditional programs" in different educational sites. However, the collection grew to exceed the conceptual parameters of this initial dialogue. Indeed the very concept of "backlash" is problematized throughout the volume. For me this problematization provokes crucial questions about the sometimes inadvertant continuity of so-called liberal, progressive, or even leftist agendas and practices in education with conservative agendas. The essays here also raise very important questions about the economic and ideological processes of globalization, capitalist consumer culture and values, and regimes of race, gender, empire and heterosexuality within and across educational sites.

The collection contains new and substantive analyses of "nation-making" and citizenship in the context of education (see essays by Bannerji, Cooper, Blackmore, Solomon, Roman and Stanley), discourses and pedagogies of gender and (hetero) sexuality in schooling (Eyre, Kenway, Elliot, Smith, Pitt), and the politics of race[1] and postcoloniality (Bannerji, Cavell, Srivastava, Roman and Stanley). The comparative focus on the "dangerous territories" of education in Canada, Australia, the United Kingdom, and the United States of America is especially useful in understanding the profoundly interconnected material, ideological, and discursive processes of global regimes of power and inequality. Reading this volume is both a sobering and a hopeful experience. We are left with no doubt whatsoever that struggles over difference and equality in education *matter*; that the struggles against domination and for social justice have to be waged situationally and regionally as well as globally; that the very basic ethical and moral notions of citizenship, belonging, and democracy are at stake here; and finally, that self-critical hard work is necessary to transform these unjust educational regimes. Contributors to this volume redefine the "territories" of power and privilege in education, expose dominant ideologies, and show that cultures of dissent exist and can be nurtured. Of course, dangers and the risks continue to exist. Speaking truth to power continues to be dangerous.

To this ongoing conversation in *Dangerous Territories*, I add my reflections about the political, intellectual, and institutional stakes involved in carving and defending curricular, disciplinary, and relational borders in academic sites. These reflections are the result of two recent experiences that serve to locate me, as well as to raise larger political and epistemological questions pertinent to the project of this volume. The first, a visit to the Netherlands to attend the 1993 European Women's Studies Conference organized by NOISE,[2] focuses on the potential pitfalls and danger of our intellectual and curricular practices around "multiculturalism," difference and justice. The second, a visit to the New School for Social Research in New York City to participate on a forum entitled "Living the Legacy: The State of Emergency at the New School Continues," on the dangerous effects of engaging in a racialized struggle which challenges territorial power in a seemingly liberal, progressive institution of higher education. Both experiences illustrate the significance of borders in understanding the relations of power/knowledge in the consolidation of particular regimes of gender, race, class, and sexuality—and both foreground for me the significance of the "Idea" of Europe, and the "Idea" of America (nation-making) in the construction of knowledge, curricula, and citizenship in the 1990s. African-American philosopher W.E.B. Dubois spoke of the problem of the twentieth century being the problem of "the color line." We carry this "problem" into the twenty first century. What analytical and strategic knowledges and conceptual tools do we need to NOT relive the violence of our inherited histories?[3]

National Borders and Curricular Stakes

A week before, leaving for the Netherlands, I discovered a visa was required to enter the country. I am an Indian citizen and a permanent resident of the United States. Procuring a visa involved a substantial fee ($60); a letter from my employer (the letter of invitation from NOISE was inadequate) indicating that I have a permanent job in the US; that I was going to Utrecht for a professional conference; and that my employer would be financially responsible for me while I was in the Netherlands; and finally, a notarized copy of my green card, the "proof" of my permanent residency in the United States. I never leave home without this card. In reflecting on this experience, it occurs to me that this process of legitimation encapsulates the dilemmas of citizenship, (im)migration, work, and economic privilege that underlie the concept and power of the European Union—and for that matter, the idea of American "multicultural" Democracy. National (and perhaps racial and imperial) borders are re-consolidated at the same time as economic borders dissolve in the name of a greater Europe. While earlier I had worried about whether my experiences and thinking about feminist studies in the United States would seem significant in this context, after this process of being constructed as an illegitimate outsider who needed proof of employment, citizenship, residency, and economic viability, I decided this wasn't all that different from a number of different border crossings—even disciplinary ones in the academy. Defining insiders and outsiders is what nation-states and other credentialing institutions do.

The challenges of an anti-racist feminist praxis that is genuinely and ethically cross-cultural are similar in both the European and North American context—whether one is a person of color or white. Practices of ruling and domination may vary across geographical and historical terrains, but the effects of these practices and forms of opposition or resistance to them are related and similar. I am convinced that one of the major challenges in deconstructing and transforming a European women's studies curriculum to become radically transnational rather than merely the sum of its national parts (e.g. British/French/Dutch, etc.), is the very challenge that faces women's studies programs in the United States of America. How do we reconcile the economic ascendency of the European Union with the very history of imperialism and colonialism that made this ascendency possible? How do we rewrite/undo "Britishness," "Dutchness," or "Whiteness," for example, such that the practice of feminist studies is a fundamentally anti-racist? What would it take to create a radically transnationalist feminist practice which is attentive to the unequal histories of rule in the European Union countries? Leslie Roman and Timothy Stanley discuss the construction of "nationalist" curricula in Canada and their images of fictive harmonious family-like nation ruled by discourses of "civility." Their essay provides a timely and disturbing counterpoint to the development of anti-imperialist curricula and transnational feminist practice. How do nationalist curricula undermine transnational practice?

This is the very same challenge we face in the North American academy—how do we undermine the notions of multiculturalism either as the melting pot, or as cultural relativism, both of which permeate United States consumer culture? How do we practice a critical multiculturalism that decolonizes received knowledges, histories, and identities, and that foregrounds questions of social justice and material interests by actively combating the hegemony of global capital? One of the primary questions feminist teachers and scholars have to face in the European Union women's studies network, is the meaning of "community"—who are the insiders and the outsiders in this community? How are the borders being drawn? How can we cross these borders to allow access to all? What forms of identification are needed to cross over? And what notions of legitimacy and gendered and racialized citizenship are being actively constructed within this community?

Himani Bannerji's essay in this collection is a wonderful example of the power and politics of the construction of such national "communities."

Bannerji offers an archeaology of nation-making by analyzing the management of race, gender, and class hierarchies by the Canadian State in
response to a crisis of legitimation and citizenship. Her careful analysis of
the history of the manipulation and disciplining of racialized and gender
specific labor by the State exposes the lie of "liberal democracy" and
Canadian "multiculturalism" making explicit the capitalist and materialist
underpinnings of "imagining" the nation. Interestingly enough, Leslie
Roman and Timothy Stanley's discussion of young people's negotiations of
official and popular racism in Canada suggests the concrete *forms* through
which this crisis of legitimation and citizenship functions within the context
of racialized consciousness and identity. Read together, these essays suggest
the power and complexity of nation-making, of the policing of borders, and
of the possibilities of dissent and resistance.

Similarly, Davina Cooper, Didi Herman, and Jill Blackmore offer somewhat parallel readings of nation-making in the United Kingdom, the United
States of America, and in Australia. I find Cooper's argument about the
practices of conservative religious education in the United Kingdom leading
to a "consolidation of self" rather than the marginalization of "the other"
particularly productive in understanding how hegemonic, normative
national identity is articulated. Borders define outsiders and insiders, but
they do much more—they also *actively* legitimate insiders. Self-making
needs to be analyzed as central to the crafting of White, masculinist, heterosexist, and capitalist citizenship in educational sites.

Confronting Racialized, Masculinist Institutional Power

In fact, it is exactly such "self-making" that was foregrounded during my
visit (February 1997) to participate in a forum on "the State of Emergency"
at the New School for Social Research in New York City. I want to comment on this situation because of its political urgency, because it is symptomatic of how educational institutions, even seemingly progressive ones,
invest in the making of hegemonic citizenship through institutional,
curricular and pedagogic practices, and because this is a powerful example
of coalition building and creating cultures of dissent in the academy. In an
eloquent 20 page letter to Jonathan F. Fanton, the President of the New
School for Social Research, the Coalition of Concerned Students and
Faculty provide a complex analysis of the disjuncture between the university's stated goals of "diversity"/affirmative action policies, and its actual
practices in actively undermining these very goals and policies.[3] After a
year long mobilization by the student group, END (Education Not
Domination) and faculty of color, the University continues to remain

unresponsive in the face of "the case against the university" leveled by students and by staff and faculty of color calling for an end to racialized discriminatory practices at the New School. I quote:

> We have come to understand during this year of struggle that "diversity" at The New School means diverse opinions. "Diversity" has been severed from the histories of race and racism in this country. In this formulation, definitions are important. They have their own unstated assumptions and they signal as well a will to clarify, amend, transform. We are even skeptical of using the term "diversity" here because it is difficult to rescue it from its current associations with euphemisms, lip service, and liberal obfuscation. Therefore, in the remainder of this document we will generally refer to specific histories, identities and power dynamics rather than to some vague entity called "diversity." We do, however, share a common vision of how communities of difference can work to abolish structural inequalities of different kinds, which entails opening frank and principled dialogues about our respective histories and different relationships to power and privilege. We share an ethical and intellectual commitment to understanding the histories and knowledges of particular mobilizations and struggles involving class, race, decolonization; different feminisms; lesbian/gay/queer liberation and theory; transnational and anti-imperialist perspectives and critiques. While we, of course, cannot predict the precise direction of such a process in advance, we can say that it will never lose sight of the relationship between racial difference and power. At a minimum this would mean, for instance, bringing the actual population of the New School more appropriately into line with a world shaped by the agency of people of color, women of all colors, queers, working class and poor people, postcolonial peoples, and immigrants. It would mean at the very least bringing the New School in line with the population of New York City, the community of which the University is a part. In short, it means that a new level of respectful attention to the histories and knowledges of peoples from Asia, the Caribbean, Latin America, Africa, the Middle East and Europe would become central in defining our intellectual and political agendas. (p. 2/3, Letter to President Fanton, 2/3/97)

I quote at length from this document to illustrate a number of conceptual points: (1) the link between intellectual and curricular priorities on the one hand, and administrative and hiring practices on the other; (2) the connection among anti-colonial, anti-racist, intellectual perspectives, and the history, geography, and experiential basis of such perspectives in different communities; (3) the limits of a politics of inclusion severed from struggles for social justice; and finally, (4) the at once dangerous and liberatory terrain of the university. The New School's response (or lack thereof) to this challenge can also be analyzed as a form of what Roman has called "institutionalized white defensiveness."[5]

The demands of the Coalition focus on: (1) dismantling practices of institutionalized white supremacy, white hegemony and white power in its curriculum, hiring practices, and in the New School's general social and intellectual environment; (2) ceasing all forms of class and labor exploitation; (3) discriminatory practices towards female employees and students; (4) ending the proliferation of an intellectual and social environment that is heterosexist; (5) dismantling non-participatory, anti-democratic decision making processes; and (6) beginning the process of rethinking the curriculum, specifically by offering a senior faculty position to feminist theorist M. Jacqueline Alexander, currently on a terminal visiting contract. The response of the institution has largely been a deafening silence coupled with a racialized mobilization closing administrative and faculty ranks in opposition to the Coalition—a mobilization which has all the makings of what Roman (1993, 71) calls institutionalized "white defensiveness" and "backlash" politics.

Why is this struggle important? Why do we need new anti-colonial epistemic maps, as well as the presence of marginalized majorities on the faculty and throughout our institutions?[6] Dorothy Smith's essay draws attention to the deployment of juridical discourses to maintain and defend the gender status quo against feminist critiques. The struggle at the New School illuminates the discourses and institutional and administrative practices which stubbornly maintain a White, Eurocentric, masculinist status quo, where business as usual is actually about "self-making" in a profound way. There is danger within the territory of educational institutions for those who resist and challenge the status quo. The stakes after all, are rather high: nothing less than the equitable redistribution of power and resources, and remaking the "self" and the image of the institution so that citizenship and democracy arc not the exclusive purview of priviledged communities.

The struggle at the New School, and other similar struggles are fundamentally about redefining borders, about including "outsiders" and reformulating what counts as the inside. Borders, especially those drawn to mark legitimate and illegitimate knowledges are often porous. While the geographical and cultural borders of nation-states since World War II and the decolonization of the third world were carefully drawn, economic, political, ideological processes always operated as if these borders were porous. The academy operates in similar ways (see Jill Blackmore's discussion of the restructuring of Australian education by the State's economic priorities and Howard Solomon's analysis of the entrenched policing of the boundaries of the university and the public sphere). While the boundaries around and inside institutions of higher learning are invisibly, but carefully drawn, the economic, cultural and ideological imperatives of the academy establish relations of rule which consolidate and naturalize the dominant values of a globalized capitalist consumer culture where the new citizen of the world is a consumer par excellence.

If the academy, the classroom, and other educational contexts are not mere instructional sites, but are fundamentally political and cultural sites that represent accomodations and contestations over knowledge by differently empowered social constituencies, then the processes and practices of education lead to profoundly significant notions of self, identity, and community. Thus, one of the challenges for feminist educators is the creation of truly democratic public spaces where people of all "races," classes, genders and sexualities are authorized to act as citizens—to understand, organize, and demand justice and equity. However, if economic and cultural globalization creates a context where material, economic and even psychic borders are porous, no longer neatly contained within the geographical boundaries of nation-states, then questions of democracy and citizenship also cannot be neatly charted within these boundaries. Thus, questions of difference and equality in education take on a certain urgency in a world where the fate of first world citizens is inextricably tied to the fate of the refugees, exiles, migrants, immigrants in the first world, and of similar constituencies in the rest of the world. The struggle over representation is always a struggle over knowledge. What knowledges do we need for education to be the practice of liberation? What does it mean for educators to create a democratic public space in this context? How are democracy and citizenship defined at the end of the millinium? And what kinds of intellectual, scholarly, and political work would it take to make the transition to the next millenium meaningful in terms of social justice? Finally, how do we hold educational institutions, our daily pedagogic practices, and ourselves accountable to plural and unequal subaltern truths and subordinate knowledges?

Dangerous Territories opens the doors to such questions. The volume will intrigue you. It introduces and analyzes some of the most urgent educational issues of our times—I invite you to enter with enthusiasm and care for the questions the volume raises.

Notes

1. I use the term "race" as a social set of power relations among racially constructed people and not a reified biological category.
2. NOISE is the acronym for the European Women's Studies Consortium, a network of Women's Studies faculty (and programs) from a number of institutions on higher education in various countries in Europe. The specific purpose of this 1993 conference was to discuss and finalize a "multicultural" Women's Studies curriculum *across* European contexts.
3. I use the term "we" as a way of indicating a shared public, and my own immersion in and accountability to this public. This is not the use of a royal, or homogenizing "we."

4. Letter dated 2 February 1997. For a copy of this document write the student coalition, END. Email: end@pentagon.com or fac@theoffice.net. Since February 1997, events have taken a turn for the worse, and while it is impossible to provide details and up to date imformation on the struggle at the New School, suffice it to say that one week before the official end of the 1997 Spring semester, at least a dozen students have been engaged in a hunger strike for over fifteen days, and Professor Alexander has joined them after withdrawing her name from a list of demands crafted by the Coalition. The urgency and depth of institutional struggles such as this illustrates graphically the profound intellectual, political, and personal stakes, the courage and risks involved in exposing and challenging the "dangerous territories" of academic institutions.
5. See Leslie G. Roman, "White is a Color: White Defensiveness, Postmodernism, and Anti-Racist Pedagogy," in *Race, Identity and Representation in Education*, ed. by Cameron McCarthy and Warren Crichlow. 1993. New York: Routledge, (pp. 71–88).
6. Some of these questions are developed at length in "Introduction: Genealogies, Legacies, Movements," co-authored with M. Jacqueline Alexander, in *Feminist Genealogies, Colonial Legacies, Democratic Futures*. 1997. New York: Routledge, (pp. viii–xlii).

Introduction

The Usual Suspects: Struggles for 'Difference' and 'Equality' in Education

Leslie G. Roman,
University of British Columbia (Canada)

Linda Eyre,
University of New Brunswick (Canada)

Round up the usual suspects.
—Casablanca *screenplay by Howard Koch, Warner Bros., 1943*

The collection of essays that appear in *Dangerous Territories: Struggles for Difference and Equality in Education* was inspired by a feminist panel at the 1992 meeting of the American Educational Research Association in San Francisco. It began as a passionate debate over the limits and possibilities of various "anti-oppression" pedagogies in our own North American universities and how they have been affected by Right–wing assaults on academic disciplines in the late 1980s and 1990s. Specifically, the panelists[1] addressed what we termed "backlashes" against the gains made by activists—both inside and outside the academy working within and across the struggles of various feminisms, anti-racisms, and the lesbian and gay movements. We noted the ways "backlash" politics set the terms both for how we taught about these different struggles for equality, and how we were constructed unfavorably by reactionary students, colleagues, and emergent Right–wing campus organizations. Through the refractory of university pedagogy and power relations (conceived of as classroom curricula and student–teacher interaction as well as policy implementation and wider programmatic decisions), we wondered how and in what ways we had begun to collude unwittingly in particular Right–wing reconstructions and restorations of our universities.

The conference papers dealt variously with the impact of Right–wing politics on different anti–oppression pedagogies, equity policies, and non–traditional programs (e.g., women's studies, gay and lesbian studies). We discussed how backlash politics worked to ensure: (1) the self-censorship of our political beliefs; (2) the derisive formal and/or informal evaluations from unsympathetic students and colleagues; (3) the regulatory and disciplining functions and boundaries of our disciplines; and (4) the retrenchment of material and political support for particular programs or curricular initiatives to which we were committed.

Challenging discussions between and among contributors and Linda and me (as editors) have reshaped the questions, conceptual terms, and implications for this volume. Although not all of the blinkers consequent upon the limited hegemonic locations and contexts of white North American feminisms have been removed, we continue (through engaging one another's work and feminist materialist, postcolonial and poststructural scholarship) to problematize and unravel the threads of undeserved certainty and privilege in our analyses and to challenge and transform the ground on which we pose our questions. At first, we restricted (perhaps understandably) our analyses of backlash politics to the sites and practices in and through which we worked—university classrooms and their specific "anti-oppression" pedagogies, non-traditional programs, and policies. However, based on the feedback we received from contributors, and the exciting array of work being done by radical scholars from various traditions/perspectives, we have since expanded our initial focus to include other levels of formal and informal education/pedagogy (e.g., elementary/primary, secondary, tertiary) as well as other sites and practices conventionally and problematically thought of as "outside" of universities (e.g., the interaction between religious movements and multiculturalism or lesbian and gay movements, the media's representations of specific struggles for equality such as feminism, the uses of cyberspace). We now more fully recognize the articulation, disarticulation, and rearticulation of the multiple sites and practices that coordinate the way in which the "texts" and "intertextual" relations among feminist, anti–racist, and lesbian and gay critiques of the academy's "chilly climate" interact with university discourses that have taken a conservative juridical turn (see Smith, chapter 9).

As with most edited collections, especially those emerging from conferences, our initial intent, audience(s), and conception of many of the points of reference and "keywords,"[2] to borrow a term from British cultural materialist Raymond Williams, have transformed markedly. In our original prospectus, produced immediately after the conference in San Francisco, we accepted rather unproblematically the transhistorical and binary oppositional framing of such terms as backlash/progressive, Right/Left, and so on, allowing them to function as "keywords"—words that legitimated some radical social change struggles for equality and delegitimated others battling within them. We were captives not only of our times, but also of certain populist sentiments—what socialist feminist Lynne Segal (1987) calls "the confirming" and compensatory "consolations" of [our] "relative powerlessness" (1). We echoed the popular, if not populist, sentiments of white U.S. feminist reformer Susan Faludi, whose Pulitzer Prize–winning book, *Backlash: The Undeclared War Against American Women*, jumpstarted the concept of backlash within both academic and non-academic feminist contexts.[3]

The concept of a single overarching "backlash" has enjoyed enormous appeal in certain sectors of feminism as well as other parts of the Left partly because it uses the language of common victimization and oppression to describe the battles faced by progressive movements in attacks by the Right and other groups. And, indeed, it must be acknowledged that the concept of backlash has been a useful (albeit at times reductive) rallying point for diverse groups of progressive women and/or men. It did, for example, provide those panelists who were the first contributors to *Dangerous Territories* with a raison d'être for their writing. However, thanks to enlivening and disconcerting interchanges with some of our contributors, we came to see that the concept of backlash has some major limitations. Most notably, the binary and transhistorical framework within which it functions grossly oversimplifies the constituencies, forms, contexts, and effects of both conservative and progressive/radical politics. As many of our contributors observe, serious differences between and within different (and differently) oppressed groups often get conflated (or obscured altogether) in the notion of a commonly experienced backlash. Furthermore, applying "backlash" exclusively to Right-wing political reactions fails to draw attention to reactionary and defensive politics within and across left-wing/progressive groups—whether feminist, critical multicultural/anti-racist, or anti–heterosexist.

The tenuousness and tendential nature of hyphenated alliances between conflicting constituencies are often glossed over with umbrella terms—whether they refer to the Left or the Right. Although umbrella terms such as Left and Right are often both practical and necessary when discussing specific instances of reactionary defensiveness,[4] they can become problematic. For example, in an effort to explain both the symptoms and the causes of "defensiveness" within the North American Left, U.S. sociologists Derber et al. erroneously generalize from and rely upon the responses of white heterosexual male Marxist academics:[5]

> The defensiveness of the marxists is tangible and their almost reflexive call to struggle on for the 'real' socialism bespeaks the angst of the true believer. A Left not able to contemplate the possibility of its own death may be a Left whose survival in the end will not make much difference. (1995, 3)

By defining this particular group as "the Left," the authors gloss over and exclude the gendered, classed, raced, and sexual interests of various other groups (e.g., feminists, anti–racists, lesbians, and gays) who may also identify as socialists or more broadly as Leftists. Recognizing the times when the agendas, priorities, and visions of equality articulated by particular groups (say, feminists, lesbian and gay activists, anti–racist groups) are different from those implicitly figured as the normative subjects of Left politics for Derber et al. would indeed complicate what they mean by "the Left."[6] Whose anxieties, after all, reside in the collapse of *statist* forms of Eastern European socialism? Impoverished women raising children on their own in New York, Toronto, or Mexico City? Lesbians and gays fighting for same-sex health care benefits? Immigrants to North America combatting representations of themselves as drains on a particular national economy and who face possible deportation? By raising these kinds of questions, we mean to challenge the notion that reactionary politics get generated from normatively neutral or disinterested locations and refer only to social movement activity in one nationally bounded context. The globalization of capitalism, patriarchy, and neocolonialism means that the forms of defensiveness produced have structural/material bases, although they may be expressed as powerful and emotionally charged political reactions. Defensive social relations and reactions articulate, disarticulate, and rearticulate political subjects transnationally.[7]

Of course, different forms of defensiveness (whether on the parts of individuals or institutions) are not exclusive to white male marxists in North America. Nor are they exclusive to any particular ideology—Left or Right, feminist or anti–feminist, and so forth. A consistent theme that emerges in this volume is the historical and political value of learning from the occasions of defensive stances taken *within, across,* and often *in reaction to* various Left struggles, including but not limited to particular feminisms; anti-racisms/critical multiculturalisms; and lesbian and gay politics. Our failure to contemplate the different forms of defensiveness that occur within various progressive struggles often means that we, as social change activists, are caught off guard. We are frequently unable to understand how supposed allies sometimes take political stances that look remarkably like reactionary or conservative positions taken on the Right.[8] And we frequently find it difficult to explain, within the existing binary framework used to conceptualize backlash, how political activists (whether of the Right or of the Left) are able to capture popular support for their political agendas. Indeed, as Davina Cooper argues (see chapter 2), analyses that reach the fevered pitch of moral panics with regard to Right-wing backlash ironically depict both the Left and the Right as monolithic forces. In other words, they elide the diverse constituencies of and divisions between Left and Right, focusing almost exclusively on the elaboration of the agendas of the latter. As a result, what gets ignored "on the ground" are the many diverse communities of Leftist and feminist practice that, in the search for social justice, articulate different versions of equality and radical difference.

However, as Julia Swindells and Lisa Jardine remind us,[9] the relations between the margins and centers of power often obscure one of the crucial paradoxes of liberal inclusion: that marginality and exclusion may not be as disempowering as are belonging and not belonging—of simultaneously being both an insider and an outsider. If it is the case that Raymond Williams's romanticized and masculinist view of the socialist transformation as the 'long revolution' was valid, and oppositional politics was a real possibility to emancipate the working classes, then, they argue, for women on the Left the case is somewhat different:

> [W]e came to the conclusion that our own position as women was inescapably *appositional* rather than oppositional, and that there must be a different strategy for women—the revolution longer still. Denied the clarity of marginality, and the lucidity of its versions of exclusion, we kept experiencing ourselves as included—but on the wrong terms—and were forced to conclude that women are obliged to articulate their exclusion from there. (1990, xi)

Although we reject Swindells and Jardine's universalization of the category of "women," we find resonances with their analysis of the paradoxical effects of liberal inclusionary strategies. This point is amplified as a common theme by most contributors to *Dangerous Territories* in their efforts to explain the complexities of specific struggles for equality and difference. The result is that most either redefine or exceed the liberal limits of the concept of "backlash."

Thus, the very reasons for the original appeal of the concept of "backlash" became, for us as well as for most of the contributors, causes for suspicion. We could not simply "round up the usual suspects" as suggested in the epigram taken from the nostalgic film *Casablanca*. So, the usual suspects—a notion of common or universal oppression which, in turn, creates the conditions for a single, over-arching backlash (in other words, a monological concept of "backlash" and its attendant binary anti–oppression pedagogy frameworks)—have become problematic for us, especially when considered through the lenses of the different national contexts and political perspectives of the various contributors to this volume.

At the same time, though, we as editors are not of the school of political solipsism and retreat that argues that concepts of "backlash" and "anti-oppression" pedagogies should be abandoned altogether or dismissed because they appeal to commonsense or popular usage. It is well worth remembering that concepts do not just appear in a social vacuum; they emerge from, and are articulated with and by, different social movements. Although these concepts are certainly not the exclusive "property" of Leftist, feminist, or anti-racist/critical multiculturalist groups, they do have a rich history of being used to galvanize support for various radical social movements. For example, although such phrases as the "backlash against women," when used in the women's movement, have indulged racism, classism, and heterosexism by universalizing the experience of women's oppression, as Dorothy Smith (1996) reminds us, they have also helped us to develop the conceptual and methodological tools for "recentering women's everyday/everynight lived experiences."[10] The failure to appreciate the reasons why radical social movements have used certain concepts such as "backlash" or "anti-oppression" pedagogies to galvanize support seems to us to result in accounts that are retroactively unsympathetic to the daily concerns faced by movement members in their own contexts and material situations. Exclusively post–hoc and grossly abstracted theoretical critiques of these concepts may also create other erasures—namely, questions of political economy become subordinate to those of psychic economy; issues of material conditions take a back seat to those of representation and textual analysis. Indifferent/liberal pluralist notions of "difference" achieve hegemonic status in contemporary theorizing while analyses testing the ground for radical notions of "difference" get marginalized. However, as many of our contributors demonstrate, the discursive turn to, for instance, the politics of representation need not inevitably stray from the centrality of daily material, psychic, and institutional experience in a depoliticized way.

Difficult Tasks, Dangerous Territories and Pleasurable Opportunities

We write this introduction not so much as synopsis or as didactic refrain in which readers discover (our) answers already hidden in the questions posed. Rather, we hope the introduction, like the volume itself, will-function as thoughtful provocateur, refining our earlier intentions, developing more subtle and nuanced questions, conceptual tools, and methods of analysis for ourselves and readers. Represented in this volume are scholars who write transgressively within or across feminist, lesbian and gay/queer, anti-racist, and postcolonial theoretical/political perspectives, generally informed by their respective disciplines but not imprisoned by them. One strength of *Dangerous Territories* is that the essays collected here embrace a theoretical and political commitment to exceed the disciplines. We are pleased to offer essays from scholars working such varied fields as law, history, sociology, literature, sociology of education, women's studies, curriculum studies, and history of education.

Undoubtedly, the debates presented here are argued not only from different vantage points but also from different (national, classed, gendered, and sexually oriented) locations. As editors, we worked strenuously to exceed the ethnocentric limits of both a Canadian national debate and U.S. hegemony when thinking through the central questions for the volume. This is reflected in the fact that we managed to attract contributors from the United Kingdom and Australia, in addition to those from Canada and the United States, thus breaking out of certain forms of nationalistic myopia. Nonetheless, we are acutely aware that this volume commits to print its own symbolic imperialism through the absence of research by feminist post-colonial scholars exclusively living and working in non-Western "Third World" countries, where English is *not* the predominant language spoken. Despite this obvious problem, we consider it some achievement that the volume contains contributions from scholars who do speak back to the hegemony of the United States and the West, having been influenced by postcolonial and postcolonial feminist critiques.

As we contemplated the essays in this book, it became strikingly clear that no conventional table of contents could represent their overlapping investments and multiple interventions while still conveying their points of tension and contestation. We have resolved this problem—however modestly—by adopting section headings that cut across sites and practices of education as well as theoretical and disciplinary approaches. These headings are: (1) Stating the Unstated: Nations, State Power, and Education; (2) Inside-Out: Transgressive Pedagogies and Unsettling Classrooms; and (3) Shifting Courses, Directions, and Policies: Out from the Pedagogical Ghetto.

We rejected the conventional approach to organizing the essays (i.e., according to whether they focus on sexism, racism, neocolonialism, hetero-sexism, etc.) because it would have reduced relations among and between forms of oppression and the struggles against them to, as Kobena Mercer puts it, "an all too familiar 'race-class, gender' mantra, which is really a weak version of liberal multiculturalism."[11] So readers will not find sections deal-ing exclusively with feminist struggles for gender equity, with anti-racist struggles to overturn reified notions of "race," and so forth. This would be to miss how several of the essays address the relations among and between various forms of oppression and the discourses that supposedly struggle against them (e.g., Himani Bannerji is just as concerned to ask how Canada's state-produced discourses on immigration and multiculturalism render her a racial and colonial "other" as she is to know how such dis-courses objectify and vilify her in gender-specific terms). It would be to miss how, when read relationally, these papers reveal conspicuous silences (e.g., what is a racialized neocolonial and gendered state for Bannerji is a gendered state for Jill Blackmore and an activist state for Didi Herman and Davina Cooper). It would be to gloss over Richard Cavell's analysis of how the interconnections between race, national identity, class, and sexuality challenge the practice of identifying certain texts as canonical. And it would be to skip over the fact that Howard Solomon, Aruna Srivastava, and Celia Haig-Brown have similar ideas regarding what notions of pedagogy mean when they are treated as socially transformative praxis rather than as isolated instances of "correct practice."

Indeed, the richness of these essays is determined by their unruly refusal to settle down into a standard binary logic, and what emerges from them is the energizing sound of contesting voices and positions—voices and positions which, from a plethora of theoretical and methodological perspectives, question what's Left, Right, feminist, anti-racist, postcolonial, queer, and so on. For example, Davina Cooper warns that the concept of backlash is inevitably inscribed within an American liberal feminist discourse. On that point her essay resonates strongly with those of Jill Blackmore, Richard Cavell, and Didi Herman. However, while Cooper finds the concept of backlash simplistic and unworthy of further refinement, others in the volume (e.g., Blackmore, Jane Kenway, Leslie Roman and Timothy Stanley, and Srivastava) pointedly disagree. Working from within and across different theoretical approaches, these scholars redefine backlash—disentangling it from its liberal voluntarist assumptions and refocusing it on the tactical war of position between the Left and the Right. There are many other examples of sympathetic resonances and/or point-counterpoint discussions throughout this volume, all of which could get overlooked if the papers were to be organized according to such a convention.

Part I—Stating the Unstated: Nations, State Power, and Education

This section gathers together those essays whose central concern is how state power affects the organization of both Right and Left discourses. Analyses range from macro- to micro-levels of power, their foci ranging from the objects of scrutiny for sociology, to texts detailed in literary studies, to media representations, to educational practices which are both pedagogical and policy-related. The state is figured variously as the normative assumptions and ruling practices of dominant groups or Right-wing groups, or, more promisingly, as a site of active contestation between and among fractious and differentially located groups.

Nowhere in the volume are the paradoxes of liberalism (in the form of Canadian multiculturalism and contemporary discourses about immigration) made more compelling than in Himani Bannerji's essay, "Geography Lessons: On Being an Insider/Outsider to the Canadian Nation." Bannerji transgresses disciplinary lines and crosses the borders of India and Canada to critique Canada's nation-making ideology of multiculturalism. As a poet and fiction writer born and raised in India, who later immigrated to Canada (where she currently teaches at York University), she breathes new life into the often stultifying writing style of sociology, her formal discipline. Remembering how she imagined Canada during her first geography lessons in India, Bannerji invites her readers to consider how the former's discourses around multiculturalism and moral panics concerning "invading immigrants" contribute to new forms of sexism, racism, and neocolonialism. For a nation that considers itself textually and politically stitched together into one multicultural mosaic, she traces the genealogy of these two state-sanctioned discourses and shows how they deny the very radical pluralism and difference upon which the hegemonic Canadian national imaginary is premised. According to Bannerji, state power must be understood as comprising a complex historical nexus of overlapping racial, gendered, national, and class interests.

One implication of Bannerji's arguments, particularly if read in the context of her own racialized, gendered, and neocolonial relation to the state, is the knotty complicity of Western feminist traditions (especially liberal feminism) in sustaining national boundaries and particular gendered, racialized, and nationalistic notions of "belongingness" and citizenship. Clearly, white Western feminists should pay greater attention to and learn from the actual agency and struggles of particular immigrant women, women of color, and indigenous Aboriginal women, all of whom are the subjects of state/neocolonial rule. If these counter-hegemonic "lessons" were learned, then the limitations of organizing feminism on a strictly nationalist basis would become apparent, as would the urgency to mobilize transnationally.

Davina Cooper's post-Foucauldian legal analysis draws attention to the severe limitations of the concept of backlash when it comes to understanding the complexities of power and political struggle both within and across the New Christian Right (NCR) and the New Urban Left (NUL) in Britain. The context for her feminist legal research is the NCR's legislative attempts to overturn the previous decade's commitment to multi–faith education. Cooper traces how the NCR's efforts to reaffirm links among the schools, the church, and the nation are being resisted by progressive educationalists, some of whom include self-defined Christians who had supported and developed those multi-faith educational environments in the first place. She bases her conclusions on data drawn from semi–structured interviews with a cross-section of progressive educationalists (e.g., teachers, municipal education advisors, and governors) and local politicians in several municipalities. Cooper advances some surprising conclusions about the oppositional roles progressive educators play in challenging legal definitions and in defying the NCR's religious agenda. The state, Cooper argues convincingly, is not monological; it is mobilized by multi-vocal and diverse factions within both the Left and the Right.

Didi Herman draws on her feminist legal research on lesbian and gay politics in the United States and the American Christian Right (CR) in order to critique the concept of backlash. Unlike Cooper, who rejects the concept outright, she reserves a qualified use of the term to define the attitudes of the "non-alligned public." However, in her own words, "it is at best unhelpful, and at worst obscurantist, to conceptualize [the Christian Right's] activities as 'backlash.'" Herman analyzes the eschatology and theology of the Christian Right (as presented in its publications) in order to show how its broad coalition of organizations articulates a conservative Christian vision. Herman shows how, through specific struggles, this diverse collection of conservative Christians (e.g., mainstream, conservative, and evangelical Protestants) form partnerships with conservative Roman Catholics and, less frequently, with orthodox Jews and Muslims. She rejects the notion (implicit within the concept of backlash) that power is unidirectional, arguing that this prevents us from seeing how movements develop historically and how political shifts occur both within and across them. Rather than stay with a unidirectional notion of backlash, Herman recommends that we adopt a fluid, dynamic, contradictory, and contingent notion of power relations when conceptualizing social movements.

Clearly, the implications of Herman's ideas for how we, as feminists, theorize state power would lead to our viewing the state as dynamic and contested rather than as monolithic and overdetermined. However, she certainly does not equate a dynamic, contested state with a progressive one. In fact, she provides a disturbing picture of the ways in which the mainstream CR, which has previously sought to distance itself from the extreme Right—the Klansmen, the militiamen, and so on—now finds itself actively "flirting with" the latter's "theological experts." These "experts," Herman shows, endorse a Christian, white, masculinist, and openly heterosexist American nation that would promote the death penalty for homosexuality, holocaust revisionism, racial segregation, white separatism, and the merging of church and state. Given the fact that they share so much Christian theology, it is not only short-sighted but quite likely lethal to assume that the mainstream CR and the extreme Right will never merge. In any case, as Herman argues, by relying on a simplistic notion of backlash in order to analyze various state institutions and/or social movements, "we may lose sight not only of the bigger picture . . . but also of the greater danger."

In contrast to Cooper and Herman, Jill Blackmore finds the concept of backlash sociologically useful and employs it to describe and explain two dynamically interconnected processes in relation to women's work in Australian higher education: (1) the American anti-feminist media discourses used to rearticulate local Australian feminisms through "discourses of derision"[12] and (2) educational restructuring, rationalization, and privatization. Blackmore notes that discourses blaming the women's movement for such things as poor child-rearing, family breakdown, and so on are not new. However, she argues that discourses blaming feminism for being irrelevant to younger women, creating the so-called crisis-in-masculinity, and/or causing unnecessary state expenditures *is* new. Her analysis of these emergent discourses shows that feminist struggles for gender equity in universities have been successful—but unfortunately so have Right-wing responses to them. She demonstrates how anti-feminist representations and restructured working conditions combine to "discipline feminism." According to Blackmore, though positively promoted as the new realities of postmodern universities, the emergent material discourses of flexibility, efficiency, and productivity often result in insecure, casualized, and intensified labor, particularly for women faculty, staff, and administrators. These discourses also often result in the loss of state-funded gender equity programs and policies. Blackmore's combined discursive/materialist critique is refreshing, even if her conclusions are less than optimistic.

Part II—Inside-Out:
Transgressive Pedagogies and Unsettling Classrooms

In naming this section, Linda and I specifically refused the binary opposition Inside/Outside; we did this to demonstrate that academic and educational matters are not separable from social movements. The contributors to this section turn the problematic binary notion of inside/outside on its head (or rather, *inside-out*) by emphasizing that there is no (university) classroom free of the inequalities that exist in the larger society in which they are located. Nor are there any universities which are not implicated in normalizing "differences" as inequalities, though certainly many instructors and students daily resist and transgress these practices.

The strategy, adopted by some Right-wing ideologues, of chastizing or baiting the Left (including feminist, gay and lesbian, and anti-racist activist scholars) with chatter about so-called "political correctness" is an attempt to regulate what and whose knowledge, voices, and experiences can be taught.[13] As poststructuralist feminist historian Joan Scott[14] argues, the Right-wing attack on universities through the use of the notion of "political correctness" endangers not only the quality of dialogue and interchange, but also the meaning of the intellectual enterprise of public education: "This kind of pressure on universities, mobilizing deep-seated anti-intellectual sentiment, is far more dangerous to the academic enterprise than debates about the limits of free speech, the rights of minorities, and the politics of knowledge" (119). To successfully counter the political correctness attack requires engaging with a variety of theoretical approaches and methods for analyzing the cultural politics of education. The contributors to this section offer such an engagement.

Richard Cavell, in the context of an English graduate seminar on postcolonialism he taught at the University of British Columbia, speaks to the strategy of "cross-dressing"; that is, of juxtaposing works not routinely taught in relation to one another in order to avoid contributing to the canonization of particular texts and content as "postcolonial." Cavell finds that students resist his strategy, favoring certain canonical notions of content, history, authors, and ways of reading. It is this resistance that leads him to challenge the academy's practice of affixing difference to a linear trajectory, location, context, and time. Cavell's essay offers an explicit challenge to liberal concepts of backlash and equality as well as to the politics of a Left that would "presume to speak for all women, all gays, all persons of color, and so on."

Similarly, Aruna Srivastava, a feminist anti-racist who teaches in the English Department at the University of Calgary, echoes Cavell's refusal to treat particular texts as canonical. Like Cavell, she struggles with complaints from students who ask why, in an English class, they are spending so much time talking about anti-racism and feminism. Srivastava addresses the many ways in which professional values and the institution of the university force her to be complicit with racism and white supremacy. In working to build anti-racist coalitions that bridge universities and non-academic community groups, she discusses many institutionally inscribed dilemmas and contradictions. In so doing, Srivastava addresses the way in which the possibilities for conducting anti-racist pedagogy both exceed and implicate the university classroom, calling upon activist scholars to rethink how to keep alive potent traditions of political resistance in social movements.

In contrast to Srivastava, Alice Pitt, who teaches in the Faculty of Education at York University, believes the term "resistance" refers not so much to the feminist movement qua political movement as it does to the processes of identification and psychic formation that implicate feminism and feminist pedagogy in what she calls "minoritizing positions." Pitt uses poststructural and psychoanalytic theories of learning to explain the resistances voiced in the narratives of two women students in an introductory women's studies course—two students who have learned that the course includes the topic of lesbianism. Pitt shows that their respective narratives are deeply interconnected, despite the fact that, on the surface, they appear to be very different from one another. Student A openly repudiates the "lesbian other" by declaring that lesbianism is a personal choice, having nothing to do with her life or the lives of other women, and by arguing that the topic of lesbianism belongs in courses dealing with "gay liberation"; student B embraces lesbianism as a specifically feminist critique of heterosexuality and voices an interest in lesbianism that is coincident with her "coming out." Pitt demonstrates that these two narratives are part of a disturbing trend within feminist pedagogy—the disavowal of differences within and among women. As Pitt argues, women's studies pedagogy (and, by implication, feminism in general) involves many scenes of misrecognition and the denial of difference. As Pitt points out, both students "refuse to know anything about relationality or about how their respective positions entail implicating the other as 'not-woman.'"

As they are for Pitt, psychoanalytic and feminist pedagogical notions of resistance are also of significance for Patricia Elliot, who analyzes her female students' resistance to learning about gender inequalities. Elliot examines how the women in her gender and society course at Sir Wilfrid Laurier University employ what she calls a "selective reality" and a "fantasy of gender equality" in order to defend their belief that gender equality has already been achieved. Elliot indicates that many of her women students routinely disclosed personal experiences of sexism while simultaneously denying the impact of sexism both in their lives and in society. She narrates experiences that are all too common for untenured feminist instructors: (1) unconscious resistance toward their feminist analyses of gender inequity and (2) hostility toward themselves, their courses, and feminism in general.

Part III—Shifting Courses, Directions, and Policies: Out from the Pedagogical Ghetto

This section includes essays by authors who shift from one site of educational practice to another in order to rethink the relations between the so-called private and public spheres of educational practice. Some, such as Celia Haig-Brown and Linda Eyre, look at curricular guidelines on equality and assess their implications for the classroom. Others, such as Jane Kenway, Howard Solomon, Leslie Roman and Timothy Stanley, Linda Eyre, and Dorothy Smith, attempt to overcome the ghettoization of different anti–oppression pedagogies by "shamelessly occupy[ing]" (Solomon, this volume) the intersecting and blurred territory/borderlands of public and private, popular and academic, non-formal and formal educational institutions, and so forth. The essays in this section encourage engagement across different educational contexts, practices, and sites. Many are compelling precisely because they refuse to settle curricular/pedagogical matters in a ghettoized manner. The movement between and across sites of practice is precisely what is required if struggles for social justice are ever to amount to anything other than brave and/or token gestures.

Dorothy Smith's feminist materialist/discursive analysis focuses on how the controversies emerging from student complaints of sexism, racism, and heterosexism within the university are part of an intertextual conversation that extends well beyond the academy. Controversies in several Canadian political science departments have become the focus of national and international attention and one of them—at the University of Victoria—forms the subject of Smith's analysis. A feature of these controversies, argues Smith, is their textual and documentary character as well as their reliance on external experts. She illustrates how those parts of the everyday feminist and anti-racist critiques that are most salient to routine "chilly climate" concerns get transformed within a juridical framework and, consequently, organize the debates to follow. She shows how the juridical framework radically alters the discursive rules for evidence, for processual standards, for determining what voices can be heard, and for constructing the relationship between those who made critiques and those about whom the critiques were made. Smith shows how transferring these critiques to a juridical framework deflects attention away from their original foci—objections to the daily institutional practice of having to put up with hostile anti-feminist, racist behavior and/or attitudes—and toward a "conflict and contestation" between students and faculty/administrators. In this relationship there are two sides, accuser and accused; and what is at issue is "the truth." Those who voice or who have voiced the critiques (namely students) now find themselves under attack, accused in various ways of failing. For example, they have failed to conform to proper procedures, they have failed to hear "both sides" of the case, they have failed to secure adequate documentation, and so on.

Smith pores over the masses of documents and texts produced by the UVIC controversy and shows how we, as feminists and anti–racists, have become captured within the juridical frame. She employs Jurgen Habermas's conception of an ideal speech situation (i.e., one in which each speaker/hearer recognizes the other as subject, in which the aim is understanding, and in which one party does not attempt to overcome or intimidate the other party) in order to analyze what feminists mean by the "chilly climate" critique. Smith argues that the notion of "chilly climate" expresses various inequalities, not as specific actions but rather as ordinary practices that are at odds with the ideal speech situation of rational discourse. Thus, in identifying barriers to full participation on the part of women and other marginalized groups, "chilly climate" critiques appeal to the alleged foundational values/ principles of universities (i.e., the right to full participation in rational discourse). The juridical turn, on the other hand, radically weakens those critiques by reducing everything to the task of identifying specific actions as some form of wrongdoing.

Like Smith, Howard Solomon also consciously transgresses the role of intellectual and activist, thus crossing the often treacherous divide between the academy and the community "outside" Tufts University, Massachusetts, where he teaches gay and lesbian history. Solomon speaks eloquently of his struggles to challenge existing conceptions of scholarly merit—conceptions that make it clear that publishing in high-status referreed journals will be valued over developing courses in "marginal" areas (e.g., gay, lesbian, and bisexual studies) or dedicating one's time to teaching well and working with diverse community groups. Daring to appropriate the exclamatory admonition "what a shame you don't publish!," Solomon considers how activist intellectuals can use discourses of institutional shaming in order to pursue radical social change. He analyzes how, at Tufts, the criteria for measuring academic merit was transformed partly as a result of his "shameless" attempts to persuade his colleagues to take a proactive role in re-evaluating the university's policies and procedures for granting promotion to full professor. Solomon's inspirational essay challenges activist intellectuals to be "shameless" in their attempts to get universities to acknowledge the interrelationship between teaching and research, community knowledge/practice and theory, and teaching and service. His promotion was not merely indicative of individual achievement—it was also indicative of his involvement in the time-honored public intellectual tradition of working to "queer" the borders of the university.

Linda Eyre, like Solomon and Smith, also creates an alternative to the ghetto of certain forms of anti-oppression pedagogy which effect little more than liberal inclusionary ideologies. She does this by examining purportedly anti-heterosexist pedagogical approaches to sexuality education in Canada. Basing her critical analysis in part on the insights of leading lesbian and gay scholars, she examines three pedagogical practices typically employed by sexual health educators in secondary schools—the add-on approach, the guest-speaker approach, and the anti-homophobic-workshop approach— allegedly to challenge traditional (hetero-normative) sexuality education. Eyre, having been a high-school teacher, a curriculum development specialist in education, and now, a professor of Education at the University of New Brunswick who works with future health educators, has at one time or another used all three approaches and found them wanting. With great precision, she describes the limits, possibilities, and contradictions inherent within conventional anti-heterosexist pedagogical approaches to health education. And she painstakingly examines how new Right discourses—by appropriating the language of equality, discrimination, stereotyping, and inclusion—subtly seduce educators into thinking they are being progressive when in fact they are being just the opposite.

Leslie Roman and Timothy Stanley analyze Grade seven student discourses in a public school in Vancouver, British Columbia, reconsidering what young people have to teach anti-racist educators about their understandings of race, racism, and anti-racism. Instead of assuming that classrooms and schools are extensions of a fictive harmonious national family that nurtures individual growth and civic responsibility, they show how schools are sites of symbolic contestation, in which struggles over the meanings of national belongingness and citizenship are acted out. The gendered grammars of racism, nationalism, and neocolonialism, they argue, are produced in the overlapping and conflicting sites of the family, the state, the school, and the media, where the current moral panics about the so-called "racial and national invasion" of particular groups occupy center stage in both official and popular discourses. In this context, they argue, young people are not simply passive receivers of knowledge waiting to be affected by the "right/correct" interventions and curricula, as is often assumed in academic research and in progressive boards of education. Roman and Stanley demonstrate why it is important to develop a postcolonialist curricular agenda that offers alternatives both to multiculturalism's exaggerated focus on discrete cultures and to anti-racism's hollow rhetoric about "stopping racism." In order to effectively challenge the blurred and overlapping discourses of both official and popular moral panics, we need to have pedagogical and political strategies that are more than mere add-ons to the curriculum. The challenge for anti-imperialist postcolonial curricula is to acknowledge diversity without either reifying or annihilating differences. Recognizing what cultural studies analyst Paul Gilroy calls "a new language of cultural democracy"[15] means ensuring that teaching about peoples' different histories does not present new barriers to anti-imperialist coalition politics.

Celia Haig-Brown traces the complex, contradictory, and ambiguous locations of British Columbia's gender equity policy. Like Eyre and Roman and Stanley, she argues that there is no end to the political process of working through the contradictions of such policies; rather, they must be addressed in such a way that one may "determine both what they offer and what they hide." Drawing on the work of Foucault, as well as that of postcolonial feminist Chandra Talpade Mohanty and other poststructural feminist scholars, Haig-Brown analyzes her students' responses to a "policy-based, government-funded university course entitled 'Gender Equity: Issues in Teacher Education.'" In so doing, she examines how the government's gender-equity policy "both promotes and impedes the transformative goals of feminism." Haig-Brown also discusses coalition work both inside and outside the classroom.

Jane Kenway's poststructuralist feminist look at cyberspace provides analysis of both the dangers and the opportunities it presents to feminist educational work. For Kenway, the notion of backlash (which she takes to refer to "the postfeminist reassertion of those oppressive versions of masculinity associated with dominance, violence, the subordination of women and girls, and the subordination of all versions of masculinity that reject dominance and respect differences") overstates the dangers of cyberspace by focusing almost exclusively on the reinscription of new forms of dominating masculinity rather than on new opportunities for women as well as new forms of non-dominating masculinity. At the same time, though, Kenway does not wish to exaggerate the feminist opportunities of the Internet; certain of its contextual features and uses "cast a shadow over feminism in cyberspace." In Australia, she notes, only recently have there been serious efforts to teach technology across various levels of schooling. Kenway believes that it is extremely important to uncouple the connection between science and technology and to make stronger connections between converging technologies in the social sciences, humanities, health, and the arts, for, as she says, "teaching *about* technology is just as important as teaching *with* it."

Conclusion: Radical Difference and Struggles for Equality

The risk of radical difference is a question of naming and unnaming, of re-naming ourselves in the context of strategic coalition-building. No common noun or umbrella term (e.g., Left) adequately describes in some transhistorical manner the range of identities and political struggles constitutive of radical social movements. However, as cultural studies scholar Kobena Mercer aptly notes, the extent to which social justice and equality struggles have pluralized radically the domain social antagonism is a "way of acknowledging the transformations associated with the social presence of new social actors/movements"[16] (1992, 425). At the very least, it is a way of going beyond the narcissistic conceit of certain hegemonic elements of the Left/progressive politics—whether male Marxists, white and/or heterosexual middle class feminists, and so forth—who are only able to think of remaking progressive/radical politics in their/our own romanticized images.

If radical difference/pluralism is to go beyond individualism in struggles for equality, then it must clarify the stakes of how time, particular events/groups, and political/socio-economic relations get articulated in educational practice, political activism, discourse, and popular memory. However, recognizing the different and often conflicting claims of "difference," as cultural activist and artist Rasheed Araeen (1994) reminds us, is *not* the only challenge; there is still the question of "how and where [we] locate these claims historically" (9). Locating such claims is also a matter of the difficult and risky business of deconstructing whose difference/identity matters to whom and in what particular contexts of differential power.

Just as pressing are the prospects for developing and sustaining new forms of transnational feminisms, critical multiculturalisms/anti-racisms/anti-imperialisms, and sexual politics to energize Left coalitions. This becomes especially relevant when in many respects the Left is fractured and composed of diverse groups, struggling to find the bases for common cause and alliance. With the acknowledgment of plural epistemologies and partial knowledges comes a certain degree of humility that any of us can always know what a broader vision of radical democracy should look like in any guaranteed (rather than provisional) way. But having forsaken the obvious guarantees provided by claims favoring universalism and essentialism, we wish also not to stray from the unavoidable *normative* task of theorizing provisional futures which try to negotiate the tension between hanging on to notions of equality and difference at the same time. This means getting messy—discussing the many difficulties as well as the successes of alliances, acknowledging where positions and/or constituencies or the positions taken by members of the Leftist/progressive groups—including feminists, anti-racists, and lesbians and gays, and so forth—are conflicted and when they are *not*. How radical democratic social movements will negotiate the contested terrain of making many new Left, feminist, queer, and anti-racist/anti-imperialist futures is what is at stake in the desire to exceed the polemics of the debates over "backlash" and "anti-oppression" pedagogies.

Without further ado, the unsettled and unsettling essays . . .

Notes

We are indebted to David Jardine, Arlene Mc Laren, and Joanne Richardson for their critical comments. The central ideas raised in this introduction are the focus of a longer and significantly different essay by Leslie G. Roman solicited for publication in *Discourse: Studies in the Cultural Politics of Education*. We wish also to thank the Faculty of Education, University of New Brunswick, for its support for this project and for a small grant that contributed in part to our East Coast-West Coast collaboration.

1. The panelists were Linda Eyre, Celia Haig-Brown, Mimi Orner, and Leslie Roman.

2. "Keywords," according to Williams are connected in two senses:

> they are significant, binding words in certain activities and their interpretation; they are significant, indicative words in certain forms of thought. Certain uses bound together in certain ways of seeing culture and society, not least in these two most general words. Certain other uses . . . open up issues and problems . . . of which we all needed to be very more conscious. (Raymond Williams, Keywords: A Vocabulary of Culture and Society [Oxford: Oxford University Press, 1976], 13)

3. See Susan Faludi's *Backlash: The Undeclared War Against American Women* (New York: Crown, 1991). Faludi's own conception of "backlash" distinguishes it from both a general "hostility to female independence" and a "fear and loathing of feminism" which shows no "acute" reactions to feminism or women. Rather, a "backlash" for her is "episodic" and resurges or flares up "when triggered by the perception—whether accurate or not—that women are making great strides" (xix). Faludi initially rejects a conspiratorial theory of agency in backlashes, but the tone and the subsequent examples contradict her position, which suggests a simple cause–effect model of social forces and action—one feminist/progressive, and the other antifeminist and conservative, engaged in struggle. For a crititique of this model, see J. Newson, "Backlash Against Feminism: A Disempowering Metaphor," *RFR/DRF* 20: 93–97.

4. Here, we draw upon Leslie Roman's formulation of the term, which emphasizes both the structural and the emotional bases of political formations, such as the white defensiveness that forms the basis of David Duke's, successful white supremacist political campaign for Congressional office in Louisiana. See Leslie Roman's use of the term in "White is a Color: White Defensiveness, Postmodernism, and Antiracist Pedagogy," in *Race, Identity, and Representation in Education*, edited by Cameron McCarthy and Warren Chrichlow (New York/London: Routledge, 1993), 71–88.

5. See Charles Derber, Karen Marie Ferroggiaro, Jacqueline A. Ortiz, Cassie Schwerner, and James Vela-McConnell, *What's Left? Radical Politics in the Postcommunist Era* (Amherst: University of Massachusetts Press, 1985).

6. In giving credit where it may be due, we suspect that it is not just the collapse of statist Eastern European socialism and communism that causes white male heterosexual Marxists in North America to be defensive. Rather, it is also the presence and demands for equality, curricular reform, and social justice made by feminists, anti-racists, gays, and lesbians in the North American contexts in which they live and work. These demands challenge and redefine who speaks in the name of the Left. Angela McRobbie makes a similar argument with respect to the male socialist Left in England in her chapter "Looking Back at New Times and its Critics," in *Stuart Hall: Critical Dialogues in Cultural Studies*, edited by David Morely and Kuan–Hsing Chen (London/New York: Routledge, 1996), 238–261.

7. For an excellent discussion of transnational articulations of capitalism, patriarchy, and neocolonialism, see *Feminist Genealogies, Colonial Legacies, Democratic*

Futures, edited by M. Jacqui Alexander and Chandra Talpade Mohanty (New York/London: Routledge, 1997).

8. For example, some male neo-Marxist scholars who picketed and protested during the Canadian Union of Public Employees (CUPE) clerical workers' strike in 1991 at the University of British Columbia also had no difficulty employing the right-wing discourse of "reverse discrimination" and violations of their "academic freedom" when, later, in their own Political Science Department, women students and students of color asserted their unequal treatment by male faculty in that department.

9. Julia Swindells and Lisa Jardine, *What's Left? Women in Culture and the Labour Movement* (London/New York: Routledge, 1990).

10. See Dorothy Smith's rejoinder to Judith Stacy and Barrie Thorne in *Perspectives: The American Sociological Association Theory Section Newsletter* 18 (3): 7–8.

11. Kobena Mercer, "'1968': Periodizing Postmodern Politics and Identity," in *Cultural Studies*, edited by Lawrence Grossberg, Cary Nelson, and Paula Triechler (New York/London: Routledge, 1992), 425.

12. See Jane Kenway's conceptualization of "discourses of derision" in "Left Right Out, Australian Education and the Politics of Signification." *Journal of Educational Policy*, 2 (3): 189–203, esp., 192.

13. One of the current ironies about risk-taking in pedagogical situations is that although risks to create counter-hegemonic pedagogies and curricula do get taken, the consequences for taking them often prevent the risks from being spoken about in print. We attribute this silence not to any lack of thought or warehouse of first-hand experience on the parts of faculty who write here. Rather, we attribute this to some of the institutionally produced power relations, which disable/silence certain kinds of speaking and speakers.

14. See Joan Scott, "The Campaign Against Political Correctness: What's Really at Stake," in *After Political Correctness: The Humanities and Society in the 1990s*, edited by Christopher Newfield and Ronald Strickland (Boulder: Westview Press, 1995), 111–27.

15. See Gilroy's discussion in "Nationalism, History, and Ethnic Absolutism," *History Workshop* 30 (1990, Autumn): 114–20.

16. Kobena Mercer, "'1968,'" 424–27.

Part I

Stating the Unstated:
Nations, State Power, and Education

Chapter One

Geography Lessons:
On Being an Insider/Outsider
to the Canadian Nation

Himani Bannerji
York University (Canada)

My first encounter with Canada occurred during my geography lessons as a young girl. There, in an atlas of physical geography, colored green, pink, and yellow, I came across Canada—a place of trees, lakes, wheat fields, ice caps, and an ancient rock formation cut through with glaciers. I don't remember reading anything of the history of this country in my geography book, but somehow there were faint echoes of people and nature blurring into each other—"red Indians," "eskimos," "igloos," "aurora borealis," and "reindeer." From where did these images come if not from my geography book? From literature and scattered visual images perhaps? There were, after all, the books of Fenimore Cooper or Jack London, which irrespective of national boundaries created mythologies of the "North," the "Indian," and wove tales of discovery of the Arctic—of Amundsen and others lost in blizzards on their dog sleds. Eventually, on my fourteenth birthday, I received a book called *The Scalpel and the Sword*, and I decided to be a doctor, like Norman Bethune.

What I am trying to recount is what Canada meant for me—all this jumbled-up information, this fusion of people and nature, my imagination moved by forests and the glow of Arctic ice. Certainly, "Canada" was a mental rather than a historical space. It was an idyllic construction of nature and adventure.

Many years later, the Canada I stepped into was vastly different from the Canada I had constructed in my childhood. When I immigrated to Montreal, I stepped out of my romantic construction of Canada and into a distinctly political-ideological one—one which impressed me as being both negative and aggressive. From the insistence and harshness with which I was asked whether I intended to apply for "landing"—a term I did not understand and that had to be explained—I knew that I was not welcome in this

"Canada." I told the officer defiantly that this would never be my country; I had come as a foreign student and would leave upon receiving my degree. That is how it has remained to this day. Had I been received differently, had I been made to feel more "at home," would this be my home, my Canada?

This remains a hypothetical question, since upon "landing" six years later and being labelled an "immigrant," a "visible minority woman," I have remained in limbo. Even after years of being an "immigrant," and upon swearing allegiance to the same Queen of England from whom India had parted, I was not to be a "Canadian." Regardless of my official status as a Canadian citizen, I, like many others, remained an "immigrant." The category "Canadian" clearly applied to people who had two things in common: their white skin and their European North American (not Mexican) background. They did not all speak English. There were two colors in this political atlas—one a beige-brown shading off into black and the other white. These shades did not simply reflect skin colors—they reflected the ideological, political, and cultural assumptions and administrative practices of the Canadian State.

"Canada" then cannot be taken as a given. It is obviously a construction, a set of representations, embodying certain types of political and cultural communities and their operations. These communities were themselves constructed in agreement with certain ideas regarding skin color, history, language (English/French), and other cultural signifiers—all of which may be subsumed under the ideological category "White."[1] A "Canada" constructed on this basis contains certain notions of nation, state formation, and economy. Europeanness as "whiteness"[2] thus translates into "Canada" and provides it with its "imagined community." This is a process that Benedict Anderson (1991) speaks of, but he glosses over the divisiveness of class, "race," and ideology—the irreconcilable contradictions at the heart of this community-nation-state project. Furthermore, he does not ask about the type of imagination at work in this project. He does not ask either *whose* imagination is advanced as the national imaginary or what this has to do with organizing practical and ideological exclusions and inclusions within the national space. These questions become concrete if we look at how I was received in Canada. Why was I thus received? Was it just an accident? An isolated instance? What did it have to do with *who* I was—my so-called gender and race? Did this story of mine begin with my arrival, or was I just a tiny episode in a pre-existing historical narrative? Can I or similar "others" imagine a "Canada" and project it as the national imaginary?

So if we problematize the notion of "Canada" through the introjection of the idea of belonging, we are left with the paradox of both belonging and non-belonging simultaneously. As a population, we non-Whites and women (in particular, non-White women) are living in a specific territory.

We are part of its economy, subject to its laws, and members of its civil society. Yet we are not part of its self-definition as "Canada" because we are not "Canadians." We are pasted over with labels that give us identities that are extraneous to us. And these labels originate in the ideology of the nation, in the Canadian state apparatus, in the media, in the education system, and in the commonsense world of common parlance. We ourselves use them. They are familiar, naturalized names: visible minorities, immigrants, newcomers, refugees, aliens, illegals, people of color, multicultural communities, and so on. We are sexed into immigrant women, women of color, visible minority women, Black/South Asian/Chinese women, ESL (English as second language) speakers, and many more.[3] The names keep proliferating, as though there were a seething reality, unmanageable and uncontainable in any one name. Concomitant with this mania for the naming of "others" is one for the naming of that which is "Canadian." This "Canadian" core community is defined through the same process that others us. We, with our named and ascribed otherness, face an undifferentiated notion of the "Canadian" as the unwavering beacon of our assimilation.

And what is the function of the many names applied to us? They are categories for organizing the state apparatus, its regulations and policy functions, and for enabling the ideological organization of "relations of ruling."[4] These categories enable the state to extend its governing and administrative jurisdiction into civil society, while, at the same time, incorporating the everyday person into the national project. One might say, then, remembering Althusser, that they are appellations for interpellation.[5] These names are codes for political subjectivities and ideological/pedagogical possibilities, and they have embedded in them both immediate and long-term political effects. They help to construct "Canada" and to place us in certain roles and niches of the nation; and those who are not "Canadians" cannot directly project "Canada." This "Canada's" placement of "others," because it creates feelings of belonging and alienation, not only produces psychological and cultural problems regarding power, but is also integral to the structure of the Canadian polity itself. Its categories of otherness delimit the membership of this nation and this state (Ng 1993). This situation reveals not only a raced or ethnicized state, but also—more importantly—a crisis in citizenship and a continual attempt to manage this crisis. It tells us that, in the polity of Canadian liberal democracy, there is always already a crisis of gender, race, and class. This becomes obvious if we look at the status of women, in particular the status of White women, in terms of their participation in the construction of "Canada." Their protracted struggle for enfranchisement, for inclusion in the nation, is marked by the fact that their gender was a barrier to them in spite of their status as mothers and daughters of the Canadian White male "race." Although Canadian suffragists such as Nellie McLung,

following their White U.S. sisters, resented Chinese and non-White enfranchisement, they themselves were considered to be second-class citizens.[6]
Privileged by class and race, but handicapped by gender, their situation
exposes the fact that citizenship does not provide automatic membership in
the nation's community. Living in a nation does not, by definition, provide
one with a prerogative to "imagine" it. From the very inception of democracy, Athenian and after, the making of a national imaginary, the construction of its ideological political form and content, has been conditional. Such
privilege, manifested as a belonging and conforming to regulatory norms
and forms, has been restricted through criteria that are both constructed
through and anchored in the social relations of the civil society. Being working class, being "raced," and being of a certain gender, all restrict access to
citizenship in the here and now by modifying the conditions of freedom,
property, and literacy.

Under circumstances in which wives and daughters of the White bour-
geoisie do not qualify for citizenship, the issue of the enfranchisement of non-
White women (usually working class) becomes ever more problematic. The
latter are virtually erased from the political map. The non-White working-
class male is at least referred to in the course of White bourgeois women's
drives for social agency and citizenship, but their female counterparts are not
even mentioned as potential members.[7] The othering or difference that is
produced through the state's racist or ethnicizing policies with regard to
importing and administrating labor[8] could only be further intensified
through gendering. General disenfranchisement, deportation, head taxes,
barrack lives, and so on (followed in more recent times by various types of
immigration and refugee statuses, the reintroduction of a form of head tax
through application fees, etc.) gave momentum to further oppression
through patriarchy. Together, "sexing" and "racing" mark moments in a pro-
bation which qualifies one for a merely *formal equality* a nominal citizenship.[9]

The making of Canada is thus accomplished through the exclusion and
marginalization of women. Even formal equality has been hard for women
to come by. Although not explicitly stated in the Consitution, this exclusive
gendering is clearly present in the case of imported labor. At lower levels of
labor, particularly, there was (and is) an active attempt to seek able–bodied
young men in the industrial/manufacturing sector and young women in the
service sector or for industrial piece-work.[10] This, too, was racialized and
ethnicized as White and non-White, with the former being given permission to create families, to "settle" Canada and outnumber its indigenous
peoples, and the latter, Chinese and Indian indentured workers, being
restricted through head taxes, quotas, and miscegenation laws. A non-
White laborer lived in a state of continual vulnerability, driven underground in search of jobs, company, and sex.[11] Even in the 1950s, when

emigrating from the Third World with families first became possible, the emphasis was on masculinizing the labor force. "Independent immigration," therefore, has been a male preserve, with most women entering Canada "sponsored" by, or as "dependents" of, the "head of a family." This is the case even when women are as skilled (or unskilled) as their husbands. This patriarchal gesture of the state gave women's husbands (or male sponsors) complete control over them, while domestic workers (also, for the most part, women) were in the grip of their "Canadian" employers. Battering, rape, and general degradation could not and cannot be effectively resisted without risking the breakdown of these sponsorships, the withdrawal of work permits, and deportation. So, not only is there a mandate for importing able-bodied adult male labor and female reproducers (whose social production costs have been borne by another country), there is also a continual attempt to patriarchalize Canada's social organization. Thus, in Canada, gender and race have always mediated the overall social production and relations of class.

This patriarchalization has been at work since the era of the fur trade. It intensified when the White settler colonial state emerged, having race and gender deeply engraved in both its definition and its administration.[12] The socio-economic and cultural disenfranchisement of indigenous peoples has been both genocidal and patriarchal. Through the Indian Act, for example, racist and sexist constructions of "the Indian," "Indian culture," and "the Indian woman" became both possible and practicable.[13] This went together with ensuring that the White woman was out of bounds for non-White men, a process that did not exhaust itself with old-style settler colonialism. Canadian social organization was based on race, which was defined as being constituted by those of "pure blood" (either "Indians" or "Europeans") and those of "mixed blood" (the Métis).[14] The Indian Act created a zone of non-identity for indigenous women, and it ensured that they lost their economic bases. By marrying out of their prescribed locations and blood spaces as "Indians," they lost their "Indian" status in their own communities and did not gain White status in the non-Native communities.[15] This was a part of the overall process of excluding women from "Canada," and it came down most heavily on "raced" others.

In more recent times, the organized subordination of women comes out clearly in the context of the pro-choice movement, which is led by middle-class White women. Given that we live in a so-called liberal democracy (which supposedly enshrines individual rights and freedom of choice), and given that we live in what C. B. Macpherson has called a "market model of democracy" (Macpherson 1977; 1973, 157–203), there should be no proscription against obtaining abortion on demand. But in spite of their formal equality with men as "citizens" and their being defined as possessive individuals, as owners of their own persons and other property, women's rights to abortion on demand is opposed by the Canadian state. And, their White, middle-class status notwithstanding, the leaders of the pro-choice movement were revealed to be, in political-ideological terms, of minority or non-age status. Unlike a man, who could consent to surgical procedures on any part of his body, a woman was against a legal wall. In fact, women turned out to be wards of the state, which, as their paternal guardian, got to decide what was good for them. With the help of protective/preventive laws and masculinized expert medical services, women were held in permanent tutelage. This role of reluctant breeders is forced, particularly, on White women, as they are of the majority culture and are thus held responsible for counterbalancing the "unassimilables" (i.e., non-Whites) among us. Besides, as non-White women are considered to be overly fecund, there is a terror that they might change Canada's racial composition. Bloc Québecois leader Lucien Bouchard, while on his separatist campaign, has put the responsibility of the success of his national project squarely in the lap of Quebec's White women, since it is they who must breed in order to prop up the declining "White race."[16] In various euphemistic forms, this argument has underpinned Canadian immigration, refugee, and cultural policies. It is not hard to see that the Canadian state's overwhelming sense of guardianship over women's bodies amounts to a demand for White women to reproduce more and for non-White women to reproduce less. The overall mandate for women, here as in China (which has become a byword for repressive reproductive regimes), is to reproduce in keeping with the economic, cultural, and political ambitions of the state and within an overall population policy projected for the country. In the end, nationally appropriate reproduction becomes the White woman's burden, and it is not coincidental that this dovetails with the White supremacist desire to "Keep Canada White."

The fact that the state seeks to hold the White woman's womb hostage has profound repercussions for non-White women. Caught in the same legal labyrinth as are their White counterparts, their motherhood is by implication also regulated. In the United States, a vast number of Black women do not reach natural menopause (Sheehy 1991); they are given complete hysterectomies or tubal ligations as early as during their thirties. It would be interesting to do a comparative study of the difficulties faced by Black and White women, respectively, in their attempts to obtain abortions in Canada; it would also be interesting to look at this research in terms of class. At this point, however, I can only point to the general discouragement meted out to non-White people with regard to reproduction. Since there is already an attempt to criminalize "immigrants" or "visible minorities," any non-White woman's violation of the state's mandate against abortion on demand threatens to further criminalize her.

The issue of "motherhood" should lead us to think about the status of women in Canada in general, and about women's location in the racialized and gendered political economy. It is interesting that when even minimum cognizance is taken of the exclusion of women, the state (e.g., Mike Harris's Ontario) rushes in to smash whatever ineffectual equity programs may have been put in place due to pressure from the women's movement. On the other hand, the state continues, in the language of Christian charity, to demonize women as recipients of social welfare.

The state constructs not only women in general, but also poor women, and impoverished women of color in particular, as political/social subjects who are essentially dependent and weak (Fraser and Gordon 1994; Alexander and Mohanty, 1997). As such they are seen as a burden on the state and the economy; that is, on the more competent, economically productive, masculinized "tax payer." The welfare recipient is often portrayed as a "she"—a "welfare mother" or a "single mother." Thanks to the combined effort of the state and the media, poverty is "feminized." It is seen as located in women's own social subjectivity, as their own creation. A whole world is conjured up—a world of mothers, strollers, babies, and recalcitrant, badly brought up children. This "female culture of poverty" is then condemned by the school system, child psychologists, the Ministry of Social Services, and the Ministry of Correctional Services. In fact, we are currently witnessing the revival of an eighteenth- and nineteenth-century category known as "the poor." "The poor" are now emerging as a character type, as (almost) a separate species. As with women, so with the poor in general: their character is their destiny. Not only does this category hide the production of poverty by the state and the ruling mores of capital, it also results in a kind of political paralysis through the ontologization of poverty. The only action taken on behalf of the poor has to do with charity and the reinforcement of the nuclear family—action that assuages the consciences of the charitable rather than the hunger of those in need. It is worth considering what a very different political and social persona would be projected if, rather than being categorized as "the poor," this same group of people was categorized as "the proletariat."

Racialization affects "the poor" just as it does others, such as unemployed workers. The category "immigrant/refugee welfare recipient," for example, includes both men and women who are thoroughly demonized as perennial welfare recipients and manipulators of unemployment insurance and workers' disability pension. The odor of dishonesty that haunts the world of "the poor" in general is most intense around those who are non-White. Whole communities live under suspicion and surveillance—Somalis, Tamils, Jamaicans, and so on. This raced poverty is both masculine and feminine, and even its feminine face does not fall within any code of chivalry or compassion and charity. Because of the alleged illegitimacy of their presence in Canada, these people are not candidates for such treatment. This segment of "the poor" is thus quickly covered in a mantle of crime. The world of non-White poverty inspires media/state–produced images of desperate young men always ready to commit crime. What is aimed at them is "order"— either that of the police officer's gun or that of the deportation law. Both poor non-White men and non-White women are under permanent suspicion of "welfare fraud," a heightened version of what confronts poor Whites.

That my assertions are not a matter of individual paranoia is evident in the fact that Ontario has established a "hotline" to prompt us to report anonymously on our neighbors and anyone else whom we think might be cheating "the system." This "snitch line" violates human dignity/human rights, creates a state of legal surveillance, and organizes people into vigilante-style relationships with one another. It brings racism and sexism to a boiling point by stimulating an everyday culture of racist sexism, and it creates an atmosphere that can only be described as fascistic. Clearly, reporting "the Jew" among us is not over yet!

Since these race-gendered class forms of criminalization, marginalization, and exclusion arise in present-day Canada—a supposedly liberal democratic state—the situation with which we have to deal becomes highly complex. Canada is not talked about in the same way as is, for example, South Africa. Its "Indian" reserves are not seen as Bantustans (the latter were apparently inspired by the former).[17] Canada as a liberal democracy cannot, in spite of the Reform Party or the police view of non-White communities, practice legal apartheid. The Canadian state, according to its Charter of Rights and Freedoms, claims not to discriminate on the bases of race, gender, and so on. But it is obvious that, by its very organization of social communities in "race" and ethnic terms, the state constantly creates "Canadians" and "others." This happens not only in the realm of state-constructed policy, but also in that of everyday life—within what Theo Goldberg (1993) calls a "racist culture." This "racist culture" is in a mutually constitutive relationship with the state.

If we do not accept this, then the racist violence of the Canadian Airborne Regiment in Somalia in the course of its peace-keeping duties for the United Nations becomes an instance of insanity. But if we see racism as a hegemonic social and political culture and practice participated in by the police, the military, the other aspects of the state, the church, the educational system, and our everyday life, then what happened in Somalia begins to make some sociological sense. This pervasive "racist culture," which is textured through and through with the cult of "raced" masculinity, cannot but claim its victims. To be a "White man," then, is not a simple physical fact; it is a moral imperative and an ideology.[18] Sometimes it works in a crude manner, as in White supremacist groups; sometimes it is more refined, as in the languages of civilization and expertise. But it is not all that far from Canadian engineering students' sexist-racist rites to the Airborne's hazing and killing in Somalia. Canada's fundamentally patriarchal character is evident from Somalia to Oka, from Gustafson Lake to Ipperwash,[19] and in the police shooting of Black youths, including that of Sophia Cooke, and the street-corner strip-search of another woman, Audrey Smith. Canada's racist patriarchal nature is further exemplified by the fact that it is so often culturally represented abroad by the Royal Canadian Mounted Police on postcards manufactured for tourist consumption. A secret police that is publicly advertised as "Canadian culture"—quite a plug for White masculinity.

In the face of my assertion that "Canada," as a national imaginary, is a sexist-racist entity, some will advance a phenomenon known as "multiculturalism."[20] I will be told that, due to this phenomenon, which needs especial scrutiny with regard to citizenship of "others," the whole world looks up to Canada. Although, in practice, multiculturalism has never been effective, it can and does serve as an ideological slogan within a liberal democratic framework. It supplies an administrative device for managing social contradictions and conflicts. This is important since "Canada," as a nationalist project, is perceived to be a homogeneous, solid, and settled entity, though its history constantly belies this.

This is why the language for imagining "Canada" is fraught with such notions as "solitude" and "survival." There is in this national space a legitimation crisis.[21] Other than the dissent and struggle of the indigenous peoples, the raced-gendered "others" who remain a source of dissentience, the national project is deeply riven by the rivalry between Anglophones and Francophones—Canada's "two solitudes."[22] Equally patriarchal and race-inscribed, these two solitudes remain central cultural/political actors, covering over the seething "Indian question," which constantly erupts in the form of land claims and demands for self-determination and self-government.[23] A creation of violent and illegal settlers (to whom no one had issued "landing" permits), "Canada" remains an unformed union, its particularist and partisan state formation frequently showing through. Yet a state cannot become liberal and democratic without an element of transcendence.[24] And what, after all, could give Canada the appearance of transcendence as well as "multiculturalism," with its slogan "unity in diversity"? The drive for making an Anglo-North American Canada is partly assuaged by this ideological gesture. "Immigrants," especially "visible minorities," become useful with regard to challenging the substantive claim of more well-entrenched "others" (i.e., the Québecois or indigenous peoples), who cannot be deported to their "home" countries. Nominally and opportunistically introducing those others as entities in the national imaginary, the notion/nation of "Canada" attempts to overcome its legitimation crisis. It is in this way that every social and economic demand can be gutted and reduced to the level of the cultural/symbolic. Ironically, immigrant "others," who serve as categories of exclusion in Canada's nation-making ideology, become an instrument for creating a sphere of transcendence. The state claims to rise above all partisan interests and functions as an arbitrator between different cultural groups. This is the moral high ground, the political instrument with which the state maintains the hegemony of an Anglo-Canada. We might say that it is these oppressed "others" who gave Canada the gift of multiculturalism. In any case, armed with the ideological tool of multiculturalism, Canada manages its crisis in legitimation and citizenship. It offers the Québecois and the First Nations peoples a part in the "national unity," albeit an empty one, while denying them their own governments as separatist enterprises.

Fractured by race, gender, class, and long-standing colonial rivalries, the construction of "Canada" entails two major forms of interconnected crises—that of citizenship and that of the legitimation of a "national" state formation. Differential status in citizenship is paired with a dual state formation, each aspect of which exerts pressures on the other. A White settler colonial state and a liberal democracy, while historically and contingently connected in many cases (such as in Australia, the former South Africa, the United States, the former Rhodesia (Zimbabwe), or Canada) are two separate political projects. They are not genealogically connected in terms of their political ideals and governing structures. This becomes clearer when we look at Britain, which had a vast colonial empire and ruled it autocratically, while developing a liberal democracy inside the country. In liberal democracy, even if it is only in the sphere of polity, the same state structures and legalities govern the entire subject population and show a reliance on the notion of enlightenment. The liberal democratic state, at least at the level of *formal equality*, is the antithesis of a colonial state. But in Canada, as in the case of Australia, for example, certain features of the colonial state coexist with those of a liberal democracy (Watkins 1977). Different laws, with special departments such as the Department of Indian Affairs in Canada, govern the population differently. Indian reserves have laws governing them economically, politically, and socially which are different from the laws governing the rest of Canada. Viewed from the standpoint of indigenous peoples, the state of Canada is based on class, gender, and race, and it continues to administer these reserves as would a colonial state. Even the territorial question is still unsettled, while containment strategies typical of colonial states continue to be in evidence around the administration of reserves. These colonial relations manifest themselves in conflicts around the James Bay Project, Oka, Gustafson Lake, Ipperwash, and so on. Debates on Native self-determination or First Nations self-government further reveal the colonial relations between Canada and its indigenous peoples. According to some scholars, Canada's dual state formation (a liberal democracy with a colonial heart) is matched by a dual economy. Theories of world system and dependency, usually applied to ex-colonized countries, are considered to be applicable to Canada.[25] It is claimed that there is a metropole-peripheral economy within, while the country as a whole displays features of advanced industrial capitalism along with its dependency on foreign, especially U.S., capital.[26] This convoluted state of affairs has given rise to peculiar social formations, whereby colonized nations continue to exist within the "Canadian" nation state. Acknowledged as the First Nations, Native peoples are like the Palestinians, who form a nation without a state and are subject to continual repression. The role that "race" has played in the context of colonization is obvious. Subsequently a dependent but imperialist capital has continued to organize an economy and a society based on "race." It is not surprising that talk of cultural identities in this country quickly veers toward racialization. Not only is "the Indian," so called, a category of "race," but so are other cultural categories used for non-White immigrants tinged with "race."

These colonial relations and representations of "Canada," which run like rich veins throughout its state formation, were overlayered with liberal democratic aspirations in the course of the latter half of the twentieth century. The state faced many contradictions and complexities in this project due to the persistence of the colonial relations and also to the country's own inability to have a bourgeois revolution. Lacking a fully articulated bourgeois class in leadership Canada has in effect a double dependency—on Britain for governmental and certain cultural forms, and on the U.S. for capital as well as for social and political culture.[27] Like all liberal democracies it is not only capitalist, but, as I said, colonial and dependent and autonomously imperialist at the same time. The problems of coherent state formation multiply as a result.

In fact, in the face of Canada's settler colonial origin and the weak development of its capital and capitalist class, the state in Canada has been a direct agent for capitalist development and has performed a substantial role in the accumulation of capital. It has also been the chief agent for procuring labor and creating a labor market, and has assisted in the regulation and exploitation of labor. Canada has depended on imported labor and has organized the labor market along lines of "race" and gender. This was not often an activity undertaken by the accumulating classes but primarily performed by the state, which took over a vast portion of the role of facilitation.[28] The current obedience of the state to NAFTA, or corporate transnational capital, is highly symptomatic of this. "Race" or ethnicity, translated into immigration policy quotas, has actually located different types of labor in different productional recesses.

By locking immigrant workers into zones of menial labor and low wages, the state has brought down the wage structure of the country as a whole. It has actively de-skilled and marginalized Third World immigrants by decertifying them and forcing them into the working class. Long before the present economic crisis, this device had created a reserve army of labor consisting of both males and females. As any study of homeworkers, piece-workers, cleaners of public spaces, or domestics will show, non-White or "immigrant" women occupy the worst position among these marginalized labor groups (Johnson and Johnson 1982). These, then, are the people—straddling the line between surplus exploitation and unemployment—who stand permanently on the threshold of Canadian citizenship. Their paper-thin status is revealed when some family members are deported while others, such as children born in Canada, are allowed to stay. If these are not sufficient reminders of the crises of citizenship faced by non-White "others," one need only remember the Japanese internment.[29]

This situation is guaranteed to produce a double crisis of legitimation, one for the state and one for its citizens. The heart of the matter lies in the fact that a colonial, partisan Anglo-Canada has arrogated to itself the task of constructing "Canada" while being economically dependent on foreign investment capital. This Anglo-Canada has neither moral high ground nor economic solvency to justify its hegemony. The notions of "Canada" and "Canadian" are mocked by gigantic question marks.

During the course of its tortuous formation, Canada has continued to exude irreconcilable contradictions. In following the imperatives of liberal democracy, in being motivated by the ideal of pluralism, and in responding to popular protests against inequality, Canada promulgated both multiculturalism and affirmative action, which both contained dissatisfaction and legitimated existing inequalities. At the same time, through various debates, the state called for sexist and racist responses to all its so-called multiculturalist and equity-oriented proposals. For example, at this moment, the fig leaf of equity and affirmative action has been altogether dropped in Ontario. By constantly calling on and constructing an entity called "Canadians" and pitting it against immigrants, the state has actually stimulated White supremacist attitudes and helped to establish their organizations, as was revealed by a government agent with regard to the Heritage Front.[30] By constantly signifying the White population as "Canadians" and immigrants of color as "others," by constantly stereotyping Third World immigrants as criminals, terrorists, and fundamentalists, the state manages to both manipulate and cancel its alleged dedication to multiculturalism.

A most dangerous state use of racism occurs with regard to its own socioeconomic failures and its inability to cope with the violence inherent within structural adjustment. Since the state and the media jointly portray immigrants from non-White, poor countries as "the problem," it is not surprising that the White population looks at them as the villains of the peace—as "those people who took away our jobs." These immigrants, in turn, look among themselves to find someone to blame for the economic and social disaster they face. Interestingly, this attitude does not apply to eastern Europeans, who are poor but White.

Due to its selective modes of ethnicization, multiculturalism is itself a vehicle for racialization. It establishes Anglo-Canadian culture as the ethnic core culture while "tolerating" and hierarchically arranging others around it as "multiculture." The ethics and aesthetics of "Whiteness," with its colonial imperialist/racist ranking criteria, define and construct the "multi" culture of Canada's others. This reified, mutated product, accomplished through a web of hierarchically arranged stereotypes, can then be both used against "ethnic" communities and commoditized with regard to fashion and current market tastes. Festivals of "ethnic" communities, from the Toronto Caravan to Caribana, provide excellent examples. Such "ethnic" constructs have serious consequences in the perpetuation of violence against women. Frequently, in the name of cultural sensitivity and respect, the state does not address violence against women when it occurs among the multiculturally defined "ethnic" communities. It is rumored that the accused's behavior is a part of "their culture," and that "they" are traditional, fundamentalist, and uncivilized. In this way, an entire population is demonized even though particular men become exempt from indictment. Similarly, Canada's Islamic population has become permanently associated with terrorism and every Arab is seen as a potential terrorist.

One more issue that needs to be stressed with regard to multiculturalism is the fact that it arises at the convergence of a struggle between the state and otherized, especially non-White, subjects. Their demands for justice, for effective anti-racist policies and administration, for the right to a substantive social and cultural life, are overdetermined by the agenda of the state. As long as "multiculturalism" only skims the surface of society, expressing itself as traditional ethics, such as arranged marriages, and ethnic food, clothes, songs, and dances (thus facilitating tourism), it is tolerated by the state and "Canadians" as non-threatening. But if the demands go a little deeper than that (e.g., teaching "other" religions or languages), they produce violent reaction, indicating a deep resentment toward funding "others'" arts and cultures. This can be seen in the Reform Party's stance on immigration and multiculturalism.

The convergence of gender and race oppression in Canada became explicit in the reactions to the New Democratic Party's (NDP) proposal for affirmative action. It was a proposal that extended inclusivity to Canada's women, visible minorities, Aboriginal people, Francophones, and disabled people. The reaction was severe, and it reverberated throughout the entire country—professors and truck drivers displaying the same response. National newspapers advertised the proposal as "Whites need not apply" or "White males need not apply." This is a curious reading, since it completely overlooks the fact that the legislation is in keeping with liberal pluralism, which entails minimal representation. The violent responses also made one realize that the ideologies of race and gender, respectively, are connected. If White women, disabled people, and Francophones are not to be recognized as White, we are left to ask: "What is Whiteness?" The issue of gender is also revealing. If Francophones and disabled people, no matter what their color, are not to be recognized as "males," then what is masculinity? Does speaking French exclude people from being "White males"?

This instance serves to show that "Canada," as a national imaginary, its multiculturalism and its lip service to Quebec's Canadianness notwithstanding, is actually an Anglo-White male idea that blurs the class lines. There is little in the state's notion of multiculturalism that speaks to social justice. More than anything else, multiculturalism preserves the partisan nature of the state by helping to contain pressures exerted by "others" for social justice and equity.

We might, at this point, be asked what legitimized Canada, what provided the basis for its national project, before the arrival of the concept of multiculturalism. What was its justificatory, politically existential discourse? It seems that it was the notion of "survival."[31] The White settler colonial entity devised for itself a threatened identity, whereby the colonizer (erasing colonialism) was faced with the danger of extinction. In the works of Margaret Atwood (1972b), such a state of affairs is advanced as a truism, as a fact of "Canada." In Atwood's novel *Surfacing* (1972a), for example, a woman discovers her violated- and invaded-self in, or as, an equally violated and invaded wilderness. In spite of her gender and feminism, her race and class allow Atwood to project this particular vision of Canada. But this metaphor of the political psyche of Canada as a threatened femininity/nature obliterates indigenous people, swallowing them up in the myth of an empty wilderness that is to be invaded and populated by White people. In doing this, Atwood follows a literary and artistic tradition already in place, for example, in many of the works of the Group of Seven (Watson 1994). The "Canadian," as the dreamer of the nation, must come to terms with the wilderness in order to find and found "Canada." S/he is White/European. The indigenous peoples are either not there or are one with the primal, non-human forces of nature. The threat to Canada, then, comes not only from south of its border but from within itself—from its denied, unincorporated, alienated nature and its human forms. In reaction to this can the settler, "the Canadian," take an option that Atwood's heroine in *Surfacing*, being a "woman" and pacifist, cannot? Can he, as he is a man, feel justified in killing or conquering that which he cannot comprehend or finally conquer? The "survival" ideological space holds that possibility in suspense. The other threat to Canada comes from without—from its fear of being overrun by, and incorporated into, the United States. This formulation, while anti-American and mildly anti-imperialist, erases Canada's own colonial and imperialist nature and aspirations. And this erasure certainly does not help to create politics or policies that challenge Anglo-White nationalism, with its masculinist inflection, and that call for other ways of imagining and administering Canada.

The possibilities for constructing a radically different Canada emerge only from those who have been "othered" as the insider-outsiders of the nation. It is their standpoints which, oppositionally politicized, can take us beyond the confines of gender and race and enable us to challenge class through a critical and liberating vision. In their lives, politics, and work, the "others" hold the possibility of being able to expose the hollowness of the liberal state and to provide us with an understanding of both the refined and crude constructions of "White power" behind "Canada's" national imaginary. They serve to remind us of the Canada that *could* exist.

Notes

1. On the construction of "Whiteness" as an ideological, political, and socio–historical category, see Allen (1994), Frankenberg (1993), Roediger (1993), Roman (1993), and Ware (1991).
2. On Europeanness as "Whiteness," see Stoller (1995).
3. See Carty and Brand (1993) and Carty (1994).
4. See D. E. Smith (1987), 3, 5–6, for a definition of this term.
5. For Althusser's concept of interpellation, see Althusser (1971, 162–70).
6. Much has been written on the suffrage struggle and second–class citizen status of White bourgeois women. For particular connections between these themes and the issue of race, see Stoller (1995) and Davis (1983).
7. See hooks (1981), chapters 4 and 5; Collins (1990), chapter 4; and B. Smith (1982).
8. On how the Canadian labor market and class system is organized through race and ethnicity, see Bolaria and Li (1988) and Avery (1995).
9. Much work still needs to be done with regard to considering class formation in terms of both race and gender, but Brand (1991) makes a beginning. See also Brand and Bhaggiyadatta (1985).
10. This is powerfully brought forth in the issue of the importation of domestic workers to Toronto from the Caribbean. See Silvera (1989).
11. See Bolaria and Li (1988), chapters 5, 7, and 8; and Arnopoulos (1979).
12. On Canada as a White settler colony and race/gender inscriptions in the formation and workings of the state, see Kulchyski (1994), Tester and Kulchyski (1994), and Monture-Angus (1995).

13. See Francis (1992). Also, Monture–Angus (1995) says: "The definition of Indian is a legal one based on the necessity of identifying the population against which bureaucrats will administer the *Indian Act* regime. This definition is based on blood lines and residency on a reserve" (122, n. 5).

14. See Campbell (1983) and Emberley (1993).

15. See chapter 5 in Kulchyski (1994).

16. This was part of Lucien Bouchard's campaign speech prior to the Quebec referendum in October 1995.

17. On the similarities between bantustans and reserves, see Bolaria and Li (1988), pages 70–71. In 1985 Glenn Babb, then South Africa's ambassador to Canada, himself made reference in a public speech to the apartheid regime's debt to Canada's reserves in formulating the bantustan policy.

18. On "White masculinity," see, among others, Sinha (1995) and Terkel (1992).

19. These places are contested spaces in Canada. They are sites of struggles over land claims, over treaty and non-treaty lands. Oka, where there was a police and military offensive against the indigenous peoples in 1990, is in Quebec. Gustafson Lake in British Columbia and Ipperwash in Ontario both saw struggles with the RCMP and provincial police in 1995, resulting in a death from police shooting in the latter.

20. On the history of multiculturalism, see Fleras and Elliot (1992).

21. For a discussion of this concept, see Habermas (1975).

22. For details of the French and English conquests of Canada and subsequent contestation between the two colonies, see Ryerson (1960) or Morton (1994). Quebec and English Canada have gone through a colonial relationship that, according to Anglophone Canada or Ottawa, has been transformed into a liberal democratic incorporation. A vast portion of Quebec's population have, however, continued to perceive this as a modernized colonial relation.

23. The condition of crisis created by a state that is a White settler colony seeking to become a liberal democracy becomes clear when we look at Tester and Kulchyski (1994), who explore the genocidal consequences of Inuit relocation. There are numerous articles and books on the land claims issue. See, for example, Boldt and Long (1985).

24. On the transcendent nature of the state as an ideal democratic institution, see Miliband (1973).

25. On world system and dependency theories as readings of the First and Third Worlds in terms of capitalism, imperialism, and dependency, see Wallerstein (1979) and Gunder Frank (1978).

26. See Bolaria and Li (1988), chapters 2 and 3. This dynamic is explored in various ways by the Canadian Left nationalist political theorists, such as Teeple (1972). For a marxist critique of the Left nationalist position see Moore and Wells (1975).

27. This dependency is not simply a matter of adopting a British style of government (parliamentary democracy) or an American style of capitalism. Canada was a colony of Britain for a long time, and then, until recently, a dominion. Even now the Crown of England has a significant governmental relationship with the Canadian government. This is evident in the face of the Queen on Canadian currency or swearing allegiance to Her Majesty during citizenship

ceremonies or in having to refer to the Crown and the House of Lords in matters of Native land claims. As for Canada's U.S. connection, political theorists of the Canadian Left such as Ian Lumsden, Mel Watkins, and others since the 1960s have drawn attention to a long-standing imperialist presence of U.S. capital in Canada. Canadian publishing, music, film, and cultural production and industry have been increasingly under attack from the U.S. culture industry and export market, and a steady dependency is being cultivated in the popular culture sector. This "Americanization" of Canadian culture has been both noticed and resented by writers such as Margaret Atwood or magazines such as *This Magazine* and *Canadian Dimension*.

28. See Law Union of Ontario (1981), as well as Canada (1974, 1986).
29. See Bolaria and Lee (1988), chapter 3.
30. For details on the Heritage Front and other neo-Nazi/White supremacist groups, see *Hearts of Hate*, a video produced by the National Film Board and aired on the Canadian Broadcasting Corporation in 1995. An exposé carried in the *Toronto Star* in 1994 uncovered evidence that one of founders of the Heritage Front, Grant Bristow, was a paid agent of the Canadian Security and Information Service (CSIS).
31. Regarding the concept of "survival," see Atwood (1972).

References

Alexander, M. Jacqui, and Mohanty, Chandra Talpade. (1997). "Introduction: Genealogies, Legacies, Movements," in *Feminist Genealogies, Colonial Legacies, Democratic Futures*, edited by M. Jacqui Alexander and Chandra Talpade Mohanty. vii–xxxvi. New York/London: Routledge.

Allen, T. 1994. *The Invention of the White Race: Racial Oppression and Social Control.* London: Verso.

Althusser, L. 1971. *Lenin and Philosophy*. London: New Left Books.

Anderson, B. 1991. *Imagined Communities*. London: Verso.

Arnopoulos, S. 1979. *Problems of Immigrant Women in the Canadian Labour Force.* Ottawa: Canadian Advisory Council on the Status of Women.

Atwood, M. 1972a. *Surfacing*. Toronto: McClelland & Stewart.

———. 1972b. *Survival: A Thematic Guide to Canadian Literature*. Toronto: Anansi.

Avery, D. 1995. *Reluctant Host: Canada's Response to Immigrant Workers, 1896–1994.* Toronto: McClelland & Stewart.

Bolaria, B. S., and P. Li, eds. 1988. *Racial Oppression in Canada*. Toronto: Garamond.

Boldt, M., and J. A. Long, eds. 1985. *The Quest for Justice*. Toronto: University of Toronto Press.

Brand, D. 1991. *No Burden to Carry: Narratives of Black Working Women in Ontario, 1920s to 1950s.* Toronto: Women's Press.

Brand D., and K. S. Bhaggiyadatta, eds. 1985. *Rivers Have Sources, Trees Have Roots: Speaking of Racism.* Toronto: Cross Cultural Communications Centre.

Campbell, M. 1983. *Half-Breed*. Toronto: Goodread Biographies.

Canada. 1974. *A Report of the Canadian Immigration and Population Study: Immigration Policy Perspective.* Ottawa: Manpower and Immigration.

———. 1986. *Equality Now: Report of the Special Committee on Visible Minorities.* Ottawa: House of Commons.

Carty, L., ed. 1994. *And Still We Rise.* Toronto: Women's Press.

Carty, L., and D. Brand. 1993. "Visible Minority Women: A Creation of the Colonial State." In *Returning the Gaze: Essays on Racism, Feminism and Politics,* edited by H. Bannerji. Toronto: Sister Vision Press.

Collins, P. H. 1990. *Black Feminist Thought: Knowledge, Consciousness and the Politics of Empowerment.* London: Harper Collins Academic.

Davis, A. 1983. *Women, Race and Class.* New York: Vintage.

Emberley, J. 1993. *Thresholds of Difference: Feminist Critique, Native Women's Writings, Postcolonial Theory.* Toronto: University of Toronto Press.

Fleras, A., and J. L. Elliot, eds. 1992. *Multiculturalism in Canada: The Challenge of Diversity.* Scarborough: Nelson.

Francis, D. 1992. *The Imaginary Indian.* Vancouver: Arsenal Pulp Press.

Frankenberg, R. 1993. *White Women, Race Matters: The Social Construction of Whiteness.* Minneapolis: University of Minnesota Press.

Fraser, N., and L. Gordon. 1994. "A Genealogy of *Dependency*: A Keyword of the U.S. Welfare State." *Signs: A Journal of Women in Culture and Society* 19 (2): 309–36.

Goldberg, David T. 1993. *Racist Culture.* Oxford: Basil Blackwell.

Gunder Frank, Andre. 1978. *Dependent Accumulation and Underdevelopment.* London: Macmillan.

Habermas, J. 1975. *Legitimation Crisis.* Boston: Beacon.

hooks, b. 1981. *Ain't I a woman: black women and feminism.* Boston: South End Press.

Johnson, L., and R. Johnson. 1982. *Seam Allowance: Industrial Home Sewing in Canada.* Toronto: Women's Educational Press.

Kulchyski, P., ed. 1994. *Unjust Relations: Aboriginal Rights in Canadian Courts.* Toronto: Oxford University Press.

Law Union of Ontario. 1981. *The Immigrant's Handbook.* Montreal: Black Rose Books.

Macpherson, C.B. 1973. *Democratic Theory: Essays in Retrieval.* Oxford: Oxford University Press.

———. 1977. *The Life and Times of Liberal Democracy.* Toronto: Oxford University Press.

Miliband, Ralph. 1973. *The State in Capitalist Society: The Western System of Power.* London: Quartet Books.

Monture–Angus, P. 1995. *Thunder in My Soul: A Mohawk Woman Speaks.* Halifax: Fernwood.

Moore S., and D. Wells. 1975. *Imperialism and the National Question in Canada.* Toronto: Published by the authors.

Morton, Desmond. 1994. *A Short History of Canada.* Toronto: McClelland & Stewart.

Ng, R. 1993. "Sexism, Racism, Canadian Nationalism." In *Returning the Gaze: Essays on Racism, Feminism and Politics,* edited by H. Bannerji. 182–96. Toronto: Sister Vision Press.

Roediger, D. 1993. *The Wages of Whiteness: Race and the Making of the American Working Class.* London: Verso.

Roman, Leslie G. 1993. "White is a Color: White Defensiveness, Postmodernism and Antiracist Pedagogy." In *Race, Identity, and Representation in Education,* edited by C. McCarthy and W. Chrichlow. 71–88. New York/London: Routledge.

Ryerson, Stanley. 1960. *The Foundation of Canada.* Toronto: Progress Books.

Sheehy, G. 1991. *The Silent Passage: Menopause.* New York: Pocket Books.

Silvera, M. 1989. *Silenced: Talks with Working Class Caribbean Women about Their Lives and Struggles as Domestic Workers in Canada* (2nd ed.). Toronto: Sister Vision Press.

Sinha, M. 1995. *Colonial Masculinity.* Manchester: Manchester University Press.

Smith, B. 1982. "Racism and Women's Studies." In *But Some of Us Are Brave,* edited by G. Hull, P.B. Scott, and B. Smith. New York: Feminist Press.*

Smith, D. E. 1987. *The Everyday World as Problematic.* Toronto: University of Toronto Press.

———. 1990. *The Conceptual Practices of Power: A Feminist Sociology of Knowledge.* Toronto: University of Toronto Press.

Stoller, A. L. 1995. *Race and the Education of Desire: Foucault's History of Sexuality and the Colonial Order of Things.* Durham: Duke University Press.

Teeple, G., ed. 1972. *Capitalism and the National Question.* Toronto: University of Toronto Press.

Terkel, S. 1992. *Race: How Blacks and Whites Think and Feel about the American Obsession.* New York: The New Press.

Tester, F. J., and P. Kulchyski. 1994. *Tammarniit (Mistakes): Innuit Relocation in the Eastern Arctic.* Vancouver: University of British Columbia Press.

Wallerstein, Immanuel. 1979. *Capitalist World Economy.* London: Cambridge University Press.

Ware, V. 1991. *Beyond the Pale: White Women, Racism, and History.* London: Verso.

Watkins, M., ed. 1977. *Dene Nation: The Colony Within.* Toronto: University of Toronto Press.

Watson, S. 1994. "Race, Wilderness, Territory and the Origins of Modern Canadian Landscape Painting." *Semiotext[e]* 6 (17): 93–104.

Chapter Two

'At The Expense of Christianity': Backlash Discourse and Moral Panic

Davina Cooper
University of Warwick (United Kingdom)

My Lords, I am very grateful for the opportunity to open this debate, because it reflects widespread concern. Parents and teachers from as far afield as London, Bristol, Derby, Preston, Newcastle, Bradford and Manchester have expressed grave anxiety over the failure of many schools to keep the law . . . to offer pupils opportunities for religious worship or instruction in the basic tenets of the Christian faith. In a nutshell, this debate is about the concern that, as a nation, we are in danger of selling our spiritual birthright for a mass of secular pottage.

Baroness Cox, Hansard, 26 February 1988, col. 1453.

Introduction

In 1988, English identity and culture lay in turmoil; after more than a decade of secular multiculturalism, a nation's children lay bereft. Confused, disoriented, unable to tell right from wrong, here was a generation in dire need of salvation—or so went the narrative of the New Christian Right (NCR) as it attempted to reinscribe the terms of religious settlement in Britain's schools. Its mission was twofold: (1) to remake schools as communities of belief and (2) to locate Christianity at the heart of those communities. No longer would it be simply one national faith amongst many;[1] instead, by highlighting Christianity's historical status and majoritarian position, the links between church and nation would be rearticulated and entrenched.

In this paper, I explore the character and impact of the NCR's religious education project through a textual analysis of recent legislation and circulars. To understand the law's agenda and impact, we need to locate developments within the broader politics of the Thatcher period. This has received extensive attention elsewhere,[2] so I will offer only a thumbnail sketch of key themes. Hall (1988), a prominent, radical commentator of the period, described the Right-wing politics of the Thatcher years as a hegemonic project of populist authoritarianism based on social discipline and hierarchical leadership. Elements of this can be found in the agenda of "law and order," "traditional family values," and patriotic nationalism. Within this context, as several writers have commented, education provided a key site of mobilization (Chitty 1989; Dale 1989; Jones 1989). Developed in Right-wing think-tanks during the 1970s, Conservative education policy deployed a populist "parents–know–best" rhetoric to undermine non-selective education, professional authority, and a questioning, child-centered approach to learning.

Yet it is important not to overestimate the strength of New Right agendas within the Conservative politics of the 1980s. While Hall (1988) argues that "moral politics" formed an extremely important aspect of the Thatcherite agenda, other writers are more equivocal. Durham (1991, 124–25), for instance, indicates that central government in the 1980s was criticized for not taking moral issues such as sex and homosexuality sufficiently seriously.[3] While moral issues became increasingly central to the political battles of the late 1980s, government interest remained uneven (Durham 1991). High-flown rhetoric tended to coincide with unwillingness at the level of policy implementation (and with even more unwillingness at the level of enforcement). For many Conservatives, including, arguably, Thatcher, government priorities were to install a neoliberal marketplace (both internally and externally) and to privatize (or reduce) public services. Where more moralistic policies were introduced, for instance, with regard to assisted reproduction (Cooper and Herman 1991) or with regard to prohibiting the promotion of homosexuality (Sanders and Spraggs 1989), these tended to be token offerings meant to appease the loose coalition of Right-wing activists, peers, and MPs that make up the NCR.[4]

Ranged against the NCR was an alternate constellation that coalesced as the New Urban Left (NUL) (Gyford 1985, 17). Distanced from the Labour Party establishment, this group included public- and voluntary-sector workers, local councillors, and community activists. Like the Right, it also extended itself, depending on the issue or conflict, to incorporate other voices.

The NUL was a key force in struggles for decentralization, in attempts to create equal opportunity policies, and in attempts to oppose the Right's sexual agenda (Gyford 1985; Lansley, Goss, and Wolmar 1989; Cooper 1994). However, it proved much less central in the struggles around Christianity. While the terrain of religious education formed a primary site for the NCR and for many other Conservatives, the Left was ambivalent. The Parliamentary

Labour Party, for example, aspired to present itself as pro-Christian and pro-discipline, while many on the NUL saw the issue as relatively insignificant. Thus, opposition to the Right on this issue came not so much from political activists as from progressive educators—many of whom had played little part in non-educational struggles.

In exploring the way in which Christianity in schools became constituted as part of a wider political project, my objective is twofold. First, I analyze the legal texts and policy developments that led to the resettlement of Christianity within the British school system,[5] and, second, I consider whether the events that took place were manifestations of a backlash. It may seem commonsensical to understand the Right's reaction to a decade of multi–faith progress in terms of backlash; however, I go on to show how this same concept may be used to frame the way in which progressive forces have responded to Right–wing legislation. In so doing, I critically consider the explanatory value and drawbacks of discussing such issues in terms of backlash.

The concept of backlash is grounded in a three–part, chronological model of change: (1) time period A (society is in equilibrium but certain areas, such as education, are vulnerable to takeover or alteration by more radical forces);[6] (2) time period B (through exerting their power, radical forces manage to win control over certain aspects of society); and (3) time period C (society becomes out of balance and forces of reaction mobilize to intervene). I problematize this simple model of backlash by drawing on a post-Foucauldian analysis that conceives of power as productive, unquantifiable, and equivocal (Cooper 1995). As I try to show, the backlash paradigm deploys a zero–sum notion of power, emphasizes agency, and depicts history as periods of reaction parasitically contingent on epochs of change—all of which leads to various kinds of marginalization. At the same time, it cannot be denied that the concept of backlash provides an influential, interpretive framework through which events are often "understood." And while this framework may be problematic, its hegemony must be acknowledged.

My argument and analysis are based on research carried out as part of a wider project that deals with the relationship between law, power, and local governance.[7] My research focuses on the contradictory effects of juridification on legal consciousness, policy implementation, non-compliance, and power relations. I draw on interviews with educators (teachers, municipal education advisors, and governors) as well as with local politicians in four British municipalities. These people are based in London, West Midlands, and West Yorkshire and have different political histories and cultures, ranging from Left-wing urban community politics to neoliberal individualism. Interviews were semi–structured and relatively informal; they focused on constructing narratives of local conflict and emphasized people's understanding of, and response to, law and illegality. Although I interviewed a political cross-section, I was particularly interested in talking with educators and others engaged in interpreting legal texts against the grain and/or in practicing defiance.[8] Interestingly, these people were often progressive, self–identified Christians who had a history of involvement in developing multi-faith educational environments. Their aim was to develop respect and understanding for religion in a context in which Christianity was embraced as an equal rather than as a dominant belief system.

Legislating Christian Prayer

Christianity has long been an ambivalent force within the British education system. Under the 1944 Education Act, religious education (RE) and daily collective worship were prescribed elements within the school day. However, both requirements were flouted with impunity in many schools, particularly during the 1970s and early 1980s. Where religious education was retained during this period, it was often taught (especially in multi-faith localities) from a standpoint that regarded a range of faiths as equally valid. Similarly, school prayer was reconstituted into stories, poetry, and songs that were performed at school assemblies. While some retained a Christian character, others were multi-faith, loosely spiritual, or fully secular.

In 1988, this trend away from mono-faith instruction was punctured by the arrival of the Education Reform Act (ERA). This act was an extensive piece of legislation, encompassing a national curriculum and the shifting of financial power to school governing bodies and away from local education authorities (LEAs). Conservative Christians, led by NCR proponents, saw the act's passage as an opportunity to refortify the 1944 settlement on religion in schools. Deploying a discourse of moral degeneration, NCR and other Conservative peers pressed for amendments that would entrench religion in schools and render explicit what they believed was implicit in the 1944 act: the essentially Christian character of prayer and instruction.[9]

Yet, despite widespread support in both the House of Lords and the House of Commons, opinions varied. The primary objective of the NCR was religious segregation (i.e., separating children on religious/racial grounds). More traditional Conservative Christians, however, adopted an assimilationist approach. Their goal was to maintain Christianity's centrality for *all* children while avoiding other faiths opting out.[10] The NCR played the more dominant role in demanding legislative change, chastising the established church for allowing the 1944 act to fall into disuse. However, the final settlement reflected a more moderate Conservative position.

The 1988 ERA introduced two major provisions dealing with religion in state schools. First, all pupils were to take part in a daily act of collective worship (S. 6(1) ERA). The responsibility for arranging this lay with the head teacher, and, if she/he did not wish to lead the assembly, she/he had to get someone else to do so. As with RE, worship was to be of a "broadly Christian," albeit non-denominational, character (S. 7 ERA). Not every act of religious veneration had to be broadly Christian, however, providing a *majority* of them were in any given semester (S. 7(3)).[11] Initial ambiguity as to what this entailed was later clarified in Circular 1/94, which stated that collective worship must "contain some elements which relate specifically to the traditions of Christian belief and which *accord a special status to the person of Jesus Christ*" (para. 63).

Neither the 1988 ERA nor the 1993 Education Act abrogated the right of individual withdrawal established under the 1944 legislation. Schools must honor any parental request to excuse their children from collective worship. Schools must also comply with any parental request for their children's exemption from religious education. In neither instance are parents obliged to give reasons for their requests. Where schools have a large number of pupils for whom broadly Christian worship is inappropriate, it is possible to apply for a wider exemption. The 1988 act lays down a procedure for obtaining a "determination" for all or certain groups of students so that they can either engage in a common multi-faith assembly or worship within mono-religious groupings. The decision whether or not to grant a determination is made by the local Standing Advisory Council on Religious Education (SACRE).

The second key element of the law concerns religious education. Religious Education is part of the basic curriculum for all students within maintained schools (S. 2(1) ERA). Syllabi are to "reflect the fact that the religious traditions in Great Britain are in the main Christian whilst taking account of the teaching and practices of the other principal religions represented in Great Britain" (S. 8(3) ERA). These must also be non-denominational, although "teaching about a particular catechism or formulary . . . is not prohibited" (Circular 1/94, para. 32).

Initially, the "in the main Christian" requirement only applied to new syllabi. Although Section 11 of the Education Reform Act enabled Local Education Authorities to convene a conference for the purpose of reviewing their syllabi, this was not compulsory. Local Education Authorities thus had a loophole through which to retain old syllabi that contravened the 1988 requirements. This loophole was closed by the Education Act, 1993, which compelled authorities who had not already done so to convene a syllabus conference by 1 April 1995 (S. 256) for the purpose of bringing their syllabi into line with the law.

The central government also adopted other methods to restrict local discretion, including producing, in 1994, model syllabi. Non-statutory documents, these syllabi set out the preferred way for fulfilling the legislative requirements. Model syllabi incorporated the "key" religions within Britain, while asserting Christianity's privileged position and significance.

Community, Nationhood, Other

The following discourse analysis of legal texts highlights several Foucauldian themes (e.g., discipline, management of the self, and the production of knowledge). However, the approach I take differs from that of many Foucauldians in that I continue to utilize a notion of ideology, by which I mean the conceptual, normative, and ontological frameworks to which discourse gives expression. Thus, I do not oppose ideology to science or suggest that it is a form of false consciousness. Yet, in identifying underlying ideologies one is in danger of assuming that any given text articulates a single meaning—that it has a "right" and a "wrong" reading. This privileging of text over audience was identified and explored within media studies, where writers developed a schema that incorporated oppositional and negotiated, as well as dominant, readings (Morley 1983, 1989). This attention to the possibility of multiple readings is sometimes lost in discourse analysis when it assumes we can get at what the text is *really* saying through close, in-depth analysis. Because I wish to focus on *Conservative* textual meanings, my reading depends on the links between the texts and their NCR/Conservative advocates. Later, I explore more negotiated or oppositional readings. My analysis revolves around the following themes: (1) the value of religion and Christian predominance, (2) the character and role of education, (3) the national "we" and the construction of the "Other," and (4) children's rights.

Religious Need and Christian Predominance

At its most basic level, the ERA inscribes the importance of religion. This is predicated on, but also reinforces, a particular religious paradigm. Faiths are conceived as discrete and unmixable, the notion of hybrids nonsensical. Religious essence is epistemologically fixed, although cultural manifestation may vary according to different periods and localities. Thus, faiths are not evolving historical phenomena contingent upon social conditions and community development.

As I go on to discuss, the promotion of religion has a nation-building role. It also functions as a solution that creates or highlights a deficiency.[12]

For example, Circular 1/94 states: "The government is concerned that in-sufficient attention has been paid explicitly to the spiritual, moral and cul-tural aspects of pupils' development" (para. 1). This "insufficient attention" is held to be responsible for such social predicaments as vandalism, joy-riding, theft, drugs, under-aged sex, and violence.

> We want more Christianity; we want children taught right and wrong.
> Those are brilliantly coded messages which appeal to ordinary people . . .
> It's good for our children . . . and they'll grow up not to rob banks and
> kill people. And anybody opposing that is actually opposing what's good
> for our children. Therefore you can't be a good person, can you?
> (London Labour councillor, February 1994)

Religion and the re-emergence of traditional Conservative values appear to offer a solution to the problem of a fast–changing society with its dys-functional families.[13] Yet religion constructs the problem to which it is supposedly the solution in a very precise manner; that is, as individual and moral (as opposed to social and political), for it needs to be one theistic faith can solve.

It is important to note that not *any* religion can halt the perceived decline in social values. A key facet of Right–wing populism is the damage that "other" religions might inflict, particularly upon Christian children. In the last decade, there have been several instances of White, Christian parents withdrawing their children from multi-racial/multi-faith schools on the grounds that they were being inculcated into other faiths and cultures.

At the center of the religious imperative within the 1988 ERA is Christianity's normative and explanatory value. Although the former is less explicitly developed,[14] the importance of the latter with regard to making sense of and perpetuating Britain's heritage is deemed crucial (Hull 1993; 1994): "An understanding of religion, especially the Christian religion, is essential to an understanding of the society, history and heritage of these islands."[15] As a number of parliamentarians argue, children who do not understand Christianity will grasp neither Britain's history nor its culture. Secular education, or multi-faith teaching in which Christianity is not dom-inant, produces ignorance, confusion, and an inability to appreciate the classics.

Defining Religious Education

The pluralist approach to RE developed by a number of LEAs during the 1970s and 1980s attempted to treat all religions as equally valid, highlighting both their similarities and their differences. While a heritage discourse was adopted, it emphasized the heritage of Britain's *present* multicultural communities rather than romanticizing a historic, monocultural past. Indeed, the latter was discursively problematized, as progressive curricula highlighted the ways in which Britain's past was constituted by diverse racial and cultural traditions.

The revised Conservative conception of heritage rejects the teleology of progressivism, presenting a White, Anglo-Christian past that neither mirrors nor prefigures current multicultural developments. However, while RE under the ERA is articulated with a particular notion of heritage, its actual role constitutes a site of tension.[16] Conservatives and the NCR are divided on whether RE concerns (1) the nurturance of faith or (2) education. For example, unlike collective worship, schools are unable to obtain exemption from the Christian requirements of RE since, whether children are Sikh, Muslim, Jewish, or Christian, they all live in a country whose Christian heritage and history they must understand.[17] At the same time, advocates of the nurturance approach argue that instruction in Christianity is primarily aimed at filling the spaces left by parents in their transmission of cultural heritage and identity. Here we witness a discourse of parental inadequacy that is at odds with the "parents'-rights" rhetoric of the 1980s (e.g., Newburn 1992, 191), and which is linked to the notion of the confirmed professional. According to this view, Christianity must be taught by believers rather than by secular educationalists.[18]

> I am sure that the vast majority of those who call themselves Christian . . . do not themselves feel capable of teaching their children properly about Christianity and how to be good Christians. They very much hope that this will be done for them by someone whom they think is better qualified than they. Therefore can my noble friend assure the House that Christian clergymen will be invited into schools to teach Christianity?[19]

Along with RE as education, RE as nurturance is also embedded in certain aspects of the law. For example, Circular 1/94 states: "The precise balance between Christianity and other religions should take account both of the national and the *local* position. . . . Account should be taken of the local school population and the wishes of local parents" (para. 35). Implicit in this statement is the suggestion that the character of religious education is premised, at least in part, on affirmation of faith. Schools should respond to what parents wish their children to know.[20] This contrasts with notions that education should emphasize learning about the unknown.

Nurturance is also articulated to a discourse of simplicity.[21] While education is concerned with inquiry—examination of the "facts"[22]—affirmation is grounded in *accessible* belief. "How does one begin with young children? . . .

Where will they start? I suppose they will start with the idea of gentle Jesus, meek and mild, and God as a benign father sitting up in the sky."[23] What the young need are simple, basic truths—Bible stories—not the intellectual questions that concern agnostic theologians engaged with a range of faiths.[24] As several parliamentarians and others have stated, a multi–faith approach to RE that comparatively explores a range of different faiths may end up confusing children.[25] They may not understand their own identity, and, in particular, they may lose the ability to differentiate between the "we" and the "non-we."

Rejection of a multi-faith, mixing-bowl approach to RE is most concretely manifested in the model syllabi, which are structured around teaching one faith at a time. It is also evident in the provision that RE syllabi set out the content of teaching in each faith (see Circular 1/94, para. 33–4).[26] By obliging syllabi to demonstrate how, at each key stage, the "relative content devoted to Christianity predominates" (para. 35), it becomes significantly harder for them to integrate different faiths on a thematic basis.

Nurturing the Christian "We"

Faith affirmation is particularly apparent in relation to collective worship (i.e., school prayers). RE syllabi are expected to take into account "the teaching and practices of the other principal religions represented in Great Britain" (S. 8(3) ERA); however, worship can be "wholly . . . of a broadly Christian character" (S. 7, ERA). Thus, while the Christian subject should know something about other faiths practiced in Britain, it is deemed unnecessary, even inappropriate, to attend their worship.[27]

The discursive focus on the needs of Christian children (which is at the center of the law) has interesting parallels with Foucault's historical analysis of the development of middle-class sexuality from the eighteenth century onwards (1981, 120–21). Foucault argued that the middle classes developed disciplinary techniques in relation to their own, rather than in relation to the Other's, sexuality as a strategy of self-affirmation (123). A similar approach is apparent here. As parliamentary debates made clear, the main function of the legislation was not "the enslavement of another" (123), but the recreation of a sense of belonging and national identity among White Christians whose ties to blood, history, and the land appeared to be under attack.[28] Thus, the legislation refers repeatedly to Christianity, while other faiths remain unspecified; they are simply the forbidding, foreign Other, against which Christians define themselves. Clearly, despite the focus being on the needs of Christian families, their identity cannot be constructed without the depiction of a non-Christian Other.

While the non-Christian Other that is demonized is not so much Islam, Judaism, or Hinduism as the "mishmash," "hotch-potch," or "mixing bowl," it is these faiths that are denaturalized, cut loose from their embedded position within a multicultural fabric. This is achieved through a range of disciplinary techniques, one clear example being the process of exemption from Christian assemblies (S. 12 ERA). While conforming with the Christian worship mandate requires little self-reflection, obtaining an exemption necessitates that a school demand, scrutinize, and evaluate the background of its pupils (Circular 1/94, para. 70) to ensure they are appropriately Other.

Parents are also forced to define themselves in particular ways, since only certain interpretive understandings of family background are deemed relevant. For instance, parents who define themselves as non-religious cannot count this towards an exemption, since the latter can only be obtained on the basis of "other-faith" membership. Likewise, atheist/humanist Jews have to classify themselves as Jewish rather than as non-religious.[29]

While this illustrates one of the ways in which the legislation renders secularism invisible, it also highlights how the law is identity-affirming for Christians. Secular Christians "belong" whether they wish to or not, for the dominant position of Christianity denies them choice. If they corporately seek a determination, the law renders their choice non-existent.[30] By law, their collective rejection of Christian prayer is a non-event that must remain unrecognized. In contrast, while Christianity retains its private, normative status, other religions are obliged to declare themselves in order to win consideration. Interestingly, they are also forced to confront Christian hegemony if they wish to be both recognized and exempted from mono-cultural, Christian worship. Parents who do not complain and who do not withdraw their children from assemblies do not provide the requisite evidence for a determination to be granted (Circular 1/94, para. 71).

It is not only the exemption *process* which generates disciplinary techniques of classification, scrutiny, and visibility with regard to the Other; dividing children for separate assemblies also categorizes them according to faith, normalizing certain identifications and accentuating others. As they pass each other on their way to separate prayers, children's bodies become disciplined to follow their facilitator and to recognize the direction other children take as "not theirs."

Capacity to Consent

The final element of Conservative discourse I wish to identify concerns young people's ability to consent. While they are registered pupils, youngsters have no formal right to opt out of daily collective worship and religious education unless their parents write a letter. Although children are not compelled by law to pray, attendance alone is insufficient. "Taking part in collective worship implies more than simply passive attendance" (Circular 1/94, para. 59), although it is unclear how much more can be expected.[31]

Coercion is rooted in the Conservative denial of young people's religious autonomy (and the assumption of a single, familial faith). Young people, even those who are eighteen, cannot choose whether to participate in religious worship or study. Any sense that they may have a religious identity separate from that of their parents is denied by the statutory provisions which, throughout, refer to safeguarding *parental* rights and interests. In light of young people's relative autonomy in other areas, most obviously their right to abandon secondary education upon reaching the age of sixteen, their inability to absent themselves from daily prayer is anomalous.

In Britain, perhaps the closest analogy to this is the inability of men under eighteen to consent to sexual acts with other men. Both the male age of consent and the enforcement of prayer and religious education suggest a paternalistic imperative to enforce the norm—to protect young people from their own potentially corrupting desires. Furthermore, the enforcement of Christian prayer and religious education is a way of perpetuating a particular community. Young people's identity as belonging both to their school and to their nation is maintained and reinforced by the shared experience of prayer and religious heritage. Yet the maintenance of this community accentuates the exclusion of others; that is, the articulation of school with Christianity reproduces the Other as outsider.

Progressive Reaction: Interrogating Backlash

Oppositional Tactics

So far, my analysis of Conservative Christian ideologies embedded within the law can be narrated in terms of backlash: Right-wing activists and politicians, outraged by the swamping of Christianity by other faiths, fight back. Their actions resonate with the silent "general public," alienated from multiculturalism but too intimidated to speak out. As I mentioned earlier, I do not deny that backlash is discursively important, largely because of its naturalized, interpretive implications (i.e., it explains change in a way that feels intuitively right). However, I argue against reading change and/or conflict as backlash, and, in order to highlight certain problems of doing so, I introduce into my discussion the progressive educators' reaction to the 1988 ERA. As backlash tends to be seen as the exclusive province of the Right, it is instructive to consider the extent to which progressive resistance to changes may also be conceived of within its terms.

In researching the impact of religious education law, one of the most striking findings was the degree of opposition it engendered. This is not to deny that the legislation and movement around it led to more religious education and prayer in schools, with Christianity receiving an increasingly central role. It also does not deny the extent to which the Right was able to set the terms of the debate (Cooper 1995). At the same time, however, compliance has been neither straightforward nor wholly sympathetic. Thus, we could argue, the legislation generated a backlash from the liberal establishment, which opposed changes that would undermine the previous multi-faith settlement.

An incredible variety of establishment and progressive figures spoke out against the law, pressuring the government to modify or abandon its position. They included church leaders, the new educational inspectorate, and even Prime Minister Major's old headmaster. At the level of educational practice, different oppositional positions were adopted. The majority strategy was to accommodate the least contentious aspects of the law, such as regular RE, while ignoring or modifying those elements considered most problematic. For instance, many educators made superficial changes (e.g., re-Christianizing Christmas festivities, including the word "God" in assembly, highlighting Christianity in RE, etc.) while trying to retain a basic, multi-faith perspective. Others blatantly refused to comply, citing secular or pluralist reasons for their opposition. While there is no single set of statistics on levels of defiance, a range of data suggests full compliance by schools is at or near five per cent.

Problematizing Backlash

Various conceptual limitations of the concept of backlash are discussed elsewhere in this collection.[32] Here, I choose to focus on how the concept of backlash fails (1) to sufficiently account for the production of resources and (2) to sufficiently account for the production of motivation. While often ignored, these factors highlight the contingency, complexity, and equivocality of social change—phenomena the concept of backlash often marginalizes.

"Backlash" suggests that forces opposing change draw their resources from some external source. In other words, the disliked change is opposed with tools already fashioned and distributed rather than with tools organically related to and emanating from the target of their protest. However, not only did the Right draw on multiculturalism in its struggle, but progressive educators—countering Conservative legislation—responded in similar fashion, drawing on Right-wing texts. However much the child of NCR/Conservative Christians, the ERA also created resources for other forces. This occurred partly because its ambiguous meanings made negotiated readings possible, and partly because of its explicitly liberal elements—elements emanating from the nature of governmental decision-making and legitimacy requirements.

Progressive educators, for instance, in order to affirm multi–faith RE, exploited the legislative requirement that other religions be included in the syllabus. However unlikely it was that this provision would be enforced by the central government, it provided some recognition of Britain's status as a multi-faith society. Similarly, the procedures established to gain exemption enabled schools, for the first time since 1944, explicitly to provide a single, lawful, non-Christian assembly.

More paradoxically, increasing legislative closure also worked to empower minority communities. By drawing attention to, and accentuating, Christian dominance within British-maintained schools, separatist claims for other-faith schools were strengthened. The 1988 ERA offered ideological resources to all those who wished to maintain the separateness of their faiths. It was also a factor in drawing progressive educators together to protest Christian hegemony; the more central government pushed, the more others could point to its policies to emphasize both the importance and the vulnerability of multiculturalism.

While the creation of such resources by the Right may seem to benefit the progressives, the capacity of legislation to structure the value and character of these resources must not be underestimated. For instance, in a context in which the key units are discursive, the ability of the Education Reform Act to construct the debate in terms of how to give expression to Christianity's predominance (culturally and/or numerically) is important. While progressive educators could draw on ambiguous wording to justify their approach, and while a few explicitly rejected the terms of the debate, the capacity to explore other questions (such as the place and character of religion in schools, and, more radically, how to contest Christian hegemony)[33] was practically impossible.

Along with underestimating the extent to which political resources emerge from (and in the process of responding to) a targeted change, the backlash paradigm fails to acknowledge the wider origins of political motivation. Backlash tends to see motivation either as a response to a preceding (and diametrically opposed) transition (Faludi 1992, 13) or to a fear of wider changes resulting from small advances (14) rather than as a discursive effect of a complex range of ongoing socio-economic, cultural, and political processes.[34]

Conservative attempts to rewrite the law, one can argue, were as much motivated by intra-Right struggles for dominance[35] (and the NCR's need for symbolic achievements) as they were by proponents of multicultural and secular education. Indeed, one can argue that the multi-faith settlement, in which Christianity was demoted, was largely constructed by NCR rhetoric. Similarly, progressive educators' opposition to the law was not motivated solely by the ERA; it was also incited by ongoing educational cutbacks and contradictory shifts in senior teachers' power. These events not only provided resources, they also affected agendas and agency. Religious education became an issue around which schools could assert their political convictions and professional authority—both of which were more fundamental than was compliance with the law.

In addition to its aforementioned conceptual limitations, the concept of backlash also raises normative problems. Within popular, everyday usage, it appears to be embedded within liberal discourse and its dislike of radical change. Backlash suggests that rapid progress is undesirable because it generates acute fear and defensive responses; it is the populist, intuitive reaction of those who feel that democracy is not functioning. In other words, when those in power take advantage of their political, bureaucratic, or professional mandate to institute non-consensual change, people may feel they have no alternative but to take direct action themselves.[36] Liberals may dislike what is happening, they may feel that the backlash is going too far, but they see it as inevitable, even necessary, if a more acceptable equilibrium is to be attained.

This liberal model of backlash has two crucial, normative implications. First, change is best when it occurs slowly and with popular support. Backlash, in contrast, leads to a see-sawing between two polarized positions—a see-sawing that benefits nobody and that does not generate lasting progress. Second, it is believed that the proponents of radical change are largely responsible for any resulting backlash. Thus, not only should they be criticized for ignoring popular feeling, but they have no valid basis for complaint when they become the recipients of a backlash.

For liberals, both radical change and its concomitant backlash pose dangers insofar as they could potentially undermine democracy and the law. However, it is this very potentiality that accounts for the backlash paradigm receiving support from more radical quarters: the vision of opposed forces fighting it out as society swings first one way and then another (Faludi 1992). Yet, as is the case with liberal discourse in general, this grants too much emphasis to agency and single determinants. While it might be politically tempting to see change as the product of forces battling for supremacy, ultimately, this vision will end in disillusion.

Conclusion

I have explored the introduction of religious legislation in Britain as part of an attempt by Right-wing Christian forces to challenge multiculturalism and to reassert a church-based, disciplined, nation-oriented identity. In doing so, I have examined the usefulness of the concept of backlash with regard to understanding (1) the legislation's emergence and (2) the ensuing resistance to it by progressive forces. While the concept of backlash is important because it condenses hegemonic understandings of political action and social change, it is problematic because it privileges a view of society in which action is equated with provocation.

If we recognize that political agendas are constituted by a wide range of factors, and that resources are always being produced and are always in flux, it will be clear that a diversity of political targets and forms of action are necessary. Fixating on backlash can lead to a political activism obsessed with the forces of reaction. Not only does this allow the so-called backlash to set the terrain and the terms of debate, but it also underestimates the extent to which social processes may render it obsolete. This is not to argue that sites of backlash such as religious education should be ignored; it is to argue that one must counter Right-wing agendas on more levels than a simple focus on backlash will allow.[37]

Notes

1. This begs the question whether or not Christianity ever played such a peripheral role.
2. See Durham (1991), Hall (1988), Levitas (1986), and Seidel (1988).
3. I follow other writers in using the term "moral" to refer to a social/domestic/familial agenda based explicitly on Conservative-Christian values. However, there are problems in using "moral" in this restricted way, as it suggests a division between the economic sphere and the moral sphere.
4. See Durham (1991, ch. 9), however, who problematizes the assumption that the moral lobby is necessarily Conservative or part of the New Right.
5. For a more extensive account, see Cooper (1996).
6. This notion resonates with an Althusserian (1971) analysis that considers education as an Ideological State Apparatus (which is more prone than are Repressive State Apparatuses to temporary colonization by oppositional forces).
7. This research was run jointly with Ann Stewart, also of Warwick University, and was funded by the Economic and Social Research Council under the rubric of the Local Governance Programme. Award No. R000232035. My thanks to Madeleine Warhlberg and Pat Hawthorne for their research assistance.
8. By asking which schools and actors had been particularly active in opposing the law, I was able to identify a number of interviewees. As with other field research, in which I have interviewed actors from different political backgrounds, levels of disclosure tended to vary. While few people asked about my own background, accepting me as a legal academic, when relevant I disclosed my own experience

as a 1980s Labour councillor opposed to the policy. This generally tended to produce more relaxed and apparently confidential responses. Within a highly polarized, politicized context, many local government actors are wary of detailing instances of illegality to a (political) stranger.

9. See Baroness Cox, Hansard, 26 February 1988, col. 1454. There is some debate over why Christianity was not explicitly named in the 1944 act. In other words, was it consciously unnamed in order to make the legislation more widely acceptable, or was the assumption that prayer and instruction would be Christian so powerful that it did not need stating?

10. See Earl of Arran, Hansard, 26 February 1988, col. 1485.

11. However, if prayers are "mainly" rather than "wholly" Christian, the inclusion of non-Christian material must be justified (see Hull 1993).

12. For a discussion of the relationship between Christianity and public morality, see Jackson (1992, 103–5).

13. See Ashbourne, Hansard, 26 February 1988, cols. 1467–8; Coombs, Hansard, 23 March 1988, cols. 402–3.

14. At different points in the debates, attacks are made on a relativist position that refuses to differentiate between truth and falsehood with regard to the normative beliefs of different faiths. Advocates and supporters of the legislation emphasize the general value and contribution of Christianity to social life. See, for instance, the letter from a headteacher (published in the Times Education Supplement, 17 June 1994), which states that, as a result of Christian values, England remains "the most kindly, tolerant and law-abiding society in the world."

15. Beith, MP, Hansard, 23 March 1988, col. 405.

16. For a useful discussion of different approaches to religious education in the United States America, see L. Mueller (1986).

17. See, for example, Lord Arran, Hansard, 26 February 1988, col. 1486.

18. Logically, this should follow for the teaching of other faiths. It is for this reason that subscribers of the nurturance approach to RE do not want children of different faiths being taught together. Since they are literally learning to believe, it would be entirely improper to have multi-faith classes.

19. Lord Swinfen, Hansard, 26 February 1988.

20. For instance, see Ron Dearing, chair, School Curriculum and Assessment Authority, who stated that, with regard to young children, classroom work should focus on the traditions they bring with them (Guardian, 6 July 1944).

21. For a discussion of the ways different discourses intersect, see J. Palmer and F. Pearce (1983).

22. Within the British system, this is the notion of education that is currently dominant.

23. The Earl of Cork and Orrery, Hansard, 26 February 1988, col. 1471.

24. For instance, see Chris Wright, Times Education Supplement, 19 August 1994, who argues that pupils need to master basic ideas, not to engage in sophisticated, academic speculations regarding the nature of faith.

25. For a more critical perspective on this point, see Jackson (1992).

26. However, it is interesting that, despite adopting this approach, the model syllabi reveal the extent of similarities between religions. This may reflect either real commonality or current, hegemonic, religious education discourse.

27. The asymmetry of treatment between children of different faiths is explicit throughout the legislative provisions. For instance, in dealing with an application for exemption from "broadly Christian collective worship," Circular 1/94 states that "care should be taken to safeguard the interests of any parents of children for whom broadly Christian collective worship would be appropriate" (para. 71). However, in the absence of such an application, "pupils who do not come from Christian families should be able to join in the daily act of collective worship even though this would, in the main, reflect the broad traditions of Christian belief" (para. 65).

28. Racialized references are relatively obscure. While the articulating of England with Christianity suggests a predominantly White population, parliamentary debate did refer to the existence of Black Christians (although they tended to be somewhat exoticized).

29. One of the ideological implications of this aspect of the law is its assumption that children come from mono-faith households; there is no discussion of, or provision for, children whose parents are of different faiths. Thanks to Carl Stychin for raising this point.

30. The Education Act, 1993, incorporated a provision allowing the secretary of state to overturn a determination "unreasonably" granted. The event precipitating this amendment was a parent's complaint that her children's school had wrongly received a determination on the basis of parental wishes. She argued that most of these parents were of Christian heritage and thus did not fall within the criteria for an exemption. The secretary of state accepted her grievance but said he did not have the power to overturn the determination. This power was subsequently granted (S. 12A ERA).

31. Children who receive permission from their parents to withdraw from collective worship may be legitimately forbidden to attend assembly while worship is taking place (1/94, para. 86).

32. See also J. Newson (1991), who discusses backlash in the context of men's opposition to women's advancement. She argues that the metaphor of backlash deflects attention away from the reality of women's achievements and is, therefore, demoralizing and disempowering. It also results in having to justify ground already gained rather than arguing for further progress.

33. By using the phrase "Christian hegemony" I am not saying that Christians necessarily support, or participate in, Conservative hegemonic politics; I am saying that British society is organized around, and naturalizes, broad-based Christian values and culture, while the church-state nexus is institutionalized in the specific form of the Church of England. Within Christianity's hegemony, there is clearly space for different articulations; however, to the outsider, they remain fundamentally Christian.

34. Newson (1991) makes a similar point. However, although she rejects a simplistic cause-and-effect model, she retains a mechanical metaphor insofar as she suggests two lines of motion—one Conservative, the other progressive—engaged in

struggle. This paradigm thus continues to emphasize agency and social forces and to marginalize structural factors.

35. The 1980s witnessed ongoing tensions amongst Conservatives over where the balance should be struck between parental freedoms and state control. For instance, in political discussions over sex education in the mid–1980s, there was a clear distinction between those parliamentarians who argued that all pupils should receive a curriculum agreed upon by the central government and those who believed that the solution to progressive sex education was to allow parents to withdraw their children from the offending classes.

36. For a useful discussion of this perspective, see J. Newson (1991, 93) on common-sense interpretations of the massacre of women students at the Université de Montréal.

37. This echoes an older, well-rehearsed question: Should fringe fascist movements be ignored on the grounds that attention increases their influence, or should they be treated as a priority? While I would argue that it is important for some forces to directly counter fascist politics, other movements should target the causes of fascist appeal and/or advocate and struggle towards an alternative vision.

References

Althusser, L. 1971. *Lenin and Philosophy and Other Essays*. London: New Left Books.

Chitty, C. 1989. *Towards a New Education System: The Victory of the Moral Right?* Sussex: Falmer.

Cooper, D. 1994. *Sexing the City: Lesbian and Gay Politics within the Activist State*. London: Rivers Oram.

———. 1995. *Power in Struggle: Feminism, Sexuality and the State*. Ballmoor: Open University.

———. 1996 "Strategies of Power: Legislating Worship and Religious Education." In *Strategies of Transgression: The Impact of Michel Foucault on the Social Sciences*, edited by M. LLoyd and A. Thacker. Macmillan: Basingstoke.

Cooper D., and D. Herman. 1991. "Getting the Family 'Right' ": Legislating Heterosexuality in Britain, 1986–90. *Canadian Journal of Family Law* 10: 41–78.

Dale, R. 1989. *The State and Education Policy*. Milton Keynes: Open University.

Durham, M. 1991. *Sex and Politics*. Basingstoke: Macmillan.

Faludi, S. 1992. *Backlash: The Undeclared War Against American Women*. London: Vintage.

Foucault, M. 1981. *The History of Sexuality*. London: Penguin.

Gyford, J. 1985. *The Politics of Local Socialism*. London: Allen and Unwin.

Hall, S. 1988. *The Hard Road to Renewal*. London: Verso.

Hull, J. 1993. "The Fundamental Distinction: A Review of DFE Draft Circular X/94 Religious Education and Collective Worship." 11 October. Unpublished.

———. 1994. "The New Government Guidelines on Religious Education." *British Journal of Religious Education* 16: 66–69.

Jackson, R. 1992. "The Misrepresentation of Religious Education." In *Ethics, Ethnicity and Education*, edited by M. Leicester and M. Taylor. London: Kogan Page.

Jones, K. 1989. *Right Turn: The Conservative Revolution in Education*. London: Hutchinson Radius.

Lansley, S., S. Goss, and C, Wolmar. 1989. *Councils in Conflict: The Rise and Fall of the Municipal Left*. Basingstoke: Macmillan.

Levitas, R., ed. 1986. *The Ideology of the New Right*. Cambridge: Polity.

Morley, D. 1983. "Cultural Transformations: The Politics of Resistance." In *Language, Image and Media*, edited by H. Davis and P. Walton. Oxford: Basil Blackwell.

———. 1989. "Changing Paradigms in Audience Studies." In *Remote Control*, edited by E. Seiter, H. Borchers, G. Kreutzner, and A-M. Warth, London: Routledge.

Mueller, L. 1986. "Religious Rights of Children: A Gallery of Judicial Visions." *New York University Review of Law and Social Change* 14: 323–51.

Newburn, T. 1992. *Permission and Regulation: Law and Morals in Post–War Britain*. London: Routledge.

Newson, J. 1991. "'Backlash' Against Feminism: A Disempowering Metaphor." *RFR/DRF* 20: 93–97.

Palmer, J., and F. Pearce. 1983. "Legal Discourse and State Power: Foucault and the Juridical Relation." *International Journal of the Sociology of Law* 11: 361–83.

Sanders, S., and S. Spraggs. 1989. "Section 28 and Education." In *Learning Our Lines: Sexuality and Social Control in Education*, edited by C. Jones and P. Mahony. London: Women's Press.

Seidel, G., ed. 1988. *The Nature of the Right: A Feminist Analysis of Order Patterns*. Philadelphia: John Benjamin.

Chapter Three

'Then I Saw a New Heaven and a New Earth':[1] Thoughts on the Christian Right and the Problem of "Backlash"

Didi Herman
Keele University (United Kingdom)

Intuitively, it seems that the rise of an explicit anti–gay politics is a response to the perceived successes of a new political movement—namely, the lesbian and gay rights movement. Similarly, anti-feminism appears to be a reactionary impulse, a retort to the demand for gender equality. These responses/reactions are located within a range of 'backlash' tendencies that came to the fore in the mid-1980s. They are constituted by a series of manoeuvres that take aim against advances won by feminists, gay activists, liberal educationalists, and so on, and they evince a desire to return to an alleged status quo where orthodox truths are not questioned and where traditional authorities are not undermined.

In this short piece, I would like to challenge some of the above assumptions. To do this, I intend to draw upon my research on lesbian and gay politics and the Christian Right, particularly in the United States.[1] Briefly, my argument is that many of these developments, particularly anti-gay activity, are being spearheaded by a social movement with a long history and a clear vision: conservative Protestantism as led by an elite I shall call the Christian Right. It is at best unhelpful, and at worst obscurantist, to conceptualize this movement's political activities as "backlash."

I will begin by defining my terms. I use the phrase "Christian Right" to refer to a broad coalition of organizations and individuals who have come together to ensure that their conservative Christian vision is ensconced in the political structure of the nation. While the Christian Right speaks on behalf of a particular constituency, the latter is composed of a diverse collection of conservative Christian believers who may or may not support its political agenda.[2] I use the phrase "conservative Christian" to refer primarily to mainstream, conservative, evangelical Protestants. While conservative Roman Catholics and, less frequently, orthodox Jews and Muslims are often partners in specific struggles, the leadership of the Christian Right is largely Protestant, as is the theology motivating most of its actions. When I use the term "mainstream," I *exclude* the extreme Christian Right—the Klansmen, the militiamen, and so on—who share a large part of Christian Right theology but who tend to exist on the margins of legality. More important, the mainstream Christian Right seeks actively to distance itself from this extreme element.[3]

Finally, and crucially, I use the phrase "conservative, evangelical Protestantism," as do many others (Bruce 1984, 4–8), to describe a specific set of religious beliefs that, largely, may be boiled down to two key tenets: (1) biblical inerrancy and (2) premillennial dispensationalism. Very simply, biblical inerrancy is the belief that the Christian testament and, to some extent, the Hebrew bible are to be taken literally as the word of God. The idea that these documents are to be read in their 'social context' or interpreted in light of changing values is an abomination. Premillennial dispensationalism is the eschatological position held by the majority of American conservative Protestants. It holds that the world will descend into chaos and war; that the true believers will be raptured to heaven; that the anti-Christ will rise and seek to take over the world (the Tribulation); that Christ will return to defeat him (Armageddon) and usher in the millennial (the thousand-year reign of Christians on earth); and that, at the end of the millennial, Satan will again rise and be defeated and earth will be replaced by heaven (which will be populated by Christ and the saints).[4]

To unbelievers, this scenario sounds like fantastic science fiction—to some it may even sound completely absurd. But I want to argue that this eschatology must be taken seriously, for those who believe it believe it fervently and base much of their politics upon its truth. It is also worth noting that millions of Americans share this theology—it is by no means confined to a "fundamentalist fringe."[5]

A key component of this and other apocalyptic belief systems (e.g., orthodox Marxism) is that the end of our current dispensation is near. Writers in the apocalyptic genre constantly read the signs of the times and interpret the biblical prophecies (e.g., John's Revelation) in light of current events. In other words, conservative, evangelical Protestants see the coming end all around them; needless to say, the rise of the feminist and lesbian and gay movements is understood in this context. Within this framework, feminists, lesbians and gay men, and liberals in general, whether or not they know it, are, quite literally, doing the "devil's work." They are part of a larger force of evil, driving the United States to the brink and contributing to setting the stage for the final Tribulation.

Having characterized the movement that forms the subject of my analysis, I now wish to move on to a substantive engagement with the concept of backlash. There are four dimensions to my argument. First, the Christian Right is, itself, a "victim" of backlash and not simply, or unilaterally, a perpetrator of backlash; second, the Christian Right is not a monolithic bloc; third, while some Christian Right activists do idealize a mythical past, a cursory glance at their literature shows that they were *never* happy with the status quo and have no wish to return to it (e.g., their vehemence against immorality was as strong in the 1950s as it is now, even though they now idealize this earlier period); fourth, and perhaps most important, the Christian Right has a comprehensive, progressive future vision: it is, I would argue, a paradigmatic movement for social change having neither more nor less to do with backlash than do the feminist and gay rights movements. As the first two points are fairly self–evident, I will discuss them only briefly and then go on to concentrate on the last two.

"Victims" and "Perpetrators"

The concept of backlash tends to suggest a unidirectional flow of action. First, a force for change appears and has some success (e.g., the lesbian and gay rights movement), then a counterforce emerges to thwart this success (e.g., anti-gay activism). Within this understanding, backlash has both a clear perpetrator and a clear victim. The perpetrators are the attackers, the members of a regressive bloc calling for a halt to perceived changes in sexual relations. The lesbian and gay movement is the victim—fighting for equality, it finds itself confronting reactionary forces that, in the name of tradition, are set on denying change.

In my view, deploying backlash in this way serves to cloud historical shifts and contemporary politics. First, the lesbian and gay movement itself is, within this understanding, a form of reaction. Demands for lesbian and gay equality are an attack upon the hegemony of heterosexual culture; that is, they constitute a reaction against the imposition of a particular construction of normalcy. In this sense, the lesbian and gay movement is the counterforce, the backlash, and the Christian Right merely the establishment "victim" fighting for survival. Second, with respect to certain social movements (e.g., feminism), the simple notion of victim/perpetrator obscures an understanding of how movements develop historically. Given the different forms feminist struggle has taken over the last century, it may be more helpful to conceptualize social movements as fluid, dynamic, contradictory, and contingent rather than simply as forces meeting counterforces in the evolutionary spiral for supremacy (which is precisely what the concept of "backlash" seems to imply).

Split at the Root?

As was indicated above, it is worth emphasizing that social movements are not cohesive blocs of power with collective and harmonious visions and politics. In the case of the Christian Right in North America, internal strife and division is intense, extending to both short-term strategizing and long-term goals. The Christian Right is riven with a matrix of fissures, including: Protestant versus Roman Catholic; diverse forms of Protestantism; elites versus grassroots; and challenges from within by, amongst others, feminist evangelicals.[6] If the Christian Right is a backlash, then it has spawned offspring who have turned against their parent. There are backlashes within the backlash, and the relationship between these "children of backlash" and the original target—say, the lesbian and gay movement—are complex and ambivalent.

Rather than viewing any of these phenomena as backlash, I prefer to conceptualize conservative Christianity, and its contemporary political advocate, the Christian Right, as a bona fide social movement in its own right. The Christian Right is not new and neither are its internal divisions. It *seemed* new (or backlash-like) in the 1980s because it had, in fact, lost its hegemony and was struggling to regain it.

The Time Has Always Been Now

The standard story with regard to backlash is that it is the result of a desire to return to an idealized period—a mythic past. But conservative evangelicals were never interested in returning to "the good old days"; for them, those days were always simply an earlier stage in an inevitable process of cultural decay. Christian Right constituents were as unhappy with the status quo and its predecessors as were the Left—perhaps even more so.

Throughout the latter half of the twentieth century, the leading publication for conservative Protestantism has been the journal *Christianity Today*. To the extent that conservative evangelicalism has a Left, Right, and Centre, *Christianity Today* is today a Centrist publication, sometimes at odds with Christian Right leadership, sometimes supportive.[7] During the 1950s and 1960s, however, *Christianity Today* was the leading forum for conservative Christian discontent, and its editors provided a strong critique of what they perceived to be prevailing social disintegration. To illustrate my argument that anti-gay politics, as exemplified by the Christian Right, is not a simple backlash, I want to point to the ways in which conservative Christianity conceptualized the 1950s and the early 1960s (some time before the rise of second-wave feminism or lesbian and gay rights politics). The pages of *Christianity Today* provide most of the requisite information. Given the focus of this chapter and of *Dangerous Territories* as a whole, I will highlight the domains of sexuality and education.

For conservative Protestants, one of the great issues of the 1950s and 1960s was sexual immorality: "A virulent moral sickness is attacking American society. Its obvious symptoms may be seen at any newsstand in large cities or small. American society is becoming mentally, morally and emotionally ill with an unrestrained sex mania."[8] This remark, the opening to an article published in 1958, signalled the start of *CT*'s concern with changing sexual mores. The authors went on to complain of the glorification of "prostitution, sadism, orgies and sexual perversion," "sordid acts of fornication," and the effects of all of this on "impressionable young people."[9] Women, the authors argued, "are completely depersonalized and are shown merely as pliant machines which men utilize for brutish pleasure." (6) Like others to follow, this article related "unrestrained sex mania" to anti–Christianity and to the era's general overall assault on the church. "If our churches fail to answer it," the authors cried, "they will rue the day that their timidity and inaction gave a victory, by default, to the advocates of paganism." (8)

This anxiety about rampant sexual licence is heightened in an article published in 1959. Here, the author is concerned about "obscene advertising," "pornographic business," "juvenile delinquency," and the "erratic sexual life" of young people.[10] These developments are condemned as "viruses [that] infest and infect not only the young but the adult generation of our population . . . infecting their numerous consumers with bodily, moral, and mental diseases." (3) The author goes on to argue that the spread of these viruses leads inevitably to training young people "in the difficult art of mass murdering of innocent people" (just how this comes about is not clear) (4).

The tone of this piece, and others like it, signifies the level of crisis at that time. The 1950s were seen, by many conservative Christians, as a period in which sexual depravity was about to cause the imminent downfall of the nation. In 1960, events had escalated to such a point that *CT* published an editorial roundtable discussion on "America's sex crisis."[11] Here, various members of the *CT* editorial board express profound distress at how "sex obsession is destined to destroy our nation." (6) Remarkably, one participant blames the "new freedom of women" (I say "remarkably" because this is still a period in which women were seen to know, and to be confined to, their "place"). It is also worth noting that some participants criticized the church for making sexuality a taboo subject and for not encouraging the frank discussion of "healthy sexuality."[12]

Throughout the early 1960s, article after article railed against "an ever–widening cancer of corruption,"[13] the effects of sexual licence on "immature youth,"[14] and "the new morality" in general.[15] One writer found that the "morals revolution" had even begun to affect the Christian college.[16] Once again, the "emancipation" of women is blamed for this situation, as is the growing consensus that sex is either simply about pleasure or requires only love.[17]

Homosexuality is also discussed explicitly during this period. An increase in same-sex sexuality is viewed as evidence of sexual depravity generally. Homosexuality is not singled out; rather, writers portray it as one of a list of sexual ills. Pitirim Sorokin accuses the theatre of promoting "sensational plays alluringly displaying 'the third sex' and other sex abnormalities."[18] In a slightly later article, he notes an "increase of the homosexuals and other 'sex-deviants,' attested by decreasing prosecution and increasing legalization of such relationships."[19] Another writer goes so far as to find that there is a "cult of the homosexual in our times [that] is hard to grasp for those who do not meet the force of its drive."[20] Other contemporary targets of the CR (e.g., the National Education Association and the Hollywood film industry) were also believed to be in enemy hands.[21] Youth crime, alcoholism, and one-parent families were topics that were as familiar then as they are now.[22]

Education in general was a constant source of discontent. American young people are portrayed as being in imminent danger of moral decay (KiK) and the schools are clearly identified as sites of struggle between evangelicals and those doing the devil's work: "We should be roused from slumber by the spectre of a society where every school may become an instrument of state policy, every classroom a centre for inculcating a totalitarian creed, every lecture an occasion for delineating truth and goodness as personal prejudices instead of durable distinctions."[23] This author uses the "spectre" of the Soviet school system to show that godlessness leads to "the worship of [the] antichrist" and that this is the direction in which the United States is headed. According to him, Christians "must not surrender [their] public schools needlessly to the spirit of the age."[24]

Schools are seen as a key battleground in the fight against Roman Catholicism and against Left-wing ideology generally, for "educational administrators have by and large nurtured socialistic tendencies."[25] Universities, too, are believed to be almost lost to the degeneration process, and this is still several years before the period of campus radicalism. Universities are "vast temples of spiritual ignorance"[26] and are "intense[ly] liberal."[27] The university student is "easily influenced" and is "pliable and submissive to what is being said, whether fact or fiction,"[28] while the "no-gospel of secularism has darkened the minds of many members of academic communities."[29]

This picture of how conservative Protestants perceived life in the 1950s and early 1960s shows that the CR was as incensed, as critical, as vehement, and as active then as it is now. Furthermore, its concerns were strikingly similar to those now being espoused: American culture stood on the brink; end times were imminent; and cultural degeneration was always seen in the light of prophecy:

> The long night of human barbarism seems to have begun. To many observers, the horizon of this third night exhibits little, if any, prospect of a sunrise. . . . Descending from its pinnacle of lofty achievement, the Christian West in becoming pagan is headed for inevitable doom. The light men shun today is blinding, for the post-Christian era revolts against the most sacred inheritance of the race. To assume that an anti-Christ culture will escape perdition is sheer madness.[30]

Unless we say that backlashes last decades (in which case the point of the term is unclear), it would seem that the concept itself sheds little light on the sources and trajectories of "morality politics."

I suggest that we explore current social struggles for what they are—struggles for hegemony between competing belief and value systems. The CR has a long history of social criticism, and, as I now go on to discuss, it also possesses a comprehensive, progressive social vision. The CR is a utopian movement dedicated to the establishment of Christ's kingdom on earth.

A Forward March

Conservative Protestantism looks forward to a world where peace reigns, hunger and want are unknown, and happiness—even ecstasy—is every-where. This world, of course, would be populated entirely by orthodox Protestants (everyone else being dead). This is not a movement that looks back with longing; it is a movement that looks forward with anticipation. Given the popular association of the CR with Right-wing politics, it may seem disingenuous to portray it as utopian, ultimately seeking to establish a kingdom of peace and tranquillity. But, with certain caveats, it is precisely this to which the CR aspires.

In my view, in order to understand key social struggles it is essential to realize that, just as the feminist and lesbian and gay rights movements seek to recreate sexuality in a world where gender is differently situated, so do conservative Protestants, as represented by the CR seek to build their own version of the good life. Much current social conflict, particularly in light of the failure of mass class mobilizations, is concerned with the clash between these competing utopian paradigms and their attendant representatives. The concept of backlash does not do justice to these dynamics.

I do, however, think that backlash has some utility when defined specifically as an attitude on the part of the "non-aligned" public. In other words, feelings commonly associated with backlash—alienation, resentment, and so on—can be co-opted by populist discourses emanating from various social-movement actors. It is in this way that the CR has successfully exploited what are largely non-religious sentiments held by poor White Americans—particularly the so-called "angry White male." Here, backlash may help to describe a culture in which individuals are prepared to fight against the perceived gains of upstart "others" because it is believed that the success of the latter has directly resulted in the failure of the former. Take, for example, the current outcry against affirmative action. For the CR, any attempt by government to usurp the powers of God is an abomination (conservative Christianity has always been hostile to the secular state and to any expansion of its welfarist agenda). Although affirmative action policies may not be a natural front-line activity in the fight to save souls for Jesus, they can represent an exercise of immense state power and, thus, are opposed by most conservative Christians—an opposition that nicely dovetails with a general Right-wing agenda.[31]

Concluding Remarks

Historically, conservative evangelical Protestantism has been divided between those who believe that Christ will return to usher in the thousand-year reign of Christianity (the premillennialists) and those who believe that Christ will not return until this reign has already occurred (the postmillennialists). The dominant strand of American conservative Protestantism, for most of this century, has been premillennial. This has been partly responsible for the previous sluggishness of evangelicals when it came to getting involved in politics; the most important thing was to save souls for Jesus before the Tribulation began.

The movement of conservative Protestants to the front of the political stage has not been without internal cost. Indeed, one could argue that conservative evangelicals are becoming more and more *postmillennial* in their thinking. The very existence of something we can call the "Christian Right" suggests a movement actively seeking to change social life in the here and now—a force struggling to (re)establish the United States as a Christian nation.

If this is so, it brings the Christian Right perilously close to movements from which they publicly seek to distance themselves—the Christian Identity movement (a White separatist movement) (see Aho 1990; Barkun 1994) and the Reconstructionist movement (a postmillennial movement) (see Anti-Defamation League 1994, 118–29; Boston 1993, ch. 9). From somewhat different ground, each of these "extreme Right" movements advocates an immediate return to biblical law. Mainstream conservative Christians tend to reject this philosophy, arguing that they simply wish to see a less Godless nation, not one run according to ancient prescriptions.[32] But this stance is somewhat disingenuous, as conservative Christianity could not be clearer in its theology (biblical inerrancy) and in its prophecy (sooner or later, the world will be run by "the saved").

It is possible to see the Christian Right's flirtation with extremes in its endorsement of particular theological "experts." For example, David Barton, who appears regularly on the mainstream religious Right circuit as a "constitutional historian" (arguing the case that the Founding Fathers never intended to separate church and state)[33] is also a frequent guest of Christian Identity groups known for promoting Holocaust revisionism, race separation, and the death penalty for homosexuality (Anti-Defamation League 1994, 54–56). Similarly, R. J. Rushdoony, the leading American Reconstructionist, has been enthusiastically feted by CR leaders (Anti-Defamation League 1994, 125).

Clearly, the Christian Right is, in a very real sense, playing with fire in its continuing struggle to achieve its vision of the good life. I make this point to underpin my argument that, through deploying the term "backlash," we may not only lose sight of the bigger picture, we may also lose sight of the greater danger.

Notes

1. The epigram is taken from Revelation (21:1). This essay, written for this collection in early 1995, begins to map out an area further elaborated in Herman (1997). See also Cooper and Herman (1995) and Herman (1994).
2. Comprehensive studies of the Christian Right can be found in: Bromely and Shupe (1984); Diamond (1989); Hertzke (1988); Hunter (1991); Jorstad (1987); Liebman and Wuthnow (1983); Lienesch (1982); and Moen (1989).
3. However, see comments in the conclusion to this essay.
4. Versions of this scenario can be found in hundreds of books that sell millions of copies each year. Two of the most popular writers are Hal Lindsey (1994) and Pat Robertson (e.g. 1991).
5. For a history of the apocalyptic genre in America, and a discussion of its continued appeal today, see Boyer (1992).
6. On some of these points, see the studies mentioned in note 3.

7. An interesting example of this can be found in James Dobson's (president of Focus on the Family, one of the leading Christian Right organizations) exchange with *Christianity Today* in 1995. See J. Dobson, "Why I Use Fighting Words," *Christianity Today* 39, no. 7 (1995): 27–30.

8. Ralph A. Cannon and Glenn D. Everett, "Sex and Smut on the Newsstands," *Christianity Today* 2, no. 10 (1958): 5.

9. Ibid., 6.

10. Pitirim A. Sorokin, "Demoralization of Youth: Open Germs and Hidden Viruses," *Christianity Today* 3, no. 20 (1959): 3. Homosexuality is mentioned specifically, but I address this subject separately below. See also the author's peculiar follow–up piece, "The Depth of the Crisis: American Sex Morality Today," *Christianity Today* 4, no. 20 (1960): 3–5.

11. "Sex in Christian Perspective," *Christianity Today* 4, no. 20 (1960): 6–8.

12. Later conservative Christians took up this challenge, and, indeed, a large literature on sex and sexual pleasure within marriage has been produced.

13. Stanley C. Baldwin, "Sodom in America," *Christianity Today* 8, no. 2 (1963): 14.

14. "Diagnosis Is Not Enough," *Christianity Today* 8, no. 2 (1963): 24–26.

15. Howard Carson Blake, "The New Morality," *Christianity Today* 8, no. 12 (1964): 7–9.

16. David L. McKenna, "The Morals Revolution and the Christian College," *Christianity Today* 8, no. 19 (1964): 10–13.

17. Ibid.

18. Sorokin, "Demoralization of Youth," 4.

19. Sorokin, "The Depth of the Crisis," 3.

20. Howard Carson Blake, "The New Morality," *Christianity Today* 8, no. 12 (1964): 8.

21. See, for example, "NCC, God, and the Schools," *Christianity Today* 3, 18 (1959): 20–22; Richard C. Halverson, "Any Good from Hollywood?" *Christianity Today* 2, no. 6 (1957): 8–10.

22. See, for example: Sorokin, "Demoralization of Youth," 3; Emma Fall Schofield, Will Alcohol Destroy Our Youth?" *Christianity Today* 3, no. 20 (1959): 6–8; J. Marcellus Kik, "Combatting Juvenile Delinquency," *Christianity Today* 3, 9 (1959): 13–16.

23. Carl F.H. Henry, "Christian Responsibility in Education," *Christianity Today* 1, no. 17 (1957): 11.

24. Ibid., 13–14. See also "NCC, God, and the Schools" (editorial), *Christianity Today* 3, no. 18 (1969): 20.

25. "America's Future: Can We Salvage the Republic?" (editorial), *Christianity Today* 2, no. 11 (1958): 4. See also "Foundations: Tilt to the Left" (editorial), *Christianity Today* 2, no. 15 (1958): 18.

26. "Christ and the Campus" (editorial), *Christianity Today* 3, no. 16 (1959): 20.

27. Robert M. Smith, "Famine on University Campuses," *Christianity Today* 6, no. 10 (1962): 13.

28. Ibid., 15. See also "The Storm Over Academic Freedom" (editorial), *Christianity Today* 7, no. 14 (1963): 20.

29. Ernest Gordon, "The Word and the Campus," *Christianity Today* 8, no. 16 (1964): 5.
30. "The Christian-Pagan West" (editorial), *Christianity Today* 1, no. 16 (1956): 34.
31. Interestingly, during the 1950s civil rights struggles, *Christianity Today* went back and forth over whether or not to support civil rights laws. While always condemning enforced segregation, these conservative Protestants preferred to keep the state out of the enforcement business generally. I explore this further in Herman (1997, ch. 5).
32. For example, all Christian Right leaders I interviewed repudiated reconstructionism.
33. See, for example, David Barton's appearance on James Dobson's radio show, distributed by Focus on the Family as "America's Christian Heritage" (cassette), 1993.

References

Anti–Defamation League. 1994. *The Religious Right: The Assault on Tolerance and Pluralism in America*. New York: ADL.

Aho, J. A. 1990. *The Politics of Righteousness: Idaho Christian Patriotism*. Seattle: University of Washington Press.

Barkun, M. 1994. *Religion and the Racist Right: The Origins of the Christian Identity Movement*. Chapel Hill: University of North Carolina Press.

Boston, R. 1993. *Why the Religious Right Is Wrong: About Separation of Church and State*. Buffalo: Prometheus.

Boyer, P. 1992. *When Time Shall Be No More: Prophecy Belief in Modern American Culture*. Cambridge: Harvard University Press.

Bromley, D. G., and A. Shupe, eds. 1984. *New Christian Politics*. Macon: Mercer University Press.

Bruce, S. 1984. *Firm in the Faith*. Aldershot: Gower.

Cooper, D., and D. Herman. 1995. "Getting the Family 'Right': Legislating Heterosexuality in Britain." In *Legal Inversions: Lesbians, Gay Men, and the Politics of Law*, ed. D. Herman and C. Stychin, 162–79, Philadelphia: Temple University Press.

Diamond, S. 1989. *Spiritual Warfare: The Politics of the Christian Right*. Boston: South End.

Herman, D. 1997. *The Antigay Agenda: Orthodox Vision and the Christian Right*. Chicago: University of Chicago Press.

———. 1994. *Rights of Passage: Struggles for Lesbian and Gay Legal Equality*. Toronto: University of Toronto Press.

Hertzke, A. 1988. *Representing God in Washington: The Role of Religious Lobbies in the American Polity*. Knoxville: University of Tennessee Press.

Hunter, J. D. 1991. *Culture Wars: The Struggle to Define America*. New York: Basic Books.

Jorstad, E. 1987. *The New Christian Right, 1981–1988*. Lewiston: Edwin Mellen.

Liebman, R. C., and R. Wuthnow. 1983. *The New Christian Right: Mobilization and Legitimation*. Hawthorne: Aldine.

Lienesch, M. 1982. "Right–Wing Religion: Christian Conservativism as a Political Movement." *Political Science Quarterly* 97: 403ff.

Lindsey, H. 1994. *Planet Earth—2000 AD*. Palos Verdes, CA: Western Front.

Moen, M. 1989. *The Christian Right and Congress*. Tusaloosa: University of Alabama Press.

Robertson, P. 1991. *The New World Order*. Dallas: Word.

Chapter Four

Disciplining Feminism:
A Look at Gender-Equity Struggles
in Australian Higher Education

Jill Blackmore
Deakin University (Australia)

Introduction

The backlash against feminism evident in Australia during the late 1980s and early 1990s arises out of national economic recession and workplace restructuring. I argue that educational restructuring has itself become a form of backlash, in that the discourses of efficiency and effectiveness shaping the radical restructuring of higher education in Australia since 1987 have silenced earlier discourses of equity. This chapter considers two dynamically interrelated aspects of the backlash in higher education: (1) the discourses that constitute the Australian media representation of backlash (with particular reference to case of alleged sexual harassment at an Australian university), and (2) the rapidly changing material conditions of academic work (particularly as they affect women), and their implications for feminist pedagogy.

In 1995, Helen Garner, a well-known feminist author and member of the Melbourne literary set, wrote what would become a bestseller within a week of its publication. *The First Stone* is about a sexual harassment case brought against Dr. Alan Gregory, the master of the prestigious Ormond College at the University of Melbourne. The book aroused more media interest than did the original sexual harassment case. The legal case, which went to appeal, was ultimately dismissed because both sides were deemed to have equally defensible positions, hence creating "reasonable doubt." By then, Gregory had resigned, and he is now having difficulty regaining an academic position.

The First Stone was a media event, not so much because the alleged sexual harassment occurred at an elite university as because Garner, a well-known, middle-aged feminist author, sympathizes with the male defendant. Indeed, not only does Garner sympathize with the male defendant, she castigates "young" feminists for their intransigence, their "priggishness," their lack of a sense of eros, their "wimpishness," and their willingness to use institutional legal processes to gain redress for minor sexist (sexual?) encounters—the kind of encounters most women deal with by delivering the master "a swift kick in the balls." In particular, she was galled by the refusal of the claimants and their "supporters" to speak with her. Garner's position was well-known even before the appearance of her book, as she wrote a sympathetic letter to the master at the time the court case was made public. The media have paid little attention to why such an incident was not appropriately handled at the college level.

Feminism is a media issue in 1990s Australia. Articles about feminism appear every day in a range of popular/academic journals and newspapers. This interest is not new and, indeed, could be seen to be due to 1980s feminist activism, strong national and state legislation with regard to equal employment opportunity, and much-publicized policies concerning equal opportunity in education. Such changes were said by Hester Eisenstein, a gender-reform practitioner and feminist author, to result in a form of "gender shock." In 1980, Eisenstein commented that the level of feminist discourse in the media and popular culture was significantly higher in Australia than in the United States; she also pointed out that Australian feminism was much more critical and confrontational than was American feminism.[1] There is also considerable confusion between American and Australian forms of affirmative action. In Australia, equal opportunity legislation is premised on individual merit, and now a quota system. The 1980s was a period of possibility, marked by individual women succeeding as leaders in political parties, trade unions, and public- and private-sector management. Indeed, one would expect to find, given the media attention granted these individual women, that there has been a significant shift in the numbers of women in executive and management positions. Yet the statistics show that women occupy only two-point-five per cent of executive positions in politics, management, and education and only twenty-four per cent of middle management positions in Victoria (Victoria Auditor General's Office 1995).

In the 1990s with regard to feminism, we are witnessing the increased privileging of what Kenway (1987) calls "discourses of derision."[2] While conservative discourses have always blamed the women's movement for poor child-rearing, violence, family breakdown, and unemployment, feminism is now also being blamed for the "crisis of masculinity," for going too far, and for being irrelevant to younger women (the presumption being that equity has already been achieved). It is the interaction and juxtaposition of various contradictory and overlapping discourses about feminism that constitute what has become known as a "backlash." This backlash, while not originating in any specific or locatable source, operates like a "productive network" that "runs through the whole social body" in ways which impart more power to certain discourses than to others (Gordon 1980, 119). In turn, these discourses produce, and are the product of, particular material conditions (Hennessey 1993).

What is equally significant is that the media, through their production of and emphasis on conflict, play a significant role in the construction of the backlash. This is achieved not only through providing air time and print space, in the name of "journalistic balance," to a small contingent of Right-wing male journalists who constantly attack "hardline" feminists and "political correctness," but also through the way the media itself represents feminism. For example, much of Australian anti-feminist discourse is framed by the American versions of backlash performed on the public lecture circuit by such "stars" as Camille Paglia, Katie Roiphe, and Susan Renfeld. These versions are then played out and rearticulated in local debates such as the Garner affair. Kate Spearritt of the Young Women and Feminism Group (part of the Women's Electoral Lobby) comments: "The parade of American feminists in Australia says more about the globalization of culture than Australian feminism." (1995, 23) Yet feminist journalists, politicians, social commentators, and academics expend considerable effort in reacting to such culturally imported versions of backlash. The media, who have themselves undergone a shift to the Right in recent years, by simultaneously generating and reproducing pro- and anti-feminist discourses promote the view that feminism is internally disrupted and fragmented. Both the Garner debate and the United Nations Women's Conference in Beijing are represented as examples of feminism in dissension and strife. Feminism is a media issue, and conflict within feminism is thus a media event.

At the same time, backlash is not merely the product of the media. I would argue that backlash has always been here, with resistance to gender equity going underground in the 1980s only to emerge reformed and recycled in more subtle and insidious ways in the 1990s (Cockburn 1992). The current media representations of backlash are, I suggest, merely an overt and public manifestation of an ongoing set of institutional processes that resist gender-equity reform. Backlash is a powerful part of the discursive field surrounding feminism and feminist practices in education, and it has been made possible by a changing political and economic context.

On the same day, while front-page headlines in The Australian read, "Garner Attacks Feminist Critics," its Higher Education Section headlines read, "Outrage as Chair Pulled from Under Women's Studies," "Sydney Uni Vice Chancellor in Damage Control," and "Day Labourers of Academe."

The first article refers to the failure of the Faculty of Arts to appoint a chair in women's studies at Adelaide University, despite it being a high priority of the male vice-chancellor. This failure was largely due to the fact that the faculty had stalled for three years (an example of institutional resistance at a time when the Women's Studies Centre itself was under threat of being swallowed up in faculty rationalization). The second headline refers to Dame Leonie Kramer's comment that there were few women in executive positions in universities because they "went all limp when the hard decisions had to be made." (Kramer is chancellor of Sydney University and is well known for her Right-wing educational stance and anti-feminism.) In an open letter, senior women academics and administrators refuted her position (The Australian, Higher Education Section, 6 June 1995). The outgoing male vice-chancellor sought to assure all females applying for his position that Sydney University was an equal opportunity employer and that they were most welcome. The third headline refers to the emergence of an underclass in the academic labour market. With reductions in federal funding, universities are increasingly being forced to sell themselves both nationally and internationally. In order to meet rapidly changing student needs and reduced financing for staff, universities are also increasingly turning to sessional and fixed-term appointments. The trend is towards both the further casualization and feminisation of the academic labour market (Castleman et al. 1995).

Since 1987 there has, in Australia, been a radical restructuring of the relationship between education, the economy, and the state. This restructuring is advocated by both Labor and Liberal parties alike, and it is meant to improve efficiency and national productivity in an era of economic rationalism. The trend in education is part and parcel of the shift away from a welfare state towards a contractual state and its concomitant reduction of public-sector funding in education, health, and welfare (Yeatman 1990). Discourses of efficiency and effectiveness have been privileged over discourses of equity and diversity; and management discourses have supplanted educational discourses in newly devolved systems of educational governance (Blackmore 1991, Blackmore and Sachs 1995–7). Restructuring has: (1) privatized the costs of education so that they fall on the user and the individual provider; (2) commodified research, curriculum, and pedagogy; and (3) created a casualized academic labour market (Blackmore 1994, Blackmore, Dugwin and Leavold 1994). Through seemingly "rational" reform, educational restructuring has facilitated the reassertion of the "politics of advantage" for men, with the result that notions of merit favor those in elite positions in universities (Eveline 1992). Likewise, university leadership has been reconstructed as being about managerialism, entrepreneurship, and hard-nosed decision-making as opposed to education (at the same time, the material conditions of academic work are being undermined).

First I examine the various discourses that constitute the current media backlash, then I examine the material and discursive conditions that facilitate their dominance in the university sector. Bearing in mind that discourses arise out of specific material contexts and have particular effects, I then consider the implications of how feminist work is discursively positioned within universities. I draw upon recent research projects that focus on the repositioning of women within the Australian education system in the wake of widespread public-sector and industrial-relations reform (Blackmore and Sachs, 1995–7, Blackmore, Dugwin and Leavold 1994).[2] Two themes which recur throughout are (1) how policy, as a product of political contestation, mediates the relationship between women and the state in education, and (2) how policy is itself a product of, and informant for the media (Falk 1994).

Discourses of Derision[3]

The range of discourses around feminism and education are various, overlapping, and contradictory. These discourses are called upon at specific sites of university decision-making and are encapsulated in policy texts. Such discourses have significant material effects on educational practice.

We-are-in-the-Era-of-Postfeminism

This discourse cites the presence of a few individual women in a range of leadership positions; the existence of anti-discrimination legislation, affirmative action legislation, equal opportunity policies; and, more recently, the educational achievements of women. Newspaper reports such as "Women Beat Men in Uni Studies" not only construct the issue of gender equity as competitive but conclude that women are no longer disadvantaged (Birrell, Dobson, and Rapson 1995). The assumption is that the mere presence of such policies, along with a few individual women in positions of power and a few examples of the educational "success" of some women, means that equity exists. This discourse is in direct contradiction with the following facts: (1) equal pay, much less equal employment opportunity, does not exist for women; (2) women are, despite being high educational achievers, not accruing the same rewards in the workforce as are their male counterparts; (3) employers are less likely to pay for women's professional development and training than they are for men's (Polonsky 1990); and (4) women continue to do family and paid work with little male assistance (Beasley 1995). Studies clearly show that the market does not produce equity for women as a group in the work-place (Rimmer et al. 1994). Even those individual women who success-fully venture into the male-dominated executive corporate level (making up 2.5 percent of senior management but 24 percent of middle manage-ment in 1990) find the "chilly climate" above the glass ceiling so bad that they often exit to become self-employed (Randell 1994).

Women-Are-the-New-Source-of-Change

This particular discourse emerges at a time when there is a perceived loss of faith in leadership in Australia. It arises out of a reaction to the corrup-tion and greed of the 1980s corporate sector and, in some instances, to its links with government. This overlaps with the national-crisis-and-lack-of-creative-business-and-government-leadership discourse. In two states undergoing financial crises in the late 1980s, women were elected by their state Labor parties to succeed male premiers. While both women premiers lost their respective state elections despite their high personal popularity ratings, their respective images as ethical and moral leaders continues. Carmen Lawrence from Western Australia was fast-tracked into federal Parliament and become health minister in the Labor government; Joan Kirner, ex-premier of Victoria, continues to have a high public profile. This ties in with new management discourses that argue that female styles of leadership are "best management practice." For example, The Karpin Report (1995) on management education in Australia, put together by a ministerial working party, makes use of discourses that present women's skills with regard to human resource management as an issue of improving productivity rather than as an issue of social justice.

The emergence of these seemingly pro-feminist discourses must be viewed as part of a postmodern "pragmatic politics" of pluralism, as political parties and trade unions seek to capture the female vote. Women are now seen to be a rapidly growing presence in the workforce and to have political clout as mem-bers of an increasingly uneasy and unpredictable electorate. This occurs at a time when there is increased cynicism about politicians and when trade unions have reduced power (labor expansion occurring largely in a casualized/ feminized workforce) (Rimmer et al. 1994). The paradox is that, in an era of radical restructuring and cultural diversity, women are positioned as agents of change in a deregulated market economy that tends to increase inequalities based on gender, ethnicity, race, and class.

The idea that women provide more altruistic and ethical models of leader-ship than do men works savagely against them once they are seen to be fallible. Carmen Lawrence (the first female state premier of Western Australia), and

Joan Kirner (the first female premier of Victoria) were expected to provide a new form of ethical leadership in state politics—a role both women have publicly stated to be a heavy burden. Lawrence is now subject to a Royal Commission instituted by a Liberal state premier, Richard Court, over the tabling of a petition by one of her cabinet members several years earlier. This commission is seen by many to be, at best, a political manoeuvre prior to an election and, at worst, a petulant boy's attack on an extremely competent feminist politician. As Lawrence has publicly stated, women leaders are usually cast as either madonna or whore, and their fall from the first to the second can be swift and irreparable. The degree of media focus upon Lawrence's feminism and moral integrity (supposedly sources of her political popularity) is significant.

Generational-War

A relatively new discourse, this one propagates an ageist division within feminism, largely defining women in their forties and fifties as products of the 1960s, as hardline feminists, as bitter and humorless man haters, and as out of kilter with current issues. Feminism, it suggests, is suddenly experiencing a generational conflict. The generational issue was first aired in Good Weekend, the magazine edited by Anne Summers, author of the landmark feminist critique of Australian history, *God's Police and Damned Whores*, and former editor of *MS*. Summers (1995, 7) asked, "Where are the young feminists to champion their case?" In her reply, Garner refers to her critics as "fundamental" and "punitive" feminists, uses phrases such as "feminists with battle helmets," and refers to feminism as a "juggernaut." Once again, her response was well received and extensively quoted, particularly by the conservative male journalists who had welcomed *The First Stone*.

Feminist responses to Garner's discourse have focused on three issues. First, Garner depicts the feminist complainants in the sexual harassment case at Ormond as priggish, as not able to cope with a "bit of slap and tickle" (from a man considerably their senior and master of the college). Yet she describes these women in extremely close detail in her text, referring to their sexuality and dress and suggesting they should understand (and use?) the power of their sexuality. In turn, she depicts the master as naive and as a victim of vindictive feminists. Judith Gill (1995) suggests that Garner's positioning of herself as an old-guard feminist who has matured and who eschews sectional fighting is undermined by the "feminine" nurturant stance she assumes vis-à-vis the master.

Second, Garner argues that the complainants' recourse to institutional means to resolve the issue constructs women as victims. It rankles many feminists to hear Garner say that the use of institutional redress promotes "victimhood" and that feminists are anti-sex. She claims to have been active in supporting the developments of equal opportunity legislation and policy, yet she damns these young women for making use of these very resources. Others saw the book as reducing women's legal problems to a matter of good taste. Still others attacked Garner for wanting the young women involved in the case to be nice. As one feminist asks: "What has being nice ever achieved for women, Helen?" (Letters to Editor, *Good Weekend,* 13 May 1995, 23).

Third, some feminists argue that the notion of a generational war within feminism is "an argument that was born in America by feminist authors such as Camille Paglia and Katie Roiphe, but which lives on in Australia under the guise of a 'generational split' in the feminist cause" (Tropoli 1995, 13). Generational difference does, indeed, arise out of changed material conditions. Younger feminists angrily argue that the conditions of feminism have now changed, that they have no time to pursue academic debate because they have to work to get their education and have no guarantee of employment after graduation. Summers and Garner, they suggest, had both enjoyed a free tertiary education in the 1960s and easily got a job "just because they were clever" in easier times (Letters to Editor, *Good Weekend,* 13 May 1995, 23).

Finally, many of the responses from both "young" and "old" feminists indicate that they believe that the current debate merely reflects feminism's diversity. Many were irritated by Garner's tendency to treat feminism as a unitary, monolithic, homogeneous movement, as they thought this belied any sophisticated understanding of where feminism is in the 1990s. And some believed that the public airing of feminism's dirty linen indicated the strength of the women's movement, not its weakness.

Feminism-Is-to-Blame

This New Right discourse blames feminism for everything from youth unemployment to family breakdown and domestic violence. It taps into both male and female uncertainties about changing gender roles, the changes consequent upon women's increasing role in paid (but largely part-time) work, the increase in the divorce rate, and the increasing dependence of women and children upon the welfare state. This discourse harks back to the "good old days" when "women were women" and "men were men," and it appeals to those males who have the greatest investment in maintaining the status quo. The feminism-is-to-blame discourse has become increasingly contentious in the media, with debates raging about whether or not full-time child care benefits children. For example, Michael Duffy (1995, 36), editor of the *Independent Monthly*, suggests: "Feminism in the form we have it today could not exist without childcare." Childcare, he argues, "liberates" not only mothers to be able to go out to work without "guilt" but also "rebellious grandmothers"! Here feminism is seen to indulge the "selfishness" of young women in seeking paid work and of older women in seeking time for themselves.

Masculinity-in-Crisis

Juxtaposed with the feminism-is-to-blame discourse is the masculinity-in-crisis discourse. The latter is an offshoot of the debates about gender equity in schools (Kenway 1994), and one of its more negative versions depicts men (and boys) as victims—victims of masculinity, of lifestyle (health, work, and leisure), and, of course, of feminism. Consequently, masculinity is in a state of crisis. Warren Farrell's *The Myth of Male Power* uses statistics of crime, health, death rates, and so on to indicate that men are "weaker" than women and are victims of their physiology and/or psychology. The logic operating here is that male gender roles are as limiting for men as female gender roles are for women. Many men consider themselves to be disadvantaged by equal opportunity policies and programs, and they want similar programs for themselves. For example, there was a recent claim for funds to provide a men's as well as a women's officer at Deakin University, even though there was nothing to indicate a need for such a position (especially considering the ongoing and increasingly publicized issues of sexual harassment of females across all universities). The masculinity-in-crisis discourse leads to calls for policies dedicated, in the name of individual rights, to redressing male disadvantage. Simplistically, equal opportunity is read to mean that everyone should be treated the same way; there is no recognition of systemic disadvantage.

This male-as-victim-of-masculinity discourse overlaps with the "Iron John" version (Bly 1990), which supposedly reasserts "primitive masculinity" by encouraging men to go out into the bush to recover some "innate" natural man. In urging men to "get back to their feelings," it reasserts macho notions of masculinity premised upon biological essentialism. The emphasis of Bly's work, along with much of the masculinity-in-crisis literature, is psychological not structural. It fails to address the structural biases that give men advantage over women, and it blithely positions men as "victims of feminism." Another version of the crisis-in-masculinity discourse is found in the men's movement, which argues that males, like females, also have problems with gender formation (albeit different ones). The men's movement is attempting to establish lobby groups both within the academy and in politics. It is largely informed by gay rights and it is ambivalent with regard to feminism. However, it must be noted that it is not particularly concerned about improving gender relations with women (Kenway 1994).

A more positive version of the crisis-in-masculinity discourse argues that men need to draw and reflect on feminism in order to inform their own processes of change. This voice is beginning to emerge in the press, as many men reject having their position with regard to the "gender debate" represented by conservative males. Don Edgar (1995, 25), of the Institute of Family Studies, writes:

> For years I've been involved in the agony of watching male academics denigrate, sneer at and deny promotion to women who were in every way their intellectual and human superiors. I've seen good women subjected to treatment that I have never experienced, that no man would have dared mete out to me as a fellow male. And I have seen many of these women stand up firmly for their right to dignity and respect, without shrewishness and dogmatism, gradually bringing about change that is positive and justice for women as well as for men and the whole of society.

Edgar believes that male journalists, authors, and critics who support Helen Garner are reinforcing *male* assumptions about feminists by reinforcing the view that a so-called "bit of slap and tickle" should not be taken too seriously. They also assume an ageist competition between older feminists, who "had it hard and managed well," and younger feminists, who are the ungrateful beneficiaries of the work of the former.

Edgar's position is representative of the pro-feminist work of the new sociology of masculinity undertaken by such people as Bob Connell (1987), Jeff Hearn (Hearn and Morgan 1991), Cynthia Cockburn (1991), and Lyn Segal (1990). The new sociology of masculinity focuses upon (1) how different masculinities and femininities are constructed in relation to each other, (2) how unequal power relations are constructed in organizational life, and (3) how particular masculinities become hegemonic in particular contexts (Connell 1987). It sees particular forms of masculinity as being sustained, reproduced, and privileged by certain management practices— practices which denigrate other forms of masculinity (e.g., homosexuality) and all forms of femininity (Connell 1995; Kerfoot and Knights 1993). Connell (1987) suggests that masculine dominance is never secure and that it has to be continually won, preferably through consent rather than coercion. For example, Kerfoot and Knights (1993) speak of how there has been a shift away from the paternalistic masculinity of the modern era and a move towards the strategic/competitive masculinity of the postmodern era. The sociology-of-masculinity literature also points out how dominant modes of masculinity (e.g., competitive masculinity) co-opt potentially subversive elements and discourses.

Finally, there is a gender-reform version of the masculinity-in-crisis discourse, and this arises from 1980s feminist research and equal-opportunity activity. Because equal-opportunity discourses are open to being appropriated, rewritten, and recycled to privilege individual males in particularly individualistic ways, equality can be simplistically equated with equal treatment, individual rights can be given precedence over systemic group oppression, and so on etc. While there are thus a number of strands in the current backlash against feminism, its central focus is on the detrimental impact of feminism on masculinity. Masculinity as such is not even an issue when dealing with instances of sexual harassment, as the latter is constructed as the problem of an individual, "deviant" male. There is no questioning of institutionalized power relations or of the role particular views of masculinity play in constructing and maintaining hegemonic masculinist cultures. As Connell points out, "one of the cultural supports of men's power is the failure to ask questions about masculinity" (1995, 191).

Gender-Equity-Is-a-Luxury

Further down the page on which Garner responds to her critics, a small article quotes an employer stating that while there are increased numbers of women in the workforce, "family leave claims [are] unfair [to] employers" because they are "not affordable" in the current economic context (*The Age*, 29 August 1995). The gender-equity-is-a-luxury discourse maintains that, in a period of radical economic restructuring, issues of equity must be judged in terms of increased output rather than in terms of social justice. This discourse has gained particular strength in the education sector. As one university manager said during enterprise bargaining negotiations in 1995: "Equity is all very well if you can afford it" (Allport 1995, 3). Further indicators of new hard times for women are newspaper headlines such as: "Equal Pay for Women Will Take 200 Years" (*The Age*, 5 June 1995); "Free Trade Deals Bad for Women" (*The Age*, 11 October 1994); "Women MP Ratio Drops" (*Sunday Age*, 12 September 1993); "Gender Pay Gap Increases 13% Under Liberals" (*The Age*, 5 October 1994); and "Women Losing Out in Enterprise Deals" (*The Age*, 18 May 1994).

In 1987, seeking to make Australia a "clever country," the federal Labor government initiated a fundamental restructuring of education, linking it to national economic needs as determined by market demand. Universities were (1) to respond more quickly to market demands for graduates, (2) to be more relevant to national economic priorities, (3) to be more flexible and entrepreneurial in selling their intellectual labor, (4) to do more immediate and applied commercial research (as opposed to long-term pure research), and (5) to market education itself. Knowledge production that is commodifiable and marketable was to be favored over knowledge production which emphasizes broad social, cultural, or equity considerations (*Australian Universities Review* 1993). University management was to emulate the "best" private business practice, business was to infiltrate the university through its sponsorship of staff and research, and the higher-education sector was to be rationalized and its institutions amalgamated in a series of arbitrary couplings based on the notion that bigger is better (and cheaper). The academic labor market was to be reformed through award restructuring, enterprise bargaining, and productivity agreements (Currie 1994). The administrative apparatus necessary to achieving these ends was to be created through a devolution of responsibility from the federal government to individual universities (Wells 1995). This radical restructuring of education has, together with the trend to market and privatize higher education, produced an equally powerful backlash against feminism's gains. The backlash disciplining feminism in the academy has been produced through inter-related discursive and material conditions generated by both the media and policy.

The Politics of Advantage:
Educational Restructuring, Women, and the State

The restructuring of tertiary education should be set within the context of the changing relationship between the state, education, and the global economy, with Australia shifting away from the welfare state towards the contractual state. In Australia, as in other Western industrialized democracies, the welfare state is being dismantled and public expenditure on education, health, and welfare is being reduced as governments of all persuasions seek to bring down the national debt and to attract investment. Australia now ranks fifteenth in a list of eighteen Organization for Economic Cooperation and Development (OECD) countries with respect to the percentage of gross domestic product (GDP) spent on education (OECD 1993). According to Hester Eisenstein (1991, 8–9), a major difference between the women's movement in the United States and the women's movement in Australia has to do with how they engage with the state. American feminists working for change were located largely within the academy, particularly within Women's Studies. By contrast, Australian feminists sought to intervene in the state through the strategic positioning of people with a commitment to feminism (known as femocrats) within the bureaucracy of the state.

This 1980s political strategy was facilitated by Australian feminism's alliance, although often unsteady and always contradictory, with the Labor movement at a time when Labor tended to be in power at both the national and the state level (Yeatman 1990). It allowed unique networks of feminists to work within government and to establish further networks in education, health, and welfare. This resulted in the development of a "range of women's policy machinery and Government subsidised women's services (delivered by women for women) . . . unrivalled elsewhere" (Sawer 1990, 12). Most state and federal governments established women's advisory units or equal opportunity units, which, together with legislation on affirmative action, sex discrimination, and equal employment opportunity, legitimized and produced a well-articulated discourse on gender equity throughout the public sector. Universities, public-sector institutions funded by the federal government, were expected to create equal-opportunity units and to develop gender-equity policies by the late 1980s.

Marion Sawer (1990) and Claire Burton (1989), who have mapped out the successes and disappointments of Australian feminists, have indicated the contradictions and debates with which the latter were confronted. As in the United States there were debates between different feminist positions as to whether the femocrats had been co-opted by the state and were, in fact, more concerned about getting individual women into powerful positions and dressing in high fashion than they were about improving the lot of women generally. Others supported the political and strategic pragmatism underlying the femocracy, arguing that (1) much of what individual femocrats were doing was invisible to outsiders; (2) there had been a range of successful policy interventions, particularly in industrial relations, education, and social welfare; and (3) femocrats simply did not have the power or resources to produce more radical change. What all agreed on was that male resistance was ever-present. It was only after significant strategic intervention by individual femocrats, along with public lobbying, that equity was included in the 1988 white paper on higher education and that the policy statement *A Fair Chance for All* (dealing with the position of women in higher education) was produced (Ramsey 1995; Bradley 1995).

Unfortunately, such policy texts continue to be more symbolic than real. While universities negotiate with the government, and mission statements flaunt equity, gender equity continues to be left out of substantive debates on resource allocation, curricula, and career paths for women academics (Blackmore 1992; Gale 1995).

The femocrat debate needs to be positioned within wider theoretical debates about the role of the state vis-à-vis feminism (Franzway, Court, and Connell 1990; Watson 1990)—debates that produced sophisticated theories constructing the state as a set of processes rather than as a monolithic entity. What emerges from analyses of this period is that feminism's reliance upon a paternalistic state to intervene on its behalf has not produced the hoped-for outcome. For example, a recent union study of women in tertiary education indicates that between 1985 and 1992 the number of females above the position of senior lecturer rose from 6 percent to 10 percent; the number of female senior lecturers rose from 10.8 percent to 19.1 percent; the number of female lecturers rose from 28.2 percent to 39.9 percent; and the number of females below the position of lecturer rose from 45.2 percent to 51.3 percent. Overall, the total number of female academic staff increased from 21.6 percent to 31.9 percent (Castleman et al. 1995). Much of this increase was due to the statistical effects of amalgamation of universities with colleges of advanced education (which have a higher ratio of female staff than do universities) rather than to recruitment. So at the very moment when the gender-reform interventions of the 1980s might be expected to bear fruit, they do not.

Furthermore, at the very moment when women's educational success is being proclaimed (Birrell et al. 1995), the state is withdrawing from, and reducing funding for, education, health, and welfare. This shifts educational costs onto individual students (with the Higher Education Contribution Scheme supplanting free tertiary education) and universities (which are now expected, in entrepreneurial fashion, to package and sell their product). Government policy for dealing with the lack of jobs for those leaving school has produced a shift away from funding for graduate students (whose ranks, since 1974, had been expanding largely due to the addition of mature women) towards funding for undergraduate students in science, engineering, and technology. This also means a shift away from female-dominated service disciplines such as teaching, nursing, and the humanities. The privatization of educational costs, in the form of a graduate tax, has significant equity implications. Women tend to be concentrated in traditional service areas—areas in which the state is the major employer; but the state, unlike the private sector, is now shifting the cost of professional development onto the individual (Polonsky 1990). And even in industries willing to fund training, research suggests that men are more likely to benefit from this than are women (Sloan et al. 1990).

This highly competitive educational market is consumer-oriented, favoring short-term profit over any long-term development that might result from pure research. At the same time, while the safety net of national awards still exists (although increasingly under threat), enterprise bargaining favors strong unions. As in New Zealand, the feminization and casualization of academic work, the shift to individual contracts, and the decreasing power of the union movement generally jeopardize many feminist gains (Hammond and Hardbridge 1993; Caruso 1995). Caruso (1995) argues that in Victoria, for example, salary packaging advantages higher-paid staff, women sacrifice their salary for child-care benefits, flexibility favors institutions and clients rather than workers, and the reduction of tenure quotas at the lowest points of the lecturer scale (where most teaching occurs and where most women are located) creates a piecework approach to teaching—an approach premised on payment for output. For the majority of female academics, institutional flexibility means increased insecurity and reduced career opportunities due to the outsourcing of academic work and the increasing number of contract staff at all levels (Lever-Tracy 1988). Downsizing means that women, usually late entrants, are the first to lose their jobs (Blackmore 1994). Sessional staff and those on annual contracts renewable for up to ten years are being "let go." This failure to renew contracts is not seen to be an "industrial" or "equity issue," as these women "chose" to be on contract.

This restructuring has been characterized in all education sectors by the shifting of responsibilities (but not policy formation or overall budget) to localized sites. The logic here is to leave decisions to those who best know the clients' needs. This shift in the context of marketization, has inevitably been accompanied by privatization and reduction in funding (Blackmore 1992). It also justifies strong centralizing tendencies in the form of accountability mechanisms such as performance indicators, performance management and bonus systems, and quality assurance programs. Again, this commodification of academic labor is biased against women academics, as performance indicators are largely defined so as to privilege research over teaching, quantity of publications over quality of publications, short-term outcomes over long-term outcomes, and funding over substance (Wells 1995). It also further advantages male academics in the hard sciences and business and disadvantages female academics in humanities and education (not to mention exacerbating biases with regard to what constitutes valued knowledge).

This "devolution," together with the rationalization and amalgamation of universities, has weakened the structural position of equal opportunity (EO) in the universities of the 1990s (Gale 1995). Mergers and amalgamations further undermined the representation of women at all levels of decision-making (Blackmore 1992). Equity was rarely addressed in merger agreements, and, with the plethora of interim committees that arise during an amalgamation, equal opportunity committees were often not even formed—despite the Affirmative Action Agency's recommendations. As often as not, equal opportunity officers were forced to react to policy documents rather than to help form them. In other words, equal opportunity officers were unable to produce fundamental change (Weineke and Durham 1992). In many amalgamated universities equal opportunity positions are part-time and equal opportunity officers are "integrated" into human resource management. Gender equity has been mainstreamed and downstreamed. Equity has become the responsibility of individuals, often male managers/academics who have a vested interest in the status quo. Equity is everyone's and no-one's responsibility—certainly not something built into the positions of heads or deans, as it is in some senior executive positions in the public sector. Various competing claims on limited funding means that equity quickly "drops off the agenda." The premature mainstreaming of equity, while seen to be strategically necessary in the long run, has meant the decimation of various proactive initiatives, including support for policy implementation and the monitoring role of equal opportunity units. Set this in the context of the slashing of health, education, and welfare sectors (the largest employer of females and the site of the most advances for women in terms of equal opportunity), and we have a frightening scenario (Victoria Auditor-General's Office 1995; Burton 1990).

Equity rhetoric has been dropped, as efficiency discourses increasingly come to dominate newly amalgamated institutions which are facing funding cuts. Institutionally based management discourses undercut equity discourses, which used to provide a voice for women staff and students. The politics of male advantage is reasserted whenever equity and efficiency compete (the latter usually meaning maintaining the status quo vis-à-vis distribution of resources and power). As the OECD puts it:

> Privileged groups . . . constantly seek to maintain that privilege. When structures and procedures are made more open, the expectation of greater equality of educational chances has frequently been disappointed by the ability of the better off to establish new criteria of success and by strategies that sidestep equalising policies. (cited in Joint Committee 1922, 24–25)

Early in the 1980s we learned that, due to lack of political will, apathy, and outright resistance, it was naive to rely on universities to voluntarily comply with equal opportunity policies. Universities saw equal opportunity as reducing their autonomy at a time when the higher education reforms were concentrating more control in the hands of the males at the top. Equal opportunity officers were appointed as "change agents," but those in privileged positions resisted any change that would have led to a redistribution of their power (Yeatman 1992). Indeed, new management structures strictly controlled equal opportunity implementation through such strategies of resistance as failing to provide information that would allow equal opportunity officers to adequately monitor various situations and expecting them to do everything relating to any equal opportunity document themselves. Universities want to be known as equal opportunity employers, but their dedication to equal opportunity has been largely symbolic.

The gender-equity strategies of the 1980s will not necessarily work in a deregulated, decentralized, and increasingly diverse education sector. The dominance of discourses of efficiency, effectiveness, and line management in universities have positioned those who argue for equity as inflexible, as against organizational and national interests, as resistant to change, and as generally "out of date." It is within this context that gender equity is (or, to be more accurate, is not) being delivered.

Feminist Pedagogy: Sustained or Constrained?

These, then, are the discursive and material conditions under which feminists work in universities. The postmodern, market-oriented, flexible university is the result of "devolution." Its hallmarks are: intensification of academic labor; lack of job security; surveillance techniques to ensure quality assurance; and quantifiable outcome-oriented performance management. Increased time and money are expended on quality assurance, while the capacity of staff to produce high-quality education is undermined by the under-resourcing of teaching and by time-consuming management demands for accountability. System wide, the quality assurance processes by which university outcomes are measured and ranked asserts a definite hierarchy. It reflects a bias towards quantitative measures that favor the older and larger institutions (which have good research-funding histories with regard to science, medicine, and engineering faculties and a good student mix) over newer universities (which have absorbed excess enrolment, taken a wider range of students, addressed issues of social justice, focused upon teaching, and hired a large number of female staff) (De Angelis 1992). At the level of practice, quality assurance (a recycled Australian version of Total Quality Management) seeks to integrate all aspects of the university through eliminating waste by providing employees with opportunities to voice their concerns over quality. This form of self-governance provides the university with an element of control over previously autonomous working conditions, and, although it facilitates flexibility, it also increases standardization. Self-governance through performance management mediates the tension between the university's need to rely upon the intellectual creativity of its academics and its need to control them.

Devolution, downsizing, outsourcing, and the standardizing procedures of quality assurance have a significant impact, not only upon academic work, but also upon pedagogy. Downsizing has meant an intensification of academic labor and a concomitant push to increase the number of postgraduate students, a rise in staff/student ratios, and a reduction in casual staff and resources—all of which affect teaching. Contract staff have been cut in areas of high student demand, resulting either in tenured staff shifting into areas in which they lack expertise or in work being outsourced to sessionals. While the rhetoric concerns the diversity of student needs, the fact that female students do not have access to senior female staff (who could be both mentors and models) reduces the pool of potential female academics (Sloan et al. 1990).

Furthermore, the under-resourcing of teaching has meant a shift from "fat" to "lean-and-mean" pedagogies, with reduced tutorials, increased tutorial size, and less student contact. Research indicates that, in disciplines in which women are a minority, the so-called "fat" pedagogies provide supportive conditions for women and other minority students—a finding with significant implications for social justice. It also has significant implications for feminist pedagogies that see student-staff interaction and collective activity as important elements of inclusive practice (Luke and Gore 1992). By contrast, quality assurance emphasizes narrow, standardizing assessment procedures which, in turn, control curriculum and pedagogy.

The changes in academic work and the academic labor market resulting from restructuring cannot be separated from the quality of education offered to students in tertiary education. With regard to academic work, contractual and competitive relationships have supplanted collegial relationships; an orientation towards concrete outcomes has constructed divisions between high-status researchers (usually male) and low-status teachers (usually female); there is a clear distinction between high-status institutions (which emphasize engineering and the sciences) and low-status institutions (which emphasize the humanities); and academics are encouraged to be entrepreneurial knowledge-brokers rather than reflective and transformative intellectuals. Furthermore, teacher-student relationships are transformed. Because the educational market views knowledge as a commodity that can be packaged and taught regardless of context and culture, the teacher becomes a mere facilitator. In turn, the student, while rhetorically constructed as an active client, is pedagogically constructed as a passive, monocultural recipient of uncontested knowledge. Education thus becomes a good for private consumption and does not concern itself with offering wider social benefits. Pedagogy is treated as though the process of teaching is distinct from what is taught, by whom it is taught, to whom it is taught, and why it is taught.

It is not surprising that it has been feminists, with their concern about pedagogy and knowledge formation, who have attacked such simplistic views. They have argued that what is selected as high-status knowledge merely indicates power relations based on class, gender, and race and that technicist views of learning provide its recipients with limited access to their own cultural experience (Luke and Gore 1992). The curriculum being packaged and sold fails to address issues of diversity and difference amongst students. Indeed, while postmodern tertiary education claims to offer choice and diversity through multimedia techniques targeted to niche markets, it in fact provides a standardized, homogenized product typical of the Fordist mass production of cars.

Conclusion

The capacity for feminist university educators and students to contest current educational restructuring is constrained, not only because they are largely powerless within the academy, but also because of the ability of those in power to negate notions of gender equity by calling upon the various media-informed discourses of derision with regard to feminism (e.g., gender equity is a luxury, gender equity is not relevant to today's generation of women, etc.). So even when restructuring does produce gender-equity policies or sexual harassment procedures, it also offers opportunities for particular individuals and institutions to mobilize the politics of advantage and to call upon popular backlash discourses grounded in the culture of fear and insecurity. While the new frames of quality assurance and managerialism provide some possibilities for the use of discourses of transparency (e.g., Luke 1995), which would require universities to establish clearly defined and well publicized procedures and criteria to facilitate decision-making, monitoring, and accountability processes, they also allow gender-equity discourses to be used in ways which undermine the material conditions of academic work. For example, the vice-chancellors "union" argued that removal of tenure (except for "star" academics) would improve gender equity—a claim strongly contested by women academics (*The Australian,* Higher Education Section, 27 September 1995, 1). As most feminists well recognize, "the degree to which feminism is allowed—or more rarely, encouraged—in the university is to a great extent the effect of how much the discourse of 'women's liberation' has been absorbed by the hegemonic culture" (Hennessey 1993, 2). Furthermore, "discourses of derision" (Kenway 1987, 189–203) actively discourage individual women from venturing into the upper echelons of educational leadership. Senior female academics/ administrators choose not to continue upwards because to do so is to be subjected to an extreme level of verbal and/or symbolic abuse on an everyday basis, both inside and outside the "chilly climate" of the academy, as witnessed in the case of other feminist leaders. Indeed, for female aca-demics, universities truly are "dangerous territories."

Notes

1. Equal Opportunity legislation in Australia is premised upon appointment and merit rather than upon quotas.
2. See Jane Kenway's conceptualization of "discourses of derision" in "Left Right Out: Australian Education and the Politics of Signification." *Journal of Educational Policy*, 2(3) 1987: 189–203.
3. Ibid.
These research projects were funded by the Australian Research Council. See Blackmore, Angwin, and Leavold (1994) and Blackmore and Sachs (1995–97).

References

Allport, C. 1995. "Equity Is All Very Well If You Can Afford It." NTEU Frontline 3 (1): 3–4

Australian Universities Review. 1993. Special Issue: The Marketing of Higher Education.

Beasley, C. 1995. *Sexual Economyths: Conceiving of Feminist Economics*. Sydney: Allen and Unwin.

Birrell, B., I. Dobson, and V. Rapson. 1995. "Women Beat Men in Uni Studies." *The Age*, 12 April, 3.

Blackmore, J. 1991. "More Power to the Powerful: Corporate Management, Mergers, and the Implications for Women of the Reshaping of the 'Culture' of Australian Universities." *Australian Feminist Studies* 15 (Autumn): 65–89.

———. 1992. "Towards a Post-Masculinist Politics." In *A Gendered Culture: Women and Educational Management in the 1990s*, edited by D. Baker and M. Fogarty. St Albans: Victoria University of Technology.

———. 1994. "Out on the Margins: The Impact of Educational Restructuring Upon the Work of Women Educators." Paper presented to the Australian Sociological Association Conference, Geelong, Deakin University.

Blackmore, J., J. Angwin, and S. Leavold. 1994. *Out on the Margins: The Impact of Educational Restructuring upon Women Educators in ALBE and Universities*. Research Report, Deakin University, Geelong.

Blackmore, J. and J. Sachs. 1995–97. *Women and Leadership in an Era of Reconstruction*. Unpublished report of Australian Research Council funded project, Deakin University, Geelong.

Bly, 1990. Iron John: A Book about men. Reading, MA: Addison-Wesley.

Bradley, D. 1995. "Equity and Quality: Can They Coexist?" Keynote speech for Second National Conference on Equity and Access in Tertiary Education, *Proceedings*, 12–13 July, Melbourne.

Burton, C. 1990. *The Promise and the Price*. Sydney: Allen and Unwin.

Caruso, C. 1995. "Women and Enterprise Bargaining." *NTEU Frontline* 3 (1): 13–15.

Castleman, T., M. Allen, M. Bastalich, and P. Wright. 1995. *Limited Access: Women's Disadvantage in Higher Education Employment*. Melbourne: National Tertiary Education Union.

Cockburn, C. 1991. *In the Way of Women: Men's Resistance to Sex Equality in Organisations.* London: Macmillan.

Connell, R.W. 1987. *Gender and Power.* Sydney: Allen and Unwin.

———. 1995. *Masculinities.* Sydney: Allen and Unwin.

Currie, J. 1994. "Award Restructuring for Academics: The Negotiating Process." *Discourse* 15 (2): 22–33.

De Angeleis, R. 1992. "The Dawkins Revolution: Plan, Performance, Problems University Funding Formulae, Over-Enrolment and Cuts in Operating Grants per EFTSU." *Australian Universities Review* 35 (1): 6–7.

Duffy, M. 1995. "Is Childcare Bad for Kids?" *Independent Monthly*, October, 36–42.

Edgar, D. 1995. "Speaking for Myself," *The Age*, n.d., 25.

Eisenstein, H. 1991. *Gender Shock: Practising Feminism in Two Continents.* Sydney: Allen and Unwin.

Eveline. J. 1992. "The Politics of Advantage." *Australian Feminist Studies* 19 (Autumn): 129–54.

Falk, I. 1994. "The Making of Policy: Media Discourse Conversations." *Discourse* 15 (2): 1–12.

Franzway, S., D. Court, and R.W. Connell. 1989. *Staking a Claim: Feminism, Bureaucracy and the State.* Sydney: Allen and Unwin.

Gale, L. 1995. "Devolution: Issues for Women." *NTEU Frontline* 3 (1): 3–5.

Garner, H. 1995, *The First Stone.* New York: Free Press.

Gill, J. 1995. "Stoning the Women? Stoning the Crows!" *Discourse* 16 (2): 71–75.

Gordon, C., ed. 1980. *Michel Foucault: Power/Knowledge.* London: Harvester.

Hammond, S., and R. Hardbridge. 1993. "The Impact of the Employment Contracts Act on Women at Work." *New Zealand Journal of Industrial Relations* 18 (1): 15–30.

Hearn, J., and D. Morgan, eds. 1991. *Men, Masculinities and Social Theory.* London: Unwin Hyman.

Hennessey, R. 1993. *Materialist Feminism and the Politics of Discourse.* London: Routledge.

Joint Committee of Current Accounts of the Australian Parliament. 1992. *Managing People in the Public Service: Dilemmas of Devolution and Diversity.* Canberra: Australian Government Printing Service.

Karpin Report. 1995. *Enterprising Nation: Renewing Australia's Managers to Meet the Challenges of the Asia-Pacific Century.* Canberra: Australian Government Printing Service.

Kenway, J. 1994. Untitled Paper presented to New South Wales Parliamentary Inquiry into Boys's Education. Unpublished. Deakin University.

Kenway, J. 1987. "Left Right Out, Australian Education and the Politics of Signification." *Journal of Educational Policy*, 2 (3): 189–203.

Kerfoot, D., and D. Knights. 1993. "Management, Masculinity and Manipulation: From Paternalism to Corporate Strategy in Financial Services in Britain." *Journal of Management Studies* 30 (4): 659–77.

Lever-Tracy, C. 1988. "The Flexibility Debate: Part-Time Work." *Labour and Industry* 1 (2): 210–41.

Luke, C. 1995. "Quality Assurance and Women in Higher Education." *Proceedings, 5th Women and Labour Conference*, 29 September–1 October, Sydney, Macquarie University.

Luke, C., and J. Gore, eds. 1992. *Feminism and Critical Pedagogy*. New York: Routledge.

OECD. 1993. *Education at a Glance*. Paris: OECD.

Open Letter, 15 Academics 1995. *The Australian*, Higher Education Section, 6 June: 1

Polonsky, M. 1990. "A Note on the Impact of HECS on Graduate Management Courses." *Australian Universities Review* 33 (1/2): 52–4.

Ramsey, E. 1995. Management, gender and language. Who is hiding behind the slam ceiling and Why can't we see them? in Limerick, B and Lingard, B. (eds) *Gender and Changing Educational Management* Sydney: Hodder.

Rimmer, S., R. Rimmer, G. Karosi, and G. Parkinson. 1994. *Equal Pay for Women*, Department of Employment, Education, and Training, Canberra.

Sawer, M. 1990. *Sisters in Suits: Women and Public Policy in Australia*. Sydney: Allen and Unwin.

Segal, L. 1990. *Slow Motion: Changing Masculinities, Changing Men*. London: Virago.

Summers, A. 1995. "Shockwaves at the Revolution." *Good Weekend*, 18 March, 4–8.

Sloan, J., M. Baker, R. Blandy, F. Robertson, and W. Brummutt. 1990. *Study of Labour Markets for Academics*. Canberra: Australian Government Printing Service.

Spearritt, K. 1995. Letter to the Editor. *Good Weekend*. 13 May, 14.

Victoria Auditor-General's Office. 1995. *Equality in the Workplace: Women in Management*. Melbourne: Government Printer.

Watson, S,. ed. 1990. *Playing the State Australian Feminist Interventions*. Sydney: Allen and Unwin.

Weineke, C., and Durham, M. 1992. "Regulating the Equity Agenda: EEO in Higher Education." *Australian Universities Review* 35 (2): 18–24.

Wells, J. 1995. "Performance Indicators in Higher Education: Government Policy and Its Implications for Women Staff." *NTEU Frontline* 3 (1): 7–10.

Yeatman, A. 1990. *Bureaucrats, Technocrats, Femocrats*. Sydney: Allen and Unwin.

———. 1992. "Gender Change Management in Higher Education." In *A Gendered Culture*, edited by D. Baker and M. Fogarty. St Albans: Victoria University of Technology.

Part II

Inside-Out:
Transgressive Pedagogies and Unsettling Classrooms

Chapter Five

Transvestic Sites:
Postcolonialism, Pedagogy, and Politics

Richard Cavell
University of British Columbia (Canada)

"Beyond" signifies spatial distance, marks progress, promises the future; but our intimations of exceeding the barrier or boundary—the very act of going beyond—are unknowable, unrepresentable, without a return to the "present" which, in the process of repetition, becomes disjunct and displaced. The imaginary of spatial distance—to live somehow beyond the border of our times—throws into relief the temporal, social differences that interrupt our collusive sense of cultural contemporaneity. The present can no longer be simply envisaged as a break or a bonding with the past and the future, no longer a synchronic presence: our proximate self-presence, our public image, comes to be revealed for its discontinuities, its inequalities, its minorities.
—Homi Bhabha, The Location of Culture

1.

In the spring of 1993, I taught a graduate seminar at the University of British Columbia called "Cultural Transvestism and Postcolonial Discourse." By the phrase "cultural transvestism" I sought to indicate the borderline tendencies of postcolonialism—its hybridity—as well as to provide a base from which to argue the intersections and complications of gender, race, class, and colonialism. My agenda in the seminar was to facilitate the demonstration of "postcolonialism" as a theoretical position that could bring together texts normally not considered in conjunction with one another in the academy and, in so doing, to provide a forum for critiquing such texts, the academic constraints that keep them separate, and "postcolonialism" itself (which, I felt, was rapidly becoming commodified as a core set of specific texts). While crossdressing was the focus of the seminar, I hoped to examine other forms of crossing as well. In addition to canonical postcolonial texts such as Coetzee's *Foe*, Naipaul's *The Mimic Men*, Findley's *Not Wanted on the Voyage*, Rushdie's *Shame*, and Hulme's *The Bone People*, I also introduced texts designed to trouble essentialized readings of postcolonialism *as canonized*—texts such as Aquin's *Blackout*, Burroughs's *Tarzan of the Apes*, Cliff's *No Telephone to Heaven*, Furphy's *Such is Life*, Grenville's *Joan Makes History*, Hwang's *M. Butterfly*, Lawrence's *Seven Pillars of Wisdom*, Moodie's *Roughing It in The Bush*, Stowe's *Uncle Tom's Cabin*, and Kureishi's "With Your Tongue Down My Throat." The seminar was designed interactively, partly to emphasize that its production was a collective responsibility and partly to displace the notion that "postcolonialism" was a specific "content." I presented as many texts to the students as I could think of, they added yet others, then we decided collectively which texts would be studied and in what order. (Much of this was done informally, during the term preceding the seminar.) The results of this process were instructive: Coetzee got in, but Findley did not; Hulme but not Furphy; Kureishi but not Naipaul; Cliff but not Stowe; and Hwang but not T. E. Lawrence. It appeared that a certain disciplinary imperative was operating here, whereby issues of race were not to be complicated by issues of class, and according to which the category of the "postcolonial" was to be associated with texts that had been produced "outside" of Europe (with Kureishi being an interesting exception) in the second half of the twentieth century. This "historical bias" might not seem at all odd, given that postcolonialism is supposed to have arisen after the end of the great European empires. But it was precisely this historical linearity I wanted to question, both because it did not take neocolonialism into account and because it is insensitive to the complexities of resistance—a resistance that often exists coterminously with colonization itself.

After we had decided on a rough order of readings (first "theory," then "texts"—another problematical binary indicative of the instrumentalization, and thus marginalization, of theory), we remained dissatisfied with the exclusion of so many texts as well as with the implied teleology of the reading list. So we created two additional lists ("Supplements" and "Further Readings") that allowed us to juxtapose texts according to what might be called a *spatial* historicism (e.g., Butler/Kureishi/Wittig; Benetton Ads/hooks/Fanon), and which had the additional value of undermining the utilitarian theory/fiction binary and the linear relationship attendant upon it (first you do theory, then you apply it). The "lack" of direction within this spatialized syllabus enabled me to dislocate myself further as instructor.

The seminar ended up being "large" (around 25 participants in a department in which 10 to 12 is the norm), with auditors, drop-ins, and guest lecturers; we held it not in the assigned seminar room but on the top floor of the Graduate Student Centre. Weekly journals replaced individual seminar presentations (what I refer to as the "Queen-for-a-Day" phenomenon), and I made it clear from the outset that I saw my role as facilitator rather than as Source-Of-Knowledge. Grades were based on journals and a project, which did not have to be text-based. (One student produced a photographically-based work, thereby raising important issues of evaluation, through which the student read *my* role in the academy.) Upon completion of all work for the seminar, I met with each student individually in order to discuss the bases on which I had arrived at his or her grade. Given my insistence on the indeterminacy of the seminar as *site of production*, most of these meetings took place off campus.

The student evaluations were instructive. The use of journals was favored, as were the consultative processes at the beginning and end of the seminar (though subsequently a few students expressed reservations about meeting off campus and about my discussing the grading process with them). The use of discussion groups was seen as a viable response to the size of the seminar, though it was also seen as leading, at times, to a lack of focus. One student was challenged "intellectually and politically." Another felt the course was "too tightly scheduled" and had a "too extensive reading list." Instructors sometimes see these apparent contradictions as cancelling each other out (and I have certainly reacted in this way), thereby indirectly reaffirming their authority; however, these contradictions can also be read as asserting that the seminar occupies not a unified space but a number of transvestic sites that are *produced* by and through the agendas of those who participate in it, including the instructor. In these terms, the subject of the seminar (if there could be said to be only one) could be seen to coincide with the performance of its pedagogy.

2.

> By their very location in the academy, fields such as women's studies
> are grounded in definitions of difference, difference that attempts to
> resist incorporation and appropriation by providing space for histori-
> cally silenced peoples to construct knowledge.
> —Chandra Talpade Mohanty, "On Race and Voice"

This coincidence of the seminar's subject with the way in which it was taught has both disciplinary and pedagogical implications. As a teacher of what has come to be known as "postcolonial literature," I have often found myself confronted with having to decide whether the term "postcolonial" refers to a coherent body of texts or to a mode of reading texts. The distinction has far-reaching implications. If "postcolonial" refers to a body of texts, this, on the one hand, allows for the valorization of a number of texts (all of which have in common that they were produced "after" colonialism) that are now excluded from the canon, while, on the other hand, such a list runs the risk of becoming canonical in its own way. If "postcolonial" refers to a way of reading, however, it appears to lose its specificity and perhaps even its historicity, becoming merely another formalism. Both of these positions embody historical attitudes, the one reified, the other process-oriented. What I sought to argue (largely through my style of pedagogy) was a third position—a position involving theorizing non-linear modes of history and a processual notion of location. My argument was that the act of reading "postcolonially" is double, in that it responds both to the historical context of the work and to the moment of localized, materialized reading, such that through our readings we locate *ourselves* in a series of discontinuous histories. For the seminar, that process of reading was inevitably defined by— and therefore involved a critique of—the academy and our places in it.

The crucial point to be noted here is that location is a significant aspect of pedagogical practice, "explicitly articulating epistemological and ontological concerns," as Elspeth Probyn has suggested (1990, 184). Yet, as Probyn goes on to argue, "location" has become, through its constant invocation, an increasingly abstract term, less a counter discourse to universalism than another version of it. This is not, however, to suggest that notions of the local should be abandoned; rather (Probyn continues), the local should be redefined as "a fragmented set of possibilities that can be articulated into a momentary politics of time and place" (187). The point to be underlined in this formulation is that space/place/location are *produced* and, therefore, inflected by their historical moment and social context. How we locate ourselves within practices of knowledge, then, is related to how we produce space (see also Cavell 1994).

The implications for pedagogy are significant. If what is being taught is a particular attitude towards a text, a particular way of reading, then content gives way to theory, to the text re-presented as process. Reading as pedagogy becomes a locating in (spatial) history as opposed to the deciphering of a timeless meaning. This position has the advantage of encouraging postcolonial readings of ur-canonical texts as well as of not restricting the postcolonial to the written text—a restriction that severely diminishes its force. As Bogumil Jewsiewicki and V. Y. Mudimbe write in a recent issue of *Transition*, "new forms of representation—such as rap, music videos, etc., whose structures are more polyphonic than linear, and that spatialize more than they historicize the experiences of the world—are generally left totally out of the [postcolonial] debate" (1994, 47). Their comments also signal the danger that the "postcolonial," if allowed to define a specific set of texts, could become dehistoricized and thereby inhibited from critiquing contemporary, technology-based society, what Arjun Appadurai has called the "mediascape" of "fundamental disjunctures between economy, culture and politics" (1990, 6).

Perhaps the most limiting aspect of seeing "postcolonial" as designating a certain sort of text is the elision of the question of the production of textuality, thus making of "postcolonialism" merely a reified historical category, like "Renaissance." This tendency is clearly evident in the recent special issue of *PMLA* (1995) on postcolonialism, in which over half the articles are interpretations of texts. The implication is that these texts are stable and that it is possible to arrive at the hard core of their meaning through a series of hermeneutic procedures. One of the lessons of postcoloniality, however, is that texts are not simply "there" to be read; rather, they are actively produced "here" according to locational determinants. Thus, texts are constantly shifting sites of production and reception, as Jean Rhys demonstrates so tellingly in *Wide Sargasso Sea*'s rewriting of *Jane Eyre*. Rather than being commodified as the latest model of "litcrit," postcolonialism can become politically transformative at the moment it begins to juxtapose the imperial production of texts with the decolonizing process of critically re-reading them. What this double reading recognizes is that the history of the production of knowledge is inevitably associated with the "other" (most clearly in the case of anthropology). Postcolonialism seeks to dislocate this nexus, turning the light of inquiry back onto the *production* of otherness. And, if "postcolonialism" is a product of the academy (which it is), then it is also a site of resistance to the academy precisely through its ability to foreground the moment of the production of knowledge and, thereby, to highlight the inflectedness of knowing. A comment Juliet Mitchell makes in *Psychoanalysis and Feminism* has, thus, a degree of paradigmatic veracity: "I am interested not in what Freud did, but in what we can get from him, a political rather than an academic exploration" (1974, xx). In the view that I have been developing here, this would constitute a postcolonial reading of Freud, demonstrating, in the process, sites of confluence among histories of colonization, psychoanalysis, and gendering (as emblematically foregrounded in the African icons of Freud's consulting room).

If "postcolonial" is conceived of not as a content but as a way of reading, a pedagogy whose anti-colonialism is focused upon cultural objects and one of whose major and most productive sites is the university, then content-oriented curricula, which are the major sites of canon production (including postcolonial canons), would be resisted. As Rajeswari Mohan states:

> The important question in these pedagogic deliberations is not what texts to teach but how to teach them, and in the nineties this may be the question that frames the multicultural enterprise in general. Already,

> multiculturalism exerts pressure on existing disciplinary configura-
> tions and their various legitimating narratives as newly authorized
> knowledges challenge the content as well as the methodologies of disci-
> plinary enquiry. (1995, 385)

To read texts in juxtaposition both to other texts and other histories (including those defining the moment of reading) is to work towards that "new and overwhelming space which annihilates time and imperial purpose," of which Ashcroft, Griffiths, and Tiffin (1989, 34) speak in *The Empire Writes Back*. Implicit in such readings is the realization that the history of empires is double—that it is made up both of colonization and of resistance, and that the relationship between the two is one not of succession but of co-determination. Such readings, as Jewsiewicki and Mudimbe remark, are "probably the only way to subvert the recurring metaphor of paternal authority so central to the postcolonial world" (1994, 49). They go on to note that when the central activity of postcolonialist critiques becomes not the content of the texts but their juxtaposition (which acknowledges the historical moment of reading) postcolonial cultures will be opened to a post-Freudian analysis (50).

3.

> Let us attempt to read the possibility of our unwilling or unwitting per-
> petration of a "new orientalism" as the inscription of an "overall strat-
> egy." . . . If we keep the possibility of such inscriptions in mind, we
> might read differently the specific examples of the working of "local
> forces," close to home.
>
> —Gayatri Spivak, *Outside in the Teaching Machine*

A number of the pedagogical implications of the "cultural transvestism" seminar are addressed in *Pedagogy: The Question of Impersonation*, the first being that teaching is itself a form of transvestism, whether it express itself as the "im-personation" about which Jane Gallop writes in her introduction (1995, 1) or the "racial drag" of which Indira Karamcheti speaks (1995, 143). Clearly, these writers mean to signal not only the theatrical element that has long been acknowledged as a component of teaching but also, as the title of the collection indicates, the displacement of the person/al and the attendant paradox that the "personal in pedagogy acts not unlike the personal on talk shows, a performance that nonetheless functions as real" (Gallop 1995, 17). The implication of this assertion is that the ungrounded subject can have political agency in a way not allowed for by a "generic ethnicity" (see Simon 1995, 93). Thus, Gregory Jay writes: "To pose cultural identity in the form of a question . . . already introduces an element of agency, freedom, or voluntarism that strict essentialists or determinists reject" (1995, 120).

As Jay suggests, the question of agency provides a crucial line of demarcation between essentialist and performative notions of identity. This question also identifies one of the major "discontents" of postcolonialism, which is that it has (or appears to have) no agency outside the academy, that it is just another disciplinary practice. This discontent, however, has its source in an "inside/outside" binary that acts to contain and reify the possibilities of agency. It is useful to examine, from this position, the controversies surrounding "political correctness," which can be seen as a construction designed to contain a discourse—let us call it "postcolonial theory"—which is posited as spreading from "inside" the academy into the "real" world "outside," while at the same time "those proposing reform are depicted as outsiders whose agenda will only subvert an essentially good system" (Scott 1995, 113). Witness the volume *Debating P.C.: The Controversy over Political Correctness on College Campuses* (Berman 1992), the title of which belies itself: its essays by no means all emerge from the "campus," thereby demonstrating that the debate around political correctness (PC) refuses to stay "inside" the academy and that the book (like the notion of PC) is itself an act of containment. As Fredric Jameson remarks in an essay on cultural studies, "At a time . . . when the Right has begun to develop its own cultural politics, focused on the reconquest of the academic institutions, and particularly of the foundations and the universities themselves, it does not seem wise to go on thinking of academic politics, and the politics of intellectuals, as a particularly 'academic' matter" (1993, 17). And Gauri Viswanathan has shown that this connection between colony and college need not be thought of as "merely" ideological; as she has recently demonstrated, Yale University "has deep, abiding roots in the mercantile activities and imperial politics of England's East India House" (1994, 1). The occlusion of these linkages is directly related to the devaluation of the role of the public intellectual in the United States and (perhaps even more so) in Canada. To write regularly in the popular press is quite common among my colleagues in Europe, but to do so in Canada is to risk not being considered a serious academic, so rigidly are town and gown constructed as separate places.

The university, however, occupies a transvestic site; it is both "inside" and "outside" its sociocultural emplacement, both "public" and "private." And what emerges from *After Political Correctness* (Newfield and Strickland 1995) is an awareness that the political positions of Left and Right (between which the PC debate has oscillated) have themselves become displaced. While "the Left . . . reads [the 1970s] as a narrative of its own decline" (13), the Right continues to splinter (cf. Diamond 1995, 26–27). No longer are

Right and Left, Liberal and Conservative, the verities they were (in the Canadian context) for George Parkin Grant when he was writing *Technology and Empire* and *Lament for a Nation*. The homogenous constituencies that allowed Grant to produce such works no longer exist (if, in fact, they ever did). Today the categories of Left and Right, Liberal and Conservative, appear to have rhetorical value precisely as ways of *eliding* differences of race, class, gender, and orientation. And if master narratives of the political are no longer possible, the same can be said for the *grands récits* of culture.

This becomes startlingly clear when one examines a non-mainstream political/cultural movement such as Gay Rights, as does Andrew Sullivan (1995) in *Virtually Normal: An Argument about Homosexuality*. While the topic of the book might immediately position its author as left of center, he is in fact the neoconservative editor of *The New Republic*. Yet Sullivan rejects positions put forward on homosexuality by both "The Conservatives" *and* "The Liberals" as well as by "The Prohibitionists" and "The Liberationists," stating that "there are as many politics of homosexuality as there are words for it" (19). "Moreover," he continues, "these terms are not mutually exclusive" (20); in fact, "by 'conservative' I mean rather a variety of liberal" (95). Sullivan's own "Politics of Homosexuality" (ch. 5) seeks to "reconcile the best arguments of liberals and conservatives, and find a way to marry the two" (169–70; the metaphor is significant). He proposes to do this by affirming "a simple and limited principle: that all *public* (as opposed to private) discrimination against homosexuals be ended and that every right and responsibility that heterosexuals enjoy as public citizens be extended to those who grow up and find themselves emotionally different" (171). As in the debate over political correctness, the public/private binary asserts itself here as a strategy of containment, given that, as Foucault (1990) argues in *The History of Sexuality*, it is the State which constructs the category of homosexual. In fact, the struggle for Gay Rights has shown the extent to which the State operates what Deniz Kandiyoti (1991) calls a "gender agenda" (patria as patriarchy) through which "a sphere marked out as 'private' at one stage of nation-building may reappear with the full trappings of the 'public' at another, their boundaries being fluid and subject to redefinition" (431). Ironically, what undoes Sullivan's argument is his unwillingness to disengage from traditional categories of political thought, even though he spends much of his book pointing out their inadequacies with regard to the issue of homosexuality. Thus the most concrete political proposal he can make at the conclusion of his study is that homosexuals have "equal access to the military and marriage" (173).

If Sullivan is correct in stating that "Western society is in the middle of a tense and often fevered attempt to find its own way on the matter [of homosexuality]" (18), then this suggests that political issues are being engendered in terms traditional politics cannot adequately address. Paul Gilroy has suggested that this is because the

> old industrial order has begun to decompose and social and political collectivities based away from the workplace have become as vocal, militant and politically significant as the residues of the workers' movement. . . . These new movements are part of a new phase of class conflict so far removed from the class struggles of the industrial era that the vocabulary of class analysis created during that period must itself be dispensed with, or at least ruthlessly modernized. (1987, 225)

Gilroy goes on to note that these changes have resulted in a renewed emphasis on the body, and this observation may be linked to Kandiyoti's contention that to question gender is to question one of the foundational bases of political expression.

All of this renders highly problematical Susan Faludi's notion of "backlash," which, increasingly, has come to define the reactionary rhetoric of the 1990s. Yet, when Left and Right have become destabilized into New Left and New Right, when "Conservative" is sometimes defined as "Liberal," of what value are Faludi's essentialist assumptions? And who are the "American Women" referred to in her subtitle (*The Undeclared War Against American Women*), given that "lesbian" is not in her index but "housewives" is? These questions are rhetorical, of course, but it is precisely in political rhetoric as disseminated through the media that Faludi seeks to locate the backlash phenomenon:

> The press first introduced the backlash to a national audience—and made it palatable. Journalism replaced the "pro-family" diatribes of fundamentalist preachers with sympathetic and even progressive-sounding rhetoric. . . . The press didn't set out with this, or any other, intention; like any large institution, its movements aren't premeditated or programmatic, just grossly susceptible to the prevailing political currents. Even so, the press, carried by tides it rarely fathomed, acted as a force that swept the general public, powerfully shaping the way people would think and talk about the feminist legacy and the ailments it supposedly inflicted on women. (1991, 77)

While the terms of this argument are naive, Faludi nevertheless identifies the importance of the media in the production of "backlash" rhetoric. The effect of this "mediatization" is to "discursify" political issues, thereby dislocating them from any presumed origin and placing them within discourse itself. In this way, political issues can no longer claim authoritative sites of discourse, as in "who speaks for the Left" (or "for the Right"), but must engage in strategies of (re-) appropriation. As Paul Gilroy writes, these strategies seek "the transformation of new modes of subordination located outside the immediate processes of production and consequently require the reappropriation of space, time, and of relationships between individuals in their day to day lives" (1987, 225).

Appadurai places this struggle in the larger context of "the new global cultural economy [which] has to be seen as a complex, overlapping, disjunctive order, which cannot any longer be understood in terms of existing center-periphery models (even those which might account for multiple centers and peripheries)" (1990, 6). "Economy," Appadurai notes (as does Gilroy), can no longer be defined solely in terms of capital; rather, it is comprised of ethnoscapes, mediascapes, technoscapes, finanscapes, and ideoscapes— where "-scape" points to "fluid, irregular shapes" (6–7).

> These terms with the common suffix -scape also indicate that these are not objectively given relations which look the same from every angle of vision, but rather that they are deeply perspectival constructs, inflected by the historical, linguistic and political situatedness of different sorts of actors: nation-states, multinationals, diasporic communities, as well as sub-national groupings and movements (whether religious, political or economic), and even intimate face-to-face groups, such as villages, neighborhoods and families. (7)

And if this decentering suggests that "backlash" cannot be seen as a univocal phenomenon of a unified "Right," it also suggests that a transformative politics of the "Left" can no longer presume to speak for all women, all gays, all persons of color, and so on.

The notion of "category crisis," which Marjorie Garber (1992) develops in *Vested Interests: Cross-Dressing and Cultural Anxiety*, is useful here. Arguing that category crisis is "not the exception but the ground of culture itself" (16), Garber defines the term as "a borderline that becomes permeable, that permits of border crossings from one (apparently distinct) category to another." Thus, "a transvestite figure, or a transvestite mode, will always function as a sign of overdetermination—a mechanism of displacement from one blurred boundary to another" (16) as well as "*a space of possibility structuring and confounding culture*" (17; emphasis in original). It is this power of displacement that makes notions of the transvestic especially productive in theorizing race, class, gender, and sexual orientation, for it complicates such categories through a constant shifting of figure and ground (where race, for example, is now figure to the ground of gender, now ground to the figure of class, and so on).

Yet what I am arguing here might, once again, appear to beg the question of agency: if one of the major signs of postmodernity, of the simulacral, is the "discursification" of the political, does this not appear to deprive the political of any forum other than the discursive? One way this question can be addressed is by placing it in the context of what Peter Dickinson (and others) have called the discursive representation of Acquired Immune Deficiency Syndrome (AIDS). Dickinson notes that AIDS has occasioned "a whole new industry of discursive inquiry" (1995, 219) that tends to make abstract the very real suffering of individuals. Yet it would be a mistake, he continues, to devalorize this discursive aspect of AIDS, for, "as Foucault reminds us, discourse is itself an *event*, an event, moreover, that involves not only the text or utterance but also their position within a given social space" (1995, 221). To this formulation of discursification I would add the concept of linguistic performativity (which underlies much of Judith Butler's theorizing of gender)— quite simply, the concept that words *do* things, that they are both abstract *and* located. As Butler (1993) writes in *Bodies That Matter*, "if the power of discourse to produce that which it names is linked with the question of performativity, then the performative is one domain in which power acts *as* discourse" (225). This *materiality* of signification returns us to the question of academic agency so often invoked by postcolonial critique and serves to remind us of the interestedness of language; as Fanon puts it at the beginning of *Black Skin, White Masks*, "I ascribe a basic importance to the phenomenon of language" (1967, 17). Homi Bhabha develops this notion in *The Location of Culture*:

> "What is to be done" must acknowledge the force of writing, its metaphoricity and its rhetorical discourse, as a productive matrix which defines the social and makes it available as an objective of and for, action. Textuality is not simply a second-order ideological expression or a verbal symptom of a pre-given political subject. . . . The political subject—as indeed the subject of politics—is a discursive event. (1994, 23; emphasis mine)

Discourse, as a polyvocal site of translation, of what I have elsewhere called "liminal incommensurability" (Cavell 1996, 3), constantly militates against universalism and essentialism. It is, in fact, precisely such an argument for difference *within* the heavily politicized term "equality" that animates Catherine MacKinnon's *Only Words*. This book argues in the strongest possible way for the importance of discursivity in the political arena: "Social inequality is substantially created and enforced—that is, *done*—through words and images. Social hierarchy cannot and does not exist without being embodied in meanings and expressed in communications" (MacKinnon 1993, 13). In her discussion of the "law of equality," MacKinnon cites the Supreme Court of Canada's definition of the Charter of Rights and Freedoms' notion of equality as one that is "more substantive than formal, directed toward changing unequal social relations rather than monitoring their equal positioning before the law" (98). In contrast, the United States defines inequality

> as distinction, as differentiation, indifferent to whether dominant or subordinated groups are hurt or helped. . . . The positive spin of the Canadian interpretation holds the law to promoting equality, project-ing the law into a more equal future, rather than remaining rigidly neu-tral in ways that either reinforce existing social inequality or prohibit changing it, as the American constitutional perspective has increasingly done in recent years. (98)

MacKinnon manages what Sullivan does not, namely, to dislocate the cen-tral term of her argument; whereas Sullivan wishes, finally, to reassert the "normal" as univocal and hegemonic, MacKinnon argues that "equal" occupies more than one site—that it is not a universal given but a condition towards which society must work.

A good deal of the efficacy of MacKinnon's argument emerges from her refusal to consider the concepts she is dealing with apart from their contextual implications, so that "principle [is] defined in terms of specific experiences, the particularity of history, substantively rather than abstractly" (109). In her insis-tence on the confluence of experience *and* history, MacKinnon identifies a postcolonialist pedagogy which asks that we locate ourselves in difference.

4.

> I address you from your place [*place*] in order to say to you that I have no place [*place*], since I am like those who make their trade out of resemblance—the poets, the imitators, and the sophists, the genus of those who have no place. You alone have place and can say both the place and the nonplace in truth, and that is why I am going to give you back the floor. In truth, give it to you or leave it to you. To give back, to leave, or to give the floor to the other amounts to saying: you have (a) place, have (a) place, come.
>
> —Jacques Derrida, "*Khōra*"

Acknowledgments

I am grateful to Leslie Roman for comments on an early draft of this paper and to Peter Dickinson for his advice and insights throughout.

References

Appadurai, A. 1990. "Disjuncture and Difference in the Global Cultural Economy." *Public Culture* 2 (2): 1–24.

Ashcroft, B., G. Griffiths, and H. Tiffin. 1989. *The Empire Writes Back: Theory and Practice in Post-Colonial Literatures.* New York: Routledge.

Berman, P., ed. 1992. *Debating P.C.: The Controversy Over Political Correctness on College Campuses.* New York: Dell.

Bhabha, H. 1994. *The Location of Culture.* London: Routledge.

Butler, J. 1993. *Bodies That Matter: On the Discursive Limits of "Sex."* London: Routledge.

Cavell, R. 1994. "Theorising Canadian Space: Postcolonial Articulations." In *Canada: Theoretical Discourse/Discours théoriques*, edited by T. Goldie, C. Lambert, and R. Lorimer. 75–104. Montréal: Association for Canadian Studies.

———. 1996. " 'Same Difference': On the Hegemony of 'Language' and 'Literature' in Comparative Studies." *Canadian Review of Comparative Literature* 23 (1): 1–8.

Diamond, S. 1995. "Managing the Anti-PC Industry." In *After Political Correctness*, edited by C. Newfield and R. Strickland, 23–37. Boulder: Westview Press.

Dickinson, P. 1995. " 'Go-Go Dancing on the Brink of the Apocalypse': Representing AIDS—An Essay in Seven Epigraphs." In *Postmodern Apocalypse: Theory and Cultural Practice at the End*, edited by R. Dellamora, 219–40. Philadelphia: University of Pennsylvania Press.

Faludi, S. 1991. *Backlash: The Undeclared War Against American Women.* New York: Doubleday.

Fanon, F. 1967. *Black Skin, White Masks.* New York: Grove Weidenfeld.

Foucault, M. 1990. *The History of Sexuality: Vol. 1 An Introduction.* Translated by R. Hurley. New York: Vintage.

Gallop, J. 1995. "Im-Personation: A Reading in the Guise of an Introduction." In *Pedagogy: The Question of Impersonation*, edited by J. Gallop, 1–18. Bloomington: Indiana University Press.

Garber, M. 1992. *Vested Interests: Cross-Dressing and Cultural Anxiety.* New York: Routledge.

Gilroy, P. *There Ain't No Black in the Union Jack.* 1987. London: Hutchinson.

Jameson, F. 1993. "On 'Cultural Studies.' " *Social Text* 34:17–52.

Jay, G. 1995. "Taking Multiculturalism Personally: Ethnos and Ethos in the Classroom." In *Pedagogy: The Question of Impersonation*, edited by J. Gallop, 117–128. Bloomington: Indiana University Press.

Jewsiewicki, B., and V. Y. Mudimbe. 1994. "For Said." *Transition* 63: 34–50.

Kandiyoti, D. 1991. "Identity and its Discontents: Women and the Nation." *Millenium* 20 (3): 429–43.

Karamcheti, I. 1995. "Caliban in the Classroom." In *Pedagogy: The Question of Impersonation*, edited by J. Gallop, 138–46. Bloomington: Indiana University Press.

MacKinnon, C. 1993. *Only Words.* Cambridge, Massachusetts: Harvard University Press.

Mitchell, J. 1974. *Psychoanalysis and Feminism.* London: Allen Lane.

Mohan, R. 1995. "Multiculturalism in the Nineties: Pitfalls and Possibilities." In *After Political Correctness: The Humanities and Society in the 1990s*, edited by C. Newfield and R. Strickland, 372–88. Boulder: Westview Press.

Newfield, C., and R. Strickland. 1995. "Introduction: Going Public." In *After Political Correctness: The Humanities and Society in the 1990s*, 1–20. Boulder: Westview Press.

PMLA. 1995. Vol. 110, no. 1. (Special issue on postcolonialism.)

Probyn, E. 1990. "Travels in the Postmodern: Making Sense of the Local." In *Feminism/Postmodernism*, edited by L. J. Nicholson, 176–89. New York: Routledge.

Scott, J.W. 1995. "The Campaign Against Political Correctness: What's Really at Stake." In *After Political Correctness*, edited by C. Newfield and R. Strickland, 111–27. Boulder: Westview Press.

Simon, R. 1995. "Face to Face with Alterity: Postmodern Jewish Identity and the Eros of Pedagogy." In *Pedagogy: The Question of Impersonation*, edited by J. Gallop, 90–105. Bloomington: Indiana University Press.

Sullivan, A. 1995. *Virtually Normal: An Argument About Homosexuality.* New York: Knopf.

Viswanathan, G. 1994. "Yale College and the Culture of British Imperialism." *Yale Journal of Criticism* 7 (1): 1–30.

Chapter Six

Anti-Racism Inside
and Outside the Classroom

Aruna Srivastava
University of Calgary (Canada)

A conference, early 1995. The subject of my paper: "Race and Ethnicity in the Classroom." Now, I am to write a new version, almost a year (and several battle-scarred stories later). I wonder how I can "show" the disjunctions and conjunctions of thought over time and space and experience. I decide to use italics for what I write now, plain type for what I wrote and said back then, when things seemed a little plainer.

Any time I am asked to talk about anti-racist teaching, I face the numbing questions: is it possible? can it work? what's the point? For me, there *is* a point; anti-racist teaching can and does work, but rarely very well, and never perfectly. In the conference setting, when I want to talk about race, ethnicity, and teaching, I don't know whether to present a well-formatted, thirty-minute paper or to pointedly enact my pedagogical and research beliefs. *Here, I enacted a compromise, a sort of self-policing which still says that my conference pedagogy cannot be oral, cannot be fragmented, cannot be participatory, as is my classroom pedagogy. A few months later, another conference, I finally decide not to stand and deliver my part of a collaborative presentation and, again, lose courage, scribble wildly the morning before to get something down that I may then read, something for the annual report. At the earlier conference I found myself confronted with a new kind of self-doubt, a sense of paralysis, knowing that colleagues from my own department would be there to watch—to watch me not be a proper scholar. I began to wonder, why am I beginning to doubt the formerly comforting gaze of outsiders?*

> *We exist in an environment where the decision not to write is eminently rational. We realize that our scholarship is suspect because our areas of interest are unacceptable, that average work, work comparable to that of our peers, is unacceptable. We cannot afford to make mistakes because*

everything we do is scrutinized with such attention to detail and minutiae
that it would paralyze most creative people. (Espinoza 1995, 423)

What intrigued and worried me about my reaction was that I was really in a
very good position; I was a member of a department made up of supportive,
feminist colleagues, two of whom would be there. Where had my comfort in
their presence gone?

I have realized in preparing for today that the trouble with talking
about anti-racist teaching is that, in fact, I cannot talk about it without
referring to (1) institutional structures of power, domination, complicity;
(2) individual cases of the same; and (3) why pedagogy should interest
any of us. My anti-racist teaching is based, as is that of many teachers
more radical than I, on Paulo Freire's notion of liberatory education and
his opposition to what he calls the banking model of education (student
as consumer, teacher as disseminator of information, power, authority).
It is also based on feminist pedagogical practice and the agony of trying to
be a practicing feminist in the university classroom. And I recognize
something quite disturbing: as we feminists have gained power and status
in the academy, our focus on, and even our passion for, radicalizing pedagogical structures has waned. I sometimes want to stop my own work to
reflect on this phenomenon. *Of course, the answers are there. As Jennifer*
Gore points out, even radical pedagogies are based on startlingly unliberatory
notions of institutionalized pedagogy, and in the case of feminist pedagogies,
institutional wars have fragmented our struggle for emancipation; Women's
Studies may well have been the site of feminist resistance for a while, but fem-
inist scholars in various disciplines have tended to ignore each other's work in
pedagogy, and, more important, have failed to realize the importance of what
bell hooks calls "self-actualization" (see especially Teaching To Transgress,
1995). As Gore puts it, our outward pedagogic focus was based on modernist
notions of change, progress, and student improvement rather than on our
own ethical position: "Little is articulated in the discourse of feminist peda-
gogy about the relationships one ought to have with oneself" (1993, 87). Her
indictment is quite harsh, even as she recognizes the possibilities of feminist
pedagogies in the academy: "While the academy is seen to constrain feminist
pedagogy, it also plays a role in structuring and supporting the discourse and
practice of feminist pedagogy. . . . That feminists are surviving [in the acad-
emy] clearly indicates duplicity. . . . Meanwhile feminist teachers will need
to be careful to construct practices consistent with their rhetoric, or else con-
front themselves as hypocrites" (pp. 83–84, 90).

As do many other radical pedagogues, hooks points out that, in a dysfunc-
tional academy, body and mind are split, and coercion is the main rule of

power. In this context, her call for self-actualization is both difficult to heed and incredibly important:

> Progressive, holistic education, "engaged pedagogy" is more demanding than conventional critical or feminist pedagogy. For, unlike these two teaching practices, it emphasizes well-being. That means that teachers must be actively committed to a process of self-actualization that promotes their own well-being if they are to teach in a manner that empowers students. . . . It is rare that anyone talks about teachers in university settings as healers. And it is even more rare to hear anyone suggest that teachers have any responsibility to be self-actualized individuals. (1995, 15–16)

Self-actualization: both the individual therapeutic process (however achieved) and a political realization—a recognition of ourselves in history and in the context of differential and fluid relations of power; indeed, the actualization of the self necessarily entails the ability to articulate ourselves in institutions, to recognize how our actions are oppositional, how they are complicit in academic structures of oppression. Gore's focus on the hypocritical nature of much feminist teaching, and her call for an ethical stance, demands that we always recognize context, that we not spare ourselves and our interests in our critiques of the academy—the "not me" syndrome. Chandra Mohanty (1994, 162) suggests that creating "cultures of dissent" in the academy is one way of fighting the prevailing depoliticization and dematerialization of knowledges:

> Creating such cultures is fundamentally about making the axes of power transparent in the context of academic, disciplinary and institutional structures, as well as in the interpersonal relationships (rather than individual relations) in the academy. It is about taking the politics of everyday life seriously as teachers, students, administrators and members of hegemonic academic cultures.

I often wonder why my own career interests, fuelled by colleagues and administrative structures, so often take precedence over what I believe to be important work—liberatory education in the university context (an analysis, critique, and educational practice which makes the classroom the site of change, of political practice, of research, and which demands that our intellectual work never preclude our activism). *That is, as many critical educators have suggested, liberatory education insists, both inside and outside the classroom, that "who we are, how we act, what we think and what stories we tell become more intelligible within an epistemological framework that begins by recognizing existing hegemonic histories. . . . Resistance lies in self-conscious engagement with dominant, normative discourses and representations and in the active creation of oppositional analytic and cultural spaces" (Mohanty 1994, 148).*

Great words, words in which I believe, especially with regard to my commitment to communities of color. What makes this emancipatory process anti-racist is the creation, within the academy, of oppositional space for people of color and for the critique of normative whiteness. My anti-racist teaching, therefore, is increasingly about institutional racism, my part in it, and how I am taken in by it.

I would like to start with this challenge, which I take from hooks (1995, 142): "I want to reiterate that many teachers who do not have difficulty releasing old ideas, embracing new ways of thinking, may still be as resolutely attached to old ways of *practicing teaching* as their more conservative colleagues." To a certain extent, I think this is true of all of us, even those of us who feel we have changed the way we teach and think about teaching. As hooks points out, curriculum revision is not the same thing as pedagogical change and revision: "I know so many professors who are progressive in their politics, who have been willing to change their curriculum, but who in fact have resolutely refused to change the nature of their pedagogical practice" (1995, 140–41).

Anti-racist teaching has to be informed by a discussion and awareness of our fears as teachers and students, our own personal and institutional bottom lines: we need to talk about the general distrust in the academy for personal narratives, for hearing the voices of our students and of ourselves. The issues we raise as problems include covering the material, class size, grading, respect for our authority, limitations of space and time, political correctness, our vulnerability as professors and students, and so on. We can talk about these things endlessly, but while we do so we need to keep this central question in mind: How do we perform anti-racist teaching?

*By now, this paper begins to move upward and outward from the classroom: what is anti-racist teaching **outside** the classroom? In most of our discussions, including a recent presentation of this (longer) paper, we invariably turn to the what-to-do-ifs of our particular classroom experiences and thus collude in silencing the real systemic issues, such as: How does anti-racist teaching work in a racist institution? Leslie Roman suggests, after Sandra Harding (1987, 1–14), that an anti-racist pedagogy would*

> entail studying up in the power structure (the board and the locker rooms where institutional decisions are made), as well as studying down. . . . It would entail democratizing the process of research such that the rights of the oppressed are protected by asking tough political, epistemological, and methodological questions concerning whose interests are served in any research endeavour. (1993, 78)

Formerly, while recognizing the problem of studying down, I did not sufficiently attempt to "study up," and, in all the conference discussion groups I attended (both then and now), in the end, we talked about what we knew, what we could name, and what we could control; that is, we talked about our experiences in our classrooms rather than about the institution in which we worked and our investments in it.

Let me now focus my discussion around (1) the fundamental question behind the 1995 conference on race, ethnicity, and multiculturalism (i.e., in the anti-racist classroom, how do we negotiate race and ethnicity, especially given the confusion around how we and our students understand multiculturalism?), (2) a brief anecdote on the nature of silence, and (3) a student complaint.

Multiculturalism: certainly students seem to have absorbed the liberal message of official Canadian multicultural policy, which legislates cultural pluralism. Indeed, the investment in Canada-as-multicultural is intense, often defining a student's sense of this country's nationhood. *The anti-racist critique of multiculturalism is therefore extraordinarily difficult for them to understand or even to acknowledge, for it profoundly threatens their sense of Canadianness. What differentiates Canadian multiculturalism from other national forms of multiculturalism is not its often insidious cultural pluralism and relativism (which may be seen quite clearly in American, British, and Australian forms of multiculturalism) but its imaginative hold on its citizens. In Canada, anti-racism is precluded because multiculturalism rigorously elides both race and racism and, hence, any historical consciousness. Within a Canadian context, I would take issue with the first part of Mohanty's (1994, 156) discussion of the academic institutionalization of multiculturalism: "While multiculturalism itself is not necessarily problematic, its definition in terms of an apolitical, ahistorical cultural pluralism needs to be challenged." In my reading of it, Canadian multiculturalism is not separable from its official manifestations and rhetoric and is, in fact, "necessarily problematic" for the reason Mohanty outlines: its "ahistorical cultural pluralism." The rhetoric of Canadian multiculturalism is identical to "diversity" rhetoric in the United States, and its manifestations in the academy are depressingly similar: there is a highly public rhetoric of approval around curriculum change, a less focused commitment to affirmative action or "equity," some hysteria around political correctness, and many of the strategies of containment that Mohanty and others discuss. In other words, beyond rhetoric, a bit of "consciousness-raising," and a liberal discourse around diversity, academic freedom, and difference, universities have changed very little in the last twenty years. To maintain this stasis, the university "has to enact policies and programs aimed at accommodation rather than transformation"* (Mohanty 1994, 156).

Let us now consider silence. Silence in the classroom tends to be seen as monolithic: it means assent, it means boredom, it means resistance. Last weekend, I spent a great deal of time in a hospital in Edmonton with a close friend who is critically ill with multiple sclerosis. He has lost his ability to speak, to eat, and to move. It took three full days for me to be able to quickly determine, through signs and head movements, Gregg's needs. As many of us know, the inability and/or unwillingness to speak is usually taken to mean lack of desire to communicate, lack of thought, and/or lack of need. I learned how to frame questions he could answer and how to figure out what he wanted. I made an alphabet board. But what I failed to recognize was that his all-round silence, though enforced, was multifaceted. My last day there, I puzzled at great length, to his and my increasing frustration, about some seemingly complex utterance he was making. I finally realized that I had presumed that all his "talk" would be based on needs and wants, while what he was actually doing was attempting to make an observation about something I had read to him. Later, when I wondered why he was being so quiet—was he frustrated, tired of it all?—he said that he simply wanted to be quiet. This episode forced me, again, to recognize that my obsession with silence in the classroom needs a great deal of work, and that, however we may deny it, most of us continue to privilege the spoken and/or written word as the only significant marker of thought and reflection. *Of course, I have habituated myself to institutional conventions, such as the annual report, the importance of "original" writing, and so on. We see, in our classroom performance and expectations, much of what we ourselves have been disciplined to perform and expect. What about my own silences and speech, then? At what point will I talk about racism in the context of myself-in-the-academy? "My truths require that I say unconventional things in unconventional ways. Speaking out assumes prerogative. Speaking out is an exercise of privilege. Speaking out takes practice. Silence ensures invisibility. Silence provides protection. Silence masks" (Montoya 1995, 536).*

So I wrestle almost daily with questions regarding my silence, my refusal to fight for myself and/or for students who, for better or worse, have come to see me as protector and mentor. When does the unlearning of this paralysis take place? When do I go to my colleagues, to my union, to administrators, all of whom may or may not have some response to the systemic racism I see and feel daily? It amazes me that, often, I still refuse to fight; I still believe the institution's self-perceptions of fairness and inscrutability. Here, I appreciate the insights of Leslie Roman, who, in reflecting on an earlier draft of this paper, noted that I presented my own paralysis as an individual act, or failure to act, rather than as a negotiated response to a systemically racist institution.

My second anecdote concerns a letter I received a few days ago from a student who had withdrawn from my new class on Alberta writers. The complaint is lengthy, and it focuses on the cost, choice, number, and bias of the texts I had chosen. For me, the most fundamental and objectionable of her complaints had to do with curriculum. Objecting to the regional focus of the course (what did Alberta writing have to do with Canadian literature?), she went on to suggest that a truly representative course would not focus so heavily on writers of color and Aboriginal writers.

One of the things I came to realize in responding to the above complaint was that I had to treat it as a pedagogical moment; that is, I had to recognize that her complaint was based on lack of knowledge about how the institution worked. As an anti-racist moment, it offered me the opportunity to take a stranger to task for the racism that her assumptions revealed.

I see my specific brand of anti-racist teaching in the university classroom as centering around the need for empathy/diplomacy. In other contexts, such as anti-racist workshops, empathy/diplomacy is not always appropriate for those of us who are people of color working in White or mixed groups; outside the university classroom I am more comfortable with the anger that often erupts, *has* to erupt, for any unlearning to take place. Because of my power, and because of the hopelessly liberal structures and expectations of the classroom, I find myself feeling more convinced than ever that direct challenges to student racism have to be tempered by empathy/diplomacy. Hooks describes a radical classroom space as one in which there occurs a truly democratic process, whereby all students know that they will be heard and respected (1995, 76). In general, I have grave doubts about the emphasis that anti-racist work places on the production of empathy; for me, it too often colludes with liberal, humanist notions of universalism, equality, and identification (all of which I attempt to expose for their pernicious cultural power).

So why the double bind: Is it true that all students need to be heard, that all students respond uniformly to my power? Is my dis-ease with empathy in community work so easily displaced in the classroom?

> We call the belief that we can somehow control our consciousness despite limitations of time and positionality the empathic fallacy [which consists of] believing that we can enlarge our sympathies through linguistic means alone: by exposing ourselves to ennobling narratives, we broaden our experience, deepen our empathy, and achieve new levels of sensitivity and fellow-feeling—we can, in short, think, talk, read, and write our ways out of bigotry and narrow-mindedness, out of our limitations of experience and perspective. (Delgado and Stefancic 1995, 218)

Robert Nowlan suggests, however, in responding to a Black student about the overt expressions of racism in his composition classroom, that bringing to (critical) consciousness the duplicitous racism of White students is essential, that they have to express their rhetoric of equality alongside their largely unconscious racist beliefs. For him, the classroom is a place where this process may occur:

> White people have to be shown that the consequences of their everyday actions (and inactions) contradict the anti-racist values they profess to

support, and that therefore they do not really support these values at all—
they pay them lip service but do not support them in reality, and, in fact,
in actual practice support the opposite. (1995, 245)

A question I have often asked, and find myself increasingly uncomfortable with,
is, who is our constituency, the White majority of the class, or the uncomfortable,
targeted student(s) of color? Indeed, perhaps I am no longer convinced that empa-
thy is the answer—certainly not if it is being confused with civility, just as "safety"
is confused with "comfort": when do I let my own political and personal senses of
violation be known? "There seems to [be] a tendency [in much feminist teaching]
towards extreme politeness, attempts made to listen to and accept multiple view-
points even when one is in strong disagreement" (Gore 1993, 90).

Undoubtedly, though, empathy exercises, such as Barbara Findlay's
(1988, 1) target-group exercise, work well in the classroom, in part because
they suspend the perceived need for rational discourse and involve students
in learning about oppression. Furthermore, the exercises themselves, while
extraordinarily useful, are open to critique (e.g., for what they assume, their
binarism, and their lack of subtlety). They also break decorum, and I am
keenly aware that one of my strongest shortcomings is my desire to avoid
conflict and confrontation in the classroom; like many, I have used the concept of safety as a kind of refuge (and, in so doing, have been tyrannized by
it); and while I still value safety as a grounding idea, I believe, as do many
others, that the risks required by anti-racist work cannot and should not
guarantee a safe space—a fiction if ever there was one.

Diplomacy, empathy: clearly there has to be a place in the classroom and in
the academy for both, and it is comforting (and not inaccurate), as a friend has
suggested, to think that the production of empathy and the use of diplomacy
can be and often are strategic. Often, they function to warn me against the ten-
dency to disavow the real institutional and cultural power I have as a professor.
My students of color and my Aboriginal students can be well served by careful
diplomacy and empathy, can learn much about their own internalized oppres-
sion, as White students learn about internalized and systemic domination. But
I am deeply uncomfortable with Robert Nowlan's aforementioned address to
his Black student's anger at White racism, and I am deeply suspicious of the
way in which strategy can be transformed into excuse and comfort. Again, the
spectre of complicity forces me to interrogate the way in which I function in the
academy, the way in which "those of us . . . in the academy . . . potentially col-
lude in [the] domestication of race by allowing ourselves to be positioned in
ways that contribute to the construction of . . . images of pure and innocent
diversity" (Mohanty 1994, 161).

Critical, feminist, anti-oppression educators point out that it is crucial for
us to interrogate our sense that the classroom should not be a place for emo-

tion, anger, or conflict. The classroom cannot help but be, at times, chaotic, confusing, and disordered, a place of pain, denial, anger, and anxiety—all of which we expect, we have to expect, when challenging others and ourselves to examine, even simply to reveal, the ways in which all sorts of racisms have inflected our/their identities. The vulnerability to which we expose ourselves and our students is enormous; and the work in the classroom is often physically, emotionally, and intellectually exhausting. *Still, our conceptions of mutually supportive dialogue prevail, even if we recognize the importance of engaging in the personal. We may recognize that conflict and anger are appropriate for the student body but not for us. For the racialized female teacher, whose "personal" is already visibly embodied, what other ruptures and questions are there? Indira Karamcheti likens herself to Caliban, and recognizes that, for her, "the personal" is always already being performed in the classroom by virtue of her visibility. Students will articulate their own (dis)respect for the authority of the racialized female instructor in any number of ways, commenting on her name, her dress, her accent, her command of English, the appropriateness of her body to her subject matter, and so on. As I have experienced it, one reasonable response to these racisms, these exoticizations, is anger—a Calibanish anger exploding in curses: "A harder issue for me is the problem of anger, the issue of rage named in the idea of cursing. Anger, [unlike analysis], is useless, destructive, degenerative, at least in reputation. Certainly, anger seems to me antithetical to the dialogues of teaching, yet anger is a real and present fact of the personal" (Karamcheti 1995, 144).*

Clearly, professors who are women of color engage in strategies of silence and pedagogical containment for far different reasons than do White (male or female) professors:

> So, the racial/gendered subject simply avoids the potential for violence to her history, background and culture. She is keenly aware, however, of that potential and that it is, in many instances, simply suspended in the classroom. Once outside of that rarefied space, the violence may reveal itself in all of its craziness, all of its horror. Thus, the revolutionary inclinations of the black woman professor may become a mere gesture, as they are tempered by her desire to have some respite, albeit temporarily, from the racism which has been her unwelcome companion from the day she came to understand what a difference a color makes. (Johnson 1995, 135)

But are there strategies for dealing with race? The question itself is problematic, "dealing" with race merely as an issue, an idea, a topic best to be avoided. In my classrooms, currently, I have a racial and ethnic mix of students, although most are White and very few (usually one in a class of forty or so) are Aboriginal. The continuing frustration for me, of course, is that anti-racist work, anti-racist reading, is directed largely to White students. Students of color and Aboriginal students often find that one of the uncomfortable effects of my pedagogy is that they feel singled out, silenced, often angered by the exposing of a racism they have frequently survived by pretending not to see. As well, there is an incredible (to me) investment in ideological multiculturalism; that is, highly individualistic, ahistorical takes on race, gender, class, sexuality, along with (perhaps because we live in Reform Party country) moral panic. For Albertans, Sikhs, turbans, the Royal Canadian Mounted Police (RCMP), and the Canadian Legion are the markers of that panic, and these issues always come up at the beginning of my classes, followed by the usual litany of oppressed-White-male stories—*stories which, for those of us professing to be racialized subjects, "other" us completely, perhaps ensuring that we fall back on a strategy of silence*:

> *As if to substantiate the Academy's misgivings about "diversity," out in the wilderness of the non-academic world roams a white male with all of his star qualities, but allegedly without his due. He is a caricature with whom many sympathize; he is accorded most favored person status. Deep in the wilderness of the academy, there is an exceptional blackwoman; however, her just deserts remain contested. She is constructed as a gorilla. Does anybody in the Academy care that she might be in harm's way? (Russell 1995, 500–501)*

Part of my anti-oppression work is to open up each of the above myths to examination, to history, and to ideological analysis. Very loosely, in order to ensure that some of my students take away with them a question or two about their own investment and participation in racist structures, I apply a reader-response approach to all of our texts. Yet I still haven't solved the problem of "how to deal" with students of color and Aboriginal students who do not have a voice (trying to keep in mind my newly learned lesson about silence). The ideal solution is to have more of them in our classes; for now the solution is how not to perpetuate racism and ethnocentrism by exoticizing them—a process that, in theory, sounds easy but, in practice, is quite difficult (e.g., all eyes swivel to a Korean Canadian student when we discuss a Japanese Canadian text). I believe that we need to have working groups consisting of students of color, working-class students, and women, respectively (or whatever constituency needs to be represented and to represent itself). And this is precisely where my fear of backlash takes over and inhibits the pedagogical process. I am scared to set up such groups, scared of my students' response, more scared of my colleagues' response; I *know* that to do this would transgress all sorts of boundaries.

And so I rely on the liberally determined model of "multicult" or pluralism—that ideal world where all groups have equal voice, where power imbalances do not exist. *I know that this model of cultural pluralism*

> *fails to acknowledge the notion of a racist society that is not neutral, nor run on negotiated consensuses but in terms of a power structure that is*

> *racist and guided by political, social, and cultural values of the dominant*
> *group. . . . Education has to be seen as part of the product of racist struc-*
> *tures and procedures within the specificity of the contemporary . . . social*
> *formation. (Brant 1986, 97)*

I know this.

The contradiction between theory and practice, between my own knowledge and my working out of that knowledge in the world sometimes astonishes me. And yet it shouldn't—at least not if I believe that pedagogy is more than a classroom experience. My sometimes minimal attempts at anti-racist pedagogy in other institutional contexts seem pathetic. In my classroom, I have the power and the time to see some of the effects of my anti-racist pedagogy, to see White students recognize (just a little) what their whiteness means, and to see students of color and Aboriginal students take pride in their own histories, ethnicities, genders, and so on. I see the latter drop the term "Canadian" and turn to local ways of expressing their identities. At those moments, I realize what incredible power we have as teachers.

> *And yet, I am imperiled by that pedagogical double bind: It is only within*
> *a structure in which the assumptions of teachers of all persuasions are con-*
> *tested by equally powerful peers that the double bind of oppositional ped-*
> *agogy can be overcome. In a curriculum in which clashing views did not*
> *simply co-exist side by side but directly engaged one another, teachers*
> *could become more aggressive in expressing political beliefs with less fear*
> *of coercing their students. (Graff 1995, 282)*

Indeed, I cannot envision an institutional setting where Graff's scenario might take place. I team-teach a first-year English course to 250 students; in this course, we (the five instructors) attempt to abide by Graff's model of "equally powerful" but dissenting views; that is, we attempt to ignore differences in professional rank, experience, pedagogical beliefs, and so on. We have been, I think, reasonably successful in demonstrating the co-existence of disparate ideas and philosophies. Where we have not been successful is in recognizing and accounting for our own resistances, those of our students, and those of our teaching assistants. What we have been quite blind to is the tyranny of what Graff calls the "course fetish" (279); we have failed to see that our curriculum, our departmental and administrative structure, does not encourage "direct" engagement with "equally powerful" peers. Thus, my attempts to read The Tempest *or* Oroonoko *in the light of colonialism and racism have largely fallen on angry ears: "What does this have to do with the text, with literature," they (mostly, but by no means exclusively, confused new university students) ask? "Teaching in a traditional discipline from the perspective of critical pedagogy means that I often encounter students who make complaints like, 'I thought this was supposed to be an English class, why are we talking so much about feminism?' (Or, they might add, race or class)" (hooks 1995, 42).*

In my department—and my department is quite progressive—I haven't found a way to extend my anti-racist pedagogy to my colleagues and superiors, except in a somewhat childish, dig-in-my-heels kind of way. I find myself overcome with anger at the extraordinary hold of bourgeois, academic values, and yet I am kept from expressing that anger by my fear of upsetting decorum. I turn away (often), remain silent, put my energies elsewhere (where they seem more effective); and, in so doing, I recognize my complicity in perpetuating the structures of my profession. *"If half of the current battle for diversity is acclimating students to different styles of teaching . . . the other half is educating our well-meaning colleagues whose preference for existing models of scholarship and teaching cause them to trivialize our work"* (Post 1995, 424). *And it is that other half that has most confused me, not least because I had envisioned myself as a legitimate professional within the academy, a professional not bound by the frequently articulated anger of the "diversity candidate" in the United States (whose intellect and place are always being questioned): "Post-appointment she will be treated like an intellectual waif. She cannot legitimately claim any special competence in any subject or field. Her considered judgments regarding course coverage, teaching methodology, examinations and grading can be challenged with impunity" (Russell 1995, 500). Yet I feel just a frisson of recognition (or is it paranoia?) in recalling those endless discussions about pedagogy, about the evils of plagiarism, grade inflation, and departmental racism. With regard to the latter, I would be treated to well-meaning but inevitably imperialistic tut-tut exclamations of "I'm sorry you feel like that"—exclamations that pathologized racism as my own personal experience rather than recognizing it as part and parcel of the institution itself.*

I know, along with Geoffrey Brant (1986, 102), that "intentionality does not measure racism," that institutional racism "exists within the 'ethos' or sociocultural environment of the organization" and relies on structuring practices which are "often intangible and are sometimes vehemently denied by White people." I also feel the effect, when reading Brant's text, of the marginalia pencilled in by an irate reader: "Crap," he (?) says to Brant's theorizing of institutional and systemic racism, and "CRAP with capital letters," later in the text, when Brant diagrams the complexities of the domains of oppression in children's lives. The book is littered with these expostulations (a particularly lengthy section that outlines how racist education functions in Britain elicits the following comment: "reduced to colour," presumably indicating this person's disaffection with the notion that White supremacy in education is self-perpetuating). I find myself English-professorly interested in the text and subtext here, the strategies of containment and denial that turn this book into (for that unknown reader, at any rate) nothing of import. I shudder when I think s/he might now be an educator.

And it seems to me that my task, and perhaps that of other anti-racist teachers, is to contemplate our pedagogical commitment within the academy, within our departments, and to run the very real risk of estrangement, the risk (I think) that now prevents us from doing much more than contemplating, in silence and wonder, the chilling hold of liberalism. *As so many theorists of race and anti-racism have suggested, the only way to do cultural work is to recognize that it is, in fact, cultural work, not "purely" or limitedly academic. The disciplines and isolation of institutional life make those of us who have complicated investments in academe, those of us who are subjected to the domination of institutional norms, histories, and denials, forget that it is working across these boundaries and borders, in coalitions (as fractious as these may be), that allows us to mount the most effective resistance. And that the double bind and paralysis of the racialized woman professor is part of the logic of the institution, a logic whose purpose is, in fact, to disempower, to pathologize, to discipline, to engender a forgetting of community. I know that I have allies who will work with me, even fight for me, and yet, as Cornel West (1995, 22) wonders in the following citation, can the "Critical Organic Analyst" hope to do much in such an institution?*

> *The most desirable option for people of color who promote the new cultural politics of difference is to be a Critical Organic Analyst . . . a person who stays attuned to the best of what the mainstream has to offer . . . yet maintains a grounding in affirming and enabling subcultures of criticism. Prophetic critics and artists should be exemplars of what it means to be intellectual freedom fighters, that is, cultural workers who simultaneously position themselves within (or alongside) the mainstream while clearly being aligned with groups who vow to keep alive the potent traditions of critique and resistance.*

References

Brant, G. 1986. *The Realization of Anti-Racist Teaching*. London: Falmer Press.

Delgado, R, and J. Stefancic. 1995. "Images of the Outsider in American Law and Culture: Can Free Expression Remedy Social Ills?" In *Critical Race Theory: The Cutting Edge*, edited by R. Delgado, 217–27. Philadelphia: Temple University Press.

Espinoza, L.G. 1995. "Masks and Other Disguises: Exposing Legal Academia." In *Critical Race Theory: The Cutting Edge*, edited by R. Delgado, 451–58. Philadelphia: Temple University Press.

Findlay, Barbara. 1988. *For All of Who We Are: A Study of Oppression and Dominance*. About Law Pamphlet Series. Vancouver: Lazara Press.

Freire, P. 1995. *Pedagogy of the Oppressed*. New York: Continuum.

Gore, J. M. 1993. *The Struggle for Pedagogies: Critical and Feminist Discourses as Regimes of Truth*. London: Routledge.

Graff, G. 1995. "The Dilemma of Oppositional Pedagogy: A Response." In *Left Margins: Cultural Studies and Composition Pedagogy*, edited by K. Fitts and A.W. France, 275–82. New York: SUNY.

Harding, S. 1987. *Feminism and Methodology: Social Science Issues*. Bloomington: Indiana University Press.

hooks, bell. 1995. *Teaching to Transgress*. London: Routledge.

Johnson, C. 1995. "Disinfecting Dialogues." In *Pedagogy: The Question of Impersonation*, edited by Jane Gallop, 129–37. Bloomington: Indiana University Press.

Karamcheti, I. 1995. "Caliban in the Classroom." In *Pedagogy: The Question of Impersonation*, edited by J. Gallop, 138–46. Bloomington: Indiana University Press.

Mohanty, C. T. 1994. "On Race and Voice: Challenges of Liberal Education in the 1990s." In *Between Borders: Pedagogy and the Politics of Cultural Studies*, edited by H. Giroux and P. McLaren, 145–66. New York: Routledge.

Montoya, M. 1995. "Un/masking the Self While Un/braiding Latina Stories." In *Critical Race Theory: The Cutting Edge*, edited by R. Delgado, 529–39. Philadelphia: Temple University Press.

Nowlan, R. A. 1995. "Teaching Against Racism in the College Composition Classroom." In *Left Margins: Cultural Studies and Composition Pedagogy*, edited by K. Fitts and A. W. France, 245–53. New York: SUNY.

Post, D. W. 1995. "Reflections on Identity, Diversity, Morality." In *Critical Race Theory: The Cutting Edge*, edited by R. Delgado, 419–30. Philadelphia: Temple University Press.

Roman, L. 1993. "White is a Color! White Defensiveness, Postmodernism, and Anti-Racist Pedagogy." In *Race, Representation and Identity in Education*, edited by C. McCarthy and W. Crichlow, 71–88. London: Routledge.

———. Forthcoming. "Spectacle in the Dark: Youth as Transgression, Display, and Repression." *Educational Theory* 46 (1).

Russell, J. 1995. "On Being a Gorilla in Your Midst: Or, the Life of One Blackwoman in the Legal Academy." In *Critical Race Theory: The Cutting Edge*, edited by R. Delgado, 498–501. Philadelphia: Temple University Press.

West, C. 1995. "The New Cultural Politics of Difference." In *Race, Representation and Identity in Education*, edited by C. McCarthy and W. Crichlow, 11–23. London: Routledge.

Chapter Seven

Reading Resistance Analytically: On Making the Self in Women's Studies

Alice Jane Pitt
York University (Canada)

Introduction

Teaching and learning feminism have always been both risky and pleasurable. The risks, as Teresa de Lauretis (1987) reminds us, concern the experiences of becoming feminist in a sexist society. In part, becoming feminist is difficult because it is entails the persistent critique of dominant cultural representations of women and the equally persistent marginalization of feminist representations. Paradoxically, within such difficulties lie pleasures; for example, the possibility of forming a new (and oppositional) identity. While much of the writing about feminist classrooms has emphasized how they offer knowledge that enables feminist struggles, it also draws attention to women's refusals to take up such knowledge (Briskin and Coulter 1992; Lather 1991; Lewis 1990; Martindale 1992). There is much resistance to learning from feminist knowledge, and these narratives of resistance trouble and complicate the view that Women's Studies provides a learning environment that recognizes women's intellectual and emotional needs. It is the dynamic of resistance that I wish to problematize here. Following poststructuralist and psychoanalytic theories of identity and learning, I read two stories of engagement with feminist knowledge—stories which are in tension both with each other and with dominant feminist pedagogical assumptions. As we shall see, each story implicates its narrator in a notion of identity that both requires and excludes difference. I explore what is at stake for feminist practices of equality when one student's narrative is read as enabling feminist struggles while the other student's narrative is read as disabling them.

The stories concern two students in an introductory Women's Studies class who responded in very different ways to the inclusion of the topic of lesbianism in their course.[1] Student A complained that lesbianism was a personal choice and that it had no place in a course that addressed women's oppression. Lesbian struggles for basic human rights, including the right to visibility and representation, were constituted as belonging solely to that arena of politics called "gay liberation." As such, lesbianism had nothing to do with her or, for that matter, with "women." Student B believed that not enough was said about the lives, sexualities, and cultures of lesbians. Whereas student A rejected lesbianism as irrelevant to her identity as a woman, student B embraced lesbianism as a specifically feminist critique of patriarchal heterosexuality. Perhaps not coincidentally, student B's interest in lesbianism coincided with her interest in "coming out."

These two responses appear to be diametrically opposed when read in relation to the twin commitments of feminist theorizing and teaching: (1) to address women's experiences and identities as marked not only by gender but also by race, class, sex, age, ability, and geography, and (2) to theorize gender itself as a category that gains intelligibility only when read through the lenses of multiple axes of identity-formation. The study of domination and subordination among women reflects ongoing feminist struggles to interrogate what it means to be a woman in a society that is class-based, sexist, racist, and homophobic. These struggles situate the responses of both students in relation to the pedagogical demands of Women's Studies. Student A's response can be interpreted as signalling her refusal to come to terms with her own position of dominance as a heterosexual woman. This is a refusal to learn that, however difficult it is to be female in a sexist society, privileges accrue to heterosexual women precisely because they are heterosexual. Moreover, to define heterosexuality as normal entails defining other sexualities as deviant and, hence, marginal. Given that the desire to acknowledge heterosexual privilege and to decenter heterosexuality has become central to feminist pedagogy, student A's response to including lesbianism in her Women's Studies course can be read as a story of resistance. On the surface, student B's response does not appear to be a story of resistance. Her desire for lesbian representation and for the possibility of self-representation as a lesbian is, however, both subject to and a subject of resentments. These resentments assume a variety of forms, including public displays of homophobia and refusals to consider gay and lesbian rights as civil rights. Such expressions exceed the intimacy of feminist classrooms.

If we begin with some insights offered by psychoanalytic understandings of learning and resistance, we learn that student responses are rarely as transparent as we might wish. Shoshana Felman provides a way of thinking about resistance to knowledge that allows us to close the gap between our two students' responses to lesbianism and, hence, between an interpretive practice that reads response A as evidence of resistance to knowledge and response B as evidence of learning. Following the work of Jacques Lacan, Felman argues that "teaching, like analysis, has to deal not so much with lack of knowledge as with resistance to knowledge" (1987, 79). In comparing teaching with analysis, Felman is saying something about learning. Analytic learning, whether it occurs in the privacy of the psychoanalyst's office or in the public space of the classroom, comes about as one works through one's resistance to knowledge—resistance being defined as the refusal to accept the relevance of certain knowledge to oneself. Covered over by such a refusal is a powerful and largely unconscious desire to ignore one's implication in the knowledge one already holds.

Resistance, then, is less an impediment to learning than it is the basis of learning. Still, our investigation of resistance to knowledge becomes quite slippery when we take into account student B's desire to embrace knowledge about lesbianism. If, as Felman's account implies, learning has less to do with the mastery of knowledge and the affirmation of identity than it has to do with gaining insight into one's implication in knowledge, then we are left wondering what is at stake when feminist knowledge insists upon the relevance of the "strange" identities of socially marginalized groups.

In the remainder of this chapter, I explore the question of feminist knowledge and how it is engaged in introductory Women's Studies courses. Women's Studies does not merely present knowledge about women and feminism; it enacts feminism as a sequenced set of curricular materials as it attempts to address women as subjects whose social positionality is marked by gendered inequality. I look at feminist knowledge and attempt to show how its assumptions give it coherence.[2] I ask what governs the dynamics of engagement within feminist pedagogical practices which set the terms by and within which women may respond to the question, "Can I recognize myself as a woman in this course?" Three questions serve to elaborate what is at stake for learners as they become participants in these dynamics: (1) What are the dynamics that structure the way in which feminist knowledge is assumed to become relevant to women? (2) How do these dynamics conceptualize the self? and (3) How do these dynamics organize they ways in which difference can be imagined?

The dynamics that organize and render coherent the way in which Women's Studies introduces feminist knowledge are rooted in radical feminism. In turn, radical feminism depends upon a series of interdependent categorical imperatives that structure the limits of its capacity to exceed its origins in humanistic notions of the individual and knowledge. As I trace how the dynamics of radical feminism are organized by what Eve Sedgwick (1990) calls a minoritizing world view and a belief in identity as a self-evident and unitary construct, some curious effects become visible. One effect concerns the durability of the power of White, middle-class, heterosexual women to "mark" with meaning the identities and experiences of women historically marginalized within feminist discourse. A second effect concerns radical feminism's own narratives of lesbian sexuality and how the figure of the lesbian retains the logic of minoritization and, in so doing, effects new categories of exclusion.

We shall see that the stories of both student A and student B implicate their narrators in a minoritizing view of identity and, hence, in the dynamics of engagement of Women's Studies. Reading their stories as sharing a structure of minoritization speaks directly to the limits of sociologically grounded interpretations of student responses to our pedagogical efforts. Drawing upon psychoanalytic understandings of learning, I consider how sociological interpretations are symptomatic of a tendency within feminist discourse to refuse the implications of understanding gender as a social relation that is lived as ambivalence. Here, the term "sociological interpretation" signifies the facile mapping of identity onto larger sociocultural dynamics. The question is not, what does identity explain? but, rather, how are identificatory dynamics provoked by feminist pedagogy?

Identity and the Dynamics of Minoritization

The production of subject positions within an introductory Women's Studies class relies heavily upon what Sedgwick calls a minoritizing view of identity and social difference. With regard to homosexuality/heterosexuality, Sedgwick defines this view as

> the contradiction between seeing homo/heterosexual definition on the one hand as an issue of active importance for a small, distinct, relatively fixed homosexual minority (what I refer to as a minoritizing view), and seeing it on the other hand as an issue of continuing determinative importance in the lives of people across the spectrum of sexualities (what I refer to as a universalizing view). (1990, 1)

Minoritizing and universalizing views offer a way of understanding different versions of the relationship between the self and the other. Whereas a minoritizing view constructs identity in terms of mutually exclusive binary oppositions, a universalizing view deconstructs such oppositions. The latter view allows for the idea that identity categories which appear to be mutually exclusive actually depend upon each other for their respective intelligibility.

In minoritizing views, identity originates in the self. The categories of race, class, sex, and even gender are understood as relevant only to those individuals whose identities are socially marked by them; they are not understood as part and parcel of the complex social relations that constitute all identities. In other words, minoritizing views presume a coherent identity as a point of departure: what a "subject is is already known, already fixed, and that ready-made subject might enter the world and re-negotiate its place" (Butler 1993, 115). For Sedgwick, attending to the dynamics of minoritizing and universalizing understandings of homosexuality enable one to ask: "In whose lives is homo/heterosexual definition an issue of continuing centrality and difficulty?" (1990, 40). Consideration of the renewed vigour of Conservative anxieties around homosexuality might prompt us to rewrite Sedgwick's question as follows: In whose lives *has* the homo/heterosexual definition *become* an issue? I return to this question later when I show how the stories of both student A and student B required them to believe in the notion of a ready-made subject. First, however, I want to explore how the pedagogical positions offered by Women's Studies also depend upon such a notion.

Introductory Women's Studies courses tend to invite women to identify with their teachers and with the images of women who populate the texts of feminist knowledge. These textualized women represent, on the one hand, women's experiences of oppression and, on the other hand, women's resistance to those experiences. A minoritizing view of identity haunts this approach to learning in that it assumes (1) that the identificatory processes it entails will cause no problem for the learner (Bogdan 1994; Britzman 1995; Simon 1992), (2) that the learner is rationally in charge of how knowledge will affect her, and (3) that identification proceeds from, and results in the affirmation of, identity.

Psychoanalytic theory, however, suggests that precisely the opposite is true. According to Laplanche and Pontalis: "In Freud's work the concept of identification comes little by little to have the central importance which makes it, not one psychical mechanism among others, but the operation itself whereby the human subject is constituted" (1973, 206). This definition reverses the relationship between identity and identitfication named above. It suggests that (1) identification precedes identity and (2) identification constitutes the grounds of possibility for the emergence of identity. From this vantage point, engagement with feminist textual knowledge and feminist pedagogical and methodological practices instantiates something that is in excess of how the ready-made subject learns of her place in the world. What becomes central are the dynamics by which feminism becomes the grounds of possibility for the fashioning of a new identification and, hence, a new sense of self and agency. Teresa Brennan describes this process in psychical terms: "We can postulate that an ego-ideal identification with feminism, in the form of a person, people, or a body of writing, suspends the ego-ideal's existing prohibitions, that it *permits* different thinking. For when the ego identifies its ego-ideal with a social other, it is permeable to the wish, will or ideas of that other" (1989, 10). Feminist knowledge and practices are important, then, not only because they unsettle, revise, and critique normative discourses of "femininity," but also because they produce particular narratives of gendered identity that function as sites of identification. This formulation is universalizing in that it rejects the notion of identity as a ready-made subject and regards it as a social relation dependent upon the existence of the other.

Radical Feminism's Narratives of Identity

However refined, elaborate, and divided contemporary feminist discourse in North America has become in its ongoing production of itself as a political movement and as a body of empirical and theoretical knowledge, Joan Cocks (1989) argues that dominant feminist narratives of gendered identity have their roots in "radical feminism" (see also Brown 1995). These roots, while increasingly critiqued, continue to shape (and to take shape within) feminist consciousness. Indeed, without them it becomes impossible to imagine second-wave feminism and/or beyond.

Cocks describes radical feminism as a movement which sets itself in opposition to what she refers to as "the regime of Masculine/feminine" and what other feminists refer to as a "self-perpetuating patriarchal 'system' in which oppression originates in men and is unilaterally directed toward women" (Butler 1991a, 88). Radical feminism challenges this system by situating itself "at an edge rather than a center," by defining itself as "a set of practices that go against the grain, a point of view outside the range of all permissable points" (Cocks 1989, 3). Radical feminism thus stakes a double claim: (1) from its position on the edge, it obtains a privileged view of the truth about women, both in terms of what de Lauretis (1987) calls the male-centered frame of reference and in terms of what that frame renders unrepresentable, and (2) it produces its own narratives of gender identity. While these narratives have become increasingly complex and are subject to debate, the story of origins described by Cocks is deeply entrenched within Women's Studies and, hence, within institutional practices devoted to engendering "feminist consciousness." Cocks argues that radical feminist narratives turn on a trio of inter-related presumptions: (1) they are structured by the insistence "that the primary division in society is one between women and men" (8); (2) they elaborate the ways in which "the self's interior is seared thoroughly and absolutely by the particular sex to which the self belongs" (8); and (3) any action, emotion, or cultural object "produced" by women is presumed to be characteristic of their position in a sociocultural dynamic. Even the shift in emphasis within radical feminist discourses from sex (as a biological category) to gender (as a socially constructed category) produces its own curious paradox. This is captured succinctly by Wendy Brown (1995, 41): "Consider Catharine MacKinnon's insistence that women are entirely the products of men's construction and her ontologically contradictory project of developing a jurisprudence based on 'an account of the world from women's point of view.'" Clearly, it is difficult to imagine a specifically feminist consciousness in the *absence* of an understanding of gender as a meaningful category. In other words, articulating a relation to these presumptions may be one of the early conditions of a feminist consciousness—what de Lauretis (1989) might recognize as an essential requirement for feminist subjectivity. What is important to note about these presumptions, however, is that women are presented (1) as possessing a core self that distinguishes them from men and (2) as sharing that core with all women. Here we have a feminist narrative which privileges a minoritizing view of identity.

The aforementioned trio of presumptions is being intensely debated within feminism, but it, along with the view from the margin that renders it visible, continues to operate discursively to produce two fictional and unambivalent categories of women: women and feminists. It is these subjects who populate the terrain of feminist education, and this fact may well ensure that minoritizing views are essential to imagining political action. That is, feminist pedagogy generally assumes that if there is to be such a thing as feminist collective action (as opposed to, say, mothers' action or recent female refugees' action), then it must be attributable to the fact that feminist knowledge is capable of mobilizing groups of individuals (see Riley 1988). Political action is thought to be produced by those who lay claim to a feminist subject position, which is not to be confused with a *female* subject position (Gordon 1986).

This formulation suggests that the process of identifying with feminist knowledge produces feminist identity, or, to recall Laplanche and Pontalis's terms, identification produces identity. For radical feminism, however, the distinction between women and feminists is secured through the mechanism of "consciousness-raising." Consciousness-raising promises to reveal the hidden truth about women's lives and experiences and, in so doing, to reinstall ontology (who women are) precisely at the moment when politics (what women want) becomes possible (Brown 1995, 49). The method of consciousness-raising, regarded as the quintessential feminist method by MacKinnon, imagines consciousness as something to be possessed rather than as a relation to be made. Furthermore, the notion of feminist consciousness (the desired result of consciousness-raising) entails the notion of false consciousness.

But this dualism between feminist consciousness and false consciousness breaks down over issues of gender. While feminist discourse acknowledges that it is difficult to be feminist in a sexist society (de Lauretis 1987), even more difficulties emerge when women are divided by whether or not they possess feminist gender consciousness (as opposed, say, to the [false?] gender consciousness espoused by the anti-feminist organization Real Women). What must be acknowledged is the fact that gender identity is always problematically and ambivalently lived; this is what makes resistance in the form of feminism possible in the first place.

In one sense, feminist knowledge can and often does function to secure for women an effective mimetic relationship between identity and knowledge about identity. This relationship is made possible by a discourse which denounces the notion of personal failure and replaces it with a notion of systemic discrimination; that is, feelings of inadequacy, frustration, and self-doubt are understood as the lived effects of a large (and insidious) social system. Two trajectories within feminist knowledge production sustain this discourse—the twin narratives of (1) victimization and (2) resistance to victimization.

Introductory courses in Women's Studies attempt to persuade students that feminist knowledge can effectively challenge the "objectivity" and "scientism" that help secure dominant forms of knowledge and the reproduction of women's social inequalities. However, the demands of persuasion leave little room for the critical investigation of feminist knowledge as a representational practice whose regulatory laws have their roots in post-Enlightenment humanism. Such an investigation would reveal that what makes feminist knowledge intelligible as knowledge is precisely what it conceals and excludes. For instance, learning to speak the feminist "I" invokes (at the same time as it refuses) its other, the female "I." The production of both categories of women—women and feminists—relies upon establishing and maintaining gender as a transcendental signifier, as the constitutive material of a core self (Butler 1991b). One effect of this is the persistence of the production of the categories of race, sex, and class as a second (and secondary) set of narratives. Thus, within feminist pedagogy, what I have been calling a minoritizing view takes shape both (1) in terms of masculinity and femininity and (2) in terms of race, sex, and class. These categories establish the framework within which difference can be imagined. But whether minoritizing views and the practices that sustain them turn on (1) or (2), what is forgotten is that none of these categories (and none of the identities which spring from them) exist outside social relations.

Radical feminist practices of minoritization refuse to consider the effects of racialization, sexualization, and class location upon gender intelligibility. This is because they refuse to take into account what Brown refers to as "the identificatory processes constitutive of one's social construction and position" (1995, 56). Radical feminist practices also refuse to acknowledge how female/feminist identity is rendered intelligible by what is excluded and named as "other." These dynamics are at work in student A's and student B's responses to lesbianism, but they often remain outside the frame of feminist interpretation. Thus, we might say that student A *rejects* lesbianism's relevance to Women's Studies because of her identity as a woman, even though it is precisely this "identity" which is at risk of becoming unintelligible to her; Student B, on the other hand, *embraces* lesbianism's relevance to Women's Studies because of her identity as a woman and, in so doing, is seen to be acting "authentically."

Self-identity, then, is an effect of the illusion that there exists a mimetic relationship between knowledge and identity, between what one knows and what one is. At the level of the individual, one effect of being in possession of feminist knowledge is that it may intensify narcissistic impulses to seek out sites of identification that serve to sustain a belief in identity as unitary, cohesive, and coherent—the ready-made subject armed with the "truth." When it comes to the staging of feminist knowledge as curriculum, discourses of minoritization sustain this illusion even as they are symptomatic of it.

But this illusion is constantly under threat from the "unthought," which may erupt and confuse both thought and identity. And it is the disavowal of this threat that gives resistance its power. For student A, the unthought is that heterosexuality conditions femininity and not the other way round; for student B, the unthought might be the possibility that being lesbian is an effect of identifications rather than a matter of identity. This fear of the unthought, which is for the most part lived unconsciously, is dynamic. As Peggy Phelan argues, "self-identity needs to be continually reproduced and reassured precisely because it fails to secure belief" (1993, 4). When feminist knowledge functions in this way a kind of psychic contentment prevails. Bad news (e.g., misogyny, sexism, etc.) can be tolerated if it meshes with women's experiences and offers release from self-blame. However, the investment in self-identity embedded in the promise of feminist knowledge "to deliver a satisfying and substantial real" (Phelan, 15) carries its own costs.

Marking Self-Identity and Its Other

It is precisely where processes of identification meet with, and are sustained by, confrontations between the self and the other that the costs of this particular binary opposition must be reckoned with. Phelan (1993) describes the reproduction of self and other in dominant social relations:

> One term of the binary is marked with social value, the other is unmarked. The male is marked with value; the female is unmarked, lacking measured value and meaning. Within this psycho-philosophical frame, cultural reproduction takes she who is unmarked and re-marks her, rhetorically and imagistically, while he who is marked with value is left unremarked, in discursive paradigms and visual fields. (5)

Not only does feminism attempt to invert this dominant binary opposition, it also creates its own categories of "marked" and "unmarked." Admittedly, feminist discourse has become extremely uncomfortable with its complicity in producing the White, heterosexual, middle-class woman as the category that is marked with value (and which is, thus, unremarkable). Yet its history as discourse and practice (and even the way in which it hears the demands of "subalterns" [see Patai and Koertge 1994]) produces and reproduces the mechanisms by which the other is "remarked," both rhetorically and imagistically. In this process, difference is reduced to the order of the same while self-identity struggles to recover its illusory coherence.

If we consider how the figure of the lesbian works within Women's Studies classrooms, the above dynamic becomes clearer. Again, our two students appear to be diametrically opposed. Student A refuses the difference of the lesbian and "remarks" that difference within a discourse of minoritization. Student B assumes a position within radical feminism; here, discourses of woman-identification, feminism, and lesbian feminism become indistinguishable from each other, and lesbian difference is once again refused. This is what Katie King warns about when she discusses how lesbianism came to function as "feminism's magical sign" during the late sixties and early seventies (1994).

King argues that the familiar axiom "feminism is the theory, lesbianism is the practice" was deployed in "a historical context in which lesbianism and feminism [were] not automatically assumed to be overlapping categories, and in which the phrase [was] being newly evolved in the women's movement to privilege lesbianism" (125). However, in her 1970 address to the New York Chapter of Daughters of Bilitis, Ti-Grace Atkinson, to whom the axiom has been attributed, apparently emphasized that lesbians and feminists belonged to different groups. Lesbians were a minority category of women who were in need of civil rights; feminists were adherents of feminism—a movement dedicated to political revolution. In fact, Atkinson argued *against* conflating feminism and lesbianism: "Feminism is a theory, but lesbianism is a practice" (Atkinson cited in King, 125).

The difference between feminism and lesbianism is significant, but not because of the presumed gap between theory and practice. The inaccurate but popularized version of Atkinson's quote, instead of ushering in a more universalizing discourse of sexuality that could hold onto the tensions between sexual practices and political identifications, reinstates a minoritizing view. In other words, had the original quote become institutionalized, lesbianism might have become "an issue of continuing determinative importance in the lives of people across the spectrum of sexualities" (Sedgwick 1990, 1) and, hence, a universalizing view of erotic identifications. However, what emerged instead, as gender developed into an analytic category that could encompass heterosexual women and lesbians in a common struggle against misogyny, was a dual claim: all women could be lesbians, and all lesbians could be women. According to King, this posed a new set of problems:

> Identifying with lesbianism falsely implies that one knows all about heterosexism and homophobia magically through identity or association. The "experience" of lesbianism is offered as salvation from the individual practice of heterosexism and homophobia and as the source of intuitive institutional and structural understanding of them. The power of lesbianism as a privileged signifier makes analysis of heterosexism and homophobia difficult, since it obscures the need for counter-intuitive challenges to ideology. (1994, 136)

King's assessment of the problems associated with the emergence of lesbianism as "feminism's magical sign" illuminates the problem of presuming that lesbian experience per se constitutes sufficient ground for a social and political critique. But her insights are also relevant to my discussion of the subject positions available within Women's Studies. The problem is that "the power of lesbianism as a privileged signifier" is by no means guaranteed but must repeatedly be invoked as a condition of "proper" feminist consciousness, whether or not women who call themselves "feminist" actually practice lesbian sex. But to identify with lesbianism as a privileged signifier within feminist discourse entails a dual and contradictory identification which involves (1) the acknowledgment that the lesbian is one of feminism's excluded others and (2) the acknowledgment that she is the apotheosis of the woman-identified woman.

For students who do not recognize themselves as lesbian, two identificatory positions are offered: (1) lesbians are women and (2) lesbianism is feminist sexuality. These two positions set the terms for the pedagogical demands associated with the claim that lesbianism should be represented within Women's Studies. Students can respond by either agreeing or disagreeing that the lesbian is oppressed first as a woman and second as a "sexual deviant." Both responses would be complicit with the pedagogical demands of Women's Studies, but the students who disagree would be doubly complicit in that they would affirm the teacher's assumption of their presumed homophobia.

The second position, that lesbianism is feminist sexuality, elaborates the feminist relationship between lesbian identity and woman-identification and returns us to student A and student B. First, there is student A's refusal to know lesbians. Her power to "remark" the lesbian is an effect of her dominant position within feminist discourse. This is true even though it is through engaging with feminist knowledge that the lesbian becomes visible and, to echo Sedgwick, a problem for feminism. It is true because feminist knowledge relies on gender as its primary category of analysis, and, as Butler argues, "the unity of gender is the effect of a regulatory practice that seeks to render gender identity uniform through a compulsory heterosexuality" (1990, 31). As long as gender functions as a transcendental category within feminism, heterosexual desire will continue to be normalized even as it contests its terms—a process which demands the production of its excluded other.

Student A's refusal to know, or know about, lesbians is an articulation of what she imagines to be the feminist subject—that is, heterosexual women. This conceptual ordering, itself an effect of the subject positions offered within Women's Studies, must exclude, as irrelevant to women, the category "lesbian." Her response, then, instantiates feminism's compulsory heterosexuality in the very moment that she enacts her own identity by identifying herself *against* an other. However, her response is not merely complicit with the terms of Women's Studies, it also reveals the "unthought"—the reliance on the ready-made subject. This is so whether the exclusion of the category "lesbian" is due to the lesbian being cast as the other within feminist discourse or whether it is due to the lesbian being cast as the privileged signifier of woman-identification. In either case, what cannot be engaged pedagogically within Women's Studies are the ways in which student A's exclusion of the category "lesbian" reinforces her own identity as natural and originary.

Student A's response to the sites of lesbian identification works to (re)assure her of her identity as a heterosexual woman even as it reveals what Butler calls "an incessant and panicked imitation of . . . naturalized idealization" (1991b, 23). But student B's response also characterizes a minoritizing view of lesbians. Unlike student A, whose self-identity depended upon the exclusion of the lesbian other, student B, to recall Phelan's terms, secures belief in her identity by identifying with both the textual representations of lesbians and the lesbian teacher who functioned as a "real" representative of the category "lesbian." Ostensibly, it is avowal of her lesbian identity that assures student B of her cohesive self. The pleasures of teaching and learning feminism are collapsed in this avowal because it secures her status as one who is willing to identify with the subject position of the lesbian as a privileged signifier for feminism. But this avowal turns out to be a disavowal when we consider that student B's self-identity is ensured by a representational visibility that frames lesbian identity as the natural and originary female identity. In other words, by staking a claim to feminism's "magical sign," student B is also taking a minoritizing position that assumes the existence of a ready-made subject.

By focusing on subject positions articulated within pedagogical practices rather than on outcomes, and by focusing on students' learning dynamics rather than on the directional pull of their responses, it becomes possible to read the narratives of both student A and student B as identificatory engagements with the subject position of the figure of the lesbian as it is constituted within Women's Studies. In spite of their differences, the two stories explored here share important structural features which tie them both to the lesbian as a contradictory signifier representing, on the one hand, a subject who has historically been excluded from dominant forms of feminist discourse and, on the other hand, a desexualized escape fantasy.

Introducing the topic of lesbianism into the Women's Studies curriculum is a thoroughly anxious undertaking caught between two tensions. The first tension concerns what to make of lesbian difference in the feminist classroom, where the terms of gender identity return sex to biology. The second tension concerns feminism's ambivalence about the meaning of lesbian identity. It is difficult to reconcile the desire to "remark" lesbian sexuality as the site of rebellion against patriarchal control with the desire to "remark" lesbian sexuality as the promise of love that knows no conflict, inequality, or, indeed, difference. In the latter instance, the lesbian becomes unmarked and, hence, "normalized" as White, middle-class, and asexual.

Earlier in this chapter, I argued that the pedagogical practices within introductory Women's Studies courses set the terms by which women may engage the question, "Can I recognize myself as a woman in this course?" My analysis of student A's and student B's respective responses to lesbianism suggests that the reply to this question cannot be adequately supplied by attempts to acknowledge social differences among women through curricular practices of representational inclusivity. What is too easily forgotten is that encounters between the self as such and representation as such cannot be reduced to scenes of recognition. Rather, such encounters set in motion psychic dynamics of identification—an ambivalent process of recognizing and recovering from the loss of the illusion that the self is a ready-made subject. Recovery, when it comes to student A and student B, is swift and decisive. Where student A finds her voice as a woman by repudiating the lesbian other, student B finds her voice by extolling the pleasures of lesbian representation. Both refuse to know anything about relationality or about how their respective positions entail implicating the other as "not-woman." Feminist practices of minoritization, to return to my earlier questions about what is at stake for women learning feminism, are provoked by viewing identity as "ready-made" and by viewing feminist knowledge as capable of revealing the "truth" about identities. And this, in turn, leads to the kind of responses provided by student A and student B. However, when these responses are read as evidence of a student's failure to achieve consciousness, we as feminists disavow our complicity in constructing/accepting a view of knowledge that has made such responses necessary. The questions we are left with concern both students and teachers: Can we imagine a feminist classroom in which everyone comes to appreciate the importance of studying how we are all implicated in the dynamics set in motion by our identificatory processes? Might the strange study of the dangers of recognition and the pleasures of misrecognition contribute to the possibility of creating feminist communities that exceed minoritizing world views?

Notes

1. These stories have been distilled from data explored in more depth in my doctoral dissertation, "Subjects in Tension: Engaged Resistance in the Feminist Classroom," completed July 1995.
2. A review of key anthologies published over the past decade (Bowles and Klein 1983; Bunch and Pollack 1983; Culley and Portuges 1985; Briskin and Coulter 1992; and Luke and Gore 1992) provides the basis for my discussion of the assumptions underpinning the development of Women's Studies in North American universities during the 1970s and 1980s. While the theoretical investigation of the dynamics of "learning feminism" has become increasingly inflected by the insights of feminist poststructural theories, writers such as Judith Butler, Donna Haraway, and Teresa de Lauretis (to name only a few) are generally considered too difficult for introductory courses. What I want to consider here concerns the pedagogical costs of treating feminist knowledge as a canon of important texts subject to feminist critique, with little concern for the identificatory processes involved.

References

Bogdan, D. 1994. "When Is a Singing School (Not) a Chorus? The Emancipatory Agenda in Feminist Pedagogy and Literature Education." In *The Education Feminist Reader*, edited by L. Stone. New York and London: Routledge.

Brennan, T. 1989. Introduction. In *Between Feminism and Psychoanalysis*. London and New York: Routledge.

Briskin, L., and R. Coulter. 1992. "Feminist Pedagogy: Challenging the Normative." *Canadian Journal of Education* 17 (3): 247–63.

Britzman, Deborah. 1995. "Is There a Queer Pedagogy? Or, Stop Reading Straight." *Educational Theory* 45 (2): 151–65.

Brown, W. 1995. *States of Injury: Power and Freedom in Late Modernity*. Princeton: Princeton University Press.

Bunch, C., and S. Pollack, eds. 1983. *Learning Our Way: Essays in Feminist Education*. Trumansberg, New York: Crossing Press.

Butler, J. 1990. *Gender Trouble: Feminism and the Subversion of Identity*. New York and London: Routledge.

———. 1991a. "Disorderly Women." *Transition* 53: 86–95.

———. 1991b. "Imitation and Gender Insubordination." In *Inside/Out: Lesbian Theories, Gay Theories*, edited by D. Fuss. New York and London: Routledge.

———. 1993. *Bodies that Matter: On the Discursive Limits of Sex*. New York and London: Routledge.

Cocks, J. 1989. *The Oppositional Imagination: Feminism, Critique and Political Theory*. London and New York: Routledge.

Culley, M., and C. Portuges, eds. 1985. *Gendered Subjects: The Dynamics of Feminist Teaching*. Boston and London: Routledge and Kegan Paul.

de Lauretis, T. 1987. *Technologies of Gender: Essays on Theory, Film and Fiction*. Bloomington and Indianapolis: Indiana University Press.

———. 1989. "The Essence of the Triangle or, Taking the Risk of Essentialism Seriously: Feminist Theory in Italy, the U.S. and Britain." *Differences: A Journal of Feminist Cultural Theory* 1 (2): 3–37.

Felman, S. 1987. *Jacques Lacan and the Adventure of Insight: Psychoanalysis in Contemporary Culture*. Cambridge, Massachusetts and London: Harvard University Press.

Gordon, L. 1986. "What's New in Women's History?" In *Feminist Studies/Critical Studies*, edited by T. de Lauretis. Bloomington: Indiana University Press.

King, K. 1994. "Lesbianism as Feminism's Magical Sign: Contests for Meaning and U.S. Women's Movements, 1968–1972." In *Theory in Its Feminist Travels: Conversations in U.S. Women's Movements*. Bloomington and Indianapolis: Indiana University Press.

Laplanche, J., and J.-B. Pontalis. 1973. *The Language of Psycho-Analysis*. Translated by D. Nicholson-Smith. New York and London: W.W. Norton.

Lather, P. 1991. *Getting Smart: Feminist Research and Pedagogy with/in the Postmodern*. New York and London: Routledge.

Lewis, M. 1990. "Interrupting Patriarchy: Politics, Resistance, and Transformation in the Feminist Classroom." *Harvard Educational Review* 60 (4): 468–88.

Luke, C., and J. Gore, eds. 1992. *Feminisms and Critical Pedagogy*. New York and London: Routledge.

Martindale, K. 1992. "Theorizing Autobiography and Materialist Feminist Pedagogy." *Canadian Journal of Education* 17 (3): 321–40.

Patai, D., and N. Koertge. 1994. *Professing Feminism: Cautionary Tales from the Strange World of Women's Studies*. New York: Basic Books.

Phelan, P. 1993. *Unmarked: The Politics of Performance.* New York and London: Routledge.

Riley, D. 1988. *Am I That Name? Feminism and the Category of "Women" in History.* Minneapolis: University of Minnesota Press.

Sedgwick, E. K. 1990. *Epistemology of the Closet.* Berkeley and Los Angeles: University of California Press.

Simon, R. 1992. *Teaching Against the Grain: Texts for a Pedagogy of Possibility.* New York, Westport, Connecticut and London: Bergin and Garvey.

Chapter Eight

Denial and Disclosure:
An Analysis of Selective Reality
in the Feminist Classroom

Patricia Elliot
Wilfrid Laurier University (Canada)

A year after taking the course that motivated me to write this paper, a student offered the following reflection on both her learning and her resistance to learning:

> It is very difficult to be a witness to your own life, to suddenly begin learning the subtle yet unmistakable ways in which a woman's life is guided by expectations, evaluations, and in many cases a lack of encouragement. These are factors that many of us, for a variety of reasons (usually the fear of truth and reality), choose to ignore.[1]

A better understanding of these unnamed factors and reasons seems to be required if teaching and learning about women's lives is to continue. Certainly, when one is faced, as I was, with an entire class of mostly women students who collectively "choose" to ignore precisely what the course is designed to examine, it is useful to have some idea of the dynamics that are in operation. My aim is not to pathologize women students who select what will count or be discounted as real, but to examine one instance of this process of selection in order to better understand and, I would hope, to interrupt its functioning.

What follows is an attempt to make sense of the apparently contradictory behavior that occurred in my class on gender and society, where the existence of gender inequality was repeatedly denied at the same time as women's personal experiences of abuse were readily disclosed. The coexistence of denial and disclosure struck me as odd, since one does not expect those who deny the oppression of women to offer personal examples of such oppression. Recent studies show that people are likely to grant the existence of oppression generally and then to deny any personal disadvantage that might be their lot as members of an oppressed group. Faye Crosby et al. (1989, 80) claim that "Women, as the victims of sex discrimination, tend to imagine, ostrich-like, a personal exemption from the rule of general sex bias that they know to operate in society." In my class, something else was happening. In theorizing what that might be, I draw on both feminist pedagogy and psychoanalytic theory.

My specific interest here is to examine how the fantasy of gender equality may have affected, or even produced, the kind of denial and disclosure that took place in the class. By "fantasy" I mean a representation *distorted* by cultural or personal defense mechanisms. The fantasy of gender equality is *not* the dream or the ideal of a non-hierarchical, non-oppressive world—it is the delusive idea that parity between the sexes has already been achieved. Whether or not feminists identify equality as the ultimate goal need not concern us here. The point is that the collective work required for achieving feminist goals, or for transforming the status quo, cannot be pursued by those who believe we already inhabit a non-oppressive society.

In the first part of my discussion, I explain Gloria Anzaldúa's (1990) concept of selective reality—a concept I find helpful in describing the kind of collective neurosis in which we participate when confronted with structures of oppression we prefer not to acknowledge. Next, I analyze resistance (as it occurred in my gender class) as an example of the practice of selective reality. My students were unable to entertain the possibility that systemic gender inequity exists, even though a high percentage of them (approximately seventeen percent) disclosed personal instances of abuse. I argue that their collective insistence on the fantasy of gender equality, plus their reluctance to consider any evidence to the contrary, constitutes a striking example of resistance.[2] Following Shoshana Felman (1987) and Jacques Lacan (1981), Gregory Jay (1987) suggests that what students resist knowing forms a structure or set of investments belonging to the "pedagogical unconscious." The last part of my discussion explores Jay's proposal to develop a pedagogy of the unconscious. Like Paulo Freire's (1970) pedagogy of the oppressed, Jay proposes a critical practice aimed at subverting selective reality. This pedagogical practice will be examined in light of recent feminist criticisms of, and contributions to, pedagogical theory.

I first encountered the concept of selective reality in the work of Anzaldúa, who describes it as "the narrow spectrum of reality that human beings select or choose to perceive and/or what their culture 'selects' for them to 'see.'" She also points out that "perception is an interpretive process conditioned by education," that selective reality is not rooted in individual incapacity (a popular liberal assumption) but is learned through a process of education and acculturation (Anzaldúa 1990, xxi). Perhaps more dangerous than a conscious belief in racial or gender superiority, selective reality is the practice of limiting or selecting what sorts of things are counted as real and what sorts of things are discounted, omitted, or relegated to the realm of the imaginary. It is not a conscious process, but it *is* political, for, as Drucilla Cornell (1993, 194) points out, politics is "not just about power but also about the very basis of what can become 'real' and thus accessible to consciousness and change."

Like the concept of ideology, the concept of selective reality helps us to understand the failure to perceive social inequalities based on class, race, or gender. Such failure cannot simply be written off as "false consciousness" concerning one's true interest (economic or otherwise); rather, the practice of selective reality appears to be based on the mobilization and normalization of powerful defense mechanisms that are very difficult (and very painful) for individuals to undo. Why do we systematically distort particular sorts of ideas and events? How does our culture (and our subcultures) come to view defensive responses as normal and expected rather than as harmful or unacceptable? What is the relationship between the degree of (repressed) pain and the tendency to distort through denial, projection, reversal, and so on? If defense mechanisms are to be successfully dismantled, then we must come to understand the ways in which they work, including the means by which they become "normal." In what follows, I examine how the defense of denial functions to maintain a patriarchal reality.

The piece of selective reality operative in my classroom is the widely shared belief that North American society has now achieved gender equality. This relatively recent perception of equality contributes as much to the maintenance of a patriarchal social order as did earlier perceptions of women as naturally inferior to men, for, by definition, it ensures that any attempt to transform the existing social order will be regarded as either superfluous or absurd.[3]

My purpose here is not to document how the belief in equality is produced; this would require a different sort of study. Rather, drawing on my own teaching experience, I attempt to demonstrate the existence and effects of a particular piece of selective reality. It is clear that one way of generating a (false) belief in gender equality, both inside and outside educational institutions, is through the routine dismissal of any contrary evidence. Instances of such dismissal are plentiful. For example, instructors who draw attention to oppressive gender norms, practices, or structures are often construed as hopelessly biased, and the credibility of their sources of information is regularly disputed by students, by colleagues, and by the media.[4] Both inside and outside the classroom, feminism serves as a scapegoat for what is wrong with society and, especially, for the interruption of previously uncontested privilege.[5] Young women fear social rejection should they identify themselves as feminists. Numerous anti-feminist articles and books appearing in, or reviewed by, "respected" national and international publications cast aspersions on the concept of women's oppression.[6] One effect of this negative media attention is that masculinist professors are able, with impunity, to castigate feminism as a violent social movement (as, recently, did one of my "humanist" colleagues).[7] What is violent, of course (aside from the numerous and increasingly well-documented instances of male violence against women), is the denial of inequality that sustains the practice of selective reality and that prevents wider participation in transformative gender politics.[8]

My own encounter with selective reality in the classroom demonstrated that engaging in transformative gender politics was a clear impossibility, an affront to my students' expectations that the course support the fantasy of equality. As one disgruntled student wrote, "Today, men are raised to respect and care for women. This respect is seen in the repeated tenderness and pleasing mannerisms expressed by the male gender." This is a clear example of an instance in which an idealized fantasy stands in for an unacceptable reality—an instance of what Phebe Cramer (1991, 216) calls "maximizing the positive." This student expressed what many others probably felt about the suggestion that gender relations were less than ideal.

From feminist pedagogical literature and previous experience, I had learned that what Paulo Freire and Ira Shor (1987) call "teaching for liberation" is more challenging and more likely to be challenged than is teaching that supports the status quo. As Margo Culley (1985) suggests, such challenges may be intensified when the instructor is female. But nothing prepared me for my students' collective rejection of self-knowledge, experience (theirs), and empowerment in favor of miracle, mystery, and authority. They sided with selective reality, the Grand Inquisitor of our classroom, subjecting the course texts (and, by implication, myself) to thinly veiled contempt. Not thinly veiled, or not veiled at all, were frequent disclosures of their own experiences of abuse, which were immediately personalized so as not to be seen as supporting a general theory of male violence or gender inequity. Indeed, painful experiences were used to justify refusing any sociological explanations of violence against women. This point requires elaboration.

What happens or fails to happen in the feminist classroom depends, among other things, on the degree of trust developed between teachers and students as well as among students themselves. In our class the degree of trust was small, partly due to a confrontation that occurred early on in the course between myself and a male graduate student who was so openly contemptuous of my feminist perspective that he voluntarily left the course. Students who knew I did not share his (culturally dominant) beliefs may have shared his contempt without having the opportunity to drop the course. Maybe they felt they would be unable to disagree with my views and therefore unable to present their own (although I had tried to be patient with the male student and to shift discussion to the question of what counts as evidence). In any case, the atmosphere was tense and not conducive to disclosing intimate details of one's personal life. In such an atmosphere, painful experiences were announced as a kind of challenge, as if any attempt to theorize them, or to read them as examples of more widespread abuse, would be either insulting or simply too painful to endure. As a result, these disclosures had a powerful silencing effect on the class.[9] When women enlist the disclosure of painful experiences in an attempt to derail class discussion, it is clearly a desperate measure—one with which any sympathetic person complies. In our class, such derailments were always successful.[10]

During the first half of the twelve-week course, I was often annoyed that this group of students failed to engage in any positive way with material that students in previous years had found stimulating. During this time, I secretly blamed them for what I took to be an unwillingness to engage, even in a negative way, with the course material. Particularly frustrating was finding myself backed into a conservative pedagogical corner where much of my energy was directed towards the negative goal of not antagonizing the students. (Like other untenured feminist instructors, I felt that it would be too dangerous to risk student complaints about my class.) Although I attempted several times to elicit discussion about what they did not want to know and why they did not want to know it, no explicit answers were forthcoming.[11] Clearly, something very peculiar was happening here!

Towards the end of the course, and immediately thereafter, I blamed myself for what I perceived to be a pedagogical failure. A perceptive essay by Amanda Konradi (1993) on the difficulties of teaching issues of sexual abuse led me to suspect that my insufficient sensitivity to students' painful experiences may have contributed to their reluctance to discuss the gendered nature of violence. As critical and feminist pedagogy demonstrates, learning about oppression evokes strong emotional responses—responses ranging from guilt and shame to anger and despair (Tatum 1992, 2). The way these emotions are addressed may be decisive in either fostering or thwarting what Culley describes as "the passage from denial and resistance, to anger, to affirmation and change" (1985, 215). Underestimating the nature or degree of these emotional responses, themselves perhaps a measure of the threatening experience of having one's interpretation of reality challenged, will most likely strengthen students' resistance to learning. What one ought to do, according to Konradi, is to presuppose the pain that discussions of violence (or, for that matter, of any form of oppression) inevitably arouse. Some of the strategies she suggests are: specifying in advance which topics will be addressed; including essays on how women combat oppression;

acknowledging the pain that will surface; listing local support services on the board; emphasizing the importance of feelings; discussing the silences; and agreeing on appropriate language. I now believe that my failure to anticipate and to acknowledge the pain that was present contributed to the students' inability (as opposed to unwillingness) to move away from denial and resistance. Moreover, my insufficient sensitivity may have enabled them to mobilize their pain against any effort to contextualize it. This brings me to the questions of how resistance in my classroom worked and what can be learned from it.

Teaching the gender course taught me what Shoshana Felman already knew, that "teaching, like analysis, has to deal not so much with lack of knowledge as with resistance to knowledge" (1987, 79). As resistance to knowing, ignorance is neither passive nor innocent, although it may well be unconscious. Felman claims that this kind of ignorance is not "opposed to knowledge: it is itself a radical condition, an integral part of the very structure of knowledge" (78).

A second-year student illustrates how this form of ignorance obstructs knowledge—in this case, knowledge of rape:

> Rape is a subject I am very uncomfortable with. Unfortunately for me, I tend to ignore the subject of rape altogether by falling into the category of "it won't happen to me." . . . I was under the impression that rapists were psychopaths who lurked in the dark alleys of lower-class neighbourhoods.

Obviously, this comment reflects a transition in the student's thought from an earlier to a subsequent (revised) understanding of rape. Insofar as she imagines herself inviolable (minimizing the danger), this student saves herself the pain both of empathizing with women who have been raped and of being concerned about her own safety. The ignorance that had previously appeared fortunate to her was, by this point in the course, being questioned and reinterpreted as unfortunate. She was becoming aware of what she had excluded (the entire subject of rape)—an exclusion that allowed her to sustain classist and other stereotypes. The media reinforce such stereotypes (witness the reporting of the Montreal massacre) by legitimizing the exclusion of alternative voices—in this case feminist voices.[12] What this student did not recognize was that her tendency to ignore the subject of rape signified, not passive acquiescence to dominant misconceptions (which could have been relinquished if proven inaccurate), but what Felman calls "an active dynamic of negation" (1987, 79).

According to some psychoanalytic theorists, the active dynamic of negation, or denial, is the basis of all defense mechanisms, including the defense of denial itself (Blum 1985, 8). Defense mechanisms are theoretical abstractions that "denote a way of functioning of the mind" and that serve "to ward off full conscious awareness and verbalization of warded off thoughts and feelings" (Blum 1985, 12; Wallerstein 1985, 222). Examples of these defense mechanisms were plentiful in my class, particularly in students' written work. With reference to a course reading that dispelled the myth that women are responsible for sexual assault, one woman wrote: "Taking into consideration how boring the article was, I found [X's] ideas to be very enlightening." In this case, the experience of enlightenment is distorted through reversal by the claim that the article was boring. Two pages later, the student disclosed her own (previously held) feeling of responsibility for a sexual assault she had survived. Another example of denial occurred with reference to the argument that sex and gender are not synonymous. "Recognizing the differences between sex and gender is one thing," this student wrote, "accepting the difference is quite another." At issue here is not a total denial of reality (of perceived differences) but a reluctance to accept it, and this suggests the preference for some alternative version of reality. Another student described her response to ideas that countered her optimistic beliefs as "a reluctance to agree that stereotypes and discriminatory messages were portrayed in a society as 'advanced' as ours."

In these examples, an alternative, idealized fantasy is imposed on reality so that the latter appears to be untrue. According to Phebe Cramer (1991, 38), when this form of denial predominates, "real events are . . . recognized only insofar as they conform to the fantasy." Furthermore, she claims that the imposition of an idealized fantasy on reality is "the most highly developed, mature form of denial: The denial occurs not in terms of a failure to perceive what is there, but rather in an imposition of a highly personalized interpretation of what the perceived events mean. The meaning is distorted to make it more pleasant" (Cramer 1991, 52). I contend that when we have large numbers of people colluding in a fantasy (e.g., only psychopaths rape), then, as Cramer claims, the fantasy *does* "come to exist as an alternative reality" (38). This is what I have called selective reality, and it is based on a collective, not on an individual, interpretation. While it is clear that, as Cramer asserts, "fantasies serve denial," it is also true that once fantasy has been accepted as reality, denial is required to keep the fantasized reality in place. As I discovered in my class, challenges to fantasized reality were immediately and strenuously resisted through a process that now merits further discussion.

Psychoanalyst Leo Rangell helpfully points out that defense and resistance occur both in psychoanalysis and in life. It is not surprising, then, to discover them in classrooms where new insights threaten to disturb well-established defenses. Because the unexpected removal of defense leads to the emergence of anxiety, it, too, must be defended against. Hence, resistance is "a defense against the undoing of a defense," or, more simply, "resistance is a defense against insight" (Rangell 1985, 150, 147).

Whether in the classroom or in analysis, the encounter with resistance indicates that some unacceptable ideas are being defended against. In my class, inquiring into the causes of resistance simply served to strengthen it and to make me (temporarily) the object of hostility. One response to an early inquiry into the non-engagement of the class with a reading was, "I don't see why we have to think about gender here"—a rather astonishing comment to make in a class on gender! Having thus encountered the unconscious desire not to know, and having unwittingly increased the resistance to knowing, I have to admit I lost hope of stimulating anything other than intense hostility. An unspoken truce seemed to be reached when I gave up trying to remove the collective resistance to knowing, and the students agreed not to undermine me and/or the course through either formal complaints or through simply refusing to speak in class. In analysis, the failure to analyze resistance would be fatal to the healing process; but in our classroom the compromise, while fatal to any liberatory learning, did allow some students to engage with the material to some extent. It is not my intention to defend what was clearly a botched pedagogical experience but, rather, to reflect on how one might work with, around, or through resistance.

One way to address what Lacan (cited in Felman 1987, 79) has called "the passion for ignorance," a passion we often share with our students, is to develop a "pedagogy of the unconscious" (Jay 1987, 790). Developing such a pedagogy strikes me as a difficult project, but it also strikes me as more constructive than the compromise route I took with my class. In what follows, I offer a few theoretical reflections on some of the issues a pedagogy of the unconscious needs to address.

In *Sisters of the Yam: Black Women and Self-Recovery* (1993, 20) bell hooks writes that, in a culture of domination, lying is not only "an acceptable social norm," it is also required. Although I would not equate lying with selective reality per se, if one is raised, as hooks claims Black children often are, "to believe that it is more important how things seem than the way they really are," then one is being "taught to exist in a state of denial." The determination of "how things really are" is, of course, problematic and contestable. But hooks points out that what is denied in this process are not only structures of domination but also feelings, experience, and the capacity to define one's own needs and desires (1993, 24). As I understand it, developing a pedagogy of the unconscious is not about forcing people to "face reality" but about undoing the mechanism of denial (or other defense mechanisms) that distorts our perceptions and our ability to think and to feel. With hooks, I believe that to accept these distortions as "normal" is to forfeit the ability to critique and to transform them. Like the psychoanalytic process, this pedagogical process does not produce the "Truth," but it *does* produce the courage to speak a little more truthfully about our lives. There are costs involved, but there are also rewards.

Practical suggestions for facilitating a classroom environment conducive to discussing potential or actual resistances can be found in the work of Konradi (1993) and Magda Lewis (1990, 1993). Konradi advocates addressing students' silences and engaging them in examining the learning process. According to Magda Lewis (1990, 473), any feminist pedagogy must "address the threat to women's survival and livelihood that a critique of patriarchy in its varied manifestations confronts." Like hooks, Lewis suggests that defensive behaviors once were, and may continue to be, a requirement for survival. She points out that, given the very real dangers involved in challenging dominant beliefs, fear is a reasonable response to challenges directed at the personal and political context of the social reality one inhabits. The relationship between fear and critique is elaborated by Joe Cheng (1993), a graduate student whose contribution to a lengthy e-mail discussion of classroom resistance is worth repeating:

> Students reject critical thinking . . . at quite a visceral level because they already realize, live the fact, that critical thinking is already political action. Since political actions can be life-endangering, they are hesitant to proceed until they know more or less how doing that thinking is going to affect the particular political constellation of their own particular lives.

Cheng's understanding of this visceral response is borne out by my students, one of whom reported that reading an essay on rape made her "cringe." Another student, who blamed herself for a recent sexual assault, wrote: "I found myself upset and frustrated at how society has somehow convinced so many women that they are to be submissive and respectful to men while men are to be in total control of themselves as well as other women."

Perhaps more frightening than the memories of abuse many of my students were willing to disclose was the idea that such violence is widespread and condoned. At least for these students, what appeared to be intolerable was the *systemic* nature of violence, defined by Cynthia Cockburn (1991, 6) as "not casual but structured, not local but extensive, not transitory but stable, with a tendency to self-reproduction." After reading about the role of the media in reinforcing misogynist views of women, another student confided her "reluctance to agree that stereotypes and discriminatory messages . . . could merge together to form accepted sets of values." Although this student recognized, at some level, the existence of such values, she withheld her acknowledgment, "hoping (as much as believing) that these terms did not exist, nor apply to me, in today's society." Whereas "seeing is believing" is the slogan of the naive realist, "hoping is believing" is the mantra of those who have learned to deny. Acknowledging the existence of systemic inequality would have obliged this student to rethink her own position in the world as well as her relationship to others. As Cheng points out, students are hesitant to embrace critical thinking, not because they are incapable of it, but because it "always precipitates a crisis, large or small, in our personal lives, and in our socio-cultural-sexual-economic-political positioning."

Lewis insists that the threat to women's sense of well-being must be addressed and validated as a way of making sense of widespread resistance to feminism:

> We cannot expect that students will readily appropriate a political stance that is truly counter-hegemonic, unless we also acknowledge the ways in which our feminist practice/politics *creates*, rather than amelio-rates, feelings of threat: the threat of abandonment; the threat of having to struggle within unequal power relations; the threat of psychologi-cal/social/sexual, as well as economic and political marginality; the threat of retributive violence—threats lived in concrete embodied ways. (1990, 485)

Upon considering Lewis's work, I conclude that attention to the unconscious dynamics operating in any feminist classroom is required, whether we wish to call this a pedagogy of the unconscious or something else. Insofar as con-cerns about emotional, intellectual, and physical safety are, as Lewis points out, inevitably raised whenever one is functioning within a feminist context, we must anticipate and address them. Lewis's strategy of politicizing class-room dynamics as well as class content seems to be an excellent one, since the social relations feminists critique are reproduced in the classroom itself. Especially relevant to my experience of unconscious classroom dynamics are her suggestions of (1) "attending to the ways in which women have been required historically to invest in particular and often contradictory practices in order to ensure their own survival" and (2) "treating women's resistance to feminism as an active discourse of struggle derived from a complex set of meanings in which women's practices are invested" (486).

According to Jay, the task of the instructor is to learn about the uncon-scious knowledge of the students by paying attention to the silences (what they cannot say) and the contradictions (what they say but cannot acknowl-edge). The purpose of learning from students about their unconscious knowledge is to reveal to them contradictions and silences that they may then explore.

Jay has this pedagogical procedure in mind when he advocates "the bringing to discourse of unconscious thoughts [as] the teacher's primary task" (1987, 789). As I understand him, instructors can offer their students three things: (1) we can offer them tools for understanding individual and cultural defenses, but we cannot provide the understanding itself; (2) we can offer them questions that probe the identity they wish to protect, but we cannot create a new identity for them; and (3) we can offer them methods for exposing dominant values and beliefs, but we cannot impose our preferences on them. It is hoped that, through participating in a pedagogy of the unconscious, students will develop a passion for interpretation that will take precedence over a passion for ignorance. This involves developing (1) an ability to identify the values and beliefs upon which their interpretations of reality rest and (2) the trust required for engaging others in productive discussion concerning conflicting interpretations.

The question of how to address conflicting interpretations accompanies any pedagogical theory. According to Chandra T. Mohanty (1990, 185), a more comprehensive view of reality would include "uncovering and reclaiming subjugated knowledges," a process that is blocked by the kind of resistance I have been discussing.[13] I find Mohanty's (1990, 185) call for "self-conscious engagement with dominant normative discourses and . . . the active creation of oppositional analytic and cultural spaces" more persuasive than those pedagogies that simply ask students to locate themselves within a given discourse. As my class demonstrated, however, there can be no "self-conscious engagement" with dominant discourses until the unconscious resistance to insight has been addressed and overcome.

Finally, it is easy to see why education is one of what Freud considered the "impossible" professions. Recent and future cutbacks to education may make it increasingly difficult to address the pedagogical unconscious and to confront the resistance that serves as a defense against insight. This will affect both anti-oppression teachers (who will no doubt feel an intensification of backlash) and students (whose learning experience will be limited). Students like those in my gender course may continue to imagine they are strong, independent, and inviolable; but they will do so only on the condition that they deny their own life histories, especially any awareness of weakness, dependency, or violation. To imagine one might gain strength through denying weakness is to participate in an elaborate and dangerous myth—a myth that has often been used to establish the (alleged) superiority of men. But neither men nor my women students have been able to acquire the strength and independence they desire by denying the existence of contrary qualities and experiences. This brings me back to Lewis's reading of resistance to feminism as an active form of struggle and, thus, to the question of hope.

According to Rangell (1985, 156), an ambivalence lies at the heart of resistance, and this ambivalence involves a struggle between insight and the blocking of insight: "Resistance . . . is a defense against insight, which is reacted to as a threat as well as a hope." I want to emphasize this claim that resistance involves both fear *and* hope. My analysis has focused on the fearful or threatening motives for resistance that led to the maintenance of selective reality in my class. The denial of women's subordination functioned, as Rangell (1985, 169) claims all successful defenses do, as a guard against anxiety and conflict, and it also worked to preserve a particular self-image. However, the hope engaged by resistance is not located in a fantasized, positive self-image but in the possibility that the insight it defends against might become conscious. The hope is not that some unbearable truth about ourselves will continue to be covered up, but that it will be recognized; the fear is that such recognition will be overwhelming. The desire for insight signifies hope for a different way of being, one that is based on self-knowledge instead of self-deception, affirmation of experience instead of denial, and self-empowerment through the exercise of creativity and awareness instead of conformity to the selective reality of the status quo.

I now believe those disturbing disclosures that took place in my classroom can be understood as signifiers of hope, as indicative of my students' desire to reclaim their ability to think, to feel, and to name their own experiences. The periodic eruption of these disclosures during the course signified that the conscious belief that women are not oppressed was repeatedly being contradicted by an unconscious testimony to the contrary. Students' resistance to feminism was thus highly ambivalent; and this ambivalence, so difficult to read, was evident in the coexistence of denial and disclosure, in the refusal to acknowledge male violence, and in the personal stories of abuse. Interpreting this ambivalence correctly when it happened might have produced a better learning experience for everyone. In retrospect, I see these disclosures as gestures of solidarity, not so much with me, as with the idea that violence and inequality *do* exist and, thus, with the hope that they will be recognized by others and collectively combatted.

Acknowledgments

I would like to thank Linda Briskin, Susan Heald, Amanda Konradi, and Janice Williamson for pointing me towards useful sources for this study; Linda Briskin, Amy Graham, Kate McKenna, and Allison Nyiri for providing helpful comments on an earlier draft; and Norma Jean Profitt for contributing insight and enthusiasm and for discussing various feminist texts with me. A shorter version of this paper was presented at the Canadian Women's Studies Association, The University of Calgary, 8 June 1994. An earlier version has been published in *Resources for Feminist Research* 24

(Spring/Summer 1995). Research funding from Wilfrid Laurier University is gratefully acknowledged.

Notes

1. Permission to quote anonymously from this student and others was obtained after the course was over. The expression "choose to ignore" is a euphemism for denial, the dynamics of which this paper explores.

2. I am using the concept of resistance in the psychoanalytic sense to account for compliance with the status quo, rather than in the popularized Foucauldian sense where resistance signifies a way of refusing the normalizing power of the status quo. Why this group of students responded differently than did previous groups is not a question I can speculate on in the absence of relevant data concerning age, race, class, sexuality, religion, and so on.

3. I say "relatively recent" because, as historians of feminism have pointed out (Jackson 1989), the perception of equality appears to emerge whenever it can be employed to silence contrary claims.

4. A good example of numerous strategies of dismissal by male faculty can be found in Susan Hardy Aiken et al. (1987). Nancy J. Davis (1992) persuasively argues that the media and political discourse both serve to undermine the existence of systemic inequality. Margo Culley (1985) suggests challenges to feminist knowledge are also challenges to female authority. This may be the case, but I suspect the issue is more complex. For recent Canadian examples see *The Chilly Collective* (1995).

5. In a contribution to public debate on this issue, librarian Alan Rutkowski (1994, A24) notes that "the simple proposition that women should be equal seems to have awakened in many a passionate concern for inter-gender fairness and justice that remained dormant so long as male dominance was unquestioned."

6. Four recent examples are Amy Friedman (1992), Wendy Kaminer (1993), Karen Lehrman (1993), and Katherine Roiphe (1993). A recent issue of *The Women's Review of Books* (vol. 11, February 1994, 7–17) is dedicated to responding to some of these attacks.

7. By contrast, mathematics professor Matin Yaqzan's dismissal of date rape as a predictable inconvenience was not well received by the Canadian media, although his views were deemed publishable by the University of New Brunswick's student newspaper, *The Brunswickian* (5 November 1993).

8. In November 1993, Statistics Canada released the results of its comprehensive survey of violence against women, a survey that confirmed feminist claims that sexual assault is endemic. *The Globe and Mail* found the news that "50% of women report assaults" shocking enough to make it a front page headline (Alanna Mitchell, *The Globe and Mail* [Toronto], 19 November 1993, A1).

9. These disclosures were made mostly in seminar groups consisting of 15 to 20 students, not in the "lecture" sessions consisting of 40 students. Even so, the

seminar groups were the most tension-ridden, particularly since they were designed for discussion and critique.

10. One of my readers suggested that these discussions may have been hijacked instead of merely derailed. I do not believe the disclosures were premeditated, as a hijacking implies. In fact, I now believe they were not consciously intended at all.

11. In the smaller seminar groups where the tension and/or silence was obvious, I invited students to discuss with me possible reasons for this. I also encouraged them to address problems they might have with the readings or with the way the course was being taught. I asked my teaching assistant to do the same. It soon became apparent, however, that drawing attention to the atmosphere only made it worse. No one responded in class to these invitations, and two students who consulted me privately said they didn't understand why this class was having the negative effect that it was.

12. On 6 December 1989, fourteen women were massacred at the Université de Montréal by a misogynist whose anti-feminism was systematically downplayed in the media. For various accounts see Louise Malette and Marie Chalouh (1991). Magda Lewis (1990, 468) discusses this incident in the context of resistance to feminism in the classroom.

13. The psychoanalytic concept of resistance does not imply passivity, but it should not be confused with a conscious refusal of the status quo. As a mechanism that distances us from our feelings or that prevents us from knowing how we feel, resistance may be necessary to feeling safe, but it is not necessarily a politically progressive mechanism.

References

Aiken, S. H., K. Anderson, M. Dinnerstein, J. Lensink, and P. Maccorquodale. 1987. "Trying Transformations: Curriculum Integration and the Problem of Resistance." *Signs* 12: 255–75.

Anzaldua, G., ed. 1990. *Making Face, Making Soul/Haciendo Caras: Creative and Critical Perspectives by Women of Color.* San Francisco: Aunt Lute Foundation.

Blum, H. P., ed. 1985. *Defense and Resistance: Historical Perspectives and Current Concepts.* New York: International Universities Press.

Briskin, L. 1990. "Feminist Pedagogy: Teaching and Learning Liberation." Feminist Perspectives Paper No. 19. Ottawa: CRIAW/ICREF.

Cheng, J. 1993. Contribution to "Resistance in the Classroom," Women's Studies List, April 29.

The Chilly Collective, eds. 1995. *Breaking Anonymity: The Chilly Climate for Women Faculty.* Waterloo: Wilfrid Laurier.

Cockburn, C. 1991. *In the Way of Women: Men's Resistance to Sex Equality in Organizations.* Ithaca: ILR Press.

Cornell, D. 1993. *Transformations: Recollective Imagination and Sexual Difference.* New York: Routledge.

Cramer, P. 1991. *The Development of Defense Mechanisms.* New York: Springer-Verlag.

Crosby, F. J., A. Pufall, R. C. Snyder, M. O'Connell, and P. Whalen. 1989. "The Denial of Personal Disadvantage Among You, Me, and All the Other Ostriches." In *Gender and Thought,* edited by M. Crawford and M. Gentry, 79–99. New York: Springer-Verlag.

Culley, M. 1985. "Anger and Authority in the Introductory Women's Studies Classroom." In *Gendered Subjects: The Dynamics of Feminist Teaching,* edited by M. Culley and C. Portuges, 209–17. Boston and London: Routledge and Kegan Paul.

Culley, M., and C. Portuges, eds. 1985. *Gendered Subjects: The Dynamics of Feminist Teaching.* Boston and London: Routledge and Kegan Paul.

Davis, N. J. 1992. "Teaching About Inequality: Student Resistance, Paralysis, and Rage." *Teaching Sociology* 20 (July): 232–38.

Ellsworth, E. 1989. "Why Doesn't This Feel Empowering? Working Through the Repressive Myths of Critical Pedagogy." *Harvard Educational Review* 59 (August): 297–323.

Felman, S. 1987. *Jacques Lacan and the Adventure of Insight.* Cambridge: Harvard University Press.

Freire, P. 1970. *Pedagogy of the Oppressed.* New York: Seabury.

Freire, P., and I. Shor. 1987. *A Pedagogy for Liberation.* South Hadley, Massachusetts: Bergin and Garvey.

Freud, S. 1979. "The Loss of Reality in Neurosis and Psychosis. In *On Psychopathology,* edited by A. Richards, 219–26. Harmondsworth: Penguin.

Friedman, A. 1992. *Nothing Sacred: A Conversation with Feminism.* Ottawa: Oberon.

hooks, b. 1993. *Sisters of the Yam: Black Women and Self-Recovery.* Toronto: Between the Lines.

Jackson, M. 1989. "Sexuality and Struggle: Feminism, Sexology and the Social Construction of Sexuality." In *Learning Our Lines: Sexuality and Social Control in Education,* edited by C. Jones and C. P. Mahony, 1–22. London: Women's Press.

Jay, G. S. 1987. "The Subject of Pedagogy: Lessons in Psychoanalysis and Politics." *College English* 49 (November): 785–800.

Kaminer, W. 1993. "Feminism's Identity Crisis." *Atlantic* 272 (October): 51.

Konradi, A. 1993. "Teaching About Sexual Assault: Problematic Silences and Solutions." *Teaching Sociology* 21 (January): 14–26.

Lacan, J. 1981. *The Four Fundamental Concepts of Psycho-Analysis.* Edited by J. Miller, translated by A. Sheridan. New York: W.W. Norton.

Lehrman, K. 1993. "Off Course." *Mother Jones* (September/October), p. 45.

Lewis, M. 1990. "Interrupting Patriarchy: Politics, Resistance, and Transformation in the Feminist Classroom." *Harvard Educational Review* 60 (November): 467–88.

———. 1993. *Without a Word: Teaching Beyond Women's Silence.* New York: Routledge.

Malette, L., and M. Chalouh, eds. 1991. *The Montreal Massacre.* Translated by Marlene Wildeman. Charlottetown: gynergy.

Mohanty, C.T. 1990. "On Race and Voice: Challenges for Liberal Education in the 1990s." *Cultural Critique* 14: 179–208.

Rangell, L. 1985. "Defense and Resistance in Psychoanalysis and Life." In *Defense and Resistance: Historical Perspectives and Current Concepts*, edited by H. Blum, 147–73. New York: International Universities Press.

Roiphe, K. 1993. *The Morning After: Sex, Fear, and Feminism on Campus.* New York: Little, Brown.

Rutkowski, A. 1994. "Feminism Offers the Labour Movement a Future." *The Globe and Mail* (Toronto), 4 May, A24.

Tatum, B. D. 1992. "Talking About Race, Learning About Racism: The Application of Racial Identity Development Theory in the Classroom." *Harvard Educational Review* 62 (Spring): 1–24.

Wallerstein, R. 1985. "Defenses, Defense Mechanisms, and the Structure of the Mind." In *Defense and Resistance: Historical Perspectives and Current Concepts*, edited by H. Blum, 201–25. New York: International Universities Press.

Part III

Shifting Courses, Directions and Policies: Out from the Ghetto of Pedagogy

Chapter Nine

Report and Repression: Textual Hazards for Feminists in the Academy

Dorothy E. Smith
Ontario Institute for Studies in Education (Canada)

This paper addresses the interaction of two texts at a juncture between two discourses: a feminist discourse critical of the academy, epitomized in the concept of a 'chilly climate' for women; and a juridical discourse, extending a quasi-legal language into the institutional setting of the academy and, in this instance, deployed by male faculty to force the withdrawal of a critical feminist review of their department.[1] These two texts are a sequence, the first a report, written by a committee chaired by Professor Somer Brodribb, a junior faculty member in the Department of Political Science at the University of Victoria and addressed to that Department; the second a letter from eight male tenured faculty members of the same department demanding from the junior faculty member an apology for and retraction of certain aspects of the report that they held to have impugned their reputations. These two texts opened debates and controversies, reviews and reports, and were fed into formal and informal networks in the academic community, in the women's movement in Canada and beyond, in networks among political scientists in Canada, and, very rapidly, into the discourses of the public sphere: news media, newspaper columns, and so forth.

My interest in examining these texts comes in part from a concern with the increasingly pervasive attacks in public discourse—in the news media and in books—aimed at repressing the advances that the university has made toward being more inclusive of gender, racial, and cultural difference, and a diversity of voices (Richer and Weir 1995). The letter in which the male faculty responded to the critical report from feminists in the University of Victoria's Department of Political Science adopted a juridical stance, using the language of allegations, charges, evidence, and so on. The same juridical discourse organizes debates in the public media reporting or commenting on similar controversies at this or other universities: faculty unjustly accused; false or misleading allegations; failure to conform to 'due process'; groundless accusations of serious, even criminal, misconduct; and so on, are the themes of these debates. John Fekete's (1994, 198) critique of what he calls "a new authoritarianism" in universities describes 'professors on trial.' His account of the Report of the Climate Committee at the University of Victoria relies on the productive work accomplished first in the male faculty members' letter and then in a paper written by one of them (Magnusson 1993). He tells us that the report "suggests . . . a pattern of corrupt and violent behaviour" (289) and that "sex-crime charges" were made (294). *Alberta Report* (1995, 38) describes the Climate Committee's Report as making "baseless" accusations "of fostering academic bigotry and sexually harassing female undergrads" against "unnamed male professors". The introductory paragraph of a front-page article in the *Globe and Mail*[2] (Saunders 1995) presents a critique of what is described as the use of sexual harassment codes to discipline professors "for ironic comments, passing glances and lectures that students or fellow faculty find upsetting" (A1). The article argues that ". . . for professors accused of wrongdoing, the normal rules of justice and due process frequently do not apply" (A1). Citing the University of Victoria situation as an example, the article suggests that some universities have allowed "individual professors—or even entire departments, through so-called 'chilly climate' investigations—to be disciplined for a wide range of actions that stop short of genuine sexual harassment . . ." (Saunders 1995, A3). This discourse denies credibility both to the feminist critique and to the issues of 'climate' that we are raising, by suggesting that the specifics of the critique are either groundless or trivial (the *Globe and Mail* article has the subheading "ruffled feathers on campus" [Saunders 1995, A3]).

I am not arguing that this sequence of two texts represents a turning point; rather, it epitomizes an increasingly general deployment of a juridical discourse as a means of defending the gender *status quo ante* in universities against feminist (and anti-racist) critique. I am particularly interested in the sequence because it marks a disjuncture, and its elaboration in the social consciousness has been registered tellingly by a woman faculty member: "One of the hardest things about working in my Faculty is that they don't know they have a problem. The majority of my Faculty would say they don't discriminate. Yet they make such obvious sexist comments" (quoted in Backhouse, Harris, Michell and Wylie 1995, 120). While feminists have no difficulty in recognizing in the Report written by the Climate Committee of the University of Victoria's Political Science Department the lineaments of barriers we have experienced, men do not.

Feminists who read the Report may say, as I did when I first read it, "Well, it may not be put together as effectively as it might have been, but I know just what they're talking about." We are reading as knowledgeable practitioners of the discourse within which the Report is written. It is familiar ground. But it is clear that it is not at all obvious to the male faculty who respond to it.

A Universe of Men

For the centuries of their history in Europe, universities have been exclusively for men. For centuries knowledge and learning were among men and men spoke to and wrote for other men. Back in 1964, Jessie Bernard discovered what she called the 'stag' effect: When men were asked to name those they held to be significant in their field, they named only men, even when there were women who had done work considered to be important. Here was a residue sedimented by an exclusively masculine history. I imagine that men took the maleness of their university and discursive colleagues for granted. It did not occur to them that they were excluding women because women were simply not there. Men's achievements were oriented to work done by other men, aiming for other men's esteem and recognition. Their everyday working lives were lived in a world in which women were never colleagues. If there at all, women were secretaries, research assistants, sessional instructors, cleaners, food servers, or students—but never equals and co-participants. At home, there were wives and daughters, irrelevant to their work. I imagine how they talked only to other men about things which mattered, and that the things which mattered were what men talked about. Their camaraderie included men's jokes and comments on the physical attractiveness or otherwise of the women they encountered. They did not think of women students as those who might become colleagues; they looked at them from within the circle of male collectivity as sexual objects. Occasionally a male faculty member married a student; there was occasional sex, an occasional affair.

I am helped here by reading Alison Lee's account of the gender organization of a high school classroom in which a course in geography was being taught:

> [T]he most lasting impression I have of this classroom is of boys' voices . . . of male voices physically swamping girls' . . . [the boys'] voices were often loud, the physiological difference combining with the classroom spatial arrangements and their apparent sense of freedom to produce their voices in ways which asserted their presence fairly effectively . . . there was a marked absence of girls' voices, despite their physical presence in the room. (1996, 72–73)

How familiar this is to those of us who have been reading the feminist studies of female-male interaction and have come to be able to observe what goes on around us! Lee continues:

> Boys swamped girls in visible ways as well, through their numbers, the massing of their bodies in clusters around the room, their occupation of most of the space. Indeed, there was a strong sense of centre and periphery in the distribution of bodies in space. Girls sat together in the front left-hand corner and seldom left this space. Individual boys and groups of boys, on the other hand, moved regularly around the classroom space, visiting each other. (Lee 1996, 73)

Allowing for differences in going from the local to the institutional level, we can surely find an analogous gender organization in those university departments still bearing the sediments of their masculinist history.

When women were present in an academic role—as students, research assistants, researchers, instructors, and occasionally as faculty—they were not members of the university on the same footing with men; their work did not count; they were not people who had things of significance to say; as students they were not colleagues in the making. If a woman were doing valuable work, it could be appropriated without scruple or acknowledgment. Only men could be the subjects of scientific sentences, since, in the virtual world of scientific discourse, only men were constituted 'author.' Were a woman to occupy a position of authority, the contradiction between that position's authority and her subjectlessness as a woman would create uneasiness. A male colleague wrote of a woman university administrator of some years past that: "She received an elaborate courtesy that was not born of respect but rather, of unease . . . she was not perceived as another academic administrator to be judged on the basis of her competence, but as a different kind of creature" (quoted in Backhouse, Harris, Michell and Wylie 1995, 100). In university classrooms, men oriented (and orient) to men as those who were or were becoming members of the same academic world. A collectivity of men could (and can) be activated across the faculty-student status boundary by telling jokes about women, denigrating women's competence, and being sarcastic at women's expense (particularly, of course, when women are present). A woman physics major at Duke University in the 1990s tells this story:

> On a physics test, her professor included the following example:
>
> Starting with the lungs and using Bernoulli's equation, describe in full physical detail the production of the sound 'Ohhh' by our lone sophomore female physics major. An anatomical sketch would be helpful. (quoted in Sandler, Silverberg, and Hall 1996, 33)

Women's local relationship to the universalized male subject was built into and reproduced by gendered speech genres in which women were excised as subjects, in which they were sexual objects and served as sexualized metaphors for objects, in which the standpoint of (White) men was exclusive vis-à-vis those it constituted as other—women and non-White peoples among them. The experiences of men of a certain class and race bled into the paradigms of the humanities and social sciences, and even into the natural sciences (Spanier 1995, 149).

I imagine the absolute normality of the regime of masculinity in the university; I imagine it being just the way people lived and worked; I imagine the everyday ordinary language of hallway, cafeteria, bar, and classroom as building in the exclusion of women as subjects/speakers. The world of discourse conformed to this same order, so that what was socially conscious could only feed back the same structures into the dailiness of faculty and student life. A self-insulating, self-reproducing system created a past that is present today because for most of those involved, its history is decanted in its everyday ordinariness.

The Feminist Critique

For women students and faculty in the university, a feminist discourse named what we had experienced but had not known how to speak. To women who know enough of feminist discourse to know how to name and see what is going on around them in the university, the taken-for-granted everyday practices of a men-only society display an everyday, ordinary, and pervasive sexism. This is the reason the phrase "a chilly climate for women" resonates. It originated in a report written in 1982 by Roberta Hall and Bernice Sandler, where it was used to describe "the myriad small inequities that by themselves seem unimportant, but taken together create a chilling environment" (Sandler, Silverberg, and Hall 1996, 1). The notion of climate does not define specific acts or kinds of behavior; it locates the generalized character of a regime that is vested in the routine and everyday and in the ordinary as well as the technical languages which regenerate the local orderliness of the everyday work of a university. It is all around us and nowhere in particular, like the weather. Analogously, the exclusions of non-White people, organized *variously* through state and economic organization, are articulated as the taken-for-granted local practices of universities.

In the spring of 1993 a group of women students and a junior member of faculty of the University of Victoria (Canada), constituted as the Committee to Make the Department More Supportive of Women (set up a year earlier), the 'Climate' Committee for short, made a report to the Department of

Political Science. Like other such initiatives, the Report's diagnoses and solutions appeal implicitly to principles of rational discourse fundamental to the university and seek to correct barriers women discover to their full and equal participation in the academic discourses to which the university is committed.

Jürgen Habermas (1970) theorizes an ethic of rational discourse as an ideal speech situation in which there is full mutual recognition of each participant as a subject and in which there is a symmetry of presence of subjects for each other. In the ideal speech situation, no one participant is privileged in the performance of dialogic roles, with the implication that though one may teach, the other too is recognized as a subject who may argue and question.

Theorizing an ideal speech situation enables identification of sources that 'deform' its realization. Deformations may arise "by the social structure on the basis of asymmetries in the performance of dialogue rules" (Habermas 1970, 144). The historically sedimented masculine university creates major gender asymmetries; its discourses have not recognized women as subjects. A symmetry of presence of women and men as subjects for each other has been lacking. Among other practices deforming the symmetry of presence in academic contexts is men's orienting themselves to women in exclusively sexual modes: "Call me fussy," said one woman student, "I just object to someone staring at my bust all the time" (University of Saskatchewan, President's Advisory Committee on the Status of Women 1995, 186). Attending to a woman as a sexual object *in a professional context* displaces her as subject in a professional mode. Within the discourses of sciences and the humanities, men have been subjects for women, but women have not been subjects for men. And, until this women's movement, perhaps not even for each other or themselves.

Feminist discourse has developed categories that name, specify, and collect what it is about men's taken-for-granted and everyday working practices and modes of relating in the university that deform women's participation as full equals in the discourses of science and the humanities. The concept of a 'chilly climate' is one. It expresses the pervasiveness of the problem, rather than specific acts. Men, however, are for the most part not competent readers, if readers at all, of feminist discourse. Nor are they sensitized by experiencing the uneasiness, dismay, anxiety, sometimes anger, occasionally even fear which women may experience and to which feminist discourse gives a name. The feminist critique raises issues for them not at the level of the academic discourses, where criticism is a familiar hazard, but at the level of aspects of their taken-for-granted ways of doing things and the very normality of the ways in which they relate to one another and to women.

A Brief Excursus on Method

Briefly, something about the method of analysis here. I have tried to avoid becoming technical. But I want to mark a difference in a method of reading that I discovered when I was working earlier on two versions of an event that took place in 1968 in Berkeley, California (Smith 1990). We are people whose work is deeply implicated in reading. We take for granted the texts before us—that we can move back and forth in them, that we can read them in relation to one another much as did those who investigated and reported on this matter (going back and forth to try to arrive at a 'balanced' view of the matter). In the analysis of the two versions of the event referred to above, I at first compared one account with the other, looking for differences, for where they converged, and so on. But I then came upon what I have since made into a methodological instruction for myself: Imagine texts as they might 'occur' in actuality, namely in some sequence in relation to each other. In the case of the alternate versions of the event in Berkeley, one account was superseded by the other; the second account was, in fact, specifically designed to subsume and displace the first.

In my experience of these texts as a sequential course of reading, I found that the second provided a set of instructions for rereading the first, so that the latter could be read as an account that recorded only what could be observed by a passerby. The second text rewrote the events, supplying a level of organization that reinterpreted the observed events as expressions of an institutional order. When the two texts I am examining in this paper are viewed in this manner, analogous processes can be seen to be at work. The second, the letter from the male faculty member, reconstructs the feminist critique of the department made in the Climate Committee's report. It is that reconstruction which is analyzed here.

The Report of the Climate Committee

The report of the Climate Committee (hereafter the Report) was presented to the Department of Political Science in the spring of 1993. The members of the committee are identified in the final paragraph of the Report: its chair was a junior faculty member (untenured), Professor Somer Brodribb; the committee included two graduate and three undergraduate students.

The Report is not in highly formalized form. It is not on letterhead paper; it is typed, but not expertly formatted (the format of subheadings displaces levels); it is not paginated. The date appears to have been added in a different typeface (I suspect it was typewritten onto the original computer-generated text). This does not create a problem of authenticity since there is no question about when it was delivered. It is identified as the work of a committee that the Department of Political Science set up the previous year in response to concerns "regarding the discouraging and unsupportive environment experienced by . . . women students" that surfaced during the report of the department's Graduate Review Committee (Department of Political Science, Minutes, May 11th, 1992). The Report is thus clearly located as departmental business, authorized by the department.

The Report is, it says, 'preliminary.'[3] There is no extended account of its method of production. In the introductory paragraph, it is said that the Report "emerg[ed] from discussions with . . . women students." The final paragraph refers to the Committee's method of proceeding: "[It] has consulted widely with the student body and the Political Science Women's Caucus of the Course Union,[4] and through a variety of meetings, forums and exchanges."[5]

The introductory section of the Report places the responsibility for change with the department as a whole, noting that it has already recognized its responsibilities in this respect by recent hirings aimed at rectifying its gender imbalance. However, concerns are expressed that the Report may meet with "hostility, indifference, and the calling into question of women's credibility and right to participate in and make representation to the department on issues of equity." These concerns had arisen because, earlier in the year, the Women's Caucus of the Political Science Course Union had made representations with respect to the hiring process then underway in the department and had been sharply rebuffed.

The general format of the Report is this: there are five major headings under each of which instances of departmental 'practices' are described, followed by recommendations for change. The headings are: Teaching, Class Content, Funding, Sexual Harassment and Everyday Hostility, and Hiring. The Report concludes with a section titled 'Further Recommendations,' which is followed by the paragraph referred to above.

The sections display a regular structure. Each opens with a general statement about 'barriers' faced by women in the area designated by the heading. This is followed by several descriptive items that provide specific illustrations of the general statement. The descriptive items are mixed in character. Some refer to particular incidents, for example, under the heading 'Teaching,' "faculty comments such as 'feminism is just Marxism in a skirt' and 'feminism is just political puff.'" Others generalize across a range of incidents, clearly relying on the feminist discourse on the academy for the concepts that assemble them: "professors do not interrupt men who are dominating seminars or class participation, and do not encourage and support women speaking." Still others make use of such categories of feminist discourse as 'sexist' without further specification: "professors often refuse to allow women students to respond to extremely sexist and anti-feminist comments made in class by male students." All sections conclude with recommendations for measures the department should take to remedy the situations they describe. These add up to a comprehensive program of change.

The Male Faculty Response

The second text is a letter (hereafter the Letter) written to Professor Brodribb, the junior member of faculty who chaired the Climate Committee. It was written after a departmental meeting at which the Report was discussed. Written on letterhead paper and 'professionally' formatted, it was accompanied by a memorandum to Brodribb informing her that copies of the Letter had been sent to the academic vice-president and the president of the faculty association, as well as to all regular faculty members.

Using departmental letterhead appropriates for the Letter the authority of the institutional site. The Letter is professionally formatted, though there are a number of minor typographical errors. Circulating the Letter to the academic vice-president, the dean, members of faculty, and so on repositions the Report, taking it from the departmental level to the level of the university at large.

The Letter denies that the Report "reflect[s] the reality" of the Department. It asserts that the Report makes "two utterly false statments [sic]," and that these are so damaging to the reputations of male faculty in the department that discussion cannot be pursued until they are withdrawn. The Letter then quotes from the section of the Report headed 'Sexual Harassment and Everyday Hostility' as follows: "Female staff and students experience harassment and hostility. The range of behaviours that women experience include the following: sexist and racist treatment of students in the class and during consulations [sic] . . . sexual advances at social gatherings by male faculty members to students." These statements indicate, they claim, "a pattern of corrupt and repugnant behaviours" and are "so obviously damaging" to the male faculty members' reputations that they must be retracted. The formulation of statements as generalities implies that "there have been many instances" of racism and that "more than one faculty member has made sexual advances to more than one student on more than one occasion." It is their belief, they state, that "there are no incidents whatsoever of the behaviours described"; the events described in the Report have never happened. The Letter then challenges Professor Brodribb to provide evidence supporting the statements made in the Report "to the proper university authorities," using the university's procedures for investigating sexual harassment, and to agree to abide by the results of the investigation. If, however, she cannot "provide credible evidence to substantiate the assertions," then they "demand an unqualified apology and retraction" by a date six days from the date of the

Letter. Collegial discussion cannot be resumed until the matter is resolved. If credible evidence is not produced and no apology and retraction made, "then it will be necessary . . . to take further steps to protect our reputations." The clause has been widely interpreted, including by the external reviewers (Berger and Bilson 1994), as a threat to take legal action.

Reconstructing the 'Climate' Report

Michel Foucault's theory of discourse (Foucault 1972, 1981) proposes that the categories, concepts, theories, and methods of positing the objects and relations of discourse, including its epistemology, are constituted in its rules and conventions. The discourse on which the Letter relies is juridical. It is a discourse with the power to reorganize and subordinate other discourses.

Central to the Letter is the construction of its discursive objects—assertions "alleging sexist and racist behavior [sic]" and "suggesting gross sexual misconduct," indicating "a pattern of corrupt and repugnant behaviours [sic]." The imposition of a juridical template over the Report generates these objects. It is useful to follow Stanley Fish's (1967) recommendation to analyze a text as a course of reading in which its meaning is built sequentially. I have taken his advice in analyzing the Letter's 'conversation' with the Report as a sequence of steps, or perhaps devices, each next one of which relies on what has been set up previously.

Step 1. The juridically relevant segments of the Report, namely its references to sexual harassment, sexism, and racism, are brought into focus; the remainder is discarded. The effect is to displace the Report as an account of a generalized 'climate' in the Department of Political Science. The section on 'Sexual Harassment and Everyday Hostility' that contains these references is reproduced below in its entirety (the numbering is for purposes of referencing and does not appear in the original).

1. <u>SEXUAL HARASSMENT AND EVERYDAY HOSTILITY</u>:
2. Subtle (and not so subtle) forms of sexual harassment are a
3. significant barrier to women's full and equal participation in the department.
4. Female staff and students experience harassment and hostility. The range of
5. behaviours that women experience include the following:
6. – comments about the "feminist imperialists"
7. – comments like "I'm not going to be evaluated by the feminist police"
8. – sexist and racist treatment of students in the class and during consultations

9. −sexual advances at social gatherings by male faculty members to students
10. −pitting women against each other during class (eg. calling upon a devout
11. anti-feminist woman to argue it out with a feminist)
12. −interruption or blocking of conversations and exchanges between women
13. especially when these seminar discussions focus on feminism
14. −the general silencing of women in seminar classes
15. −disparaging scholarship on women, or ridiculing material that deals with
16. women's perceptions or [sic] in class and informally (eg. derogatory
17. comments about "the feminists" and "feminism")
18. −sexist humour as a classroom device
19. * We recommend that this behaviour stop.
20. * We also recommend that faculty, staff and students who are addressing
21. issues of sexual harassment receive departmental support.
22. * We recommend that the Department take leadership in formulating a serious
23. and unequivocal policy against sexual harassment. This policy may serve as
24. an example to other sections of the University community.
25. * We recommend that an effective and serious approach to women's safety
26. become part of the mandate of Traffic & Security.

Step 2. The objectionable 'assertions' are extracted from the surrounding text of the original through quotation. Two passages are selected (lines 4–5 and 8–9). Combined, they read:

> Female staff and students experience harassment and hostility. The range of behaviours that women experience include the following: sexist and racist treatment of students in the class and during consulates [sic] . . . sexual advances at social gatherings by male faculty members to students.

Stripping away the context and adjusting the continuity produces a passage representing the Report that is fitted to the Letter's account of the offending assertions as follows:

(a) The first sentence (lines 2–3 above) of the section is omitted. It defines the significance of sexual harassment as a barrier to women's "full and equal participation in the department." Omitting it removes any indication of the Report's claimed intention to treat the behaviors described as attributes of the department. Omitting any reference to the Report's recommendations regarding the department's role in making change (lines 19–26) has a similar effect.

(b) The first two items (lines 6–7) in the list of the 'range of behaviours' are omitted. This omission is not marked. The remainder of the items (lines 10–18) illustrating the theme is also omitted.

In reading the Report I found the use of the concept of 'sexual harassment' equivocal. I think this is because it locates an intersection of discourses. As formalized procedures for dealing with complaints of sexual harassment have been established in universities, sexual harassment has come to be juridically defined and to be restricted increasingly to specifically sexual forms of harassment. There has been, however, a feminist usage that defined it more broadly to include behavior that expresses hostility toward women or denigrates them as women. This usage tends to survive where universities have harassment procedures which also take up racial harassment.[6]

Starting to read this section of the Report, its introductory paragraph (lines 2–5) tells me to discard the first of these interpretations (i.e., the juridical). The 'range' of the examples (lines 6–18) confirm the second, broader, interpretation.[7] In omitting all but two of the items, the Letter restricts interpretation of 'sexual harassment' to the juridical, ruling out the broader feminist interpretation.

Step 3. Tracing a course of reading through the Letter, the reconstructed segment attributed to the Report can be seen as the object referred to in the Letter's next move—the construction of the 'assertions' as "obviously damaging to our reputations." 'Obviously' instructs the reader to register the reputational damage as what anyone could see. We have seen in Step 2 how the groundwork for this has been laid. The next move is to articulate the 'objects' within the framework and juridical language of the Letter. The items illustrating 'sexual harassment and everyday hostility' can now be read as "unfounded assertions" "alleging sexist and racist behavior" and "suggesting gross sexual misconduct," together "indicat[ing] a pattern of corrupt and repugnant behaviours."[8]

Step 4. The course of reading the Letter sets up for the reader upgrades the rhetorical value of references to 'sexual behavior':

(a) The original wording of the Report is reconstructed in a juridical language, 'sexual advances at social gatherings' (the Report) becomes 'gross sexual misconduct' (the Letter). An intertextual tie is set up between the 'assertions' and grounds for dismissal of faculty that may be written into disciplinary clauses of faculty-university contracts and/or into the formalized sexual harassment processes of the university.[9] There are implications, therefore, that more than reputation could be at stake;

(b) Stripping away all other items except the reference to sexist and racist treatment of students has had the general rhetorical effect of enhancing the offensive value of the assertions. I found the jump from 'sexual advances at parties' to 'gross sexual misconduct' rather startling. It is a rhetorical shift in the offensive value of the item as it appeared in the Report. Because they are accomplished in step-by-step fashion, the reader does not necessarily recognize how steep the shifts in rhetorical value have been. Later upgradings are also filtered through the ordinary process through which one text refers back to another, which refers back to another, and so on. Readers, however, don't generally lay the texts side by side to compare them. Being accused of making sexual advances to students at parties would hardly warrant the formality of the Letter's indictment. Upgrading the accusation's value brings it to a level commensurate with the outrage the Letter expresses. Here is the groundwork for further upgradings, first in an informally distributed paper written by one of the signatories to the Letter (who refers to "allegations" of "truly corrupt and violent behaviour") (Magnusson 1993, 5), and later, as we have seen, in John Fekete's (1994) further upgrading—'sexual advances' by faculty to students at social affairs become "sex-crimes" (294).

Step 5. Juridical discourse is, through and through, modernist in its discursive practice. Categories must have a determinate reference to events, states of affairs, and so on, independent of the statements that use them. The wording of the Report must be reshaped into formulations of definite acts performed by actual and identifiable individuals. Only then can they be treated as if they were charges or accusations. Only then can issues of truth and falsity be determined. In the first two paragraphs of the Letter, a falsehood/reality contrast is introduced—the report "provides a portrait of our Department which, in our view, does not reflect reality"; and "there are two utterly false statments [sic] in the report. ..." The sequence I have analyzed as a course of 'construction' follows. Only then can Professor Brodribb be challenged to produce "credible evidence" for "the proper university authorities." The insistence on a retraction if credible evidence is lacking relies on a whole course of construction that has transformed the Report's delineation of a climate into allegations of determinate acts committed by definite people on definite occasions and for which evidence can, in theory, be brought to establish their truth or falsity.

To my count, the Report lists twenty illustrative items; the Letter focuses on only two. Some of these items describe students in class being treated, either by the instructor or by other students, in ways that should surely be considered questionable, regardless of whether women or men are involved. Instructors are described as treating women students and what they put forward with contempt; of allowing, even encouraging, 'harassing' behavior from male students in class that is continued outside class; of allowing male students to dominate classroom discussions; of making "patronizing and demeaning comments on work submitted"; and so on. These are not made an issue in the Letter; nor are the questions the Report raises about the lack of feminist content in mandatory political science courses and the lack of feminist and Native instructors. In stripping down the Report to fit the juridical frame, the Letter disables the Report's attempt to make visible a taken-for-granted gender order that deformed the conditions of women's full and equal participation in the discourse of political science.[10]

Discussion

Imagine the Report being received in the Department of Political Science as a local critique of departmental practices. Imagine it as having been intended to instruct and to make visible rather than to accuse. And imagine then that, although they were upset and even angry, the men decided they would try to look further at what was being presented to them.[11] It is a situation that many White feminists, myself included, have had to confront in relation to non-White women.

At what point does criticism become accusation? The theory of symbolic interaction and its echoes in ethnomethodology tell us that it is the response to the act that gives the latter its determinate character. Here we see an act, the Report, given definition in the terms, syntax, and methods of juridical discourse. The public character of the Letter elevates the Report to its own status. In a sense the Letter produces the accusations of which it complains. Translated juridically, the Report becomes subject to a critique of its research methodology. The external reviewers (Berger and Bilson 1994), for example, are preoccupied with what become problems under the rule of the juridical discourse: the ambiguity of the terms used, the reliance on women's experience, the violations of due process (the accused do not know their accusers), and so on. They observe: "It is all very well to say that the purpose of the report of the Chilly Climate Committee was not to indict individuals. Yet that is its effect" (Berger and Bilson 1994, 55). But the Report has this effect only after the Letter has retroactively reconstituted it as a formalized and public or semi-public document, reinterpreted in a juridical mode.[12]

Later deployments of the juridical discourse referred to earlier (Fekete 1994; Saunders 1995) replicate this performative (Austin 1962) at the level of public discourse. Journalistic conventions call for hearing from both sides and these may be followed, as they are in the *Globe and Mail* (Saunders 1995). In spite of this a single monologic standpoint prevails—the feminist critique is included only to be discredited and mocked by trivialization. Reproduced at the level of public discourse, the juridical representation offers a device that others can use to protect established gender asymmetries in settings of higher education.

The gender deformations of rational speech that feminist discourse locates in postsecondary institutions arise as aspects of an historically normalized organization of social relations. They do not readily resolve into specific acts, let alone acts describable as "corrupt and repugnant" (the Letter). Imagine the girls in Alison Lee's geography class making their feminist critique. It would be full of those "myriad small inequities that by themselves seem unimportant" ([Sandler, Silverberg, and Hall 1996, 1];

Michèle Le Doeuff, quoted in the introduction to the Report, writes that as a philosopher, on the one hand, she faces "fierce opposition" and, on the other hand, is told that "you are making a lot of fuss about nothing" [Le Doeuff in Climate Committee 1993]). It is the daily and taken-for-granted gender organization in university departments that deforms women's opportunity to share equally in the intellectual life of societies as this is vested in universities. Gender asymmetry becomes invisible again wherever the devices and conventions of juridical discourse are imposed.

The juridical discourse overrides others, submitting them to its methods of constructing objects, its epistemological conventions, and the agonistic order of the subject positions it constitutes. It is not the only way to go. Feminists who are White have lessons for men here. We have had to recognize our own practices as racist. We may have felt anger and have surely felt guilt and shame. But we have also learned that to be racist (or sexist) is not simply a matter of individual moral choice or character, but of societies and histories we inherit and participate in but did not choose to make. We have learned to receive and to work with the critique that non-White women have brought to us. It is always painful, but we are enriched. We make discoveries about ourselves, and about the discourses and institutions in which we participate—discourses and institutions that have gender and racial asymmetries built into them. There is a lesson here for men.

Notes

1. This paper is part of a more extensive project analyzing other situations in Canadian departments of political science.

   I am indebted: to Somer Brodribb for providing documents that enriched my own sparse collection; to my co-workers, Melanie Randall and Michelle Webber, of the Centre for Women's Studies in Education's Academic Freedom Committee; and finally to James Heap and members of my 1996 graduate class on Texts and Textuality. We discussed these texts in a wonderful session while I was in the last day or so of meeting the deadline for this paper. In the end I never got around to incorporating their insights—getting the thing finished became paramount—but our discussion was immensely stimulating and helped me hang on to some of the freshness with which I undertook to write the paper.

2. A business-oriented newspaper, the *Globe and Mail* is the only Canadian newspaper with national circulation.

3. In a record of the meeting based on a compilation of notes made by participants supporting the Report, members of the Climate Committee make it clear that the Report had been intended as a basis for dialogue and was preliminary. There was discussion of assigning a work study position to it (Minutes of Political Science Department Meeting, 29 March 1993, 10).

4. The Political Science Women's Caucus of the Course Union is a union of students taking courses in the department.

5. In addition, the archives of the University of Victoria library contain a substantial package of materials, which apparently were used by the Climate Committee in preparing its Report. These materials include the Hall and Sandler pamphlet (Hall and Sandler 1982) that introduced to feminist discourse the concept of the 'chilly climate,' as well as other papers and reports on the situation of women in universities.

6. In a sense, the success of the women's movement in installing sexual harassment procedures as part of the disciplinary machinery of the university has created its own problems. The intervention of faculty associations, properly concerned with the interests of members charged under these rules, has moved such procedures in a more strictly legalistic direction. They become less flexible and hence less effective as a means of dealing with the kinds of generalized 'asymmetries' which women experience and which are named by the feminist 'chilly climate' discourse. I note that Professor Hester Lessard's report to the President as chair of the Equal Rights and Opportunities Committee charged with reviewing the university's harassment procedures "urges that climate complaints be differentiated from individual complaints of harassment" and that a new procedure for the former be set up (reported in Bilson and Berger 1994, 29). I note too, however, that in the collection of documents I possess, which is substantial, there is no indication that the issue has been taken further by the administration.

7. However, the recommendations (lines 19–26 of the passage from the Report), particularly the reference to women's safety in the last (lines 25–26), return me to an equivocal reading since they seem to refer to 'sexual harassment' in the current institutional sense.

8. Two spellings of 'behavior' appear in the Letter.

9. I have not, as yet, had an opportunity to find out whether this is a reference to the University of Victoria Faculty Association contract with the University.

10. It would be a mistake to think that these moves prevailed altogether in suppressing the Report of the Climate Committee. The Letter itself, and the initiatives of the Climate Committee in response to its implied threat, led to issues at the University of Victoria becoming widely known and discussed within the university and in the wider networks of the women's movement and beyond.

11. Alison Lee (1996) tells a story about the gender organization of the classroom she observed. She describes two interactional sequences in which a girl attempts to give direction to the group's work. In the first the girl is told to 'be quiet.' In the second, what she says is treated by one boy as a personal attack on another boy. "These two excerpts indicate a kind of social cohesiveness among the boys which not only excluded Mandy but which operates as a form of control and of resistance to her attempts to control" (Lee 1996, 77). Lee's story suggests how we might understand the faculty men's letter as performative at a different level of gender relations. Women may be present; it is good if they are present; it is another thing altogether if they seek control or to undermine the local and

extra-local organization of male collectivity in department and discipline. By resolving the 'chilly climate' critique into personal attacks on the men as individuals, it reclaims for men as a collectivity control of the departmental, even the disciplinary, territory, threatened by the feminist critique.

12. An example of the problems of translation from "preliminary" to formal public document can be seen in many passages in the external reviewers' report (Berger and Bilson 1994). For example, they write:

> Professor Brodribb says that the word "staff" as used in the report was not intended to include support staff, that it meant faculty. But Professor Brodribb and the members of the committee have never advised the staff that the report was not intended to refer to them. (Berger and Bilson 1994, 20)

These are precisely the kinds of problems that get ironed out in the process of advancing a document from a preliminary to a final and formal status.

References

Alberta Report. 1995. "A Banished Complainer: The University of Victoria Suspends a 'Harassed' Feminist Professor." *Alberta Report* (March 27): 38.

Austin, J. L. 1962. *How to Do Things with Words*. London: Oxford University Press.

Backhouse, Constance, Roma Harris, Gillian Michell, and Alison Wylie. 1995. "The Chilly Climate for Faculty Women at Western: Postscript to the *Backhouse Report*." In *Breaking Anonymity: The chilly climate for women faculty*, edited by The Chilly Collective. 97–132. Waterloo, ON: Wilfrid Laurier University Press.

Bernard, Jessie. 1964. *Academic Women*. New York: New American Library.

Fekete, John. 1994. *Moral Panic: Biopolitics Rising*. Montreal-Toronto: Robert Davies Publishing.

Fish, Stanley. 1967. *Surprised by Sin: The Reader in Paradise Lost*. New York: St. Martin's Press.

Foucault, Michel. 1972. *The Archaeology of Knowledge and the Discourse on Language*. New York: Pantheon Books.

Foucault, Michel. 1981. "The Order of Discourse." In *Untying the Text: A Poststructuralist Reader*, edited by Robert Young. 51–78. London: Routledge.

Habermas, Jürgen. 1970. "Toward a Theory of Communicative Competence." *Inquiry* 13: 114–47.

Hall, Roberta, and Bernice R. Sandler. 1982. *The Classroom Climate: A Chilly One for Women*. Washington, DC: Project on the Status and Education of Women, Association of American Colleges.

Lee, Alison. 1996. *Gender, Literacy, Curriculum: Rewriting School Geography*. London: Taylor and Francis.

Magnusson, Warren. 1993. "Feminism, McCarthyism and Sexist Fundamentalism." Department of Political Science, University of Victoria.

Richer, Stephen, and Lorna Weir, eds. 1995. *Beyond Political Correctness: Towards the Inclusive University*. Toronto: University of Toronto Press.

Sandler, Bernice R., Lisa A. Silverberg, and Roberta Hall. 1996. *The Chilly Classroom Climate: A Guide to Improve the Education of Women*. Washington, DC: National Association for Women in Education.

Saunders, Doug. 1995. "Ruffled Feathers on Campus." *Globe and Mail* (July 1): A1, A3.

Smith, Dorothy E. 1990. "The Active Text." In *Texts, Facts and Femininity: Exploring the relations of ruling*, by Dorothy E. Smith. 120–58. London: Routledge.

Spanier, Bonnie B. 1995. *Impartial Science: Gender Ideology in Molecular Biology*. Bloomington: Indiana University Press.

University of Saskatchewan, President's Advisory Committee on the Status of Women. 1995. *Reinventing Our Legacy: The Chills Which Affect Women*. In *Breaking Anonymity: The Chilly Climate for Women Faculty*, edited by The Chilly Collective. 171–210. Waterloo, ON: Wilfrid Laurier University Press.

Documentary Sources

Berger, Thomas R., and Beth Bilson. 1993. "Interim Report of the Review Committee, September 29, 1993." *The Ring* 19 (18): 4–5.

Berger, Thomas R., and Beth Bilson. 1994. *Report of the Review Committee into the Political Science Department*. Prepared for the President of the University of Victoria, January 21.

Callahan, Marilyn (School of Social Work and Advisor to the Vice-President Academic on Faculty Women's Issues), and Andrew Pirie (Faculty of Law and the Centre for Dispute Resolution). 1993. Findings of the Review of the Situation in the Department of Political Science at the University of Victoria, University of Victoria, May 11.

Climate Committee. 1993. Report of the Climate Committee to the Department of Political Science, University of Victoria, March 23.

Department of Political Science, University of Victoria. 1992. Minutes of Departmental Meeting, May 11.

Department of Political Science, University of Victoria. 1993. Minutes [note: these are notes compiled subsequent to the meeting rather than formal minutes] of the Political Science Department Meeting, March 29.

Scully, Samuel E. 1993. Memorandum to All Regular Faculty Members/Department of Political Science. University of Victoria, May 26.

Chapter Ten

"What a Shame You Don't Publish": Crossing the Boundaries as a Public Intellectual Activist

Howard M. Solomon
Tufts University (United States)

Twice I sought promotion to full professor at Tufts University, Massachusetts, first in 1992 and then, a year later, in 1993. Both times, as an intellectual activist working in the public sphere, I challenged existing definitions and conceptions of merit. The second time I succeeded, but the first time I failed. It is the first time that I write about here, and the deep shame I experienced as I traversed the contested terrain of the faculty merit process.

Far removed from the disembodied language of economic and social analysis that Susan Faludi uses in *Backlash: The Undeclared War Against American Women*,[1] the "no" vote of the tenure and promotion committee in 1992–93 seemed written on my body, as if my shoulders and my back had been physically lashed. Like some historical figure from my courses in lesbian and gay history or European social history—say a sixteenth-century Spanish Jew exposed to the Inquisition, a blasphemer in a seventeenth-century Scottish village, or a gay man arrested in a police raid in London in 1810—I felt as if I were being paraded through the marketplace, face down, under the whip. And what was my crime? Having exposed the dirty little secrets of my community through challenging its merit system. These physical symptoms—lowered eyes, bent back, pain in the shoulders (as though from carrying a terrible burden)—I now realize marked the shame of entering contested territory.[2] Looking back from the perspective of a successful reapplication and promotion to full professor in 1994, I also see that my challenge helped contribute to the transformation of that territory. There is now a campus-wide task force examining the entire promotion process, a systematic airing and honoring of long-silent issues. It is

as if the shame I experienced ultimately shamed the community into transforming itself.

The possibility of shaming exists wherever values are being contested, not
only in campus politics, but also in national politics. Within the last ten
years, ultra-conservative politicians who are battling to "reaffirm traditional
family values" and to "revitalize America" have seized upon ritualized
government-imposed shaming (e.g., the reappearance of chain gangs in
Alabama, William F. Buckley's proposal to tattoo people with AIDS)[3] as
weapons in their arsenal. This should not surprise us, but it *should* trouble us.
Shaming rituals divert public attention away from troublesome social realities and towards scapegoated victims; they propose simplistic, dramatic,
emotionally charged solutions to complex issues. Historically, conservative
societies have used shaming rituals to enhance the authority of those in
power and to resolve conflicts in the moral realm. In simple terms, the formula has been: "The greater the shame of the Other, the greater our honor."

Societies with heavy moral investments in honor and shame often make
analogous zero-sum assumptions about the material realm: economic well-
being can only happen at the expense of someone else, and vice versa.[4] No
wonder the economic changes of the 1990s are providing ultra-conservative
political forces with a ripe environment in which to shame those who represent a challenge to the status quo. The waves of this tide wash over the
university as well.

Those of us who traverse contested territory within and without the university need to understand how shame operates—not only how it debili-
tates, but also how it transforms. We need to stop obsessing about how
"awful" shame is; instead, we need to articulate how "awe-ful" shame can
be, recognizing that it marks the site for potentially profound and radical
transformation.[5] I use the shame I experienced when denied promotion to
full professor as a prism through which to analyze the intellectual activist
challenge to conservative notions of merit within the university. That prism
will reveal that, contrary to our usual way of thinking about it, shame can be
a powerful tool with which to revise both ourselves (as agents of change)
and our institutions (as places of transformation).

Transgressing boundaries and entering ill-defined and contested terrain is
dangerous and holy work. To become shameless leaders, we need to understand the sacred nature of what we do. That is what this paper is about.

Queering the Boundaries

When I decided to apply for promotion to full professor in 1991, I was
crossing ambiguous territory. Promotion cases at Tufts seemed to fall into

three groups: (1) colleagues with strong research and publishing records who applied for, and received, promotion six to twelve years after becoming tenured; (2) associate professors whose long-time service led to full professorship just before retirement—the so-called "golden parachute" promotions; and (3) a large number of associate professors in their forties and fifties, myself included, who fell between (1) and (2) and whose promotion possibilities were much more ambiguous.

For as long as anyone could remember, faculty bylaws stipulated that (1) scholarship, teaching, and service should carry equal weight (33.3 per cent, respectively) in determining tenure and (2) the same criteria should be used to determine promotion from associate to full professor. In the 1980s, after much faculty and administrative discussion, a new weighting was adopted: forty per cent scholarship, forty per cent teaching, and twenty per cent service. Public rhetoric claimed that teaching was as important as was scholarship, but most faculty and administrators privately agreed that scholarship (usually defined as research monographs or articles in refereed publications) was the more important of the two. Most of the discussion concerned applications for tenure and promotion to associate professor; no one seemed to consider that promotion to full professor might require a different weighting of the criteria.

In fact, the entire topic was conspicuously absent from campus discussion. Many people either dismissed promotion to full professor as pro forma or, worse yet, refused to consider seriously whether the criteria should be re-examined. The subject reminded me of family *schandes* (Yiddish for "scandals" or "shameful secrets") of my childhood—divorce, sex, alcoholism, cancer. No one wanted to talk about these matters; if one had to discuss them, one did so in highly coded English or impenetrable Yiddish. Here at Tufts, promotion to full professor dragged any discussion of scholarship, teaching, and service into a morass of emotional issues— unrealized scholarly dreams, disappointments of age, changing career paths—that no one wanted to acknowledge, much less address directly and openly.[6]

Ambiguity surrounding the criteria, and not knowing whether the forty-forty-twenty per cent formula really applied, served to delay and sometimes even sabotage decisions to initiate the promotion process. One of my colleagues spoke of the application in terms of ending a prolonged adolescence: "It's about time I put on long pants; I'm finally going to apply for promotion." Another said, "The hell with going through this crap. I'm happier as an outsider without the promotion." Still another said, "I only have another ten years to retirement; I can wait [for the golden parachute]." In their voices, I heard echoes of my own internalized "I'm not good enough," the *schande* of not being a full member of the community.

By any standards, my service and teaching records were first-rate. In addition to chairing the Department of History and a number of important committees and programs, I had served as Tufts' first Dean of Undergraduate Studies and Academic Affairs; had helped organize the faculty-staff lesbian, gay, and bisexual caucus; and, from 1990 to 1992, had co-chaired the campus-wide Task-Force on Lesbian, Gay, and Bisexual Issues.

I had developed areas of the curriculum (e.g., lesbian/gay history; the history of stereotyping, disease, and marginality; and gender and sexuality) that were quite different from early modern French history (the area in which I was trained and had first published). Since becoming tenured in 1974, I had published reviews and some short essays and had delivered a few professional papers—certainly nothing "major" by traditional standards. Instead, I had focused on teaching, on developing non-traditional areas, and on making the extant scholarship in these areas (especially lesbian/gay issues, sexuality, and homophobia) available to the wider community.

My application dossier reflected my identity as an intellectual activist who blurred traditional university definitions. I provided the articles, papers, and reviews published in the usual professional settings. Along with them, however, I included numerous community lectures and workshops, classroom syllabi and bibliographies, and the *Report of the Task Force on Lesbian, Gay, and Bisexual Issues,* insisting that these also reflected my scholarly effectiveness. The candidate's department is required to name eight to ten outside experts from "within the field" to evaluate his/her scholarship. I persuaded the chair of my department to include only six historians, a mere two of whom were in the fields of lesbian/gay history and French history, respectively—my ostensible "specialties." The others were historians who spoke directly to how my work as an intellectual activist furthered Tufts' self-professed commitment to a socially engaged professoriat, to providing a model of community service for its students, and so on. My other experts had even less to do with the discipline of history. One wrote from the perspective of her research on lesbian and gay teachers, another from her research on the subjectivities of race, class, and sexual identity in American education. I approached the process as an opportunity to educate everyone involved—my department, the faculty tenure and promotion committee, senior administrators—even though, obviously, my immediate goal was to get the promotion.

My scholarly identity is much broader than is my identity as a gay man teaching lesbian and gay history within the university. I define myself as an intellectual activist who, in *carrying on* (i.e., developing non-traditional areas of study), *carries out* ideas (i.e., translates them into praxis), and ensures that they are *carried across* to the public arena. As a translator, what are the images that carry me from the traditional terrain of publishing and research to the contested territory where the lines between town and gown, public and private, teaching and service intersect and blur? First of all, I draw upon the experiences of the witches, heretics, and queers who are the figures at the center of my courses: socially marginalized individuals who occupy liminal territories of meaning and mystery. I draw upon the image of Hermes, the god of translation, trickery, and commerce. He is a trouble-making, queer god, constantly *carrying on* (joking, playing), *carrying out* (putting ideas into action), and *carrying across* from one realm to another. Hermes cannot be shamed.

Like these figures, the intellectual activist occupies and defines potentially shameful territory. Performing as a public intellectual activist is a more threatening transformation of my identity, and of those of the public and academic terrains in which I work, than is my advocacy of gay issues and teaching lesbian/gay history within the confines of the university. Anna Marie Smith's analysis is useful here; she notes the qualitative difference between the "dangerous queer" and the "good homosexual . . . contained within closed frontiers."

> The goodness of the "good homosexual" consists precisely in her self-disciplining, self-limiting, fixed subject status, an otherness which knows her proper place. The dangerousness of subversive queerness lies in its unfixity and "excessiveness," its insatiable drive towards expansion and self-reproduction, its contamination of the space of normalcy through its entry of the wrong orifices, and, above all, its pursuit of unlimited pleasure.[7]

It is no accident that ultra-conservatives fixate on "outsiders"—illegal immigrants, people with acquired immune-deficiency syndrome, homosexuals, welfare cheats—whose existence is perceived as threatening to the identity of "real" American society. The intellectual activist raises similar deep-seated fears about the "sanctity of the academy," its "inviolability," and so on, when s/he shifts shamelessly in and out of the public arena, in and out of the university classroom. The sexuality of the intellectual activist per se is not the issue: the issue is that all intellectual activists are practitioners of "subversive queerness." Indeed, the identity of the university is at stake when intellectual activists queer its borders, violating the self-serving and deceptive fiction that it is fundamentally separate from the outside world.

The University Sphere and the Public Sphere

Public disputes about merit and accountability (e.g., the not-for-profit status of the university, demands of public service in lieu of taxes, etc.) have always been part of town/gown relations. What is different in recent years is the amount of rhetoric coming from national political and media figures. The current demand that academics "give back" to the community is more than garden-variety anti-intellectualism dressed up in "Contract-with-America" language. When Newt Gingrich, for example, says that colleges "are 'out of control' because of rising costs and faculty members bent on 'rejecting the culture of the people who pay their salaries,' "[8] he is exploiting the deep fears of people who believe themselves to be innocent victims of malevolent forces in a zero-sum universe: whatever the university has, it got at *our* expense.

Whether we like it or not, such rhetoric is raising important questions: What is the relationship of the university to society? Are professors public servants or simply opportunists freeloading at public expense? And what about intellectual activists who slide in and out of university and public space? Where do their loyalties reside?

Unlike people in other parts of the world, for whom the term "intellectual" broadly refers to teachers, lawyers, journalists, and so on, Americans have long been apprehensive about "pointy-headed" academic types who stray into the public arena. Anti-intellectualism is as American as the fourth of July and apple pie. At a time when the academy is defensive about public scrutiny, it is likely to be particularly uneasy about the activities of intellectual activists who shamelessly move in and out of public space.[9]

Universities are extremely vulnerable to changing public opinion, and my own institution, like others, is scrambling to respond to it. Throughout the 1970s and 1980s, for example, Tufts touted internationalism as the hallmark of its undergraduate programs. Currently, however, it couples rhetoric about global citizenship to rhetoric about community service and volunteerism (traditionally defined). At every chance it gets, the Office of Communications now touts faculty community service (e.g., the geologist who runs for school committee, the mathematician who works as a volunteer in a children's hospital). On one level, this public relations work is designed to appease those who say that we're not giving enough to the community; on another level, of course, it plays to isolationist public opinion that is more anxious about the United States' role in the international scene than it was ten years ago.

Liberal advocates of public service typically imagine a traditional, narrowly defined model of volunteerism that is perceived to be rightly separate from, and less worthy than, the university's real business of teaching and scholarship. In fact, this model of volunteerism accords with how service is being perceived in tenure and promotion cases at Tufts, where it now accounts for only twenty per cent (as opposed to thirty-three per cent) of the merit formula. Just as a narrow definition of service rigidifies the separate spheres of teaching and scholarship and renders them sacrosanct, so the classic Liberal conception of volunteerism exaggerates the differences between the university sphere and the public sphere and obviates any serious interrogation of their structural relationship.

The concept "intellectual activist" calls into question neat definitions of "volunteer" and "community service," and it problematizes the relationships *between* university and society. It also problematizes the relationships *among* the three categories "service," "teaching," and "scholarship" within the university itself. The fetishization of the refereed journal article by defenders of "traditional standards" reflects anxiety over all these relationships. The refereed article is the product of an academic economy that produces, exchanges, and consumes knowledge within its own closed borders and measures these activities by its own standards. The refereed article ("referee" = "carry back") operates within a defined territory, while the publications of the intellectual activist cross frontiers, translate ("translate" = "carry across") and corrupt the language of the academy, revealing and discrediting its secrets. What is the coin of measurement when the intellectual activist breaks the Hermetic confines of traditional scholarly activity? The very act of carrying outside is an act of betrayal. "Traddutore, Traditore," as the Italian aphorism expresses it: "Translators are traitors."

There is no question that the electronic revolution is also posing numerous questions about how we measure academic production. In an electronic world which produces publications which never go into print and academic conferences which take place entirely in cyberspace, questions such as "What is authorship?" and "When is a publication completed?" have tremendous implications with regard to how universities evaluate intellectual productivity.[10] I would argue, however, that the image of the intellectual activist is even more challenging to current methods of measuring merit than is the electronic revolution. Criticism of the public intellectual activist—that s/he publishes, literally and figuratively, beyond peer review—acknowledges, in terror, that such behavior totally rejects the industrial-capitalist model of knowledge and of the university. Reveling in unfixed, excessive circulation, the work of the intellectual activist, "through its entry of the wrong orifices, and, above all, its pursuit of unlimited pleasure,"[11] is unspeakable. Unspeakable because the old language cannot accurately describe it. Unspeakable because it rejects reproducing itself in favor of spilling its seed outside the tribe, seeking endless pleasure.

Universities are quick to reward high-profile intellectual activists who show up on *Nightline* or in the pages of *The New Yorker*—thank goodness for the bell hookses and Cornell Wests who inspire the rest of us. The fact of the matter, however, is that most intellectual activists do their work in church basements, Rotary Club meetings, high-school classrooms, retirement homes, and in the op-ed pages of local newspapers. In spite of its rhetoric to the contrary, the university continues to undervalue these work-places and the people who inhabit them. Working in these spaces muddles the neat town/gown, theory/praxis divides which a narrowly defined (Liberal) civic volunteerism perpetuates.

It also brings into public scrutiny some of the dirtiest secrets of academic culture. For example, the anxiety about working with non-university working-class groups replicates the silence around class issues that dominates the typical bourgeois classroom.[12] The devaluation of church and synagogue groups (i.e., the assumption that they are unlikely sites for intellectual transformation) reflects the anti-religious bias that permeates much of academia. And the disdain of people in post-secondary education for those who teach young children reflects what Jonathan Silin describes as our culture's "passion for ignorance" vis-à-vis childhood.[13] For example, after I had facilitated an exciting workshop on homophobia with a group of tenth-graders, one of their teachers told me that it was a shame that I hadn't become a high-school teacher. Needless to say, I was thrilled by her compliment. A week later, I recounted her comment to a senior university administrator, who interpreted it as an insult!

Such devaluations permeate the academy and the merit process as they are now constituted. Hard-wired into academic culture is a fundamental prejudice valuing grossly abstracted theory over politically engaged practice, valuing the "higher" products of vision ("theorizing" = "seeing") and speech over the "lower" products of hand and body. This false mind/body hierarchy elevates the status of physicists, philosophers, and mathematicians (who work with their minds) and lowers the status of dance and physical education specialists (who work with their bodies) and occupational and physical therapists (who work with the bodies of others).[14] It also denigrates artists and sculptors who use their bodily skills to work physical media. The traditional devaluing of those who facilitate "experiential," "laboratory," or "workshop" learning (unlike those who "give lectures" or "teach classes") reflects the deep-seated prejudice against "hands-on" production in academic culture.

Notions of "hands-on" production, "intellectual field," and "scholarly output" reflect the language of pre-industrial capitalism, a language indicative of a time when agricultural fields and economic markets had tangible boundaries and the physical space in which one worked determined one's identity. And not simply one's economic identity, for questions about the property of one's field were inherently moral: is it proper, appropriate, and clean (as in the French "propre") or is it dirty and shameful to work both within and without an identifiable field? In the language of academic conservatives, "intellectual purity" must be at stake if an intellectual activist is too accessible to non-academic constituencies.[15]

As the boundaries of regional and national markets have disintegrated in the world of postindustrial capitalism, so too have the self-defined boundaries of traditional academic disciplines. Even more than the scholar doing inter-disciplinary work *within* the university, the intellectual activist working both *within* and *without* the university is the harbinger of change. How is one to measure the activities of the intellectual activist who is unable/unwilling to honor the propriety of disciplinary and institutional definitions and who is living in a shameless, borderless world?

The postmodern university can no longer use two hundred-year-old con-ceptions of merit to measure the production, distribution, and consump-tion of intellectual capital. What will replace the industrial-capitalist model of merit and productivity? Must intellectual activists who challenge out-moded conceptions of merit be defined only as traitors?

The Professoriat and Intellectual Activism

In June 1993, after the tenure and promotion committee had voted three to two against promoting me, the chair of my department and I met with two senior academic deans. They commiserated with me and suggested strate-gies for reapplying. "It's a shame you don't publish" some of the photo-copied classroom materials submitted in (your) dossier, one of them argued, since this would be an "effective" way to persuade the committee of (your) scholarship. I was willing to risk the shame of again challenging the faculty merit process, I told them, but I would not compromise myself by cranking out an "effective" (read: "quick-and-dirty") publication simply for the sake of promotion, nor would I go through the process again without their active support. Refusing to look away, I pointed out that their own public rhetoric about merit and a changing professoriat was meaningless if they couldn't relate it to the lives of specific faculty members. Shamelessly, I persuaded them to agree to take a more proactive role in persuading the faculty (including the tenure and promotion committee) that it could no longer avoid re-evaluating its policies and procedures regarding promotion to full professor.

In June 1994, the tenure and promotion committee voted to support my application for promotion. Even more important, the academic vice-president appointed a Task Force on Criteria for Promotion to Full Professor. Several of their recommendations are related to the issues raised in this chapter: there should be some sort of periodic progress review to help tenured associate pro-fessors "understand whether [they are] ready to come up for promotion or [are] following a reasonable path toward promotion"; there should be consid-eration of the special situations of tenured associate professors who have distinguished themselves in interdisciplinary teaching or in pursuing interdisciplinary work outside of their tenured discipline; and faculty members tenured both as scholars and performers should have the opportunity to be promoted in any combination of scholarship or performance. The task force reached no consensus on whether there should be thresholds of scholarship and/or teaching performance, on whether promotion should be automatic after a fixed period of time, or on the issue of pre-retirement promotions.[16]

The eventual success of my own challenge persuades me that the university *can* be shamed into expanding its conservative definition of the professoriat so that it may embrace different models, including that of the intellectual activist. I am also persuaded that conceptualizing our work within a sacred context—moving ourselves from the "awful" to the "awe-ful"—is strategically useful. We, as intellectual activists, should not be embarrassed by the fact that we are part of a long history of sacred trouble-makers. As Judith Butler says, "Trouble is inevitable, and the task is how best to make it, what best way to be in it."[17] Coming out as intellectual activists redefines as sacred ground the territory in which we operate; our declaration of vulnerability to public shaming is a holy, sacred declaration. Like Molière's bourgeois gentleman, who discovers that he's been speaking prose for years but never knew it, intellectual activists have always done sacred work but never knew it. We need to know it.

As Matthew Fox says, "All our work is meant to be about making beauty in some capacity or other. But where there is awe and beauty there is also terror."[18] Doing the sacred work of contesting business as usual is terrifying and stressful. How, then, can we renew ourselves and the territory in which we live? Commit to a no-holds-barred adversarial posture and slash and burn our fields? Take time out and retreat, and let the fields, and ourselves, lie fallow? Or, like Hermes and the witches, heretics, and queers, who preceded us, revel in our role as sacred actors and inhabit all the territory and make it our own?

We can draw strength from spiritual traditions that honor trouble-makers. For me, the image of Hermes infuses my gay identity, empowering me to embrace ambiguity and double-spiritedness, the joy of walking both sides of the street. My commitment to Quaker practice challenges me to view all gatherings—even faculty meetings—as opportunities for spiritual growth. And my Jewish roots call me to emulate the values of the "prophet"—what Rabbi Abraham Heschel defined as someone who interferes with the demands of an unjust and inhumane society.[19]

One of the most injurious assumptions of backlash rhetoric is that social action is a process of remedying or curing—an assumption that takes for granted immeasurable differences between the all-knowing expert and the problem-to-be-fixed, between us and them. Such an assumption precludes the possibility of seeing social action as a form of healing, of seeing the naturalness of compromise and consensus, and of seeing the impossibility of separating our personal healing from the healing of the world in which we work. As bell hooks puts it, if we are to empower our students, we "must be actively committed to a process of self-actualization that promotes [our] own well-being."[20] The Jewish commitment to tikkun olam—"repairing the world"—challenges us to heal ourselves, inside and out, as we also heal the world.

The mere act of occupying different spaces—from university classroom to Kiwanis Club to high school to op-ed page in the local newspaper—and making them our own can help heal a professoriat battered by institutional in-fighting, disciplinary isolation, and the rhetoric of backlash demagogues. Expanding the definition of professor so that it includes intellectual activist and healer requires us to reimagine the contested territories in which we work and to recognize them as sacred. Above all, it requires opening up the narrow definition of university professional so that it includes "amateurs"—those who do their work out of love.[21] And that, in the final analysis, may be the most shameless challenge to the conservative backlash of all.

Acknowledgments

I want to thank Chris Beach, Rita Kissen, and Steve Marrone for their contributions to this essay.

Notes

1. Susan Faludi, *Backlash: The Undeclared War Against American Women* (New York: Crown Publishers, 1991).
2. See, for example, C. D. Schneider, *Shame, Exposure, and Privacy* (Boston: Beacon Press, 1977); Leon Wumser, *The Mask of Shame* (Baltimore: Johns Hopkins, 1981).
3. Rick Bragg, "Chain Gangs to Return to Roads of Alabama," *New York Times*, 26 March 1995, p. 16; William F. Buckley, Jr., "Identify All the Carriers," *New York Times*, 18 March 1986, p. 27.
4. On the economic and social contexts of honor, shame, and envy, see J. G. Peristiany, ed., *Honor and Shame: The Values of Mediterranean Society* (Chicago: University of Chicago Press, 1966) and George M. Foster, "The Anatomy of Envy: A Study in Symbolic Behavior," *Current Anthropology* 13, no. 2 (April 1972): 165–202.
5. I think of the Biblical examples of Moses hiding his face from the Burning Bush (Exodus 3) and of Peter falling on his face, in awe, at Christ's transfiguration

(Matthew 17). Their transformation into powerful, shameless leaders begins at the moment they confront a reality greater than themselves and experience extraordinary shame.

6. See Denise K. Magner, "Beyond Tenure: Colleges Seek Periodic Review of Professors Who Have Already Passed Muster," *Chronicle of Higher Education*, 21 July 1995, p. A13.

7. Anna Marie Smith, *New Right Discourse on Race and Sexuality: Britain, 1968–1990* (New York: Cambridge University Press, 1994), 204.

8. "Ways and Means," *Chronicle of Higher Education*, 14 July 1995, p. A20. See also John Immerwahr and James Harvey, "What the Public Thinks of Colleges," *Chronicle of Higher Education*, 12 May 1995, pp. B1–B2.

9. See Louise Menand, "The Trashing of Professionalism," *Academe* (May–June 1995): 16–19. The classic history of American anti-intellectualism is found in Richard Hofstadter, *Anti-intellectualism in American Life* (New York: Alfred A. Knopf, 1963).

10. See *Scholarly Journals at the Crossroads: A Subversive Proposal for Electronic Publishing* (Washington: Association of Research Libraries' Office of Scientific and Academic Publishing, 1995).

11. Smith, *New Right Discourse*, 204.

12. See bell hooks, "Confronting Class in the Classroom," in *Teaching to Transgress: Education as the Practice of Freedom* (New York: Routledge, 1994), 177–89.

13. Jonathan Silin, *Sex, Death, and the Education of Children: Our Passion for Ignorance in the Age of AIDS* (New York: Teachers College Press, 1995), 113.

14. The high prestige of medical doctors, and especially surgeons, seems to counter this observation. In fact, until the development of anesthesia in the mid-nineteenth century, surgeons were denigrated by university-trained physicians as mere "empirics" and "mechanics" precisely because of their direct involvement with the human body. "Any profession bases its claim for its position on the possession of a skill so esoteric or complex that non-members of the profession cannot perform the work safely or satisfactorily and cannot even evaluate the work properly." Elliot Friedson, *Profession of Medicine* (New York: Dodd and Mead, 1970), 45.

15. Jervis Anderson, "The Public Intellectual," *New Yorker*, 17 January 1994, p. 40.

16. *Report to the Task Force on Criteria for Promotion to Full Professor*, 31 May 1995. The complete text is available from the Office of Vice President for Arts, Sciences and Technology, Ballou Hall, Tufts University, Medford, MA 02155.

17. Judith Butler, *Gender Trouble: Feminism and the Subversion of Identity* (New York: Routledge, 1990), vii.

18. Matthew Fox, *The Reinvention of Work: A New Vision of Livelihood For Our Time* (New York: Harper Collins, 1995), 98.

19. Fox, *Reinvention of Work*, 264.

20. hooks, *Teaching to Transgress*, 15.

21. See Sarah Chinn, "Queering the Profession, or Just Professionalizing Queers?" in *Tilting the Tower*, ed. Linda Garber (New York: Routledge, 1994), 243–50.

Chapter Eleven

Re-Forming (Hetero) Sexuality Education

Linda Eyre
University of New Brunswick (Canada)

Introduction

The 1995/96 Canadian AIDS Awareness Campaign, sponsored by the Canadian Public Health Association, has apparently raised the ire of AIDS activists across the country.[1] In recognition of National AIDS Awareness Week, the Association distributed a series of posters promoting the message that homophobia is a barrier in the fight against AIDS. A poster that fell across my desk certainly raised my eyebrows. The image: A young White man, alone, ear-ring in left ear, collarless shirt, short hair, sideways glance, sitting on a bus. Heading out of town, perhaps? The text: "People say it takes courage to live with AIDS. Well it takes courage to deal with people who reject me because I'm gay"; and "It takes more than condoms to fight AIDS. It takes your acceptance and understanding." While attempting to work towards equality by challenging homophobia, the Canadian Public Health Association has fallen into a heterosexist trap by using gay stereotypes, in troping gay stereotypes with AIDS, and by calling for "acceptance" and "understanding" from the viewer, who is presumed to be heterosexual. The poster exemplifies the paradox I address in this essay; that is, the way in which pedagogical practices supposedly intended to work towards social change risk reproducing the very aspects of injustice that they seek to rectify.[2]

I focus on the underlying liberal ideology of supposedly anti-heterosexist pedagogical approaches to sexuality education in Canada. Drawing on critiques from gay and lesbian theory, I examine three pedagogical practices typically used by sexual health educators in secondary schools to challenge traditional (hetero)sexuality education. I have used all three approaches myself, they are often used by other sexual health educators, and they are often mentioned in curriculum resources and in health education literature. My point is not to suggest a one-correct-way of doing things, but to question the pedagogical assumptions, the inherent contradictions, and the limits and possibilities for social change suggested by each approach. I argue that, as social change activists, I/we must pay closer attention to how opposition to anti-heterosexist pedagogy in sexuality education works—how discourses that appear to work towards social justice can subtly discriminate and exclude.

The impetus for this essay comes from my own work as a high-school teacher, as a university professor who works with future health educators, and as someone who has worked on curriculum development with various departments of education. During my career, opposition to sexuality education per se has been perceived as coming from the Christian Right. School administrators and department of education consultants with whom I worked were reluctant to raise "red-flag" issues,[3] claiming the possibility of reprisals from various community religious groups. Small gains in (hetero)sexuality education at the local level were prized. However, opposition to the development of curricula presenting a more inclusive approach to sexuality education is complex. Anti-heterosexist pedagogies and practices continue to be undermined by a variety of political ideologies, ranging from those that are Far-Right (which oppose any attempt at anti-heterosexist pedagogy), to those that are New-Right (which profess nuclear familialism), to those that are liberal (which espouse supposedly liberatory pedagogies and practices).

I have also been motivated by my increasing discomfort with the outcome of my own attempts at presenting anti-heterosexist pedagogies to beginning teachers (see Eyre 1993). I have found the pedagogical practices that I use to be generally ineffective in helping profoundly homophobic students change their attitudes and practices towards gay men, lesbians, and bisexual women and men. Amid scenes of angry backlash, I have tended to blame myself for being ineffective, for being too defensive, or for having unrealistic expectations; and I have often thought my students to be closed-minded. I have tended not to question the pedagogical assumptions and contradictions inherent in my teaching approaches.

Impetus has also come from separate conversations with Ursula Kelly and Suzanne de Castell regarding an earlier paper in which I recounted my "horror stories"[4] of homophobic classroom encounters. Their comments and questions helped me realize how students' homophobic responses to my pedagogy were not necessarily a result of my being an ineffective teacher in a technical sense, but rather through the heterosexist assumptions and liberal ideologies that I brought, and no doubt still bring, to questions of identity and inclusivity. Whereas I agree with Mary Lydon (1988, 141) who says women scholars should resist "the confessional impulse," I also support Biddy Martin (1988, 13), who, in discussing the links between Foucault and feminism, says that his work "does insist that we understand and take account of the ways in which we are implicated in power relations and the fact that we are never outside of power." This essay, then, is also an attempt to recognize my own implication in deeply embedded heterosexist pedagogies and practices.

Naming Heterosexism

Educational researchers who support inclusive pedagogies have for some time challenged educators to confront heterosexism in (hetero)sexuality education curricula and heterosexualized classrooms (see Fine 1988; Lenskyj 1991a, 1991b; Sears 1992; Whatley 1992). Other writers have specifically challenged schools to confront homophobic acts of individual and institutional violence against lesbian, gay, and bisexual students and teachers (Doe 1991; Khayatt 1990; Rofes 1989; Trenchard 1992; Wicks 1991). Collectively, this work has raised questions about the invisibility and/or distortion of bisexual, gay, and lesbian sexualities in school health curricula and resources. The work supports a vision of school sexuality education that celebrates the diversity of human sexuality; counters heterosexism and homophobia; politicizes bisexual, lesbian, and gay issues; and legitimizes the experiences of bisexual, lesbian, and gay students and teachers.

Naming Discourses of Eradication

Whereas the naming of heterosexism in (hetero)sexuality education motivated sexual education activists like myself, it has accomplished little in countering the political conservatism that swirls in and around sexuality education in schools.[5] I have found the work of poststructural writers helpful both in understanding the persistence of (hetero)sexuality education in schools and in considering an appropriate response to this situation. From a poststructuralist perspective, social relationships are constituted not by one structure but by different discourses; and they are constituted "in such a way that conflict between discourses marks all symbolic activity" (Banister et al. 1994, 94). Here, the "unitary, prior, essential subject" is replaced by "a fragmented subject, constituted in difference," and power is viewed "not as a negative constrained action, but as a positive, constitutive activity, contested and resisted" (Fox 1994, 19).

Eve Kosofsky Sedgwick, Cindy Patton, and Deborah Britzman brilliantly explore how discourse, knowledge, and power work in the formation of sexual identity. Sedgwick (1990) exposes contradictions in pedagogical practices that tend to present, on the one hand, homo/heterosexual identity formation as having relevance to everyone (a "universalizing view") and, on the other hand, treat gay, lesbian, and bisexual identities as separate and fixed categories having nothing to do with the social relations of heterosexuality (a "minoritizing" view). Sedgwick argues that educators need to recognize how minoritizing and universalizing discourses can create and perpetuate marginalization.

Sedgwick further illustrates how professional discourses have shifted from Far-Right to New-Right positions. She argues that psychoanalytic discourses have merely moved from discourses about extinction to discourses about prevention. The latter are now evident in

> biologically based "explanations" of deviant behaviour that are absolutely invariably couched in terms of "excess," "deficiency," or "imbalance"—whether in the hormones, in the genetic material, or, as is currently fashionable, in the fetal endocrine environment. (1993b, 79)

Sedgwick's argument is recently exemplified in what the medical establishment now terms "Gender Identity Disorder of Childhood" (see Britzman 1995, 73). In short, being gay, lesbian, or bisexual is rarely viewed positively.

Patton (1993) illustrates how sexuality education has been influenced, simultaneously, by (1) the increased visibility of the gay and lesbian rights movements and (2) the genocidal politics of the Far Right and the neoconservative politics of the New Right. She argues that it is crucial for educators to recognize the subtle distinctions between Far-Right and New-Right discourses, even though both are intent on the eradication of gay people. Whereas Far-Right strategies attempt to stop sexuality education, New-Right discourses simply insist that it be carried out within a framework of heteronormativity.

Britzman (1995) has specifically identified three neoconservative discourses that normalize heterosexuality and pathologize homosexuality. The first supports the myth that lesbian- and gay-affirmative sexuality education will encourage heterosexually identified students to become lesbian or gay. Hidden in this discourse are the notions that absence of information about homosexuality will keep people heterosexual and that gay-positive educators must be gay or lesbian. In other words, "knowledge and people are deemed dangerous, predatory, and contagious" (Britzman 1995, 74). A second discourse concerns the myth that adolescents are too young (1) to be bisexual, lesbian, or gay or (2) to have social relations with bisexual, lesbian, and gay peers, friends, or family members. A third myth presents homosexual and heterosexual identities as separate and private, as though "ignorance about homosexuality has nothing to do with ignorance about heterosexuality" (74). Britzman argues that these three discourses work together "to produce normative notions of heterosexuality as the stable and natural sexuality" (75).

The long-awaited *Canadian Guidelines for Sexual Health Education* (Health Canada 1994), while reflecting an inclusive position, may also be seen to contribute to discourses that normalize heterosexuality. The *Guidelines* states: "In terms of access and content, effective sexual health education does not discriminate against race, gender, sexual orientation, religion, ethnocultural background, or disability" (8). But it also states: "Effective sexual health education enhances sexual health within the context of an individual's values, moral beliefs, religious or ethnocultural background, sexual orientation or other such characteristic" (8). This seems to suggest that homophobia is allowed if it falls within an individual's values or moral beliefs. This critique raises the question of individual rights versus collective rights, but, as Barbara Smith (1993) points out, homophobia is often the last oppression to be recognized, and it continues to be institutionally sanctioned. The contradiction inherent in the *Guidelines* has not gone unnoticed (see Naus 1995; Valentich and Gripton 1995).

Taking Risks/Living Contradictions

I now go on to show the contradictions inherent in pedagogical practices explicitly intended to challenge heteronormativity and heterosexism; how educators deal with these contradictions in individual classrooms may be a different matter. The three pedagogical practices that I address are: (1) the "add-on" approach, (2) the gay and/or lesbian guest-speaker approach, and (3) the anti-homophobia workshop.

The "Add-On" Approach

Some recent curricula documents in sexuality education direct educators to provide students with specific information about gay and lesbian sexuality. These documents often include (1) a definition of terms such as "gay," "lesbian," "bisexual," and "homosexual," (2) statistics on the number of people who are homosexual, and (3) theories on the "causes" of homosexuality. Curricula definitions generally focus on sex acts but are usually vague about what lesbians actually "do" (a gender issue here), and they often refer to anal intercourse solely in relation to gay men; statistics often refer to "one in ten," à la the Kinsey Report (Uribe and Harbeck 1992); and theories about the origins of sexual identity focus on whether homosexuality is biologically or socially determined. The add-on approach is used in sexuality education curricula in general and in AIDS education in particular.

Whereas the add-on approach to sexuality education fills a void in curricula that were previously silent about bisexual, lesbian, and gay sexualities, it has inherent problems. Attempts at definition suggest it is possible to reduce sexual identity to neat categories (a minoritizing view), thus ignoring the complexity of how sexual identities are constructed in relation to one another (a universalizing view) (Sedgwick 1990). Also, reducing sexual identity to specific sex acts suggests that sexual identity is only about sex and has nothing to do with issues of power, politics, or civil rights (Britzman 1995). Moreover, the pedagogical practice of discussing anal intercourse in relation to gay men only, rather than across sexual identities, perpetuates the notion that gay men are deviant, which, in turn, contributes to discourses about the evils of homosexuality (Patton 1993).

Whereas statistics can be used to legitimize gay and lesbian sexuality (Uribe and Harbeck 1992), they are just as likely to be used to support a neoconservative position: "one in ten" can be used to justify exclusion (Patton 1993). Patton describes this strategy as "a new form of governmentality, concerned with the rules by which groups may claim subject status" (161). As well, discussions on the origins of homosexuality can be used to support beliefs that homosexuality is preventable—either through genetic engineering (changing nature) or through socialization (choosing differently). Sedgwick (1993a, 257) argues that nature/nurture arguments cannot be separated from the "gay-genocidal nexuses of thought through which they have developed." Furthermore, the educational practice of linking homosexuality, anal-intercourse, and AIDS can contribute to discourses about the unnaturalness of bisexual, gay, and lesbian sexualities. As Patton says, "the 'social disease' known as AIDS is actually homosexuality" (1993, 158).

The Guest-Speaker Approach

Increasingly, members of gay and lesbian organizations are being called upon to speak to high-school or university students about what it is like to "be" bisexual, gay, or lesbian. Such stories frequently include personal accounts of identity formation, "coming out," and experiences of homophobia. This approach assumes that (1) students are not gay, lesbian, or bisexual; (2) students do not already have social relations with gay people; and (3) personal stories will help homophobic students develop "tolerance" for lesbians, gay men, and bisexual men and women.

As Mary Bryson and Suzanne de Castell (1993a, 296) argue, the guest-speaker approach has enabled lesbians, gay men, and bisexual women and men "to insist on the 'right to speak as one' [and] to make pedagogical spaces where the hitherto unsayable could be uttered." But what do students learn and at what cost? Following a gender-equity course I team-taught with Celia Haig-Brown in the summer of 1991, Celia wrote about our efforts, as heterosexually identified women, to address anti-essentialism:

> We exploit our friends. We call [on] them to be what Suzanne [de Castell] calls "performing parrots." Step right up: a real live Lesbian. She walks and talks and you can ask her anything you want. We expose our friends to ignorance and abuse. . . . Come to my class and enlighten us. When is a token not a token? How many differences[?] . . . How many lives? How much pain? (Bryson, de Castell, and Haig-Brown 1993, 48)

In personal communication, Suzanne de Castell described her talk to our class (de Castell 1991) as "personally awful." Impressed with her eloquence and humor, I had been unaware of her pain.

Lisa Jeffs (1995), a self-identified lesbian, recently wrote about the abuse she typically receives when invited to speak to high-school students about "issues of concern to lesbians, gays and bisexuals" (6). She described her feelings when, after a one-hour presentation to high-school students, a young woman said loudly: "All of them should be shot" (6). Jeffs also listed the kinds of questions she is often asked by students:

> Why do lesbians hate men? Are all gay men child molesters? If you know someone who is gay are you likely to become gay yourself? If lesbians and gays have children will they be gay too? Are there any black gays? . . . How did you get "that way"? What is it like living "that way"? Why don't you stop being "that way"? and Don't you know that you will go to hell because you are "that way"? (8)

Jeffs did not indicate if or how she answered the students' questions. Nevertheless, her descriptions of the events indicate that homophobic violence and endless discussions on the origins of homosexuality are part of her taken-for-granted experience in schools. Britzman writes:

> For the gay or lesbian teacher and students who must listen as their cohorts work through or become entrenched in their heterosexism . . . the "unleashing of unpopular things" always has the potential to not only colonize social imagination—that is bring many back to the place of departure—but also to disorganize the efforts of those who attempt to intervene. (1992, 155)

What Jeffs also does not address is the danger that she may have planted a fixed notion of what it means to "be" lesbian. This approach also suggests that bisexuals, lesbians, and/or gay men have either similar or, conversely, very different experiences of desire and discrimination, when neither of these views should be assumed (Sedgwick, 1993a). Not only may the dynamics of the interrelationships of heterosexual, gay, lesbian, and bisexual identities be missed, but, just as important, the complexities of intersecting oppressions may be overlooked. This means considering, for example, how the oppressions of gender, race, ability, and sexuality intersect, and how "a person who is disabled through one set of oppressions may *by the same positioning* be enabled through others" (Sedgwick 1993a, 253).

Also, as Bryson and de Castell argue, the context for speaking as a lesbian is often clearly defined in heterosexual terms:

> Although lesbians now are occasionally permitted to speak in the academy, we can only speak *about* but we cannot speak *as* lesbians, except insofar as we are prepared, in such speaking, to make of ourselves not lesbian subjects, but lesbian objects, objects of study, of interrogation, of confession, of consumption. Nor can we speak *to* lesbians, except as we are prepared to place them in jeopardy, to open and dissect a subjectivity created for and by the dominant other. (1993a, 301)

In addition, presenting a lesbian, gay man, or bisexual woman or man as a "feature of the day" may further pathologize homosexuality and, ultimately, drive bisexual, lesbian, and gay students into hiding.

Following similar "guest" presentations in my own classroom, I have heard heterosexually identified students say: "Well I don't agree with it, but it's okay if that's what they want to do." Whereas such comments are often delivered as progressive and democratic, they are indicative of New-Right discourses about sexual identity as a choice; in other words, one could choose differently. Also, as I have shown elsewhere (Eyre 1993), students have used the occasion to actively posture homophobia, while others have remained silent—afraid to speak lest they be thought to be bisexual, lesbian, or gay. As Deborah Britzman says: "This queer paradox—of emerging identities becoming more visible yet less understood—needs exploration" (1995, 80).

The Anti-Homophobia Workshop

Anti-homophobia workshops/in-service for teachers and special sessions for students are slowly gaining institutional sanction, albeit as part of AIDS education[6] or under the guise of "violence-in-schools" rhetoric. This approach typically explores individual practices that perpetuate discrimination and prejudice on the basis of sexual identity. The focus is usually on myths, stereotyping, discrimination, homophobic slurs, and acts of physical violence against lesbians, gay men, and bisexual women and men. This approach assumes that knowledge about homophobia will lead to change in individual homophobic practices and, ultimately, help bring about social change.

Even though anti-homophobia approaches to sexuality education name individual acts of violence against lesbians, gay men, and bisexual women and men, they are not without problems. A focus on stereotypes and discrimination might suggest that, if discrimination were eliminated, then "gay people [would] have no further political interest as a group" (Warner 1993, xi), which might suggest that gay, lesbian, and/or bisexual identities are merely "a way of being" rather than a "matter of duty and ethics" (Patton 1993, 148). In other words, an emphasis on individual homophobic acts can support a New-Right agenda by diverting attention away from larger social forces that support and maintain the normalization of heterosexuality as well as away from the growing collective political activism of gay and lesbian groups. Moreover, as Britzman eloquently states, attention to the negative aspects of being gay, lesbian, or bisexual without knowledge of "the pleasures of desire, this thing called love . . . [risks] reinscribing the very conditions of normalization one attempts to name" (1995, 84).

We Are All Implicated

Whereas all three pedagogical practices fill a void in (hetero)sexuality education by putting bisexual, gay, and lesbian identities on the agenda in the heterosexualized classroom, each could be said to contribute to discourses that "render as deviant 'queerness'" (Britzman 1995, 73). Each approach assumes that knowledge about gayness, lesbianism, and bisexuality will lead to social change, and none questions the embedded assumptions about the formation of sexual identity actively produced by such knowledge. Each approach presents homosexuality and heterosexuality as separate, fixed, and opposed categories that have nothing to do with one another. All three approaches fit into what Sedgwick (1990, 1993a) describes as "minoritizing" orientations to the study of sexual identity formation, thereby doing little to facilitate Foucault's desire to create "different conceptions and possibilities for relating" or to "threaten that 'bedrock of existence' . . . and undermine the structures on which contemporary power alignments and their solidity depend" (Martin 1988, 12).

Thus pedagogical practices explicitly intended to educate students about sexuality may, paradoxically, be influenced by subtle neoconservative discourses that continue to affirm heterosexuality as the appropriate and desirable sexual identity. As Sedgwick argues, ignorance is not neutral; it is not a lack of knowledge but an effect of knowledge: "Ignorances are produced by and correspond to particular knowledges and circulate as part of particular regimes of truth" (1990, 8).

The Work Continues

Until recently it has been assumed that the development of sexuality education was held back by well-organized Right-wing groups opposed to any form of sex education. In communities across the country, enormous energy and huge amounts of resources have been used to combat the power of these groups, often leaving sexuality educators placated by minor successes and too debilitated to take further risks. This essay has attempted to illustrate (1) the contradictory meanings inherent within "progressive" approaches to sexuality education, (2) how New-Right discourses seduce educators into believing they are progressive and future-oriented (often by the use of discourses of "equity," "discrimination," and "inclusion"), and (3) how discourses become very powerful when inscribed in pedagogical practices. Far-Right, New-Right, and progressive liberal ideologies appear to have left little room for the Left in sexuality education.

The concept of a single overarching "backlash" to describe opposition to anti-heterosexist pedagogies in sexuality education is both limited and limiting. The idea of a binary us/them did provide a sense of security for educators like myself working in similar "dangerous territories." It was a means of situating ourselves and mobilizing what was believed to be a collective vision of equality, difference, and curriculum change in sexuality education. Although some form of sexuality education is now in place in most school districts in Canada, liberatory educators must look carefully at the discourses and liberal ideologies that have shaped its implementation and are seriously undermining any challenges to its heteronormative position. A broader consideration of how progressive movements are undermined not only by the diverse politics of Right-wing forces "out there," but also, paradoxically, by different versions of sexual politics and social justice operating within Leftist groups, and in several sites of educational practice, including the state, is paramount if sexuality education is to take anti-heterosexist pedagogies and praxis seriously. Anything short of this is mere tokenism.

How do I/we learn to recognize the contradictions inherent in supposedly liberatory pedagogical policies and practices? How do I/we challenge discourses that subtly trap and dangerously invade supposedly liberatory pedagogical spaces? How can I/we gather the energy to not allow heteronormative discourses to paralyze and defeat my/our work? How can those who are already taking personal and professional risks by challenging (hetero)sexuality education be encouraged to interrogate their work and come to see how we are all implicated in its production and reproduction?

Sedgwick (1990, 40) compels liberatory educators to focus on pedagogical contradiction by interrogating their pedagogies as follows: "In whose lives is homo/heterosexual definition an issue of continuing centrality and difficulty?" Britzman (1995) recommends that sexuality educators become immersed in gay and lesbian studies so that they may gain a better understanding of the theories of identity construction. Bryson and de Castell (1993a, 285) support "an explicit ethics of consumption," where lesbian-, gay-, and bisexual-affirmative pedagogies would be guided by such questions as "At what cost?" and "To what end?" Sound advice, but questioning knowledge and ethics may not be enough to challenge the seductive discourses that operate in these doubly dangerous times of economic recession and the celebration of nuclear familialism.

In my/our efforts to interrogate pedagogical practices, let me/us not forget the daily advocacy work that is still needed. What is to be done about homophobic acts of individual and institutional violence? What is to be done about the material conditions of lesbian, gay, and bisexual students and teachers? Who will move sexuality education curricula beyond approaches that pathologize gay, lesbian, and bisexual identities to a vision that sanctions the "ordinariness of homosexuality" (Patton 1993, 143)? Will there be the necessary emotional and material support from colleagues, allies, and institutions to affect educational policies/programs and pedagogical practices? Despite the risks I/we take and the contradictions I/we live, I/we must continue to work to challenge (hetero)sexuality education, for, not to do so could, justifiably, be read as further collusion with a heterosexist agenda. In the meantime, there must be no more placating of the New Right with "opt-out" clauses disguised as democracy; no more treatment of homosexuality as a "sensitive issue"; no more troping of homosexuality with AIDS; no more slipping homophobia under the mat of "violence in schools"; no more consideration of bisexual, gay, and lesbian sexualities as chosen and specific sexual behaviors; no more wasted energies on the so-called origins of homosexuality; and no more treating bisexual, lesbian, and gay sexual identities as though they have nothing to do with constructions of heterosexuality.

Notes

1. In the winter 1995/96 edition of *Canadian AIDS News* 7 (3), 7, Liz Goodman Communications Officer, Canadian AIDS Society, alludes to the controversy created by the posters but does not elaborate on the issues involved.

2. My analysis of approaches to heterosexuality education has been inspired by Mary Bryson's and Suzanne de Castell's (1993b) critique of gender equity policy and practice, and Elizabeth Ellsworth's (1989) exposé of the contradictions, limits, and possibilities of critical pedagogy.

3. *Masturbation, abortion,* and *homosexuality* are usually grouped together as controversial issues that teachers may address (at their peril). For example, in the province of New Brunswick, where I am currently working, teachers are told that they may explain but not discuss these topics with high school students. And, discussion of any aspect of sexuality with elementary children is strictly regulated. In workshops run by the Department of Education, elementary school teachers are even told to say "parts of the body under the bathing suit" rather than "vagina," "vulva," "penis," and so on.

4. I owe this term to Leslie Roman. See Roman (1993) for discussion of "discourses of horror."

5. For example, curriculum development in sexuality education in New Brunswick seems to be at an impasse. The recent removal of the provincial consultant for sexuality/health education, the abolition of school boards, and the formation of parent advisory groups to the government may mean liberatory pedagogy has gone as far as it can go. As I write, a "Say No to Sex" program is touring junior high schools in the province.

6. See, for example, *Challenging Homophobia: An Addendum to Skills for Healthy Relationships* produced by the Social Program Evaluation Group, Queens University, sponsored by the Council of Ministers of Education Canada and funded by the AIDS Education and Prevention Unit under the National AIDS Strategy, Health Canada, 1995. Note also that although the document claims to compensate for the heterosexist approach taken in the parent document *Skills for Healthy Relationships* used in schools across Canada, it too is grounded in heterosexist assumptions. For example, some of the activities involve having "students" (presumably all students) "place themselves *in the shoes of* a gay or lesbian young person . . . [so that] they can *imagine* the prejudice, discrimination and pain that some must face" (1; my emphasis).

References

Banister, P., E. Burman, I. Parker, and M. Taylor. 1994. *Qualitative Methods in Psychology: A Research Guide.* Philadelphia: Open University Press.

Britzman, D. P. 1995. "What Is This Thing Called Love?" *Taboo: The Journal of Culture and Education* 1 (Spring): 65–93.

———. 1992. "Decentering Discourses in Teacher Education, Or, The Unleashing of Unpopular Things." In *What Schools Can Do: Critical Pedagogy and Practice,* edited by K. Weiler and C. Mitchell. 151–75. New York: SUNY.

Bryson, M., and S. de Castell. 1993a. "Queer Pedagogy: Praxis Makes Im/perfect." *Canadian Journal of Education* 18 (3): 285–305.

————. 1993b. "En/Gendering Equity: On Some Paradoxical Consequences of Institutionalized Programs of Emancipation." *Educational Theory* 43 (3): 341–55.

Bryson, M., S. de Castell, and C. Haig-Brown. 1993. "Gender Equity/Gender Treachery: Three Voices." *Border/Lines* 28: 46–54.

de Castell, S. 1991, August. Presentation given to Education 372 (Gender Equity Issues in Education), Simon Fraser University, Burnaby, British Columbia.

Doe, J. 1991. "Teaching on Thin Ice." *Our Schools/Our Selves* 3 (2): 74–79.

Ellsworth, E. 1989. "Why Doesn't this Feel Empowering? Working Through the Repressive Myths of Critical Pedagogy." *Howard Educational Review* 59: 297–324.

Eyre, L. 1993. "Compulsory Heterosexuality in a University Classroom." *Canadian Journal of Education* 18 (3): 273–84.

Fine, M. 1988. "Sexuality, Schooling and Adolescent Females: The Missing Discourse of Desire." *Harvard Educational Review* 58 (1): 29–53.

Fox, N. J. 1994. *Postmodernism, Sociology and Health.* Toronto: University of Toronto Press.

Jeffs, L. 1995. " 'So You Think I Should Be Shot?' Unteaching Homophobia." *Women's Education des Femmes* 11 (3): 6–10.

Health Canada. 1994. *Canadian Guidelines for Sexual Health Education.* Ottawa: Minister of Supply and Services Canada, Cat. H39–300/1994E.

Khayatt, M. D. 1990. "Lesbian Teachers: An Invisible Presence." In *Feminism and Education: A Canadian Perspective,* edited by F. Forman, M. O'Brien, J. Haddad, D. Hallman, and P. Masters. 191–218. Toronto: Ontario Institute for Studies in Education.

Lenskyj, H. 1991a. "Beyond Plumbing and Prevention: Feminist Approaches to Sex Education." In *Women and Education* (2nd ed.), edited by J. S. Gaskell and A. T. McLaren. 283–98. Calgary: Detselig.

————. 1991b. "Combatting Homophobia in Sport and Physical Education." *Sociology of Sport Journal* 8: 61–69.

Lydon, M. (1988). "Foucault and Feminism: A Romance of Many Directions." In *Feminism and Foucault: Reflections on Resistance,* edited by I. Diamond and L. Quinby. 135–48. Boston: Northeastern University Press.

Martin, B. 1988. "Feminism, Criticism, and Foucault." In *Feminism and Foucault: Reflections on Resistance,* edited by I. Diamond and L. Quinby. 3–20. Boston: Northeastern University Press.

Naus, P. 1995. "Applying the *Canadian Guidelines for Sexual Health Education* in a University Course and in a Community Setting." *Canadian Journal of Human Sexuality* 4 (1): 57–60.

Patton, C. 1993. "Tremble, Hetero Swine!" In *Fear of a Queer Planet: Queer Politics and Social Theory,* edited by M. Warner. 143–77. Minneapolis: University of Minnesota Press.

Rofes, E. 1989. "Opening Up the Classroom Closet: Responding to the Educational Needs of Gay and Lesbian Youth." *Harvard Educational Review* 59: 444–53.

Roman, L. G. 1993. "White is a Color! White Defensiveness, Postmodernism, and Anti-Racist Pedagogy." In *Race, Identity and Representation in Education,* edited by C. McCarthy and W. Crichlow. 71–88. New York: Routledge.

Sears, J. T. 1992. *Sexuality and the Curriculum: The Politics and Practices of Sexuality Education*. New York: Teachers College Press.

Sedgwick, E. K. 1990. *Epistemology of the Closet*. Berkeley: University of California Press.

———. 1993a. "Axiomatic." In *The Cultural Studies Reader*, edited by S. During. 243–68. New York: Routledge.

———. 1993b. "How to Bring Your Kids Up Gay." In *Fear of a Queer Planet: Queer Politics and Social Theory*, edited by M. Warner. 69–81. Minneapolis: University of Minnesota Press.

Smith, B. 1993. "Homophobia: Why Bring It Up?" In *The Lesbian and Gay Studies Reader*, edited by H. Abelove, M. A. Barale, and D. M. Halperin. 99–102. New York: Routledge.

Trenchard, L. 1992. "Young Lesbians at School." In *Learning to Lose: Sexism and Education*, edited by D. Spender and E. Sarah. 193–200. London: The Women's Press.

Uribe, V. and K. M. Harbeck. 1992. "Addressing the Needs of Lesbian, Gay, and Bisexual Youth: The Origins of Project 10 and School-Based Intervention." In *Coming Out of the Classroom Closet: Gay and Lesbian Students, Teachers, and Curricula*, edited by K. M. Harbeck. 9–28. Binghamton, NY: Harrington Park Press.

Valentich, M., and J. Gripton. 1995. "Canadian Guidelines for Sexual Health Education: Application to Social Work Practice." *Canadian Journal of Human Sexuality* 4 (1): 47–56.

Warner, M. 1993. "Introduction." In *Fear of a Queer Planet: Queer Politics and Social Theory*, edited by M. Warner. vii–xxxi. Minneapolis: University of Minnesota Press.

Whatley, M. H. 1992. "Images of Gays and Lesbians in Sexuality and Health Textbooks." In *Coming out of the Classroom Closet: Gay and Lesbian Students, Teachers, and Curricula*, edited by K. M. Harbeck. 197–212. Binghamton, NY: Harrington Park Press.

Wicks, M. 1991. "A Day Without Homophobia." *Teacher: News Magazine of the BC Teachers' Federation* 3 (7): 7.

Chapter Twelve

Empires, Emigrés, and Aliens: Young People's Negotiations of Official and Popular Racism in Canada

Leslie G. Roman
University of British
Columbia (Canada)

Timothy J. Stanley
Université d'Ottawa (Canada)

Young people, like their teachers and other adults, develop their notions of "racial" and "national" difference from a range of conflicting official and popular discourses.[1] These discourses are neither simply imposed from above nor voluntaristically acted upon from below. Instead, they are mediated by particular asymmetries of power and historical/political and cultural contexts that define and redefine the borders of nations, nationalist pedagogies, and curricula. By the same token, young people are not passive receivers of knowledge waiting to be acted upon by "the right" or "correct" interventions, as is often assumed in academic research and in pedagogical practices. Students are themselves active agents of cultural production, though their agency is not separable from larger structures of power and inequality.[2] It matters how they make sense of hegemonic struggles over the meanings of "national belongingness," "diaspora," and "exclusion." As students and young people, they have a great deal to teach "us" (particularly educators) about the contradictions of inhabiting places of neocolonialism and racism while at the same time striving for languages and community identifications that challenge their effects.

In this essay, we show how young people in a Grade Seven classroom in a Vancouver, British Columbia, public elementary school,[3] both articulate and are articulated by the conflicting discourses of race, nation, and diaspora. We briefly discuss the social composition and breakdown of the class in terms of ethnicity, race, class, gender, languages spoken, and so on, and the implications for positioning the students as speakers in the class. We show how the students attempt to articulate their understandings of the official multicultural policy (as practiced in their school) and what they imagine to be the moral responsibilities and pedagogical implications of a yet unrealized (and thus unofficial) anti-imperialist postcolonial practice.

The impetus for our analysis comes primarily from what we have learned from the students and their teacher in relation to our own specific experiences as university educators working with prospective or practicing teachers and with people who have worked on curriculum development in the contested arena of multiculturalism and antiracism. The data upon which we draw come from an assignment one of us (Roman) gave to her students in an antiracist pedagogy graduate seminar, who were predominantly practicing teachers, and the way it was carried out by one of these students.[4] It is also informed and inspired by a growing literature on antiracist and postcolonial feminist theory and empirical research.[5] This literature attempts to countenance the realities of globalization, cross-national migrations, and diasporic identifications as well as the gendered symbolism and bases of different nationalisms and neocolonial formations.[6] The analysis we offer is provisional in its development and extension of postcolonial feminist theory, and partial in both senses of the term.[7]

Crucial to the development of anti-imperialist postcolonial pedagogies is establishing an empirical basis from which to critique long-standing popular and academic conceptions of "childhood"—conceptions that construct young people as infantalized subjects who live in simple universes untainted by social divisions and conflicts, and who are incapable of complex moral judgments.[8] Likewise, in contradistinction to the ideologies and discourses of many mandated nationalist curricula, classrooms and schools are not extensions of a fictive national family that harmoniously nurtures individual growth and civic responsibility. Instead, they are sites of contestation and symbolic (sometimes physical) violence; that is, they are sites of hegemonic struggles to legitimate some social identities and communities while delegitimating others. Such struggles include, among others, those establishing meanings and identitites/communities for "national belongingness" or "citizenship" as well as those relating to their obverse, "national exclusion" or "alienness."

What young people have to teach educators and other students is illustrated by our analysis of a participatory video project conducted by a Grade Seven teacher (herein called "Mr. Peter DuBarry") with the students in a mixed (according to gender, ethnicity, class, and race) classroom in a Vancouver public elementary school (referred to as "MacArthur Elementary School").[9] The video project sought to explore how DuBarry's students understood racism and the role of teachers and students in antiracist initiatives. It began as part of DuBarry's way of fulfilling the final requirement for Roman's university graduate seminar in antiracist pedagogy and yet it was also mediated by the conceptions of permissable multiculturalist and antiracist practice already understood in the everyday workings of MacArthur Elementary School. The video project was the culminating event for the teacher both as a graduate student and as a dedicated teacher exploring how his students would respond to his questions about their experiences of racism and their understandings of the moral responsibilities of schools, teachers, and students in practicing what they saw as antiracism. Thus our interpretations of DuBarry's intervention and the students' discourses are not innocent: they irredeemably situate us within broader social relations of unequal power (most notably, those enacted between a professor and her graduate student, and those enacted between a public school teacher and his students). To say this is an unfinished and intertextual work is to say that we take seriously the risks and ethical dangers of imposing our constructions on the students' discourses. A similar danger exists with respect to how we analyze the contradictions of DuBarry's intervention with his students—contradictions evident in the assumptions underlying the questions he chose to ask them and in our discussion of those questions here.

We recognize that our project of analyzing the students' discourses is fraught with ethical and methodological dilemmas. The challenge is to permit these dilemmas to trouble our emergent interpretations and theories. We aim to minimize (if not avoid altogether) a lack of reflexivity that would do symbolic violence to the discourses of these students or to their teacher's laudable efforts. At the same time, refusing to engage critically with what the students say and do not say is no less a form of symbolic violence, since it infantalizes them as contemporary paternal wards. Similar dangers exist with respect to analyzing DuBarry's discourse. We see the process of troubling our emergent theories with our analysis of the students' discourses and DuBarry's intervention as, on balance, a necessary and worthwhile high-wire to walk. Thus, we show how the students' racialized, gendered, nationalized and/or diasporic, and class-specific understandings of themselves and others, as well as of their moral positions on the subject of racism and antiracism, cannot be read in an essentialized manner. In other words, they do not follow directly from structurally determined or dominant readings of their racialized, nationalized, gender- and class-specific, and diasporic locations. On the other hand, neither can the students' understandings be seen as detached or separable from the larger system of social determinations and processes of representation that locates them as racialized, gendered, classed, nationalized, or diasporized subjects—or as subjects seen to possess citizenship rights or not.

Contextualizing the Students' Discourses:
Conflicting Discourses of "Race" and "Nation"

Young people, like most adults, are exposed to the idea that Canada is a multicultural society by virtue of its celebration of diversity—of different "ethnocultural" groups that are pieced together in one "mosaic" called "the nation."[10] Under this rubric, schools, along with other institutions (such as the family) are expected to teach children the principles and practices necessary to achieve the "intercultural harmony and tolerance" of so-called racial/ethnic and national differences (which have been equated with so-called "cultural differences"). In the context of critiquing what he sees as the "moralist misuse" of antiracist political struggle in educational institutions, Paul Gilroy turns his attention away from the obvious forms of racism, which overtly evidence biodeterministic stigmatizations in public discourse, redirecting it toward what he calls the "new culturalist racism" (Gilroy 1990, 114). He observes that the "new culturalist racism" secures its notion of "tolerance" largely without direct or spoken reference to the residual biodeterministic category of "race" (115). For Gilroy, the new or emergent culturalist racism operates through a reductive or essentialist understanding of ethnic and national difference as well as an

> absolute sense of culture so powerful that [it] is capable of separating people off from each other and diverting them into historical and social locations understood to be mutually impermeable and incommensurable. Ethnic absolutism may not trade in the vocabularies of 'race' or 'the symbolism of colour,' and most important, it can afflict anyone. In fact, those who experience racism themselves may be particularly prone to its lure. They often seize upon its simple self-evident truths as a way of rationalizing their subordination and comprehending their own particularity. It is therefore necessary to argue against the rhetoric of cultural insiderism and the narrow practice of cultural nationalism whatever their source. (115)

Rather than relying on the older, aggressively biodeterministic discourse, the emergent discourse of ethnic absolutism, according to Gilroy, treats "culture/s" as distinct and as composed of largely distinguishable characteristics of language and religion that are " 'naturally' reproduced in families" and transmitted in the official national histories of schools (114).

Yet while multiculturalism itself often unwittingly supports or promotes an emergent discourse of ethnic absolutism, even its liberal (rather than radical) ideological notions of cultural difference are not to be taken for granted in the current conservative political conjuncture. Of late, the discourse and the policies instituting official Canadian multiculturalism increasingly confront a Right-wing popular moral panic over a perceived racial and national invasion by so-called non-Canadians.[11] By this, we mean the discursive ideology conveyed by neoconservative critics of multicultur-alism (through the dominant media and other institutions) that particular "visible minorities"[12]—a euphemism for the racially oppressed and immi-grant groups—are "aliens" whose presence threatens to drain the nation of scarce employment, educational, health, and housing opportunities. This discourse attempts to structure commonsense notions about *whose* cultural practices constitute membership in Canada's version of civility and who may (or may not) be considered worthy or deserving of citizenship rights. It is particularly evident within the current evocative and powerful discourses on "immigration" that construct select groups of immigrants, refugees, and political dissidents as "menaces to Canadianness." Within such discourses, Canada is represented as a "nation-at-risk" of losing its moral (and, implic-itly, patriarchal) authority, if not its political and economic control over "traditional" institutions.[13] Those constructed by such moral panics as "menaces to Canadianness" are not always confined to particular groups immigrating to Canada. They may also include those subjects of racism, antisemitism, colonialism, and neocolonialism who live within Canada's national borders (e.g. First Nations and Aboriginal peoples, Jewish Canadians, Chinese or Japanese Canadians, Quebecois nationalists, among others), whose demands for political enfranchisement, land claims, linguis-tic preservation and/or religious self-determination challenge dominant English-Canadian ideas of "settlement" and nation-building. At one and the same time, moral panics over immigration and racial/national invasion are in fact struggles over political belongingness and/or formal citizenship rights. They articulate a neoconservative nostalgia on the part of those Canadians who fondly draw upon a national imaginary of their Anglo-centric heritage and British colonial legacy as free from the horrors of con-quest, domination, and deterritorialization, and who call into question the struggles of those people whose demands for political enfranchisement are seen as threatening or perverse.

What is at stake in moral panics over immigration and racial/national invasion is the hegemonic struggle to define commonsense notions of civil-ity, decency, and the symbolic public, or community of belongingness, that Canada as a nation (or any nation, for that matter) is said to represent. Such discourses obscure people's diverse historical reasons and material/political conditions either for moving to Canada or for fomenting colonization within the land now known as Canada. Moreover, they project a fictive, if not reified, notion of Canada as a nation, erroneously constructing diverse White ethnic groups as homogeneous with regard to their sense of entitle-ment and national belongingness.

As part of the project of Western imperialism, moral panics over immigration and racial/national invasion are neither unique to the 1990s nor to Canada. What is significant about the current historical juncture (which is also spatial/political) are the discursive and historical geographical forms taken by the ideological clash between two official versions of "Canadianness." While the relatively recent and "emergent" version, multiculturalism, draws upon notions of Canada as a place expressing liberal tolerance of "cultural differences and diversity," an older, "residual" version, now operating within a moral panic of racial and/or national invasion, increasingly reasserts an open masculinist intolerance for perceived racial/ethnic and national cultural differences. It advocates a return to monoculturalism—the underside of multiculturalism. This residual version of Canadianness draws upon the rhetoric of a homogeneous national epic of Anglo-conformity, in which perceived "ethnic" and "racial differences" are represented as alien to Canada as nation. Indeed, multiculturalism itself is blamed for having opened the floodgates to those "aliens" who are alleged to have created national instability.

Theorizing the Silenced Discourses of Antiracism and Anti-imperialist Postcolonialism

Our analysis extends the important insights of Fazal Rizvi (1993), who draws upon the ideas of Stuart Hall and Ludwig Wittgenstein concerning the struggle of the interests at play in the articulation of grammars of popular racism.[14] We argue that an adequate understanding of "grammars of popular racism" must explicitly account not only for the rules, conventions, and moral judgments that establish the spoken discourses and practices of racialized and neocolonial exclusion, but also for the antiracist and anti-imperialist discourses that are silenced and suppressed both in the present moment and historically.

While we agree with Rizvi that young people have agency in the process of identity construction and that, as "they grow older, [they] increasingly seek to locate themselves within the contradictory discourses of popular racism" (Rizvi 1993, 126), they are not the sole arbiters of their identity construction. As Hall puts it, "identity is formed at the unstable point where the 'unspeakable' stories of subjectivity meet the narratives of history, of a culture" (Hall 1988, 44). If grammars of popular racism are to be adequately understood, as well as challenged, a more complex analysis of the practices and conventions that could violate the imperial imagination is necessary. Such violations would be seen to enable particular groups of young people to speak and to be heard.

Situating "Diversity" in MacArthur School

Background

MacArthur Elementary School reflects Vancouver's ethnic/racial diversity, serving 545 students from a variety of backgrounds.[15] Despite being located in a lower-middle-class neighborhood in the inner urban core (which is undergoing gentrification), the school also includes within its catchment area students who live in low-income housing. Sixty-one per cent of the students (i.e., 330) fall within the Vancouver School Board's designation of those who speak English as a second language (ESL), qualifying them for some form of English language service or instruction.[16] MacArthur's percentage of ESL students is slightly higher than the district average of 47.9 per cent. A minority of students (182) speak English exclusively, both at home and at school. In addition to English, the predominant languages spoken in the homes of students, according to the British Columbia Ministry of Education's classifications, are: Chinese (182), Punjabi (43), Hindi (30), Spanish (26), Vietnamese (11), Tagalog (5), Japanese (3), Italian (3), and Arabic (2). Fourteen students speak eleven other languages.

Not surprisingly, MacArthur is committed to official Canadian multiculturalism. This commitment is described in its annual "Multicultural Action Plan," which each year is assigned (for upgrading) to a group of teachers appointed to the school's multiculturalism committee.[17] According to this plan, several classes participate in conducting "heritage" studies of each student in the school. This is supposed to encourage students to "share their customs" with their classmates and to invite their parents to "speak about their traditions" or to bring objects from home that are representative of their "cultural backgrounds."[18]

Peter DuBarry's Class and the Video Project

Like the school, DuBarry's class is ethnically diverse. Of the thirty-three students enrolled in the class, thirty-two participated in the video project. Of these, fifteen were born in Canada; the remainder were born in Hong Kong, Fiji, India, El Salvador, Nicaragua, Costa Rica, the Philippines, Ecuador, and the United States. Eleven students speak English as a second language; nine are second-generation Chinese or South Asians; only eight are Canadian-born Anglophones.

Taking seriously the aims of the graduate seminar to ground in pedagogical practice elements of antiracist theory and research, Mr. DuBarry drew on readings assigned toward the end of the course to construct several questions that he then took to his Grade Seven students for their written thoughts. The questions were as follows and were given in this sequence: (1) What is racism?; (2) Is racism inherent in Canadian society?; (3) Can racism be unlearned?; (4) Why?; (5) How can racism be eliminated?; (6) What can educators/teachers do eliminate racism?; (7) What can students do to eliminate racism? (7) Have you ever experienced racism in your own culture or country?[19] He explained to them that he was taking a course on antiracism and that like them, he too had "homework" on which they could be of assistance. He gave the students the questions and asked them to take them home and write down their responses, inviting them to videotape their discussion of their thoughts in class the following day. Upon showing his students' video in the graduate seminar and later in talking about it with us, DuBarry told us that his students really liked the idea of helping him do his homework and were enthusiastic about the idea of videotaping themselves discussing and often, reshaping the questions he had given them. He also explained that they comprehended the questions, with the exception of asking him to provide a dictionary definition for the word "inherent."

To the credit of DuBarry and his students, the video project created an animated forum for discussion over a two-day period of socials. For the project, DuBarry spent nearly six hours of instructional time with his class discussing their different lived realities of racism and the responsibilities of schools to challenge it, and this resulted in a twenty-minute video. The video tape was not edited after the fact but the recorder was operated by student volunteers intermittently during the discussion. Students spoke directly to one another when asking and responding to the questions DuBarry had given them. Altogether, thirty students (twelve girls and eighteen boys) variously participated in the videotaping and discussion, out of the thirty three students in the class. (Two students, one of each sex, were absent that day). Not everyone talked on the tape, and those who did so spoke with varying frequency and duration. The students did not all employ the same discourses.

Methods of Analysis

The background to our analysis is based in part on our intensive open-ended interviewing of and conversations with DuBarry, as well as on data he and other school officials helpfully provided regarding the social composition of MacArthur Elementary and of his class. In the main, though, what we present here is based on careful semiotic analysis of the students' transcribed discussion and the commonsense ideological discourses that organized both the content and form of their understandings.[20] While watching and listening to the video and, later, poring endlessly over the transcript of the students' narratives, it became clear to us that the students mobilized certain discourses repeatedly, while other discourses were either marginalized or silenced by fellow students, and that there were conflicting understandings over what constituted racism in the school. It also became clear that there were rules of judgment and moral authority, which we call codes, that were employed by the students in order to enact their understandings of racial and national difference and/or diasporic experiences, as well as of the racial and national inequalities articulated in their discourses. Of crucial interest were the discourses that were never spoken, as well as those that were misinformed, causing us to wonder what kinds of institutional silences and failures of moral imagination might have contributed to students' understandings (and misunderstandings).

Throughout our engagement with the students' discourses, we have been repeatedly although pleasantly surprised by what they have taught us about the complexity of their moral judgments and material situations. For example, it became clear that a pervasive English-Canadian nationalist discourse, which constructs Canada as the non-racist antithesis of the United States, was echoed by the students. Despite these hegemonic strands in their discourses, we were also impressed by the forms of articulate anger and resistance coming from those students who resisted English-Canadian dominance in its gendered and racialized forms. We believe that openness to such surprises represents a test of the adequacy of our semiotic interpretive strategy and of our own postcolonial feminist analysis.

The Students' Discourses

We decoded four discourses that were in ideological play among the students as they responded to the questions, in some cases exceeding their assumptions. The discourses we found in large part follow the chronology of the questions, but we also noted where they overlapped or conflicted with one another. The students used these discourses in a volatile way, often shifting between positions (with different moral and political consequences). The four discourses were: (1) "What Causes Racism?"; (2) "Affirming and Contesting 'Canada, the Redeemer'"; (3) "The Backlash"; and (4) "Being Friends." We discuss all four discourses here, but concentrate on the last three, which are the ones that articulate the students' understandings of their own racialized and nationalized locations and subjectivities, thus telling us something about how to develop counter-hegemonic postcolonial pedagogies.

First Discourse: "What Causes Racism?"

The first question Du Barry asked his students was: "What is racism?" Despite the definitional emphasis of this question, the students talked about the consequences as well as the causes of racism. They did so using three codes: (1) "Races Are Real"; (2) "Race Is Not Real, But Racist Injury Is Real"; and (3) "Race May Be Real, but Racist Injury Is Also Real." These three codes strongly contest one another with regard to the content of their ideological terms. Much of the students' discourse centered on the terms in which they perceived "races" to exist and, especially, whether racial differences are biologically or culturally determined. They rarely strayed from what has been called the old and the new racism by both Gilroy (1990) and Barker (1981). Interestingly, these apparent disagreements were united in their strong implicit assumption that racial differences are "real" and, further, that they themselves cause racism in different forms. Significantly, only one student objected, with an awkward articulation of the "Race Is Not Real, but Racist Injury Is Real" code.

The ideological contest becomes evident when Roy, a Salvadoran refugee boy speaking for the second time, articulates the "Race May Be Real, but Racist Injury Is Also Real" code: "Racism is about people that have hate toward someone like of [a] different color, or different skin, and most of the times they just, say, get a laugh or maybe two out of hate." Susan, a Canadian-born Anglophone girl, also speaking for the second time, then attempts to articulate the "Race Is Not Real, but Racist Injury Is Real" code: "I disagree with Roy because it's not really, um, the race that counts. We're all one race and that's the human race. But, um, it's just the culture or beliefs that make us a little bit different from one another." Rajiv, a Canadian-born boy whose parents were born in India, then reaffirms the "Race Is Real" code: "Racism is when you pick [on] or put down someone because of their race. Also when society doesn't include a certain race, a certain person, or group of people, because of what language or culture they are." This discourse then continues with the debate as to whether "race" is a "cultural" or a "natural" construct.

This exchange illustrates the difficulty students have in affirming their awareness of their own or others' experiences of racist injury without falling into an intractable notion of "difference" as the inevitable cause of racism. This struggle for a language that denaturalizes "race" indicates an important institutional silence that is pervasive in the public school curriculum. What is missing is attention to "races" as mutable, historically specific, and socially constructed categories. Also absent in the students' discourses is demonstrable spoken knowledge of the ways in which various forms of disciplinary knowledge and colonial histories themselves are implicated in the project of constituting "racial" and "national" hierarchies of "difference."

Second Discourse: "Affirming and Contesting 'Canada, the Redeemer'"

This discourse affirms and contests the link between racism and Canada as "nation"; it is particularly concerned with what establishes "national belongingness." It articulates three codes, the first two of which strongly conflict with the third. Two codes—"Yes, There Is Racism in Canada, but . . ." and "No, There Is No Racism in Canada"—affirm the idea of Canada as a moral community in which racism is either an aberration of the past or is no longer a significant social problem in the present time and place of the nation. They affirm their perceptions of the absence of racism and neocolonialism as integral to the Canadian-nation-building project both in the past and in the present. Despite the fact that the "No, There Is No Racism in Canada" code embraces and redeems Canada as being exempt from racism and colonialism in a more pervasive fashion than the code of "Yes, There Is Racism in Canada, but . . ." what is common to both of these codes is how students speak of Canada in redemptive terms in contrast to the racism of other times and (national) places. When recounting their understanding (or rather, more accurately, misunderstanding) of the historical development of Canada as part of imperial nation-building, the place most often referred to as the "immoral" other of a racist-free Canada is the United States. Even when a few of the recent emigrés from countries other than the United States employ the "Yes, There Is Racism in Canada, but . . ." code, they mention their experiences of racism in Canada as isolated exceptions in their experiences in Canada. However, these two codes also meet with resistance to their problematic assumptions when other students employ the third code in this discourse. The third code, "Racism Hurts People in Canada Today," challenges the various forms of nationalist denial of racism in Canadian history (both in the past or the present) asserted by the students who employ the first two codes. Students who employ this code draw directly on their own experiences of racism and neocolonialism in Canada, generally doing so with references to hurtful experiences they have had in their neighborhoods, schools, or families. In the latter case, they draw on the knowledge they have of family members' experiences of racialization and imperialism at the point of immigrating to Canada and/or suffering downward mobility in the Canadian labor market as result of racialization of labor in Canada. It is worth noting that the third code comes about only after the first two are asserted with confidence in the chronology of the students' discourse on this question.

"No, There Is No Racism in Canada" is articulated by James, a Anglo-Canadian boy born in Canada, who cites Canada's role as a terminal for the underground railroad from the United States, erroneously implying that, in contrast to in the United States, the enslavement of African peoples did not take place in Canada. "I don't think racism is inherent in Canadian society. I mean look at the underground railroad that was around a lot a long time ago. We helped bring Black people here so they could get away from the slave camps in America." James's comments are not surprising, given the fact that they are a response to the framing of DuBarry's question—"Is racism inherent in Canadian society?"—which makes similar assumptions.[21] But James also invokes the normative "we" when speaking of himself. This "we" is a nation of redeemers who "save Black people" (them) from slavery. It can also be a nation of White male Canadians. In either case, the nation is represented as "Canada, the Redeemer," a country that redeems and saves people from the racism of the United States.

Notably, the "Yes, There Is Racism in Canada, but . . ." code is articulated by students from racially oppressed and racially privileged, as well as from immigrant and non-immigrant, backgrounds (three boys and one girl). The students articulate this code in three different ways, all of which share a common Whiggish and ameliorative view of Canada as nation. For example, one way students articulate this code is by speaking of racism as existing in the past but as not being prevalent in Canada today. Richard, whose mother is a First Nations person and whose father is an Anglo-Canadian born in Canada, speaks for the first time, saying:

> Um, yes I think racism is inherent in Canada. And I think it started with the White people who just came here because they took everything away from the Indians and they told them that it was all wrong and that their [White people's] ways were right. And if you still look at [it] nowadays, people, are people, still, um, go by those rules but it is getting better.

George, an immigrant from Hong Kong who speaks English as a second language, also speaking for the first time, similarly states:

> Racism is still inherent in Canadian society because, uh, lots of them before Chinese people came to Canada to help the Canadian[s] to build [interrupts self] build the railroad station and the Canadian government have to make them to pay more tax and but the, uh, White people don't have to. Uh, I think that's really racist, uh. Well it's getting much better right now because, uh, there's not lots of news about racism any more.

Richard and George articulate a contradictory desire to believe in the dominant notion of "Canada, the Redeemer." Both cite subaltern histories that place themselves and their family members outside the dominant nationalist historical narrative: Richard by speaking of the appropriation of aboriginal lands by European colonizers, George by citing the Canadian government's 1885 imposition of a head tax on Chinese laborers whose nationally and racially specific immigration was encouraged to aid in the building of the Canadian Pacific Railway. Yet both students qualify their historical challenges to the dominant rendering of the nation by variously asserting, "it is getting much better," thus evincing a faith in the uninterrupted historical progress of moral forces by which Canada is becoming increasingly distant from an immoral racist past and increasingly closer to a non-racist, morally redemptive present. Thus the "Yes, There Is Racism in Canada, but . . ." code has a great deal of affinity with the "No, There Is No Racism in Canada" code.

In striking contrast to the articulation of the "Yes, There Is Racism in Canada, but . . ." code, only students of color, all but one of whom are recent immigrants or refugees, employ the "Racism Hurts People in Canada Today" code. All the boys who articulate this code speak of the racially stratified labor market or access to services, citing experiences of people they know who have been discriminated against. In contrast, the one girl who articulates this code speaks about the threat posed by the cultural imperialism of White supremacy.

Brenden, a Canadian-born boy whose parents are from Hong Kong, speaking for his second time, gives a specific gendered example of the downward social-class mobility concomitant with migration: "Two of my aunts are from Hong Kong and now that they came here they have to work at sewing and all that—clothes—and when they were back there, they had, like, really big businesses. And now, here, they don't get as big chances." Beatrice, herself an immigrant from Hong Kong, in her first and only comment, added, somewhat reluctantly, "Racism is in Canadian society because other people want Canada to be one country and one color." Charanpal, a Canadian-born male student whose parents are from India, then speaks for the first and only time, declaring: "[Racism] is inherent in Canada 'cause of White people are giving [interrupts and corrects self] given more opportunities and more chances than other races." All these students build upon the disruption of the codes involved in the "Canada, the Redeemer" discourse and thus effect other openings in the classroom discussion. They articulate their ideological critique with increasing emotional commitment and courage, as evidenced by the risks taken to name their experiences in the face of a dominant discourse that would ordinarily position them as "aliens" and thus silence them.

Third Discourse: "The Backlash"

Significantly, it is immediately following the break in the dominant discourse described above that James, the Anglo-Canadian male student who earlier asserted the "No, There Is No Racism in Canada" code, reasserts a dominant discourse. We call this "The Backlash" discourse. James, speaking for the second time, says, "It's not just, um, I mean it's not like White people get special treatment. I mean sometimes, like, Black people will be against White. Like gangs will beat up a White person for being White." James's comment provides an opening for other students to similarly articulate the "Whites Are Victims of Racism Too!" code.

"The Backlash" discourse ignites the assertion of an oppositional code— "Affirming the Historic Realities of Racial Oppression." Rajiv, speaking for his second time, thoughtfully introduces this code:

> I think what some people are trying to say is that . . . racism started because of White people, where [with what] White people did to the Indians and what they [White people] did to the Black people— slaves—and what they [White people] did to the Chinese, etcetera, and stuff like that.

Immediately thereafter, Richard (whom we earlier identified as having a mother who is a First Nations persons and a father who is Anglo-Canadian) directly challenges Rajiv. Richard employs the "White People Are Victims of Racism Too!" code to erroneously claim that White people today are unfairly expected to make up for past wrongs. In so doing, he explicitly identifies with the anti-affirmative action or reverse discrimination discourse of the White students employing this code, including himself in their implicit normative "we"—an identification he maintains throughout his subsequent comments. Speaking for the second time, Richard says:

> Yeah, but not all White people do that—I mean because people nowadays are trying to make up for, uh, what their ancestors did, because they didn't think it was fair. So why should we be punished for something that they did? I mean, we're even trying to make up for it. It's not just Whites, it's other countries [that] do that—trying to do the exact same thing.

NéNé, a Filipina immigrant from an upper-middle-class family background, agrees with Richard, saying:

> I think that's true, like, not only White people are racist towards other cultures, because in, like, Black neighborhoods if any other White people go there, they go and beat them up. And there are the Chinese gangs and there are many other, like, gangs that are against White people. They're [White people] not the only people who are racist.

In sharp refutation, this leads Rajiv, who had previously been measured in his comments, to heatedly ask:

Well why does this happen? Why [interrupts self] why did this [refer-
ring to NéNé's statement that Chinese and other gangs are against
White people] happen? It is because of what happened in the past. It's
so [like when a] Black person, or [a speaker of] another language, were
on a White sidewalk, before they [White people] would, uh, beat, they
would beat him up, they would do the same thing before. And now,
[interrupts self] now they're doing it [fighting back] because of the
feelings they have inside and the anger of what happened to their culture, uh, many years before.

The discourse continues, with the contest going back and forth several
times between these two codes as articulated, with the exception of NéNé,
entirely by boys. Charles, a White male student from Alaska, joins James,
Michael, and NéNé in articulating the "Whites Are Victims of Racism Too!"
code. The only student to support Rajiv in articulating the "Affirming the
Historic Realities of Racism" code is Roy, a refugee from El Salvador, who
states: "I have a comment on James. James says that all White people, uh, do
this. But how about the L.A. cops? Do they have enough right to beat some-
body up just for walking on the streets? Doing nothing?"

As the discursive contest between the boys heats up, it seems to disallow
any space in which the girls might speak. As the boys get increasingly
involved, they direct their comments to each other, addressing each other by
their first names and speaking of racialized territories where "racial others"
are subject to beatings and gang violence. This is strikingly similar to the
masculinist discourse that Phil Cohen calls "fighting talk" (Cohen 1992, 87).

Finally, it is highly significant that, in the context of an ideological contest
over whether or not racism is inherent in Canadian society, much of this discourse gets framed in Black/White (African-American/Anglo-American)
terms. One must remember that Vancouver is a city that at the time of this
video project (and even now) had no predominantly African Canadian
neighborhoods. Second, the televized American discourse of racial tensions
in Los Angeles surrounding the Rodney King incident itself erroneously
exaggerates the Black versus White tensions where racial relations between
subordinate and dominant groups would more accurately reflect diasporic
realities of Latino/Hispanic and White settlement. Furthermore and perhaps
of most importance here, the historical subjects of racism and colonialism in
Vancouver have been primarily First Nations people and Asian Canadians.
The universalized United States referent, as seen in the students' allusion to
the Rodney King incident, denies students' personal knowledge of forms of
racism occurring in their own communities, both locally and nationally. It
also permits the insidious reappearance of the "Canada, the Redeemer" discourse, which, in turn, lays the basis for denying the existence of racism in
Canada and claiming erroneously that it exists primarily "over there."

Fourth Discourse: "Being Friends"

We call the last discourse "Being Friends," following the students' persistent insistence that "being friends" is an antidote to racism. It rearticulates both the promise and the perils of official multiculturalism as well as broader social discourses of belongingness and exclusion in the context of forming friendships. This discourse was prompted by DuBarry's questions: "Can racism be unlearned? Why?"; "How can racism be eliminated?"; "What can educators/teachers do to eliminate racism?"; and, "Have you ever experienced racism in your own culture and country?"[22]

The students' discourse breaks down into highly gendered codes, revealing the gendered symbolism of English-Canadian nationalism as read through their articulations regarding making friends with those whom they perceive to be national and racial "others." The boys employ the code of " 'Us-Versus-Them' Talk" and, to the extent that they are either permitted or willing to talk, the girls employ the code of " 'Respect-and-Reciprocity' Talk." Although both boys and girls construct a shared third code that we call "Naming the Silences," once again the boys dominate the discourse.

DuBarry's question "Can racism be unlearned?" shifts the masculinist focus of the boys from "fighting talk" to something more introspective. This seems to create room for the girls to speak. The "Being Friends" discourse thus begins with Susan, a Canadian-born Anglophone. Speaking for the third time, she says:

> I think racism can be unlearned but not totally. We have to teach others in this generation to respect others and their feelings. And when people from two or three, um, generations back, um, they were taught racism. They were taught to dislike people who are different. When they die, thirty to forty years from now, um, all [who] will be left . . . will [be] people that [who], um, believe in respect, and, um, think like that. Right? They, they'll, um, respect people that are different or just consider them one of them, and the world will be pretty much racist free, but not completely.

Her answer to the question is a qualified yes, but she does talk about norms of respect and reciprocity in human relationships as keys to overcoming racism. She speaks of gradual, generations-long change in which there are no quick fixes and in which history progresses in an inexorable, Whiggish manner.

Susan's comment is followed by the comments of several boys, who continue with the fighting talk of "The Backlash" discourse. This fighting talk, a common form of heterosexual masculine intimacy, seems to exclude many of the girls. Thus only one other girl, Samantha, who is Canadian-born and whose (Chinese) parents are from Hong Kong, speaks. This is her first and only comment: "[We or You] can eliminate racism, by educating people that people are all equal and there's no one race more superior than another." Her comment rejects racial supremacy. It is worth noting that this exchange between the two girls not only disrupts the boy's fighting talk but also reinforces their gendered bond of " 'Respect-and-Reciprocity' Talk." Interestingly, unlike the boys, the girls do not offer a spatial location either for their experiences of racism or for their understandings of antiracism. Because so few girls spoke at all and only two employed this code, we hesitate to venture more than a descriptive account of this gender difference.

The power of the masculinist discourses to cement intimacy by bringing together boys who were formerly on opposite sides of "The Backlash" and the "Affirming and Contesting 'Canada, the Redeemer' " discourses is illustrated in the following exchange. It begins with Richmond, a Canadian-born boy whose parents are from the Philippines and who is speaking for the third time; it continues with Rajiv, the Canadian-born boy whose parents were born in India, who earlier resisted "The Backlash" discourse; and it is then taken up by James, the Canadian-born Anglophone boy who initiated "The Backlash" discourse and who earlier cited Canada's role as a terminal for the underground railroad from the United States.

> Richmond: [What] kids can do to eliminate racism is probably to learn more about the different cultures that are in your classroom and maybe they're actually interesting and you can find out and then try to be friends with them.
>
> Rajiv: Well, if, if you're with a group and you have a lot of friends, right, and, uh, [if] you [the group] are just one language, you can invite other people to come into the group, and do activities with you and stuff. You know, you don't have to just have one, uh, a group of the same culture.
>
> James: Yeah, that's [interrupts self] that's right, Rajiv. And like the students can do a lot more than what a teacher should do. They can invite them into their groups and introduce them to their friends and stuff.

These views articulate the official practice of multiculturalism in MacArthur Elementary School and DuBarry's emphasis on the need to welcome new students to the class by inviting to join in activities. At the same time, the students' construction of friendship, like the belief in liberal notions of the inclusive curriculum, in some respects, mirrors colonial relations in which the colonizing project is represented as one of civilizing and morally elevating the subaltern and the racially oppressed. While the would-be befrienders, like former colonizers, construct themselves as beneficent, they construct the "others" as subjects to be invited into the colonizing group. What they appear not to fathom, and certainly do not articulate, is the possibility either (1) that these "others" are themselves moral subjects who have roles to play in negotiating or resisting friendship on these terms, or (2) that these "others" might have friendship groups that the members (in this case, the boys) from the dominant group might want to join.

DuBarry's questions "Can racism be eliminated?" and "What can educators/teachers do to eliminate racism?" allow both racially privileged and oppressed students to speak to some of the deafening institutional silences surrounding the lack of antiracist programs in their school. We call this code "Naming the Silences" because the students so articulately speak to what their school fails to imagine, much less articulate: that is, how racism and nationalism remain as largely unaddressed systemic problems whose normativity must be challenged. They give voice to their own lived experiences and to the subaltern knowledge and histories that are suppressed by Canadian nationalist pedagogies.

Students articulate this code across racial and gendered interests/subject positions. It begins with Michael (a Hong Kong-born boy who speaks English as a second language), and then is picked up by Charles (an Anglophone from the United States) and Karen (a Canadian-born Anglophone girl).

> Michael: Teachers can stop this from happening in the school and by telling them how wrong it is.

> Charles: Well, I think that a teacher can try to set a good example for every culture, like not favor just one person. Like, if someone's raising their hand and wants to answer a question, [do] not always go to the one culture, like try to let the students [to] feel that he's favoring every culture.

> Karen: I think the educators should, um, make some programs for children to go into so they can learn how to stop racism, and [then] they won't be racist themselves when they grow up.

In contrast to the naiveté and redemptive faith of official multiculturalism, the students *unequivocally* saw a role for active and systemic inventions on the parts of teachers and schools with regard to eliminating racism. Moreover, their solutions are specific and, if taken seriously, would necessitate a radical revision of most school curricula (including so-called "inclusive curricula") and their attendant practices.

It is exciting that students articulated this systemic critique across racial and gendered positions, exhibiting what Roman has called "effective coalitions for social transformation" (Roman 1993, 82). This joining together created the discursive space for racially and nationally marginalized students to speak for the first time of their own subaltern experiences of racism and nationalism. This is an example of what Edward Said has called "contrapuntal analysis" (Said 1993, 18), and it is illustrated in the following set of exchanges. Jordan is a refugee from Nicaragua, and this is his first and only comment; Timothy is a Hong Kong-born Chinese Canadian, and this is his second comment; and, finally, Rajiv is the boy who earlier challenged "The Backlash" discourse.

> Jordan: Yes, I experienced racism because one day my family were going to a provincial park, and [interrupts self] and everybody was White in the provincial park, and some people were just staring at us because we were the only brown person [sic] there. And, and, and racism is prevalent in my country, Nicaragua, because, um, the Nicaragua government told to [interrupts himself] told the poor people to build their cardboard houses around the American embassies, so they just would look bad, and there is racism in every country.

> Timothy: [In] Hong Kong we don't like the people that came from Vietnam because, um, they rob, um, they fight and they are really bad, and the government take [sic] [sends] them back [to Vietnam].

> Rajiv: Because of racism, people have called me names such as Paki and dumb Hindu and stuff like that.

Conclusion: Learning from the Students' Discourses on Popular Racism and the Silenced Grammars of Antiracism

As our analysis demonstrates, students in this ethnically and gender-mixed classroom articulated complex multiple and conflicting discourses regarding their understandings of racism and nationalism and what teachers and schools could do to challenge them. Their understandings were located both in their own experiences as racialized, nationalized, gendered, and classed subjects and in the context of MacArthur school's mediation of official and popular discourses of racism and multiculturalism. The value of this kind of analysis is its potential to point out the intimate intertextual relation between student discourses and the specific institutional, national, transnational, and local contexts in which they emerge.

We have provided evidence for our claim that young people actively negotiate their own sense of "racial" and "national" difference as "belongingness" or "alienness" based on conflicting official and popular discourses of racism and multiculturalism/antiracism pervasively available (or not) in their school, familial, and media contexts and experiences growing up in one or more national contexts. We have shown how these students at times struggle for new languages of radical humanism and democracy that resist reifying "race" as a category, while at other times they, like many adults, fall back into the hegemonic language of reifying "race" as a category and seeing racism as an inevitable result of perceived intractable "racial," "cultural," and "national differences." Their much more "primordial" or biologistic view of "race" certainly conflicts with the humanist view that eschews essentializing "racial" differences. The fact that in this particular context of a diverse classroom there is conflict over whether and whose "racial," "cultural," or "national" difference entitles people to belong or feel included in Canada speaks to the intersections of "nation" and "race" in everyday understandings, despite the prevalence of official multiculturalism. It also bears witness to some of the effects of the current discrepancies between critical multiculturalist/antiracist goals and realities in Canadian schools. The times when the students lack a language that allows them to speak about the systematic bases and effects of racism and imperialism in their daily lives point to broader institutional and social silences—silences that are not the fault of the individual young people themselves or their teacher. That some students are able to get beyond the stereotypes and essentializing discourses of "racial" and "national" difference to name the silences and speak about the some of the systemic bases and effects of racism and imperialism in their lives is testimony to the crying need to create more spaces of this kind in classrooms and schools for such discussion.

Equally compelling are the occasions when students, particularly students of color and emigrés, sharply dispute and reject notions of Canada as a nation of (White) redeemers, regarding such notions as part of a mythic past. These rejections call for more thoughtful approaches to educating educators, teachers, administrators, curriculum developers, and university instructors committed to critical multiculturalism/antiracism. Moreover, they point to the need for more critical approaches to teaching history. This means addressing, among other issues, the knotty complicity of Canada with colonialism and racism both in the past and in the present.

We have learned from DuBarry's intervention and the students' discourses why it is important to develop an anti-imperial postcolonial curricular agenda that offers alternatives to multiculturalism's exaggerated focus on separate and discrete cultures and, more importantly, to the recent articulations of the moral panic over racial invasion of Canada by presumed aliens. The conflicts between these two discourses of "race" and "nation" are nothing less than hegemonic struggles to define the contested space of "official" and "popular" ideologies regarding who belongs in Canada and who deserves citizenship rights. In order to effectively challenge these forms of racism and imperialism, alternative pedagogical and political strategies will need to be constructed, and they will need to be more than mere supplements or add-ons to the curriculum.

Given the diversity of the students' experiences, it is not surprising that they mobilize no single or overarching understanding of "race" and racism or of Canada as "nation" as evidenced by their conflicting and contesting discourses. But the expression of this diversity, or even the acknowledgment that postcolonial histories vary, does not guarantee progressive readings on the part of either the racially privileged or the oppressed. The challenge of anti-imperialist postcolonial curricula is to acknowledge diversity without reifying or annihilating differences—differences that testify to the plural and asymmetric histories and geographies of the interrelations among and between colonialism, racism, and sexism. Asymmetries in people's relationships to racial and neocolonial oppression may require us all to rethink how anti-imperialist postcolonial curricula could teach differences differently. For example, they must engage racially privileged students in the task of learning about how they benefit from a system of conferred racial privileges that simultaneously harms others and is rendered invisible by the structural workings of schools and other social institutions.

Moreover, to build upon the different experiences and discourses of the students means challenging what often gets taught as an unquestioned narrative of historical progress—Canada's narrative of nation-building. This "grand narrative" is more promisingly and appropriately taught as contested histories of gendered, sexualized, and racialized colonialism in the project of becoming a liberal state.[23] From the vantage point of indigenous groups, what has been taught as the nation's story of nation-building reads justifiably as nation-destruction and deterritorialization. Likewise, for many immigrant groups, it has been a contradictory legacy of being simultaneously outsiders and insiders—never fully belonging in the empire that considers itself a mosaic of ethnocultural and racialized differences. And, as we also learned from the gendered discourses of the students, "race," racism, and nationalism are not innocent of gendered symbolism or gendered power relations. Much could be learned from the girls' " 'Respect-and-Reciprocity' Talk" in developing alternatives to weak versions of inclusionary pedagogy. The girls seemed to favor more far-reaching and long-lasting notions of living with common (rather than divisive) transnational differences, which suggest some hopeful possibilities for notions of transnational global citizenship being incorporated into curricula.

An alternative strategy could involve what cultural studies analyst Paul Gilroy (1990, 115) calls "a new language of cultural democracy." This would mean getting beyond multiculturalism's relativistic celebration of reified cultural differences with a postcolonial pedagogy capable of recognizing peoples' different histories and relations to imperialist nation-building and diasporic migrations at the same time that it teaches antiracist and anti-imperialist coalition politics both inside and outside schools. The opportunity provided by this challenge is to effectively demonstrate to teachers and other school personnel that an antiracist politics of radical democracy entails something more than hollow rhetoric about "stopping racism." To fail to imagine alternative discourses and pedagogies in practice is to cede further ground to the current calls for monoculturalism. Lest we all forget, moral panics over racial and national invasion, which now invade even the liberal discourses of multiculturalism, articulate with the "new postmodern" discourses of efficiency, the streamlining of different equality struggles into overarching equity programs whose staffs and fiscal resources are currently being cut back. They also fit well with treating multiculturalism and antiracism as "add-on's" to curricula that are seen as no longer affordable or even necessary.

Our analysis, which owes a great debt to what we learned from DuBarry and his students, is part of an unfinished project to shift the burdens of risk-taking from isolated courageous students and teachers to schools, school districts, and faculties of education in conjunction with progressives in movements fo critical multiculturalism and antiracism. A central question for all of us is: What conditions, both in and around schools are necessary to enable us to articulate and realize this challenge?

Notes

1. This essay would not have been possible without the efforts of Mr. Peter DuBarry, the teacher who, for reasons of protecting the confidentiality of his school and his students can be acknowledged only under his self-chosen pseudonym. We would also like to acknowledge the critical insights of Doug Aoki, Frances Boyle, Yvonne Brown, Fazal Rizvi, Charles Ungerleider, Ian Wright, and various teachers who have anonymously and generously responded to the piece in its previous incarnations.

2. With the notable exception of ethnographic work by sociologists of education Richard Hatcher and Barry Troyna (1993) in England, philosopher of education Fazal Rizvi (1993) in Australia, and the survey work of psychologist Ann Phoenix (1993 and 1995), this idea is rarely discussed with regard to how young people in schools make sense of the conflicting ideologies of "racial," "ethnic," and "national" difference. Especially disconcerting is the relative paucity of qualitative studies in Canada that are directed toward learning from young people the means by which they negotiate their relationships to contemporary conflicting ideologies of racial/ethnic difference and national belongingness.

3. In the Vancouver School Board, elementary schools go from Grade One through Grade Seven.

4. The course was given through the Faculty of Education and the Centre for Curriculum and Instruction at the University of British Columbia during the Winter term of 1993. It encouraged those enrolled, most of whom were practicing teachers, to ground or test the implications of readings in the areas of multiculturalism and antiracism by developing innovative projects or written work which addressed the concerns of teachers or students, and which could be made accessible to a wider audience of educators and school communities.

5. When referring to the body of literature that critiques imperialism, we use the term "postcolonialism" advisedly because, as postcolonial critic Anne McClintock argues, it "too readily licence[s] a panoptic tendency to view the globe through generic abstractions void of political nuance" (McClintock 1995, 11). Abstractions such as "the postcolonial condition," "postcolonial discourse," and the generic "*the* postcolonial Other" cause Sara Suleri to remark that she is weary of being treated as an "Other-ness Machine" (quoted in Appiah [1992], 253). Another problematic assumption of the prefix "post" is that it can imply that the odious relations of colonialism and imperialism are somehow something that "happened elsewhere" (i.e., in non-Western countries) and were not dependent upon various Western nation-building/destroying projects. "Post" can thus erroneously imply that Western identity is untouched by the residual and emergent neocolonial conditions of imperialism. For an excellent critique of these problems, see Anne McClintock (1995). Postcolonial analyses are most useful when they aim to understand the articulation of imperialism and racism within the West as well as their effects on non-Western colonial and neocolonial peoples.

6. Among those who have paid attention to the gendered aspects of imperialism, see, for example, Agnew (1996), Eisenstein (1996), Lewis (1996), McClintock (1995), Jacqui and Mohanty (1997), Niranjana (1992), Rajan (1993), Prakash (1995), Pratt (1992), and Stoler (1995).

7. Politically, we share an investment in antiracist commitments across different academic and biographical experiences. Stanley is a middle-class male historian of education who studies racism and was born in Canada to a Chinese-Canadian mother and an Anglo-Canadian father; in his own words, he "passes" for White most of the time. Roman is a middle-class woman who was born and raised as a secular Jew in the United States; she is a relatively recent emigré to Canada, where she continues her work in cultural studies, feminist theory, and antiracist/postcolonial pedagogy. We acknowledge our (contradictory) White locations so as to provide evidence of how our different structural and political interests shape our interpretations and analyses. We neither think our specific forms of whiteness are essential locations—conflicted as they are by issues of ethnicity, class, gender, and/or religion—nor do we think they are transparent. We believe our different forms of whiteness render us complicit with certain privileges, but we have also, by virtue of Stanley's Chinese-Canadian mother and Roman's Jewish background, had experiences of racism that are not shared by other specific dominant groups of Whites. The social category of whiteness is a hybrid one, constructed from specific contextual, historical, structural, and geographical locations.

8. Lesko (1992) makes this point in relation to the literature on adolescent developmental theory and its pedagogical implications. See also Roman (1996) for an analysis of the ways in which certain kinds of state policy can render particular groups of youths transgressive yet voiceless spectacles with regard to the social policies that affect their lives. The issue of paternalistic views of youth extends well beyond theory and policy into curricular practice. For example, the Vancouver School Board regularly features among its antiracist films one

that is particularly popular among teachers, entitled "First Face" (1992), by Virginia Hama, produced by the British Columbia Teachers' Federation Lesson Aid Service, with assistance from the National Film Board and the University of British Columbia. This film reduces racism to a single instance of racist name-calling between elementary-aged children. The children, unlike those who are the subjects of this study, are conceived of as incapable of understanding or articulating any of the complexities of their experiences of racism. Instead, in a paternalistic, neocolonialist model of curricular reform, they are sent to a teacher and a principal, who instruct them in a condescending manner to cooperate in erasing a blackboard, leaving the actual bases of racist name-calling untouched.

9. "Mr. Peter DuBarry" is a self-chosen pseudonym. For the purposes of maintaining confidentiality, we have also given the school and the students involved in the video project pseudonyms. In choosing pseudonyms for the young people, we aimed to preserve the family's choice of ethnic naming. Thus, for example, if a child had first name that was Anglicized, despite being from a non-Anglo background, we honored or preserved such a choice with a comparable pseudonym.

10. For an excellent discussion of the official Canadian multiculturalism policy, see Moodley (1983). Moodley argues that Canadian multicultural policy encompasses a range of conflicting understandings of "cultural differences." "Cultural differences," in her view, can be at once "extolled and considered a hindrance to be removed in the interests of equal opportunity" (320).

11. Here we draw on Roman's (1996) definition of moral panic and its conceptual history. Briefly, "moral panic" is the term commonly used in cultural studies to refer to manufactured crises. Neil Bissoondath's (1994) scathing critique of multiculturalism is reminiscent of other "blame-the-victim" ideologies that attack the subject of various forms of oppression rather than the structure of inequalities that created them.

12. The term "visible minorities" is deeply problematic and is contested for its denial of forms of racism that demarcate people and groups along lines other than color. For a critique of the reification of "race" as a category associated exclusively with color, see Linda Carty and Dionne Brand (1993).

13. One notable but increasingly typical example of such a moral panic occurs in the lead cover story for *Maclean's*, written by Andrew Phillips and entitled "The Lessons of Vancouver: Debating Immigration . . . Who? and How Many?" (Phillips 1994, 26–35), which erroneously alleges that there have been "record high levels of non-white immigration" and, further, that they "are testing Canadians' commitment to the ideals of multiculturalism." It depicts Vancouver as having become "a magnet for Asian immigrants," whose presence threatens to destabilize so-called Canadian values by introducing "changes . . . so profound that even many who regard themselves as liberal are bound to ask themselves: Is it all happening too quickly?" The cover features a photo of students from Queen Elizabeth Elementary School; one Anglo girl in the center is surrounded by three Asian students (one Indian boy and two Chinese students, one girl and one

boy). All three are juxtaposed against the metropolis, connoting the threatened decline of life in Vancouver as Anglo-Canadians know it.

14. Rizvi cites Hall's (1986) use of the concept of articulation and Wittgenstein's development of the idea of a "grammar" of linguistic practice as a way of understanding how children learn the conventions establishing how concepts are used in relation to their function in the social world. This determines, for example, how concepts of racial difference get established within the system of racial inequality (both connotative and denotative) they articulate. See Wittgenstein (1889–1951 [Trans. 1976]), paraphrased in Rizvi (1993, 136).

15. All of the background information was supplied through personal communication (i.e., faxes) from MacArthur School and the Vancouver School Board with the assistance of DuBarry, Yvonne Brown, and Charles Ungerleider. The profiles of the school were sent on February 7, February 8, and March 8, 1994.

16. The designation of ESL students reflects perceived academic impairment; it does not necessarily reflect the allotment of district funds and resource personnel for English language instruction.

17. Interview with Peter DuBarry (February 1994).

18. See MacArthur School's "Multicultural Action Plan," Vancouver School Board, Vancouver, British Columbia, 1993, p. 20. The "Multicultural Action Plan" was faxed by Mr. DuBarry to Roman's office at the University of B.C. on February 8, 1994.

19. Of course it should be noted that DuBarry's questions build in certain assumptions and have played a role in shaping (that is, both limiting and animating) the terms of the discussion. He asked the questions as a practicing teacher (not as a trained critical ethnographer) and as a White middle-class Canadian-born male committed to going beyond tokenistic approaches to multiculturalism/antiracism. Although as analysts we have some concerns about particular questions and their assumptions, which we comment on later in the discussion, we also wish to make clear that the students' discussion is not wholly inscribed by the questions. At many points, their discussion goes in directions that exceed and complicate the questions.

20. Unlike conventional approaches to analyzing texts through content or thematic analyses, semiotic analysis aims to show how meaning is produced not as a reflection of a presumed reality or naturally given categories (e.g., "race," "women," "youth," etc.) but rather through a process of sign production and signification which can either construct or interrupt existing codes of meaning. For an elaboration of the literature conceptualizing semiotics and semiology as a method, see Roman (1996, 9, n. 33).

21. Although this question succeeded in eliciting a good deal of talk among the students (indeed, ten students from very diverse backgrounds spoke at least once), its closed-ended formulation prefigured a "yes-or-no" answer that led the students to offer *opinions* on whether or not racism is part of Canada's past. An open-ended question, such as "How is racism part of Canada's history?" could have afforded the opportunity of learning what the students knew about the histories of different racisms in Canada.

22. The first three questions assumed that racism could be eliminated through voluntarist but responsible acts by individuals, while the last question assumes that those students who might have experienced racism come from another country or culture, thus positioning as "alien" or "other" any student who possesses knowledge of racism or neocolonialism either in Canada or elsewhere. Although they were instrumental in stimulating discussion among a range of students, the questions also show how difficult it can be to avoid the everyday language involved in denying racism in Canada.

23. For a ground breaking analysis of the state as eroticized and (hetero)sexualized, see Alexander (1997).

References

Agnew, V. 1996. *Resisting Discrimination: Women from Asia, Africa, and the Caribbean and the Women's Movement in Canada*. Toronto: University of Toronto Press.

Alexander, M. J. 1997. "Erotic Autonomy as a Politics of Decolonization" In *Feminist Genealogies, Colonial Legacies, Democratic Futures*, ed. M. J. Alexander and Chandra Talpade Mohanty. 63–100. New York: London.

———. M. J. and Mohanty, C. T., eds. 1997. *Feminist Genealogies, Colonial Legacies, Democratic Futures*. New York/London: Routledge.

Appiah, K. A. 1992. *In My Father's House: Africa in the Philosophy of Culture*. London: Methuen.

Barker, M. 1981. *The New Racism*. London: Junction Books.

Bissoondath, N. 1994. "I Am Canadian." *Saturday Night* (October): 14–22.

Carty, L. and Brand, D. 1993. "Visible Minority Women: A Creation of the Canadian State." In *Returning the Gaze: Essays in Racism, Feminism, and Politics*, ed. Himani Bannerji. 169–81. Toronto: Sister Vision Press.

Cohen, P. 1992. " 'It's Racism What Dunnit': Hidden Narratives in Theories of Racism." In *"Race", Culture and Difference*, ed. by James Donald and Ali Rattansi. 62–103. London: Sage.

Eisenstein, H. 1996. *Hatreds: Racialized and Sexualized Conflicts in the twenty-first Century*. New York/London: Routledge.

Gilroy, P. 1990, Autumn. "Nationalism, History, and Ethnic Absolutism." *History Workshop* 30: 114–20.

Goldberg, D. T. 1993. *Racist Culture: Philosophy and the Politics of Meaning*. Cambridge, MA: Blackwell.

Hall, S. 1986. "The Problem of Ideology: Marxism without Guarantees." *Journal of Communication Inquiry*. 10 (2): 28–43.

———. 1988. "Minimal Selves." In *Identity: "The Real" Me*, ICA Documents, 6: 44–6. London: Institute of Contemporary Arts.

Hatcher, R. and Troyna, B. 1993. "Racialization and Children." In *Race, Identity and Representation in Education*, ed. C. McCarthy and W. Crichlow. 109–25. New York/London: Routledge.

Lesko, N. 1992. "Mind Over Matter: Towards a Postcolonial Theory of Adolescent 'Development.' " Paper presented at the Curriculum Theory and Classroom Practice Conference in Dayton, Ohio.

Lewis, R. 1996. *Gendering Orientalism: Race, Femininity and Representation.* London/New York: Routledge.

Lutz, H., Phoenix, A., and Yuval-Davis, N., eds. 1995. *Crossfires: Nationalism, Racism and Gender in Europe.* London/East Haven, CT: Pluto Press.

McClintock, A. 1995. *Imperial Leather: Race, Gender, and Sexuality in the Colonial Contest.* New York/London: Routledge.

Moodley, K. 1983. "Canadian Multiculturalism as Ideology." *Ethnic and Racial Studies* 6 (3): 320–31.

Niranjana, T. 1992. *Siting Translation: History, Poststructuralism, and the Colonial Context.* Berkeley: University of California Press.

Phillips, A. 1994. "The Lessons of Vancouver: Debating Immigration . . . Who? and How Many?" *Maclean's* (7 February): 26–35.

Phoenix, A. 1993. *Black, White or Mixed Race? Race and Racism in the Lives of Young People of Mixed Parentage.* London/New York: Routledge.

———. 1995. "Young People: Nationalism, Racism, and Gender." In *Crossfires: Nationalism, Racism, and Gender in Europe,* ed. by Helma Lutz, Ann Phoenix, and Nira Yuval-Davis. 26–47. London: Pluto Press.

Prakash, G., ed. 1995. *After Colonialism: Imperial Histories and Postcolonial Developments.* Princeton, NJ: Princeton University Press.

Pratt, M. L. 1992. *Imperial Eyes: Travel Writing and Transculturation.* London/New York: Routledge.

Rajan, R. S. 1993. *Real and Imagined Women: Gender, Culture and Postcolonialism.* London/New York: Routledge.

Rizvi, F. 1993. "Children and the Grammar of Popular Racism." In *Race, Identity and Representation in Education,* ed. C. McCarthy and W. Crichlow. 126–39. New York/London: Routledge.

Roman, L. 1993. "White Is a Color!: White Defensiveness, Postmodernism and Antiracist Pedagogy." In *Race, Identity and Representation in Education,* ed. Cameron McCarthy and Warren Crichlow. 71–88. New York: Routledge.

———. 1996. "Spectacle in the Dark: Youth as Transgression, Display, and Repression." *Educational Theory* 46 (1): 1–22.

Said, E. W. 1993. *Culture and Imperialism.* New York: Knopf.

Stoler, L. A. 1995. *Race and the Education of Desire: Foucault's History of Sexuality and the Colonial Order of Things.* Durham/London: Duke University Press.

Wittengenstein, L. 1889–1951. *The Philosophical Investigations.* Translated by G. E. M. Anscombe. [1976, ed.] Oxford: Blackwell.

Chapter Thirteen

Gender Equity, Policy, and Praxis

Celia Haig-Brown
York University (Canada)

The school system will: promote gender equity in all programs and services and work to eliminate sexism in schools.
—*Ministry of Education, British Columbia*

But as they pass from the level of public remarks and declaration to the level of actual policies, first differences of emphasis and problems of priority, then actual contradictions, soon emerge.
—*Raymond Williams,* The Politics of Modernism

Through the ensuing contradictions, as well as shifts in discourse, the subject can occupy a range of positions, thereby becoming not a unitary identity but a process of change. In process, she concludes, "lies the possibility of transformation."
—*Ellen Messer-Davidow,* Academic Knowledge and Social Change

There is no denouement, only continued working-through.
—*Nancy Caraway on Minnie Bruce Pratt's* Identity: Skin Blood Heart

Introduction

The central argument of this chapter is that the ambiguity which lies within a particular government policy of "gender equity" both promotes and impedes the transformative goals of feminism. I locate this policy within the specific context of a classroom, a place of "power at its extremities, in its ultimate destinations, with those points where it becomes capillary, that is, in its more regional and local forms and institutions" (Foucault 1980, 96). In keeping with Spivak's (1993, 25) notion of the critical as "a philosophy that is aware of the limits of knowing," I present a critical feminist view of what nineteen students and two teachers (Linda Eyre, then a doctoral student at the University of British Columbia, now an associate professor at the University of New Brunswick, and myself) wrote and thought about the policy-based, government-funded university course entitled "Gender Equity: Issues in Teacher Education." I examine how the students came to know, and to work within, the parameters of the policy of gender equity and how they dealt with the complex interrelations within the "sisterhood" of the class. Ultimately, I choose to acknowledge those possibilities, however slight, which may arise with the careful use of such government policy initiatives as gender equity.

Since Robin Morgan edited *Sisterhood is Powerful* in 1968, many anti-racist feminists (e.g., Bannerji 1995; Bourne 1984; Carby 1982) and anti-essentialists (e.g., Butler 1990; Fuss 1989) have questioned the mythical commonality of "woman's experience" for those who are trying to work together for change. While acknowledging the power and the necessity of claiming an identity as "women," they also insist on moving beyond any simplistic gender categories that define women merely as the binary opposites of men. Aboriginal, Afro-American, working-class, Latina, woman of color, and lesbian are a few of the identities women claim, often in opposition to the limitations of a White, privileged women's movement that presents itself as *the* women's movement (e.g., Davis 1981; Giddings 1984). Significantly, white, middle-class women have tended not to name their locations but to assume them as the norm: " 'Identity politics,' they claimed, is what those 'others' do" (Bannerji 1995, 21). "I don't like to be called 'White'," said a student in a recent class. On the topic of identity, lesbian feminist Monique Wittig (1992a, 20) argues provocatively that a lesbian is not a "woman": if "woman" exists only in relation to "man," lesbians "escape [that relation] by refusing to become or stay heterosexual." At the same time, the power of engaging in feminist politics and analysis "as women" is not to be ignored. As Spivak writes of the strategic use of essentialism, "the critique of essentialism is understood not as an exposure of error, our own or others', but as an acknowledgment of the dangerousness of something one cannot not use" (1993, 5).

Almost fifteen years ago, Bernice Johnson Reagon told anyone who would listen that the "barred room" where women do their identity work is

> nurturing, but it is also nationalism. At a certain stage nationalism is crucial to people if you are ever going to impact as a group in your own interest. Nationalism at another point becomes reactionary because it is totally inadequate for surviving in the world with many peoples. (1983, 358)

She wants women to recognize the importance of moving out of that room and beginning the difficult task of coalition work. As Gentile suggests, people may learn to work together across differences by "find[ing] a commonality in the experience of difference without compromising its distinctive realities and effects" (cited in Ellsworth 1989, 324). Only in coalition work is there the possibility of making real change with regard to the privilege afforded to those who are White, able-bodied, male, heterosexual, and middle-class. Ultimately, the processes through which people define and claim identities challenge any static or monolithic view of categories.

The state figured prominently in our course,[1] for gender equity was (and to a lesser degree still is) a part of school reform in British Columbia. In the early 1990s, the Ministry of Education was basing its notions of reform on a policy paper called *Year 2000: A Framework for Learning* (n.d.), which arose out of the royal commission report, *A Legacy for Learners* (British Columbia 1988). Significantly, although these two documents, and the working plans related to them (British Columbia 1990), used the term "gender equity," the term "feminism" never appeared. In three later documents (British Columbia 1994a, 1994b, 1994c), gender equity is reduced to one comment (1994c, 5); an occasional nod in the direction of a generic equity (e.g., 1994a, 9, 41; 1994b, 20); and the following comment: "The education system is committed to helping both boys and girls succeed equally well in the school system" (1994b, 2).

Before I taught this course, I planned to argue that the discourse around a policy-driven "gender equity" would ultimately undermine feminist projects. However, I have come to believe that, in focusing on specific structural limitations (such as the time allotted for the course and the government's determination to delete reference to feminism from official considerations of gender), I lost sight of agency. I now argue that the discourse around gender equity allowed many students and both teachers to critically create and recreate, in the Freirian sense, our various knowledges of feminist projects and of gender relations as well as to find a basis for praxis. If women's studies is the daughter of modern feminism, gender equity is her runaway child—a child bent on denying its feminist mother and skirting issues of power.

This chapter utilizes theory based in critical and feminist pedagogy (e.g., Weiler 1988; Briskin 1990) as well as some writings and reflections on our gender-equity course. It provides an example of how "a dialectic between critical theorizing and practice can be dramatized in our daily lives" (Roman 1993, 159). I offer a case study in Merriam's (1988, xiv) sense of the term: "A qualitative case study is an intensive holistic description and analysis of a *bounded* phenomenon such as a program, an institution, a person, a process, or a social unit" (emphasis mine).

Despite its denial of feminism, the policy initiative on gender equity, and its attached funding, gave Linda and me, as teachers, the space to open discussion and to pursue various possibilities for praxis. We brought a feminist perspective to the course by critically examining gender-equity policy and by relating it to our lives. Predictably, the recognition that power and gendered relations are inextricable led to anger. Through discussion, readings, and thought, we moved to channel some of that anger into praxis. In nine days, for four hours a day, two feminist professors/teachers and nineteen students/teachers troubled the notion of "gender equity," naming it as a socially acceptable way to acknowledge and to act on feminist projects. After the fact, we summarized our work under the topics of identity politics, considerations of essentialism, praxis, and coalition work.

Approaching the Research

I focus on student journals and writings. Journals were used as a dialogic tool, and, because of the duration of the course, they provided an additional and much-needed forum for articulating responses to the classes. They are, of course, written for the teachers and may omit real concerns that students had and chose not to reveal for fear of repercussions. Each student has given permission for the use of her or his writings.[2] Although they were invited to participate as co-authors, all had other work commitments that took priority. A number did agree to meet and comment on a draft of the chapter I circulated to them and to Linda. They had a chance to edit their quotes and I asked that they pay particular attention to how I had contextualized their words. While a few made minor changes, most left them as they were. Although this chapter's analysis is mine, its strength lies in the student writings and the fact that those who participated in the class reviewed and approved it (Lather 1991).

We began in a quandary: How, in nine days, could Linda and I provide a forum in which each voice might be heard, in which we could reveal gender equity for what it is (i.e., feminism in disguise) and simultaneously critique the historical shortcomings of White, middle-class, feminist practice? How could we sensitize students to the strategic use, as well as the dangers, of essentialism and its reductionist view of gender equity? Finally, and perhaps most important, how could we provide students with opportunities for deep, focused reflection on the gendered nature of their lives, the possibilities for re-forming it, and even for in-forming future policy? Would there be time to investigate "the ways in which [we] are complicit with what we are so carefully and cleanly opposing" (Spivak 1990, 122)? We selected readings and videos, lined up resource people, and prepared for discussions.

I began with doubts, but the course became something of a dream come true. Perhaps this tells the reader more about the limits of my dreaming than it does about the course: some students were hurt; some never seriously engaged the issues. I present aspects of the course in order to call into question the paralysis that seems to come with postmodern angst. While postmodernism has provided an indispensable addition to the analytic toolkit, some students find themselves picking endlessly through the pile of rubble left in the wake of deconstruction, with little incentive to begin the next stage of the work. I want to resist the criticism that we can never do enough, well enough—a criticism which leads many academics right back to their offices to read, think, and write for each other and nobody else. Critical pedagogues, in whose midst I like to situate myself, have written of the interstitial tensions of structure and agency (e.g., Weiler 1988).

Poststructuralist Judith Butler (1990) poses a particularly provocative view. Coincident with Reagon's refusal to see identity as final, she calls for "the reconceptualization of identity as an *effect*, that is, as *produced* or *generated*," as a way of "open[ing] up possibilities of 'agency' that are insidiously foreclosed by positions that take identity categories as foundational and fixed" (147).

Gender Equity

We began the course with an examination of the policy from which it originated, focusing particularly on two conceptual pairs: (1) gender and sex and (2) equality and equity. According to Harding, "In other eras—the nineteenth century, for example—distinctions between female and feminine, between feminine and feminist may have been virtually nonexistent, but only the ignorant confuse these terms today" (1991, 105). Simply put, gender has too often been equated with biological sex differences.

To introduce the notion of "equity," I presented students with a little history and with a distinction between equality (which emphasizes measurement) and equity (which emphasizes fairness and justice). As Smith (1987, 9–10) writes: "The concept of *equity* refers to situations which are considered just, and should not be confused with equality. . . . The crucial question is that of the circumstances in which a specific degree of inequality may be considered (in)equitable or (un)just." In Canada, federal government rhetoric includes such terms as employment equity, while government policy focuses on representative numbers of women, visible minorities, people with disabilities, and Aboriginal peoples. Gender equity is just one of the policy initiatives articulated by the British Columbian provincial government in its current sweeping educational reforms. The government's Gender Equity

Program provided the funding and the impetus for our course. Members of the program's advisory committee, which include teachers, university faculty, school trustees, and administrators, took the time to develop a guiding statement that moved well beyond the numbers game of most equity policies:

> Gender equity is concerned with the promotion of personal, social, cultural, political, and economic equality for all who participate in the education system of B.C. The term gender equity emerged out of a growing recognition in society of pervasive gender inequities. Continuing traditions of stereotypical conceptions and discriminatory practices have resulted in the systematic devaluation of attitudes, activities, and abilities attributed to and associated with girls and women.
>
> The negative consequences of stereotypical conceptions and discriminatory practices adversely affect males as well as females. However, in the short term, greater emphasis in the gender equity initiatives will be placed on improving conditions and attitudes as they affect girls and women. In the long term, these initiatives will also improve the situation for boys and men.
>
> Gender equity, as distinct from "sex equity," is not attainable solely by a quantitative balancing of females and males in all aspects of the existing system. It must entail, also, a qualitative reworking of gender assumptions within all aspects of the present system itself, both formal and informal. Concretely this means promoting gender equity in respect of (1) curriculum, instruction, and assessment, (2) social interaction within the school setting, (3) institutional conditions and structures, and (4) the socio-cultural context of public education. (Gender Equity Advisory Committee 1990)

Equity moves such as those implied in this policy statement call for systemic change and challenge the status quo. While the statement clearly addresses much of the ground covered by a general feminism, the absence of the *term* feminism is startling. At a meeting of the provincial Gender Equity Advisory Committee, I came to realize that this absence was strategic, if highly questionable. We were asked to remove the word feminism from a set of documents because, according to the chair, "It would be like a red flag to a bull."

The Course

I became involved with the gender-equity course partly by happenstance but primarily because of my growing public commitment to work for change in gender relations in the Faculty of Education at Simon Fraser University. I agreed to team teach Education 372 with Linda Eyre, whose area of academic expertise is feminism. Conflict around feminism and gender equity began with the course approval process, the details of which are documented elsewhere (Bryson, de Castell, and Haig-Brown 1993). Eventually, the course outline was approved.

Students, all of whom were involved in teaching or educational analysis, came with a variety of histories and expectations. Ages ranged from twenty-six to fifty; there were sixteen females and three males; thirteen were working at public schools, one at a community college, and one was a graduate student; the others, including a student teacher just completing his program, were looking for teaching jobs. Early in the course, two students declared themselves to be of working-class background. Another spoke of being a lesbian, and another of her First Nations heritage.

They read, listened to a variety of resource people, and participated in class discussions and presentations, while keeping journals and preparing a final paper based on their presentations. Topics addressed included an analysis of the gender-equity documents; the intersections of racism, class, and gender; the gendered curriculum; the gendered classroom; feminist/critical pedagogy; and teachers as researchers. Resource people focused on gender and language; women and history; women, Aboriginal peoples, and science; female teachers and the British Columbia Teachers' Federation (the provincial teachers' union); and women and the law. Student presentations included material on gender and math, children's literature, technology and education, physical education, administration, and feminist pedagogy.

First Day

First-day journals revealed a promising openness and hinted of work to come: several students were beginning their examination of gender relations and feminism. L wrote, "I feel bombarded by information, but at the same time revelling in the experience" (sic). D, assimilating her response to the pre-readings (which included Lewis and Simon [1986] and Gaskell, McLaren, and Novogrodsky [1989]) wrote:

> This is a whole new experience for me. . . . I looked at feminists with a negative connotation—as men-haters and lesbians. I probably gained this ignorance from listening to others' opinions & mostly through the media—newspapers, magazines, & TV. Boy do I have a lot to learn.

Another student, Y, wrote in response to the pre-readings:

> I'm working on finding the concrete examples of sexism in my own life but holding that mirror up is proving more difficult than I thought. The unquestioned acceptance of so many LITTLE things starts to eat at

you and you wonder if life will ever be the same. Can you turn back time and replay the scenes you once felt so good about and, now recognizing them for what they are, still love those moments?

I'd like to put the mirror down now.

The relationship between their readings and their own experiences began right away. KC came with a carefully chosen agenda that proved hard to broach: "My main concern is not specifically for gender equity but for equity across the spectrum." G, a student who was forced to take the course by his student-teaching supervisor, responded as follows on the first day on which students talked about why they had enrolled:

> This is my first experience working with feminists. In spite of some vague stereotype views which I've acquired in my past, I was filled with admiration when I learned about the other students. Other than sports, I have never really felt strongly about anything in life. It was great to hear how some of the women have overcome hardships and still remain eager to fight the battle.

R raised the desire for praxis, a desire that resurfaced as the course progressed and she pursued her investigation of feminist pedagogy:

> Growing up, I never questioned my equality to men. Life experiences, however, have taught me differently. I have feelings of frustration and rage. I need to find out how to channel these emotions into *positive action* in the classroom and for me personally. (Emphasis mine)

J wrote of the immediate impact of first-day discussion on her classroom practice:

> I really liked the concept Linda [Eyre] put forth about the importance of listening as well as talking in a classroom. We discussed it in my class in the afternoon and it developed into a wonderful discussion on who is in the class, what are they like, what are our assumptions and issues about who is in our class and what kind of power they hold.

Working with teachers who came to the class seeking regenerative, practical knowledge, and who began making immediate connections between discussions of sexism and their own lives, was what made this course so powerful.

Second Day: Gender and Context

Linda and I, positioning ourselves as white women of privilege, decided to challenge feminist essentialism from several angles. Rather than merely using writings by Aboriginal women, lesbians, and women of color, we wanted, if possible, to have their perspectives represented in the presentations of both resource people and students. Conscious of the dangers of tokenism, we worked with students to develop critical approaches to these presentations. By the second day, the topic of which was "Racism, Class, and Gender," people were asked to focus on essentialism, on identity politics, and on an increasingly complex construction of gender. Coupled with Rich's "Compulsory Heterosexuality and Lesbian Existence" (1986), resource person Suzanne de Castell presented four conceptualizations of gender. These conceptualizations, developed with Mary Bryson (Bryson and de Castell 1995), are positivism (biology is destiny); constructivism (gender as socially constructed); critical analysis (gender as ideology); and postmodernism (gender as difference). Speaking of herself as "differently gendered," de Castell concurred with Wittig's (1992b) view that conventional considerations of gender render lesbians invisible by constituting women wholly in terms of their difference to men.

The day provided what I saw as a foundation for coalition work: heterosexual women and lesbians working together to consider the fundamental concept of gender in order to work for change in the classroom. And, as Bernice Johnson Reagon (1983, 359) writes, "Coalition work is not done in your home . . . And it is some of the most dangerous work you can do. And you shouldn't look for comfort . . . You don't get fed a lot in a coalition. In a coalition, you have to give and it is different from your home." The day brought thoughtful responses in student journals. L wrote, "My life is enriched by consideration of another's perspective." D, who had written of feminists as lesbians and man-haters, now wrote:

> While I feel somewhat uncomfortable with lesbianism, I know I would never feel uncomfortable with her. She is a very likeable person, sincere and I really enjoyed her wit. . . . I didn't like the idea of people like her, lesbians, having been treated unfairly and sometimes, I'm sure, inhumanely.

A Chinese-Canadian student found himself thinking critically, and writing tellingly, of his own experiences of exclusion:

> I have never really been ostracized because of my race but at the same time, I can't say that I've felt accepted in all situations. I guess this is similar to women's experiences. To different degrees I guess we've both been accepted when we don't inconvenience the people in power.

B, the only Aboriginal teacher in the class, spoke from a place of solitude:

> What were the major influences which helped me survive in Canadian culture and at that a male dominant culture? Was it the fact that I was groomed by a male culture where I learned to understand the language

or was it the cultural roots of my ancestors which entailed gaining strength and respect from both male and female role models?

It's difficult to see perspectives from both worlds. I know I need to make meaning out of this experience for myself. I wonder if one can truly ignore a part of her culture and reflect from a world she is not really sure about.

She wrote of her separate identity within the classroom and, very politely, of the racism she found there:

I found there seemed to be more of a focus on feminism rather than the reading which was "Ethnic Prejudice: Still Alive and Hurtful" [Pang 1988]. I needed to make the talk meaningful to me and my experiences so I kept re-focusing on my previous experiences with discrimination. . . . It seemed people didn't want to get into an in-depth discussion on the meaning behind this reading. I didn't take it too personally . . . however I think this points to our need as educators to look at what the system is ignoring just because it's something certain individuals are not experiencing.

These comments gave me pause then, and they give me pause now: the racism is blatant. The statement "I didn't take it too personally," holds much pain. Our failure as a class to engage with an article that spoke directly to B's experiences of discrimination made her relive it. Even as we addressed race issues in the class, we were unable to exorcise, or even name, racism as such.

L also felt alone, but for different reasons:

I confess I've hurt my head and wrenched my guts over this course . . . I am struggling for direction. Still, it's not that I feel (totally) [added later] lost or alone—but rather that I feel intimately connected to what I am reading, hearing, thinking about and discussing.

Without doubt, there are heady implications surrounding this course. Basically what I am learning so far outside class is that feminist study (inquiry?) raises suspicion and initiates negative criticism. . . . Could it be that some males are afraid of more independent females who take charge of their lives because they fear exclusion, loss of power? I've encountered females as well who say they fear what unknown changes feminism might effect. To be willing to accept or feel charged with personal responsibility for facilitating change is very heady stuff.

Her pain was a matter not of cultural difference, but of the responses of those outside the classroom. The class shifted between being a place of identity work (as students struggled to locate themselves in relation to the complexities of feminism and a place of coalition work (as they struggled together to make sense of their work and to find places for praxis). As the preceding quotes demonstrate, sisterhood is not a harmonious and idyllic state but a complex and shifting set of relations.

R commented: "Up to this date I have been a 'flailing' feminist. I am beginning to understand the importance of being educated and well-read in this field." By day three, Y was deeply affected by the stories and experiences that were exchanged. And, indeed, these were startling, power-infused (as in Seth Kreisberg's [1992] notion of *power with*), and fundamental to our work.

> Today I have nothing to write. I am full to exploding with thoughts but no words will come ... only poetry that I'll keep privately and will touch me always. I continue to be moved by the sharing today. I feel very inadequate ... as though I am no one; have no substance. Do I have the right to be here with someone whose oppression has been so stingingly complete and who has survived? I have known so little. This is a poem for P.

P's biography had moved us all. One of the self-identified feminists wrote:

> One of the major reasons I took this course was to become renewed and revitalized. I am weary of the struggles with women and trades. I feel each day I am becoming more centred, more focused again on why I do the work I do and why it is important. Planning the presentation with P and K again gives me energy to work more and to work harder.

As a conclusion to her presentation, she wrote the following:

> hands do my
> work,
>   extended,
>   tool lengthened.
> Hands,
> straight fingered
> and strong.
>
> I turn them
> over,
> the surfaces
> reflecting
> back,
> my work,
> proud lines,
> creases
> deep, calloused

Yet you would
gender my hands
smooth them
back into
soft round
silence.

—Joan McArthur-Blair (with permission) 1991

Responses to Pedagogy

As time went by—too fast—Linda and I constructed our version of critical/feminist pedagogy. Midway through "Gender Equity: Issues in Teacher Education," building on the notion of reflexivity and ever-conscious of wanting to see policy in action, we asked the students to look critically at how the course was being conducted and to brainstorm about those aspects of it which differentiated it from other courses they had taken. They made the following points:

(1) Student comments are valued regardless of whether or not they agreed with what was said by the teachers.
(2) Learning is negotiable.
(3) The traditional classroom is content-driven; ours is process-driven.
(4) Teachers don't mind diverging from set topics; course is student-oriented.
(5) Experts are brought in from different areas; teachers are not *the* experts.
(6) Class is not based on competition; in most classes they worry about their mark.
(7) Class had more women than men.
(8) Students are used as resources.
(9) Students are recognized as adults; a mark does not signify where they are or who they are.
(10) There are a variety of resources, not just one main textbook.
(11) The classroom is set up in a circle.
(12) Vested interest in learning being on-going.
(13) Class empowered them to take informed social action.

These observations were considered in relation to the readings on critical and feminist pedagogy. Disappointingly, but perhaps predictably, the student who was more interested in equity in general than in gender equity in particular saw little difference between this class and others he had taken: "All of the courses I have taken in education fit this model."

Journals also provided some rich insights into student responses to our pedagogy and into their developing understandings of theory. With regard to this class being different from others, J, a student who works in technology education, wrote:

> The language of trades is male. . . . It has not changed with the influx of women into the trades occupations; it is inert, powerful, unchanging and male. Tools and fixtures are male- and female-identified, there are studs to be erected and female things to hit into place and everything that sticks out is a nipple. . . . The language must be changed for women to have a voice in the work they have chosen.

In the meeting in which we discussed her draft, J acknowledged that although she actually wrote these words, she felt indebted to two of her technology colleagues, Kate Braid and Judy Doll, for the ideas they express.

Another technology education curriculum developer cited a student's contribution to his thinking, exemplifying the legitimacy of student input, the possibility of coalition building, and the respect that many of the students demonstrated for one another. KK wrote:

> I owe much of my current rethinking of my understanding of what technological literacy may include . . . to the discussions concerning *First Nations science and technology and the thought-provoking statements that B [First Nations woman] brings to our group.*
>
> My commitment to making the technology classroom more female friendly is fueled both by the guilt I feel as a male (I feel responsible) and by an anger that so many of my colleagues still cannot, do not, or will not see the fundamental injustice of current technology education curriculum, teacher attitudes and instructional methods. Both the guilt and anger are good, as I believe that one must arrive at these before any true change can take place. *Once channelled and clearly focused these feelings may do great things.* (Emphasis mine)

Finally, R wrote: "The ideas of the class being a community rather than a hierarchy, process versus lecture and everyone a teacher, everyone a learner, are all aspects of feminist teaching."

Possibility of Coalition?

Within the class, Linda and I tried to connect overtly feminist critiques to other challenges to the status quo. For instance, Ethel Gardner, director of the First Nations House of Learning and a member of the Sto:lo Nation, presented her developing research on First Nations peoples and science.

While she did not present as a feminist, students thought it significant that the concerns she raised often paralleled feminist critiques of conventional science. Thus, her talk introduced the possibility of coalition work. The student sitting beside me during Gardner's presentation whispered, "She's using the same words that we have been using to talk about other gender issues: connections, interrelationships."

B found some solace in Gardner's presence. Acknowledging her growing alienation in the class, she wrote, "Ethel Gardner made me feel better, I can't wait to get home, I really need to go to the sweatlodge for a cleanse after this. Not that it's too negative, its just a lot to learn and deal with." As the non-Native students in the class came to a greater appreciation of Aboriginal issues, B developed her awareness of the serious issues facing non-Native women. Having just seen the video *After the Montreal Massacre*, she wrote:

> I had to put *Feminist Pedagogy* [Briskin 1990] down for a while. Somehow it really bothered me when I found out those were women from the engineering faculty. ... I heard it on the news, but for me it was a white middle-class problem which was none of my business because I chose to segregate myself right along with the sorting which is done in society.
>
> I think I feel guilty for having ignored the issue of Feminism. Why did that fool do that to those women? I said a prayer for them and I burned some sweet grass.

And, as her awareness of others' concerns increased, her frustration with those in the class who could not hear *her* concerns also increased:

> Gender, race and class in the feminist classroom. There are still people in the group I was reflecting with who think race should not be included. I think that's why I don't want to share the First Nations values; I don't feel comfortable. They're discriminating against others themselves.
>
> Should I have jumped up and down and screamed and told this individual over and over again that she's making me feel oppressed? I'm losing patience.

As I read these words, I wonder again about the success of our anti-essentialist goals and what sisterhood might mean. I wonder about the inequities faced by students who come with cultural understandings that remain unheard by others, and I wonder about the responsibility of professors who "allow" this to happen. From my privileged position, I ponder the following:

> Our educational goal must be to learn from these [inabilities and unwillingness to deal with racism], to try to avoid them in future

efforts, and to move beyond them; the last thing educational theorists should be doing is exaggerating them, reifying them, and, in the process, exacerbating them. (Burbules and Rice 1991, 413)

Is that enough? I remain grateful to B for her contributions and for the effect she had on so many of the students. I also find a crumb of comfort in her acknowledgment that the course helped her to redefine her relationship with her daughter—a relationship that surfaced often in her journal: "I was trying to fix her and mold her to the norms of society. Thanks Celia and Linda, you saved our mother and daughter relationship." Even more, I treasure the phone call I got from her in 1995 as I was working in her territory in northern British Columbia. She was still fighting, this time to get her band to take gender issues seriously.

P, another self-identified feminist, also wrote of her shifting perceptions of feminism:

> From this course, I'm beginning to realize the interconnections between sexism and classism, but also racism, heterosexism and ageism. At this stage of my growth, I believe feminism to be the term which best describes the struggle against the oppression of women by all of these factors. If this is the case, I'm even more proud to be a feminist and I want to design a big sign with "I'm a feminist" on it that I can velcro to all of my sweatshirts, etc.

A struggle with the complexity of voice and identity work emerged in J's journal as a poem:

If I speak from
my experience and   this has
speak for you it is   become my
a silencing of your   confusion during
   voice.   this
               course.

If I just speak
for me then am
I silencing the
women who have
no voice

Do I have the
power to give
a voice to women
who do not have
one.

As the course progressed, students reiterated the theme of praxis and their developing awareness of the need for coalition work. Several journal entries focused on how to effect change in gender relations. G wrote, "By being silent, one is being an ally in maintaining the status quo." Just as KK and J mentioned colleagues' responses to their enrolling in this class, so G found himself confronted by a colleague from his teacher education program.

> The word feminist invoked a negative facial expression. . . . I could sense that she was unaware of gender equity and wasn't motivated to listen to what I was saying. . . . As a man, it seems kind of strange to talk to a woman about gender equity and have her treat the topic with nonchalance.

G was wrestling with his developing feminist understandings and this experience outside the class provided an immediately problematic twist to his growing awareness. R, who had come to the class focused on action, soon needed a respite:

> The whole idea of social change is quite overwhelming and I've come to realize that when I start with change within the classroom, I am going to be up against [the] whole society, because of the context of the students, the school, peers, administrators, etc. But I've decided to not let that stop me.
>
> However, today it is weighing me down. I feel emotionally drained and exhausted. I would like to have two days between each session to think and reflect. It is too short a time to take it all in. So today I need to take a rest.

Comments such as this one constituted the most serious and oft-repeated criticism of the course. This led Linda and me to question the worth of such a crammed agenda.

One Boundary for This Case: End of the Nine Days

When the nine days came to an end, R's comments summed up much of what we all felt, "I had to ask my husband what day it is today. Is tomorrow the last day of this class already? I feel like I have been through a hurricane." Another student wrote, "I found this course really made me question my own values and behaviour both in my professional and personal life." Yet another found in the course a little bit of solace, "I have learned in your course, been re-generated in your course and wish it was on-going. I came to this course very burnt out and needing to hear some common voices. I have healed some in 9 days." Sounding a little wistful, L wrote, "There were

no promises made about coming away with a neat package. Still, I am getting much more than I expected from this course." As for JJ,

> When I enrolled in the course . . . I didn't intend to do anything but to
> attend classes and read and do the papers and get the credits. Looking
> back on this very intense few days, I realize that it is a combination of
> the topic, the readings, the speakers, and the people—oh, very much
> the people—that have helped create this very special experience for me.

And, in her final journal entry, Y focused on feminism:

> Having come to this course not as a "feminist," but as a feminist sym-
> pathizer, my stance has changed. I now believe that I am a feminist,
> although I have yet to pay my dues. That will come. Hopefully, in the
> fall . . . when I begin, in my small way, to change the thinking of young
> minds.

Gender Equity Unbounded: After the Course

Despite mostly glowing evaluations, it was not until our reunion in
November that I truly appreciated what both students and teachers had done
in this course. I began to see it as the foundation for on-going work in gender
relations. Six students—clearly not a majority, but, for me, a significant
number—and Linda and I attended the evening pot luck at R's house. After
dinner, I asked each person to speak about the on-going impact of the
course, "if there was any." R began by saying that she had taken the course
almost by accident: it fit with her summer schedule. Since the course, she had
found a colleague with a similar interest in gender equity, had become chair
of the Professional Development Committee, had proposed gender equity as
a topic for consideration, and had been vetoed by the administrative officer
in her school. She had also physically restructured her classroom, pushing
out the rows of rigid desks and moving in a circle of tables and chairs; she had
talked to a curious male colleague about how he might do the same with his
classroom. LW, a long-time self-identified feminist, audited the course and
said she was still dealing with some anger about criticism of the White
middle-class women's movement. However, because of the course, she had
recently attended some conference sessions organized by lesbian feminists—
lesbianism being an area that she had not previously considered relevant to
her understandings of feminism. P spoke on the influence B had had on her
practice. In her focus on gender issues in technology education, she had not
previously considered such issues as Aboriginal technology.

M wrote a follow-up letter outlining her thoughts. The Lewis and Simon
article continued to resonate in her life, and she introduced one of the books

suggested by guest lecturer and English as Second Language (ESL) faculty member Kelleen Toohey—Tannen's (1990) *You Just Don't Understand*—to her reading group. "It sparked a lively interchange." Continuing to question gender inequity "helps me cope with the inequities which still exist. . . . I haven't decided whether this makes me more or less angry." She then elaborated. Stimulated by the technology education people in the course, she decided to take a directed studies course on the use of the video camera. She is now competent enough to use it in her classroom and to give workshops to other staff members. She did, however, attend a recent Canon workshop, which she described as "another discourse not intended for her."

> I was the only single woman in the audience and the only one [woman] to ask questions. Of the couples in attendance, it was the men who were holding and operating the camera and asking the questions. . . . Although it makes me angry, being able to put it into a certain perspective helps me accept *myself*. (Emphasis mine)

She went on to say:

> Through the readings and the speakers [in the course], I gained an appreciation of the broader scope of the gender equity issue—that gender equity issues are not solely issues involving white, middle-class, heterosexual women, but women from all walks of life. . . . B's presence and participation has affected my perception of First Nation's people. She had a keen sensitivity to others' feeling and I will not forget her insistence on understanding "the pain" of the oppressed.

Her words resonate with those of Nancie Caraway (1991, 115): "All feminists need to see value in the experience of those 'on the edge' because such a vantage point embodies a negative moment, inherently attuned to flesh-and-blood deprivation and pain as central to political attention." And, bringing us back to policy, M wrote: "As a result of the course, I have a clearer understanding of the difference between being treated *equally*, as opposed to understanding feminine/masculine socialization influences which require *different* considerations for real equity" (emphasis in original).

Coalition Work

The course was far from perfect: it was too intense, too packed, too short. People hurt one another too often; racism was persistent. But people learned, and they learned to talk with one another. Without over-simplifying, one can say that a form of coalition work, working together across differences that were articulated and accepted as meaningful, actually began.

In responding to a draft of this paper, one student said it was important to recognize that the intensity of the class was good insofar as it enabled the development of group feeling. "Today wherever women gather together it is not necessarily nurturing. It is coalition building. And if you feel the strain, you may be doing some good work" (Reagon 1983, 362). The students/ teachers developed an understanding of the slipperiness of the province's gender-equity policy and its ties to feminism as well as of the need to move beyond any essentialist notions of male/female. Most, while seeking ideas about praxis, also found a commitment to other people in the course and learned about (1) the complexities of working together and (2) the complexities of sisterhood.

Clearly, B's presence had a tremendous impact on people. As an Aboriginal person, she found the group receptive enough to make it worth her while to go on speaking, in spite of being frustrated with what she clearly saw as racism. She said that her class journal has proven very valuable to her on-going consideration of gender. She has shared it with others and reflected on it herself. The responses to my requests for student involvement in this paper continue to be noteworthy. One student said, "I see the world different as a result of the course." Another said, "I received my guide to summer courses in the mail and I thought, 'I want to take that course again.'"

What of the notion of gender equity, its articulation in policy, and its disruption of feminist projects? There was a wonderful twist to the use of this term, in that it both obstructed and enabled the critical consideration of feminism. Many of the people who came to this course were not among "the converted." Certainly there were some feminists seeking collaboration, but there were also people for whom the words "gender equity" had nothing to do with feminism. If they had known they could be related, they might not have come; if the state had known, it might not have provided funding. But because the course insisted that gender equity and feminism are inescapably interrelated, people had the opportunity to re-search their understandings of feminism and to re-form them. And this they did. Even the converted re-thought their fondly held beliefs. Fortunately, policy cannot determine practice.

And what of sisterhood? In light of B's experiences, among others, must we declare sisterhood ultimately powerless? I have come to the point that, paraphrasing Biddy Martin and Chandra Talpade Mohanty, I want to say, "What's sisterhood got to do with it?" Not a lot, unless we recognize sisterhoods in all their situated complexities, in which case they begin to look much like most other human relationships—terribly diverse and devastatingly complex. The issue is coalition work; the issue is the risk involved in doing something with people who are not exactly like us, whoever we may be. As we found in the class, "There is no hiding place. There is nowhere you can go and only be with people who are like you. It's over. Give it up"

(Reagon 1983, 357). The teachers who came to the course are coming to know this. They began their work under the auspices of a policy with serious limitations. Perhaps if there is a lesson to be learned from this experience, it is to take advantage of whatever policy initiatives are available—to work reflexively and critically to determine both what they offer and what they hide.

Notes

1. Unless otherwise specified, when used with regard to the gender-equity course, plural pronouns refer to both teachers and students.
2. In order to minimize the potential abuse of the power inherent within a teacher-student relationship, permission was not sought until more than six months after the course had been completed.

References

Bannerji, H. 1995. *Thinking Through: Essays on Feminism, Marxism, and Anti-Racism*. Toronto: Women's Press.

Bourne, J. 1984. *Towards an Anti-Racist Feminism*. London: Institute of Race Relations.

Briskin, L. 1990. "Feminist Pedagogy: Teaching and Learning Liberation." *Feminist Perspectives No. 19*. Ontario: Canadian Institute for the Advancement of Women.

British Columbia. Ministry of Education. n.d. *Year 2000: A Framework for Learning*. Victoria: Queen's Printer.

———. 1988. *A Legacy for Learners: The Report of the Royal Commission on Education*. Victoria: Queen's Printer.

———. 1990. *Working Plan #3 1990–1999: A Plan to Implement Policy Directions: A Response to the Sullivan Royal Commission on Education by the Government of British Columbia*. Victoria: Queen's Printer.

———. 1994a. *Guidelines for the Kindergarten to Grade 12 Education Plan: Implementation Resource*. Part 1. Victoria: Queen's Printer.

———. 1994b. *The Kindergarten to Grade 12 Education Plan*. Victoria: Queen's Printer.

———. 1994c. *Putting Policies into Practice. Implementation Guide*. Victoria: Queen's Printer.

Bryson, M., and S. de Castell. 1995. "So We've Got a Chip on Our Shoulder!: Sexing the Texts of 'Educational Technology.'" In *Gender In/forms Curriculum: From Enrichment to Transformation*, edited by J. Gaskell and J. Willinsky. Toronto: OISE Press.

Bryson, M., S. de Castell, and C. Haig-Brown. 1993. "Gender Equity/Gender Treachery: Three Voices." *Border/Lines* 28: 46–54.

Burbules, N. C., and S. Rice. 1991. "Dialogue Across Differences: Continuing the Conversation." *Harvard Educational Review* 61 (November): 393–416.

Butler, J. 1990. *Gender Trouble: Feminism and the Subversion of Identity*. New York: Routledge.

Caraway, N. E. 1991. "The Challenge and Theory of Feminist Identity Politics: Working on Racism." *Frontiers* 12 (2): 109–29.

Carby, H. V. 1982. "White Woman Listen! Black Feminism and the Boundaries of Sisterhood. In *The Empire Strikes Back: Race and Racism in 70s Britain*. London: Hutchinson.

Davis, A. 1981. *Women, Race & Class*. Toronto: Random House.

de Beauvoir, S. 1952. *The Second Sex*. New York: Bantam.

Ellsworth, E. 1989. "Why Doesn't This Feel Empowering? Working Through the Repressive Myths of Critical Pedagogy." *Harvard Educational Review* 59 (August): 297–324.

Foucault, M. 1980. *Power/Knowledge: Selected Interviews and Other Writings*. New York: Pantheon.

Freire, P. 1970. *Pedagogy of the Oppressed*. New York: Continuum.

Fuss, D. 1989. *Essentially Speaking: Feminism, Nature and Difference*. New York: Routledge.

Gaskell, J., A. McLaren, and M. Novogrodsky. 1989. *Claiming an Education: Feminism and Canadian Schools*. Toronto: Garamond Press.

Gender Equity Advisory Committee. 1990. British Columbia. Ministry of Education. Understanding Gender Equity. Unpublished paper circulated to committee members.

Giddings, P. 1984. *When and Where I Enter: The Impact of Black Women on Race and Sex in America*. New York: William Morrow.

Harding, S. 1991. "Who Knows? Identities and Feminist Epistemology." In *(En)Gendering Knowledge: Feminists in Academe*, edited by J. E. Hartman and E. Messer-Davidow. Knoxville: University of Tennessee Press.

Kreisberg, S. 1992. *Transforming Power: Domination, Empowerment, and Education*. Albany: State University of New York Press.

Lather, P. 1991. *Getting Smart: Feminist Research and Pedagogy With/in the Postmodern*. New York: Routledge.

Lewis, M., and R. Simon. 1986. "A Discourse Not Intended for Her: Learning and Teaching within Patriarchy." *Harvard Educational Review* 56 (4): 457–72.

Martin, B., and C. T. Mohanty. 1986. "Feminist Politics: What's Home Got to Do with It?" In *Feminist Studies/Critical Studies*, edited by T. de Laurentis. Bloomington: Indiana University Press.

Merriam, S. B. 1988. *Case Study Research in Education: A Qualitative Approach*. San Francisco: Jossey-Bass.

Morgan, D. 1984. *Sisterhood is Global*. Garden City, New York: Anchor Books.

Pang, V. O. 1988. "Ethnic Prejudice: Still Alive and Hurtful." *Harvard Educational Review* 58 (3): 375–79.

Reagon, B. J. 1983. "Coalition Politics: Turning the Century." In *Home Girls: A Black Feminist Anthology*, edited by B. Smith. New York: Women of Color Press.

Rich, A. 1986. "Compulsory Heterosexuality and Lesbian Existence." In *Blood, Bread and Poetry: Selected Prose 1979–1985*. New York: W.W. Norton.

Roman, L. G. 1993. "'On the Ground' with Anti-Racist Pedagogy and Raymond Williams's Unfinished Project to Articulate a Socially Transformative Critical Realism." In *Views Beyond the Border Country: Raymond Williams and Cultural Politics*, edited by D. Dworkin and L. G. Roman (pp. 158-214). New York and London: Routledge.

Smith, D. M. 1987. *Geography, Inequality and Society*. New York: Cambridge University Press.

Spivak, G. C. 1990. *The Post-Colonial Critic: Interviews, Strategies, Dialogues*. New York: Routledge.

———. 1993. In A Word: *Interview*. In *Outside in the Teaching Machine*. New York: Routledge.

Tannen, D. 1990. *You Just Don't Understand: Women and Men in Conversation*. New York: Morrow.

Weiler, K. 1988. *Women Teaching for Change: Gender, Class and Power*. New York: Bergin and Garvey.

Wittig, M. 1992a. "One is Not Born a Woman." In *The Straight Mind and Other Essays*. London: Harvester/Wheatsheaf.

———. 1992b. "The Straight Mind." In *The Straight Mind and Other Essays*. London: Harvester/Wheatsheaf.

Chapter Fourteen

Backlash in Cyberspace: Why 'Girls Need Modems'

Jane Kenway
Deakin University (Australia)

Introduction

The information superhighway is a new feminist frontier. It is an emerging ideological space in and around which the politics of gender relations and identities are being revisited and where new opportunities for renegotiating gendered power relations exist. As I will show, these are dangerous opportunities; and while I do not want to exaggerate their potential, I do want to stress the importance of feminist educational work in cyberspace. This chapter has three purposes: (1) to demonstrate that dominant and dominating forms of masculinity are being reinscribed in and around cyberspace but that so, too, are other masculinities; (2) to make the case that if feminist educators focus too myopically on these reassertions of masculinity, then they are likely to miss new opportunities; and (3) to argue that overstating these opportunities is also dangerous and that attention must be paid to certain contextual factors which cast a shadow over feminism in cyberspace and which must be part of a feminist educational agenda. Let me begin with a little background about the information superhighway itself.

The Information Superhighway

The metaphor "information superhighway" refers to the unstoppable trend to replace current technologies for the delivery of information, communication, and entertainment with new. It is about a move from narrow band to broad band, which provides the capacity to deliver much more volume, much more quickly. It is also about digital encoding, which brings about the convergence of computing, telecommunications, and broadcasting into a common digital format. This means that voice, text, graphics, and video signals can be mixed and manipulated. The Internet, which links computers and telephones, is the medium attracting most educational interest.

The Internet is a network of computer networks that allows users access to data bases worldwide. As we move from narrow to broad banding, the quality and range of the textual forms to which the Internet provides access will increase. However, there is more to the Internet than access to more and better information; it also offers a different economy of communication than do other communications technologies. Until computer networks, communications technologies fell into two categories: (1) one-to-one communication (telegraph and telephone) and (2) one-to-many communication (broadcasting, print, television, movies, and radio). Computer networks, on the other hand, offer many-to-many communication in addition to one-to-one and one-to-many communication. The Internet, therefore, offers many different ways of communicating. These include real time chat sessions; person-to-person e-mail; networked discussion groups; on-line newsletters, journals, and multimedia databases; and virtual reality. In short, the Internet readily opens the way to membership in an array of new communities and makes it possible for people to become both producers and distributors of their own cultural products. It is these changed relations of production and new opportunities for association that are seen to account for the Internet's tremendous popular appeal. In 1994, statistics indicated that there were fifteen million Internet users and that this number would grow by twenty per cent to thirty percent every quarter ("Internet to Grow by Becoming Invisible," *The Economist*, reprinted in *The Australian*, 22 February 1994, 39). It is difficult to gain access to figures about differential male and female usage, but estimates are that women constitute ten percent of Internet users and that their numbers are rising rapidly.

At the same time as it is being constructed technologically, the information superhighway is also being constructed discursively, with a range of very different values and interests at stake. Those who are constructing popular understandings tend to be advertisers and journalists, technology experts, and governments. The tendency amongst these groups is to uncritically celebrate and promote new communications media and, it often seems, to cater to the vested interests of specific industries. The stress is on convenience, access, choice, enhancement, and profit. Let us look at a few examples, starting with the idea of the new networked home. Access to home-based services focuses upon an extensively networked Internet whose functions include banking, paying bills, filling in forms, and various sorts of home shopping. When the focus moves to education, the emphasis is on access to more and better information (unrestricted by geography, institutional location, or teachers) and on new opportunities for global communication between and amongst students, teachers, and "experts." When the focus is entertainment, the stress is on choice and interactivity. Multiple-channel pay television, video on demand, and interactive television are seen as opportunities for "entertainment democracy." For business and industry, the new media forms are promoted as providing new opportunities for profit.

While their views do not necessarily contribute directly to popular under-standings, many cultural, social, and educational analysts are currently exploring the implications of new communications media for various aspects of our lives. Again, let us look at some examples. Poster (1994) claims that the new communications media which will arise as a result of conver-gence are so dramatically different from those preceding them that they represent a second media age. Drucker (1993) argues that the information or knowledge economy is the major economy of today and the future. Further, Brand argues that "communications media are so fundamental to society that when their structure changes, everything is affected" (1987, xiii). The consensus amongst such commentators is that these new media forms have the capacity to reshape our work, leisure, lifestyle, social relationships, and national and cultural groupings/identities in ways that are difficult, but important, to predict.

Given the profound technological changes on the near horizon, it is cru-cial that those of us who work for gender and social justice in and through education understand them, seek to identify their short and long-term implications, and consider what they mean for pedagogy and curricula. Some key questions are: What inequalities are reinscribed or erased in cyberspace? How are masculinity, femininity, and the power relationships within and between them constructed on and around the information superhighway? What new possibilities for more just and humane ways of being does it make available?

Gender Politics on the Information Superhighway

The information superhighway is a very successful and popular metaphor. However, those who regularly employ it usually say nothing about the direction and quality of its traffic, the different activities in different lanes, who controls the lights, or who gets to travel. All of these issues have gender implications. Furthermore, superhighways are about doing it all bigger, better, and faster, and, in this sense alone, the metaphor has masculinist connotations. Indeed, there is evidence that the information superhighway offers opportunities for enhancing hegemonic masculinity. Witness the fol-lowing "call to arms."

THE AMERICAN PURIFICATION SOCIETY

Do you feel that the blacks, hispanics, and asians are taking over this once prosperous country by stealing jobs, leeching off welfare, and just plain POLLUTING our society? Do you feel that your HARD EARNED taxes are being wasted on worthless welfare mothers and criminals who should just as soon be exterminated let alone [sic] supported by OUR OWN government? Are you infuriated by abortion rights activists, who through their support of Womens' [sic] right to abortion, are actually participating in a MASS HOLOCAUST of innocent human beings? Do you share our belief that the women who participate in abortions should share the same fate as their aborted fetuses? Do you think women today posess [sic] too many freedoms and should be put in their place again? . . . Please, join up with us in our fight to cleanse this country of the scum that pollutes it and take part in the removal of those individuals involved by ANY MEANS NECCESSARY [sic]. We plan to use the Internet as our primary means of reaching out to the general public . . . To contact us . . . ADDRESS: cain@golden.ripco.com, SUBJECT: American Purification Society

This indicates that backlash activists have recognized the potential of the Internet as a medium for political mobilization. However, backlash in and around cyberspace has even wider parameters. I use the term backlash to refer to the postfeminist reassertion of those oppressive versions of masculinity associated with dominance, violence, the subordination of women and girls, and the subordination of all versions of masculinity that reject dominance and respect differences. I predict that those aspects of the information superhighway related to women's work, the networked home, and mainstream media will particularly reinvigorate hegemonic masculine social and cultural forms. However, despite a host of problems, I contend that the Internet has much potential as a feminist educational resource. But if feminist pedagogies are to properly address the gender issues that arise around converging technologies, then they must not focus exclusively on the Internet; they must also attend to changing mainstream media forms and to the gendered contexts of the production and consumption of the new media.

Feminism on the Internet

While there is a developing and controversial general feminist literature on gender issues in electronic communities, very little of this is concerned specifically with gender and education. Part of my project here is to help build the latter by drawing on the former and on other relevant literature.

The most common feminist line of argument with regard to the Internet is that it is an outcome and expression of male culture in both its most extreme and more subtle forms. This argument is put more subtly and in a less essentialist manner by Haraway (1987), who points to the "informatics of domination" attending to matters of race and class as well as to matters of gender. According to many reports, sexual harassment and pornography are rife in certain places on the Internet (Edlington 1995, 44; 48), and, as the infamous Mr. Bungle case on LambdaMOO illustrates, cyber-rape has now occurred (Dibbell 1994, 26; 32). Clearly, disembodied females still suffer degradation.

Male "Netiquette" is seen as a more subtle problem than is either sexual harassment or pornography. As Wylie (1994) reports, Susan Herring, a linguist from the University of Texas, argues that Netiquette supports typically male communication patterns:

> The Internet's libertarian survival of the fittest ideals codify men's speech patterns as the norm for Internet discourse. The aggressive, winner take all attitudes of netiquette don't appeal to the way women communicate. While women tend to create shorter posts that ask questions, hedge, seek consensus and encourage other points of view, men's posts tend to run much longer, use strong assertions, challenges and authoritative statements. . . . Netiquette rules tend to authorize insults and criticisms as proper, so long as one allows one's adversary an equal and opposite blow. . . . Women's attempts to initiate new threads get significantly fewer responses than threads started by men.

Certainly, many of the metaphors associated with the Internet have an unself-conscious male orientation. Witness Nunberg's (1995) remarks:

> When we talk about the net we invoke all the stock American heroes of the wide open spaces. You're a net surfer, you're a cowboy on the electronic frontier. You're standing on the bridge of your own private Enterprise about to boldly go where no one has ever gone before.

Although he goes on to observe that "the metaphors for the net are all wrong," he does not notice that they are all gendered. Nor does Appel (1995), who argues that "violence is the hidden icon of the Net." "As an ex military technology, it still retains a flavor of militaristic violence. Messages are 'fired off' to one another. Postings are 'killed.' Unpopular recruits are 'flamed.' 'Knowbots' and 'gobots' do our bidding. Lists are 'blitzed,' 'spammed,' and 'targeted.' . . . The Internet is a tough town."

The Internet practice of flaming (the fierce exchange of insults), and the flame wars that result (Derry 1994), certainly supports the contention that it facilitates symbolic violence. I suspect it is groups made up of young men that are most prone to flaming. The stories in Herz (1995) support this view. I also suspect that many of these young men may be what are often described as "geeks" or "nerds," those who do not fare well in male contests for power and status in so-called "real life." It is possible that these young men use their computers to enhance their sense of their own masculinity, and that flame wars in the "safety" of cyberspace are a substitute for male power on the outside. Nonetheless, flame wars clearly provide an opportunity for certain males to construct their masculinity in unpleasant ways, and they represent a particularly offensive mode of interaction—one that our research suggests is emotionally damaging but which nonetheless develops its own momentum (Fox).

It is certainly the case that the press has an exaggerated interest in the downside of the Internet (stories about cyberpunks, Net Nazis, and pornography abound) and that, as a result, it is often perceived as a "tough town" populated mainly by unpleasant and violent males. However, this tends to obscure the fact that the Internet is to some extent a more "global commons" that accommodates many different sets of interests, ranging from health support to science fiction, the occult to music, and peace activism to electronic scholarship. As these demonstrate, there are many different ways of being male, and males can and do move between them and behave differently as a result (Fox). And, as I will show later, some males are committed to reorganizing the rules of social life in cyberspace in positive ways. While it is important for feminists to document and to try to change the downside, it is also important for them to acknowledge that there is more to life in cyberspace than male violence and female oppression.

The types of problems noted above have led many women to sign on with gender-neutral signatures. They have also led some women to invent new feminist practices to contend with male Netiquette and to explore and to try to articulate a distinctive women's approach to network-based interaction (Shade 1994). Women-only electronic salons are developing apace. WIRE is one example of a women's group that has formed on the Internet and that aims to be "accessible to those without a computer jock mentality" (Weise 1993, 26), providing a "safe space" for women and girls. Others have sought to open up opportunities for women to publish on the Internet "in their own voice."

Some feminists oppose these types of responses and call them "politeness ghettos," their concern being that they imply that women are weak and need protection, that they can't make it in the "main game." Others see feminism and/or women-only groups as constituting a form of censorship. They object to the policing of what is said, how it is said, and by whom it is said. This is seen to go against Netiquette, which insists on free speech. St. Jude (otherwise known as Jude Milhon) says, "Fuck niceness!"

She wants women to "toughen up!" She believes that the Internet provides women with ideal opportunities to learn to defend themselves and even to change the views of Net bullies and bigots. She says, "Learn to fight! . . . This is the best training ground for women; we may start ten down in a physical fight, OK, but the keyboard is the great equalizer" (St. Jude cited in Cross 1995a). Given women's and girls' generally superior linguistic skills, we might well have an edge on the Internet. Indeed, some would also argue that, given the non-hierarchical and relationship-oriented processes of the Internet, it is particularly suited to women's styles of interaction. This generally enthusiastic position is endorsed by those known as cyberfeminists. Cyberfeminists are well-represented in the Australian on- and off-line publication *Geekgirl*, particularly by Sadie Plant, who, in answer to the question, "Do you agree . . . that technology is a deadly game? says 'Only for the white guys.' " (Plant in Cross 1995b).

Others see political opportunities in the anonymity of the Internet and the fluid identity games people can and often do play on it—games that allow a great deal of "gender bending" and "cross dressing" (particularly by men). People can live parallel lives, use nicknames or false names, conceal their identities, and have multiple identities—including multiple-gender and sexual identities. This is fascinating for scholars who are interested in exploring the construction of humanity, gender, sexuality, and the reconstituted subject in cyberspace, and there is some intriguing literature on this topic (e.g., Hayles 1993; Morse 1994). Allucquere Rosanne Stone (1995), a leading theoretician of identity/bodies/machines, explores this issue through some telling tales that problematize the notion of identity itself. Particularly telling is the tale of "the cross-dressing psychiatrist." The suggestion is (1) that there is no identity "masked under the virtual persona" but, rather, that the disembodied nature of the Internet allows repressed and multiple personae to come into play, and (2) that it encourages a "radical rewriting . . . of the bounded individual as the standard social unit and validated social actant" (1995, 43). Indeed, this challenges much psychoanalytic theory (for other psychoanalytic perspectives, see Sofia 1993). As Stone says, networks are social environments in which

> some of the interactions are racially differentiated and gendered, stereotypical and Cartesian, reifying old power differentials whose workings are familiar and whose effects are understood. But some of the interactions are novel, strange, perhaps transformative, and certainly disruptive of many traditional attempts at categorisation. (36)

Disembodiment allows much to happen that otherwise might not and, as Stone suggests, "new collective structures [are] risking themselves in novel conditions" (1995, 36). Less dramatically, it is not uncommon for men to "lurk" in women-only electronic salons. Some women consider this deeply offensive and "out" any men found to be so doing. St. Jude sees disembodiment otherwise:

> It may be that this is the only way the alien sexes can honestly converse—when they're bodiless, nothing at stake, behind the masks of their pseudonyms. Online you can learn to be fearless, you can afford to be bold . . . we can play amazing pranks, or we can do something even more outrageous: we can be honest. . . . This could be a breakthrough for humans learning about humans, not just men and women learning about each other. (St. Jude cited in Elmer-DeWitt 1993, 58)

She also sees liquid identity as providing women with defensive and political opportunities that otherwise would not be available to them. She argues that "girls need modems" and encourages women to be "online warriors for civilization":

> In cyberspace everyone can hear you scream. There was a woman crying virtual rape on LambdaMOO. It's a game, lady. You lost. You could have teleported. Or changed into an Iron Maiden (the spiky kind) and crimped off his dick. . . . Because the MOO's also a social space, where you can meet people with real cultural differences—like Klansmen—and make them respect you as a woman, as a dyke, as whatever. Toe-to-toe, you may change their prejudices forever. . . . Cries for niceness don't make it. (St. Jude cited in Cross 1995a)

This gung-ho suggestion to "teleport" or to technologically gag the offender from one's screen does not meet with much approval. As Dibbell observes, it certainly did not attract the support of opponents of Mr. Bungle in the LambdaMOO, who looked for more communitarian solutions to the problem. He refers to suggestions such as St. Jude's as coming from a

> gag and get over it school of virtual rape counselling with its fine line between empowering victims and holding them responsible for their own suffering and its shrugging indifference to the window of pain between the moment the rape text starts and the moment a gag shuts it off. (Dibbell 1994, 19)

Certainly, one wonders what effect either "cries for niceness" or the liquid identity of on-line warriors would have on groups such as the American Purification Society. It remains to be seen how women use the possibilities of liquid identity. Meanwhile, the more conventional response from feminists is to use the Internet for the purposes of communication, for the promotion of women's politics, and for making new connections. For example, the National Organization for Women in the United States has unveiled its own homepage on the World Wide Web: "An Internet presence . . . enables NOW both to efficiently inform the media, and thereby the public, and to collaborate with other organizations."

Social Justice, Gender, and the Internet

Many non-feminist discussions of power and control point to matters that are central to issues of gender. It is not uncommon for the press and for governments to raise issues associated with the information superhighway and social justice. In Australia, the slogan for expressing this concern is "information rich and information poor." This slogan raises the questions (1) will converging technologies create new social divisions in terms of the 'information rich' and the 'information poor' and, thus, add yet another layer of social inequality to those already existing? and (2) how can this be prevented? Also, although governments and the press frequently express concern about Internet pornography, they do so mainly with regard to child protection. Despite all this, there is little government or press interest in the gender implications of the information superhighway. Nonetheless, the slogan works very well as rhetoric, and it has potential for feminist analysis.

Access is a baseline issue and includes matters of cost, availability, and competence. Matters of poverty, social and geographic isolation, disability, gender, and generation (which, of course, overlap and intersect) are particularly pertinent here. Given that technological literacy is now a basic of education, equal access to it must be a fundamental premise; thus, it is crucial to consider how this may be brought about. For example, perhaps the provision of public-access terminals is one way of addressing the needs of those on low income. However, it is extremely important to look at what would be available on these terminals. When inverted, the "information rich/information poor" slogan points to the problem of being "rich in poor information," and it indicates enduring gender and social justice questions concerning "access to what?" What will be the quality and nature of interactions, and how will social relationships and individual and group identities be constructed within them? What sorts of knowledge is offered? Whose knowledge is it, and what does it say to users about who they are, how they should behave, and what they should value? As feminists will recognize, these are standard curriculum questions.

Utopian and Dystopian Narratives

Predictably, on the Internet there has been a proliferation of both *utopian* and *dystopian* narratives with regard to communications technologies and social justice issues. I will point to the main threads of both perspectives and briefly note some of their implications for gender.

Basic to all utopian arguments is the fact that the Internet has a fundamentally different economy of communication than do other forms of communications technology. As I noted at the outset, it allows multicasting or many-to-many communication. And, so the argument goes, the Internet offers people the opportunity to become producers and distributors of their own cultural products rather than to remain consumers of the products of others. As Weston (1994) points out, "the mouse is more powerful than the remote control." According to him, "It is impossible to understand much about the Internet's appeal by analysing its content. The Internet is mostly about people finding their voice, speaking for themselves in a public way."

In this view, the Internet is less about content and information and more about new relationships to content and information. The mass media are seen as offering "almost pure content" along with a non-dialogical relationship that insulates the few content-producers from their audiences. According to Weston, the Internet expands "the locus of direct, self-mediated, daily political involvement." Cultural producers of all sorts no longer have to kowtow before mass media agencies in order to gain a public voice. And, "what was previously local, domestic, idiosyncratic and private can, for the first time, become external and public. This is an abrupt reversal of the mass media's progressive appropriation of the idiosyncratic and private for their own institutional purposes."

There are many implications here for those who wish to rewrite gender identities. The Internet provides them with new opportunities to re-present themselves in their own voices and in their own ways. This allows them to move beyond the constraining and often demeaning constructions of gender produced by the mass media. It also allows women to move beyond the gendered barriers often put in their way by those who control publication outlets, and it makes possible an outpouring of women's art, literature, and music. In turn, this has implications for such notions as expert and novice, high culture and low culture—notions that have often placed women on the downside of the gender divide.

Some argue that this capacity provides a direct challenge to the mass media and to the established institutional order which they support—that the more public expression becomes distributed the more the institutions of modern society will be inconvenienced, destabilized, and threatened. Certainly, because it fundamentally challenges the nature of property and ownership, digitized information has the capacity to subvert the market economy. Obviously, challenges to the notions of property and ownership have important implications for women, who have often been viewed as property and who tend not to be property holders.

Taking a somewhat different tack, some argue that the Internet provides opportunities for building new communities, renegotiating the rules of social life, and provoking a more democratic polity (Reingold 1994). They argue that distributed public media require the renegotiation of the rights and freedoms associated with public self-expression, assembly, and privacy. For researchers, these are new concerns, as we are in the early days of understanding the production, distribution, and consumption of media texts and the formation and operation of virtual communities. Nonetheless, Agre (in press) goes so far as to argue that, as the collective life of the Internet community unfolds, the politics of social life are being renegotiated.

> Concepts of identity, civility, and community were suddenly transformed beyond recognition—and not just in a theoretical way, but in a way that the system maintainers and the users themselves had to work with daily. System maintainers . . . have been, in many ways, rediscovering the basics of democracy as they negotiate the social contract that balances individual freedom and social harmony while confronting a whole range of social distinctions and divisions.

As Sobchak (1994) points out, there are shades of neolibertarian individualism here. Nonetheless, renegotiating the rules of social life is an attractive proposition for women, as those rules have often been used to exclude them. This, of course, will be no easy task.

There are many Internet activists who claim that the easy replication and distribution of digitized information provides a powerful resource for social-justice activism. They see this technology as providing unprecedented opportunities both for resistance to the forces of dominance and for the development of alliances across differences. There are untold examples of this (e.g., see *.net:the internet magazine* 1995). Females tend to be good networkers, and there are enormous opportunities here. Agre (in press) takes this point further, arguing that there has been "an explosion of geographically dispersed/on line and local/on line community networking activity in the last few years." He contends that "the increasing pervasiveness of computing in society means that activism around technology increasingly becomes coextensive with social change work in general. No longer a specialised concern, computing becomes an indispensable tool and a facet of every particular site of human practice."

Dystopian themes are also present on the Internet, although they are not as common as are utopian themes. Interestingly, they are more common in the print literature *about* the Internet and its social and economic contexts than they are *on* the Internet.

A panopticon-like surveillance theme relates to the growth of sophisticated watching, listening, storing, sifting, and intrusive devices and to the eventual capacity of full-service networks to track the behavior of individuals and to develop digital profiles for various state and/or market purposes (Ratcliffe 1994). David Chaum (cited in Levy 1994) calls this a "panopticon nightmare." According to him, "Everything you do could be known to anyone else, could be recorded forever. It's antithetical to the basic principle underlying the mechanisms of democracy." Another concern arises over the implications of commercializing the Internet for its proclaimed democratic practices and communities. The fear is that the so called inclusionary ideals and vocabulary of the Internet cannot be sustained now that markets have recognized its immense potential.

The rise of the market on the Internet, combined with the technologies of surveillance noted above, raises serious issues about the further commodification of women's bodies and burdens. Networked homes and home services have the capacity to reinscribe traditional versions of femininity. It is likely that the networked home will increasingly become the networked workplace, where secondary labor markets will flourish and where paid work will be conducted at the same time as unpaid household and child-care work. Home shopping, with its ever-changing flow of seductive commodities and images, is likely to further position women as subjects for the endless array of gendered images and identities offered by the advertising industry (which will extend its reach into more and more aspects of life). While it may offer convenience, it will also privatize and individualize consumers and further lock them into market forms of exchange and the social relationships that accompany them.

Markets require a shift in focus from the community to the individual and a redefinition of such terms as rights, citizenship, and democracy. In consumer democracy, civil rights, welfare rights, and civic responsibility give way to market rights. The rise of market forms is accompanied by the decline of the welfare state. This does not bode well for those women who depend on welfare or for those women who need unions to help them to gain their rights as outworkers.

Many fears have been expressed about the psychological fallout of the information superhighway—that it will breed a cop-out society by feeding fantasy, escapism, and nostalgia. Media critic Neil Postman (1986, 1993) argues that the information superhighway is unnecessary because we already have an over-abundance of information. He writes about the loss of meaning and the trivialization associated with the media age; the feelings of alienation, confusion, and inertia that it produces; and information glut and information junkies. Apparently, some players of MUDS (Multiple-User Dungeons) play for up to forty hours a week, have trouble slipping back into real life, and "pinch time from work . . . and sleep" (Stewart 1994, 11). In Postman's view, as the home increasingly becomes the site for accessing shopping, entertainment, and work, "cocooned and isolated individuals will be produced who find it difficult to distinguish between reality and simulation" (Postman cited in Stewart 1994, 11).

New mass media forms in the "networked home" raise important issues about gender and household leisure. Pay television, with its popular sports and pornography channels, is unlikely to rewrite masculinity in a positive way. Indeed, as many feminists have argued, sports and pornography are prime sites for the construction of aggressive and oppressive forms of masculinity. Video games, both those in arcades and in homes, are renowned for their violence, and broad-banding will augment their availability and create new opportunities for interactive violence. *Mortal Combat*, a top-rated arcade game, is described as follows by Elmer-DeWitt (1993):

> Johnny Caggs kills his victims with a bloody decapitating uppercut. Raydon favours electrocution. Kano will punch through his opponent's chest and rip out a still beating heart. SubZero likes to tear his foe's head off and hold it up in victory, spinal chord twitching as it dangles from the neck.

Elmer-DeWitt notes that American kids who have video-game machines play them an average of one-point-five hours a day and that the core audience for video games is eight- to fourteen-year-old boys. How boys construct their masculinity through these games is a matter of serious concern. In an attempt to lure girls into the market, creators have begun to produce games around such toy characters as *Barbie* and the *Little Mermaid*. What can one say?

One must also consider the implications of new communications media for broader patterns of production and consumption. Saskia Sassen (1991) uses the network metaphor to point to the decentralization of production and to continued central ownership and control in what she calls global cities. In these global cities, banking, accounting, legal, and other services are provided to enable "complex organisations to manage spatially dispersed networks of factories, offices and services." Furthermore, as Probert (1993, 20) points out, drawing from Reich, the "enterprise web" is a more apt metaphor than is the "global web," as "the centre provides the strategic insight that binds the threads together. The threads of the global web are computers, facsimile machines, satellites, high resolution monitors and modems." As she goes on to observe:

> Producer services involve significant numbers of high wage professionals and technical employees, but even greater numbers of low wage clerical workers, usually women, and nothing much in between . . . the increase in low wage jobs and casual employment is linked with the

growth of the knowledge industries, the growth of high income professional jobs and the resulting gentrification of global cities. (20)

This class, she explains, has a lifestyle that has moved away from the consumption of mass-produced goods to the consumption of leisure and craft
goods, both of which tend to involve sweated work and outwork as well as a
vast increase in part-time and casual work.

This is but one of many arguments about the ways in which new communications technologies contribute to the stratification of the workforce.
The easy movement of information across dispersed locations and communities also allows for the dispersal of production across the globe, and this,
in turn, allows for new international divisions of labor that intensify the
control of workers at the same time as they intensify wage competition.
Equally, new communications media permit the rapid and intense promotion of ideas around the globe and may well have contributed to the enormous power of the ideology of global competitiveness. This ideology
currently guides the behavior of every nation and has led to massive state
restructuring, the rise of corporate welfare (government subsidies, grants,
and tax breaks for business), and the dismantling of the welfare state, thus
creating new forms of poverty while exacerbating the old.

Implications for Feminist Pedagogy and Curriculum

The new communications media, particularly the Internet, raise many new
questions for educational practice (see Tiffin and Rajasingham 1995;
Spender 1995; Luke 1995). Here, however, I focus upon the information
superhighway as a resource for education and then go on to consider its significance as a context for learning (Bigum and Green 1995).

There is no doubt that the Internet is an important global provider of
curriculum information and curriculum materials. And, as it is predictable
that neither will be gender-inclusive, there are some obvious challenges for
feminism. However, if teachers are to tap the full potential of the Internet
for curricula, pedagogy, and justice, then they must move beyond considerations of access to information and materials; that is, they must understand
what is significantly different about the Internet and explore the implications of such difference for teaching and learning. Arguably, the best way to
learn such lessons is through use, and I would strongly urge women teachers to get a modem and to use it for their own professional development.
Indeed, if women teachers remain aloof from this technological moment, it
will be dangerous for them as professionals as well as for the general movement for gender justice in education. To hark back to St. Jude, "Girls need

modems." That said, let me now turn to the new and the different and consider their implications for gender.

As I showed earlier, cyberspace, in its disembodiment and multiplicity, draws out our multiple identities. King (1995) points to some of the implications of this, arguing that each cyberspace makes possible a new identity.

> Just as our behaviour is different in real life when in church, at school, or spending an evening in a jazz bar, so too does the level of and content of discourse vary across cyberspaces. *The difference is the range possible and the juxtaposition in time of roles played.* From one minute to the next, one can redefine ones self [sic] according to the community standards of that cyberspace. One can be associating with the highest highbrow intellectual discussion of theories of philosophy, and then, with a few key strokes, change to being an active member of a truckers for peace social movement. (Emphasis mine)

In terms of gender, the notions of multiple identities and of liquid identity have fascinating possibilities. Indeed, the mind boggles at what disembodied students might do once their gender need not matter—play with gender identities, engage in role reversals, role play, and so on.

I see considerable scope for the usefulness of liquid identity with regard to reconstructing masculinity through education. Just as the computer provides boys and young men with a safe space in which to "enhance" their less civilized and less sensitive identities, so it gives them a safe space in which to try out different masculinities in different contexts and to develop their more sensitive sides. Technologically skilled and gender sensitive teachers are well placed to encourage males to travel the many different paths of cyberspace which construct them as males and which allow them to write up their various masculine identities. They are also well placed to help males reflect on these travels and to encourage them to examine and to understand why they do what they do—to see what investments they have in flaming, say, or in sexual harassment—and to search for other possible ways of being male. Liquid identity also provides young women with new gender-identity opportunities. With a few points and clicks, they can move from a girl-only space to alt. flame. They can try out the idea of being an "online warrior for civilization," have verbal tussles with cyberpunks, and they can share with other young women the difficult and different experiences of being female.

Text-based virtual realities offer enormous potential for educating students about gender, culture, and power; for constructing different gender regimes; for assessing their different complexities and consequences; and for taking on different gender personae. The opportunity exists for satirizing different conventional gender regimes and for developing unconventional and utopian forms—indeed, for renegotiating the gendered rules of social life. In a sense, students would be playing with the idea of gender but, at the same time, learning about its current constructions and their different benefits, costs, and consequences for differently located males and females (as well as for the relationships between). The value of this approach is that it has the potential to avoid both the boredom and the authoritarian preaching which feminist pedagogies often involve and which often provoke student resistance (Kenway et al., in press). Indeed, one might say that the key to change is serious pleasure.

Internet discussions and experiences of electronic scholarship have many implications for what we teach in schools and universities. A key to many of the new curriculum possibilities provided by the Internet arises from the difference between conventional pedagogy (lecture, dialogue, discussion, print) and the many-to-many model of Internet communication. Shank calls this the multilogue. Other significant features of the Internet which have implications for education are its infinite lateral connectedness and its porousness. These and multiloguing provide revolutionary resources for teaching, and they also open up new areas of inquiry while challenging both the organization of knowledge and the knowledge community itself. This has the potential to be profoundly destabilizing for all forms of order, not the least of which is the gender order. Let me elaborate.

Shank suggests that Internet practices that make it easy to belong to many different types of communities (consisting of people with wide-ranging interests and expertise) challenge the borders between disciplines, between knowledges, and between experts and novices. He argues that "discussions are inclusive rather than exclusive" and that neither levels of expertise nor disciplinary orientations can be used for exclusionary purposes: "Any one [sic], no matter what their qualifications can join in, insights from any field can be part of the discourse." He also observes that electronic archiving practices, drawing from different communities and "disparate arguments and examples," can also lead to the hybridization of knowledge and to new and shared ways of constructing meaning. Furthermore,

> the very idea of the multilogue helps preserve this egalitarian atmosphere, since there is no "teacher" or primary "discussant" to either lecture or to lead and orchestrate the discussion. Since everyone comes into the discussion sequentially, everyone has equal access to being heard.

Unsworth (in press) argues that electronic forms and practices "open up the possibility of re-creating the basic resources of all scholarly activities." As he points out, electronic publications and archives have "the disturbing quality of open-endedness, of extendibility, and of collectivity. They can be continually added to, connected to other data bases, worked on and 'owned' by many people from any location and keep growing beyond their originators." They challenge notions of authorship and ownership, scholar and layperson, and the time- and place-based nature of publications and archives. He also observes that the Internet "offers new opportunities for theorising signification, communication, literature, culture, editing, bibliographic and textual scholarship, history, and linguistics." These comments suggest that we are/will be experiencing an intellectual renaissance. There are many implications for gender here, and there is much scope for feminist-inspired student research.

The Internet should be used to encourage students to develop a new orientation to the media. They should be encouraged: (1) to recognize the different qualities of interactivity between the Internet and other aspects of the superhighway (such as video on demand or video games); (2) to understand and benefit from the fact that "information is no longer constrained by the traditional mass media" (King 1995), with its highly stylized gender modalities; (3) to move beyond a reliance on a few centralized and sexualized organizations and to capitalize on the Internet's many-to-many paradigm of communication; (4) to see the emancipatory potential of the Internet and to use it so that the voices of females, non-dominate males, and those of minority cultures can more readily be heard; (5) to recognize the socially "transformational power of cyberspace participation"; (6) to develop the very different relationship between the author and the reader that the Internet offers; and (7) to develop a strong sense of agency as producers of culture.

Technology is much more than a *resource* for learning; it is also an important *context* for learning. And it is a context about which we must become knowledgable. It is commonly expected that the convergence of new technologies and the development of the information superhighway will have an ever-increasing impact on our work, leisure, health, lifestyle, and national and cultural identities—and, as I have indicated throughout, on our gender identities. But insufficient *educational* attention is being paid to the manner in which we produce and consume such technologies. We need to consider the social and cultural ramifications of the possible transformation of the ways in which we "live, work, and play," and we need to build these into the curriculum. Be it in the workplace, the home, or elsewhere, students need to be in a position to assess the costs and benefits of the new communications media and to make choices that maximize their economic, social, and cultural benefits and minimize their risks and costs.

Some central questions are: What are the gender issues that arise when we consider the ways in which converging technologies may reshape our lives? For example, what are their implications for the physical and emotional health of males and females? What are the implications of the abstract social relationships promoted by the Internet for, say, face-to-face relationships between males and females in the home, the community, and elsewhere? What are the implications for the ways in which males and females use and regard their bodies and their leisure? Are there differences? And do these differences result in inequalities? Understanding the likely gender (and other) implications of converging technologies will have an important bearing on those curriculum areas that seek to produce healthy, well-adjusted, critical, and creative young people. And, presumably, it will be these areas that will help young people consider how they relate to Internet pornography, harassment, and extreme clashes of values and opinions on-line. Clearly, students need to be able to cope with these issues in a critical and informed manner.

To date, teaching students about technologies vis-à-vis their social/cultural and work/leisure contexts (as well as about the associated issues of gender and social justice) has not been a high priority in curriculum development. Only recently, and only in National School Curriculum policy circles in Australia, have there been serious moves to encourage the teaching of technology across curricula. In practice, however, information technology in schools and universities often either remains a separate subject or is seen as the main concern of science and math departments. Maybe the most basic challenge in this regard is to "uncouple" the connection between science and technology and to make very strong connections between converging technologies and the social sciences, the humanities, health, and the arts. Teaching *about* technology is just as important as teaching *with* it.

Conclusion

As the possible roles the information superhighway may play in curricula become better known and, thus, become part of broader curricula debates, another round of fighting is likely to occur. It is predictable that there will be the usual struggle on the part of those in power to take control of new curricula developments to ensure that they work in favor of gendered and other vested interests. This time of flux will provide dangerous but important opportunities for those who seek to rewrite curricula in gender-inclusive and expansive ways, and who seek to encourage students to explore a range of gender identities in the hope that they will settle on those that embody principles of empowerment, justice, and full humanity. Powerful knowledge is the best response to the politics of backlash within and beyond cyberspace.

References

(Note: Articles published on the Internet do not have page numbers.)

Agre, Phil. In press. "Introduction." In *Computing as Social Practice*, edited by D. Schuler and P. Agre. Albex: Published on the Internet. Permission to quote granted.

Appel, R. 1995. *Violence is Unquestionably the Unrecognized Icon of the Net!* Published on the Internet. Permission sought to quote.

Bigum, Chris, and B. Green. 1995. *Managing Machines: Educational Administration and Information Technology*. Geelong, Australia: Deakin University Press.

Brand, Stewart. 1987.*The Media Lab*. New York: Penguin Books.

Cross, Rosie. 1995a. "Modem Grrrl, St. Jude Interview." *Wired Ventures Ltd*. All rights reserved. Last Modified: Wednesday, 22 February 1995, 23:47 PST.

———. 1995b. "There Is an Intimate and Possibly Subversive Element Between Women and Machines." *21.C* (3): 17–18.

Derry, Mark. 1994. *Flamewars: The Discourse of Cyberculture*. Durham: Duke University Press.

Dibbell, Julian. 1994. "Data Rape: A Tale of Torture and Terrorism On-Line." *Good Weekend*, 19 February, 26–32.

Drucker, P. F. 1993. *Post-Capitalist Society*. New York: HarperBusiness.

Edlington, S. 1995. "Flex Crime: Sexual Harassment on the Internet." *Internet Today*, no. 4, February, 44–48.

Elmer-DeWitt, P. 1993. "The Amazing Video Game Boom." *Time Australia* 8 (39): 54–60.

Fox, E. In press. *Electronic Support Groups*. Geelong, Australia: Deakin Centre for Education and Change.

Geekgirl. on line at http: // www. next. com.au./spyfood/geekgirl/

Haraway, D. 1987. "A Manifesto for Cyborgs: Science, Technology and Socialist Feminism in the 1980s." *Australian Feminist Studies* 4: 1–42.

Haylcs, K. 1993. "The Seductions of Cyberspace." In *Rethinking Technologies*, edited by Verena Andermatt Conley. Minneapolis: University of Minnesota Press.

Herz, J. C. 1995. *Surfing the Internet: A Nethead's Adventures On-Line*. London: Abacus.

Kenway, J., J. Blackmore, S. Willis, and L. Rennie. In press. "The Emotional Dimensions of Feminist Pedagogy." In *Effective Pedagogies? Educating Girls and Boys*, ed. Pat Murphy. London: Falmer Press.

King, S. A., 1995. "The Psychology of Cyberspace." *The Chronicle of Higher Education* 41 (29): B1–B3.

Levy, S. 1994. "E-money: That's What We Want." *Wired Ventures Ltd*. All rights reserved. December.

Luke, C. 1995. *ekstasis@cyberia*. Paper under review for *Discourse*.

Morse, M. 1994. "What Do Cyborgs Eat? Oral Logic in an Information Society." In *Culture on the Brink: Ideologies of Technology*, edited by Gretchen Bender and Timothy Druchrey. Seattle: Bay Press.

.net:the internet magazine. 1995. October, no. 11.

Nunberg. G. 1995. "Virtual Rialto." Contribution to the National Public Radio program *Fresh Air*.

Poster, M. 1994. "A Second Media Age?" *Arena Journal* 3: 49–91.

Postman, N. 1986. *Amusing Ourselves to Death*. London: Heinemann.

———. 1993. *Technopoly: The Surrender of Culture to Technology*. New York: Vintage.

Probert, B. 1993. "Restructuring and Globalization: What Do They Mean?" *Arena Magazine*, 18 April–22 May.

Ratcliffe, M. 1994. "A Red line in Cyberspace." Editorial in *Digital Media Perspective*, 23 December, 1.

Reingold, H. 1994. *The Virtual Community: Finding Connection in a Computerised World*. London: Secker and Warburg.

Sassen, S. 1991. *The Global City*. Princeton: Princeton University Press.

Shade, L. R. 1994. "Gender Issues in Computer Networking." In *Women and Work: Breaking Old Boundaries, Building New Forms*, ed. Alison Adam et al. Amsterdam: Elsevier.

Shank, G., N.d. *Abductive Multiloguing: The Semiotic Dynamics of Navigating the Net*. Northern Illinois University, (P30GDS1@NIU).

Sobchak, V. 1994. "Reading Mondo 2000." In *Flamewars: The Discourse of Cyberculture*, edited by Mark Derry. Durham: Duke University Press.

Sofia, Z. 1993. *Whose Second Self? Gender and (Ir)rationality in Computer Culture*. Geelong, Australia: Deakin University Press.

Spender, D. 1995. *Nattering on the Net*. North Melbourne, Australia: Spinifex.

Stewart, M. 1994. "If You Can Turn On Your Telly, You Can Turn On to the Information Superhighway." *The West Magazine*, 24 September, 10–12.

Stone, A. R. 1995. *The War of Desire and Technology at the Close of the Mechanical Age*. Cambridge: MIT Press.

Tiffin, J., and L. Rajasingham. 1995. *In Search of the Virtual Class: Education in an Information Society*. London: Routledge.

Unsworth, J. In press. "Electronic Scholarship or Scholarly Publishing and the Public." In *The Literary Text in the Digital Age*, edited by Richard Finneran. Ann Arbor: University of Michigan Press.

Weise, E. 1993. "Women Wired for Information." *The Age* 26 October, 26.

Weston, Jay. 1994. "Old Freedoms and New Technologies: The Evolution of Community Networking." Paper given at Free Speech and Privacy in the Information Age Symposium, University of Waterloo, Canada, 26 November.

Wylie, Margie. 1994. "Sexist Netiquette." *Digital Media Perspective* 94 (12): 23.

Contributors' Biographical Notes

Himani Bannerji

Himani Bannerji is an associate professor at York University in the Department of Sociology. She has published in the areas of marxist anti-racist and feminist theories, and cultural politics. She is the author of *Thinking Through: Essays on Feminism, Marxism and Anti-racism* and co-authored *Unsettling Relations* (both published by Women's Press). She also edited and introduced the collection, *Returning the Gaze* (Sister Vision Press). She has published two collections of poetry, *A Separate Sky* and *Doing Time* as well as the essay collection, *Writing on the Wall*. Her critical essays, poetry, essays and short stories have appeared in numerous academic journals and magazines.

Jill Blackmore

Jill Blackmore is a Senior Lecturer in the School of Administrative and Curriculum Studies in the Faculty of Education, Geelong. Her main research interests are in feminist approaches to administrative and organizational theory, educational restructuring, organizational change and teachers' work, and their policy implications. Recent publications include *Answering Back: Girls, Boys and Feminism in Australian Schools*, co-authored with Jane Kenway, Sue Willis, and Leonie Rennie (Allen and Unwin), and forthcoming book with Open University Press titled *Troubling Women: Feminism, Leadership and Educational Change*.

Richard Cavell

Richard Cavell is Chair of the Program in Canadian Studies at the University of British Columbia, where he teaches in the English Department. Research interests include Canadian cultural production, theory of literature, and theories of the production of space. He is the recipient, with Peter Dickinson, of the 1996 NEMLA Essay Prize in Lesbian and Gay Studies for "Bucke, Whitman, and the Cross-Border Homosocial," forthcoming in a joint issue of the Canadian Review of American Studies/American Review of Canadian Studies.

Davina Cooper

Davina Cooper was a local politician in Britain in the late 1980s. She is currently Senior Lecturer at Warwick University Law School. She has published widely on local government, sexuality, feminist theory, and Conservative, Christian, moral agendas. Publications include *Sexing the City: Lesbian and Gay Politics within the Activist State* (Rivers Oram 1994) and *Power in Struggle: Feminism, Sexuality and the State* (NYU, Open University, 1995).

Patricia Elliot

Patricia Elliot is Associate Professor in the department of Sociology and Anthropology at Wilfrid Laurier University. She teaches courses on women, gender, feminist theory, and psychoanalysis. A former Coordinator of the Women's Studies Program, she also teaches an introductory women's studies course. She is currently pursuing research on the transgendered movement.

Linda Eyre

Linda Eyre is an Associate Professor in the Faculty of Education, University of New Brunswick, Canada, where she teaches courses in feminist theory and education, and health education. She is the recipient of the Canadian Association of Curriculum Studies Dissertation Award (1992) for her work on the social construction of gender in the practical arts. She has published in the area of gender and schooling, and sexuality education. Her current research interests concern institutional responses to issues of sexism, racism, and heterosexism.

Celia Haig-Brown

Celia Haig-Brown is an Associate Professor at York University's Faculty of Education. She is the author of two books: *Taking Control: Power and*

Contradiction in First Nations Adult Education (Vancouver: UBC Press, 1995) and *Resistance and Renewal: Surviving the Indian Residential School* (Vancouver: Tillicum Library, 1988).

Didi Herman

Didi Herman teaches law at Keele University in Britain. She writes in the area of social movements and legal struggle, and her publications include *Rights of Passage: Struggles for Lesbian and Gay Legal Equality* (University of Toronto, 1994); *Legal Inversions: Lesbians, Gay Men and the Politics of Law* (edited with Carl Stychin) (Temple University Press, 1995); and *The Antigay Agenda: Orthodox Vision and the Christian Right* (University of Chicago, 1997).

Jane Kenway

Jane Kenway teaches in the graduate program in educational administration at Deakin University and is Director of the Deakin University Centre for Education and Change. She has published widely on the topic of gender and education. Her latest book is Kenway, J. & Willis, S., (1995). *Critical Visions: Rewriting the Future of Gender Education and Work*, Australian Government Publishing Service, Canberra. Her new jointly authored book, *Answering Back, Girls, Boys and Feminism in Schools*, will be published by Allen and Unwin in 1997.

Chandra Talpade Mohanty

Chandra Talpade Mohanty is Associate Professor of Women's Studies at Hamilton College, New York and core faculty member of the Union Institute Graduate School in Cincinnati, OH. Her intellectual and political interests include the transnational dimensions of feminist theory, feminist and anti-racist pedagogy in the U.S. academy and the intersections of international development, race and gender in education. She co-edited with Lourdes Torres and Ann Russo, *Third World Women and the Politics of Feminism* (Indiana University Press, 1991). She also co-edited and introduced with Jacqui Alexander, *Feminist Genealogies, Colonial Legacies, Democratic Futures* (Routlege, 1996). Her numerous articles appear in journals such as *Cultural Critique, Boundary*, and *Feminist Review*. She edits the series, "Gender, Culture, and Feminist Politics" for Garland. Her current work focuses on citizenship, democracy, and radical, anti-racist pedagogy.

Alice J. Pitt

Alice J. Pitt is an Assistant Professor in the Faculty of Education, York University. Her most recent publications appear in *Theory Into Practice* and *Measured Lies: The Bell Curve Examined*, by Deborah Britzman. She is currently exploring the implications of psychoanalytic theory for education and curriculum theory.

Leslie G. Roman

Leslie G. Roman is an Associate Professor in the Department of Educational Studies in the Faculty of Education, University of British Columbia. She is the recipient of a Killam Memorial Fellowship for 1996/7 and a recent fellow in residence with the University of British Columbia's Centre for Research in Women's Studies and Gender Relations. She has published widely in cultural studies, feminist ethics in ethnographic research, and in the often disjunctive areas of feminist theory and anti-racist pedagogy. Her articles appear in journals such as *Educational Theory, Discourse: The Cultural Politics of Education*, and *Historical Studies in Education*. She has co-edited and introduced *Becoming Feminine: The Politics of Popular Culture* (The Falmer Press) and *Views Beyond the Border Country: Raymond Williams and Cultural Politics* (Routledge). Her forthcoming book, tentatively entitled, *Transgressive Knowledge: Comparative Studies in Feminist Theory and Pedagogy*, compares the resources of poststructural and postcolonial feminism for anti-racist and anti-sexist practice.

Dorothy Smith

Dorothy E. Smith is a feminist sociologist, author of *The Everyday World as Problematic: A Feminist Sociology; The Conceptual Practices of Power: A Feminist Sociology of Knowledge;* (both published by Northeastern University Press) and *Texts, Facts, and Femininity: Exploring the Relations of Ruling* (Routledge). She is currently professor in the Department of Sociology in Education at the Ontario Institute for Studies in Education of the University of Toronto (Canada) and adjunct professor in the Department of Sociology, University of Victoria (Canada).

Howard M. Solomon

Howard M. Solomon is Professor of History at Tufts University, teaching courses in lesbian and gay history, the history of stereotyping, and European social history. He lives in Portland, Maine where he is a community activist.

Aruna Srivastava

Aruna Srivastava teaches in the Department of English at the University of Calgary, Canada, where she teaches in the areas of Canadian and postcolonial writing, particularly by racialized writers; feminist theory, and critical race theory. Recently, she has been working on a project outlining the connections between feminist and anti-racist pedagogies. She is also especially interested in institutional pedagogies, particularly those pertaining to academic "progress," the relationship of activism to the academy, and classroom practices.

Timothy Stanley

Timothy J. Stanley teaches education foundations at the University of Ottawa. His publications have appeared in J.A. Mangan (ed.), *Making Imperial Mentalies; Historical Studies in Education; BC Studies* and *Canadian Historical Review*. He is currently researching the roles of historical narratives in contemporary racisms and student teachers' understandings of gender.

Index